MY CARDBOARD

A collection of comics from 2008-2010

Philippa Rice

Published by My Cardboard Books, April 2011. First Edition.
© 2008-2011 Philippa Rice. All rights reserved. No portion to be reproduced
without permission of the author, exept for reviews.
printed in China
ISBN 978-0-9568442-0-0
www.mycardboardlife.com

FOREWORD

We all have dreams. Children dream of being astronauts, firemen, or princesses. Some adults do too. Some adults dream of being astronaut fireman princesses, which to the best of my knowledge is a position for which one cannot apply. But that doesn't stop them dreaming. And it seems to me that if My Cardboard Life is about anything, it is about dreams and aspirations.

Cardboard Colin yearns for Pauline's unobtainable friendship, Paper Pauline longs to be a business baroness, Dr Bandaid craves romance over anything else, Cardboard Carl desires to use each and every savage beast as a household convenience of some kind – but I've said too much already. To read Philippa Rice's work is to know the dark heart of dreams, the plump fruit inches from your already over-extended grasp. In sugar-paper and glue, she tells each of us the uncomfortable truth about life: that you are always going to have to try a little harder.

John Allison
Manchester, March 2011

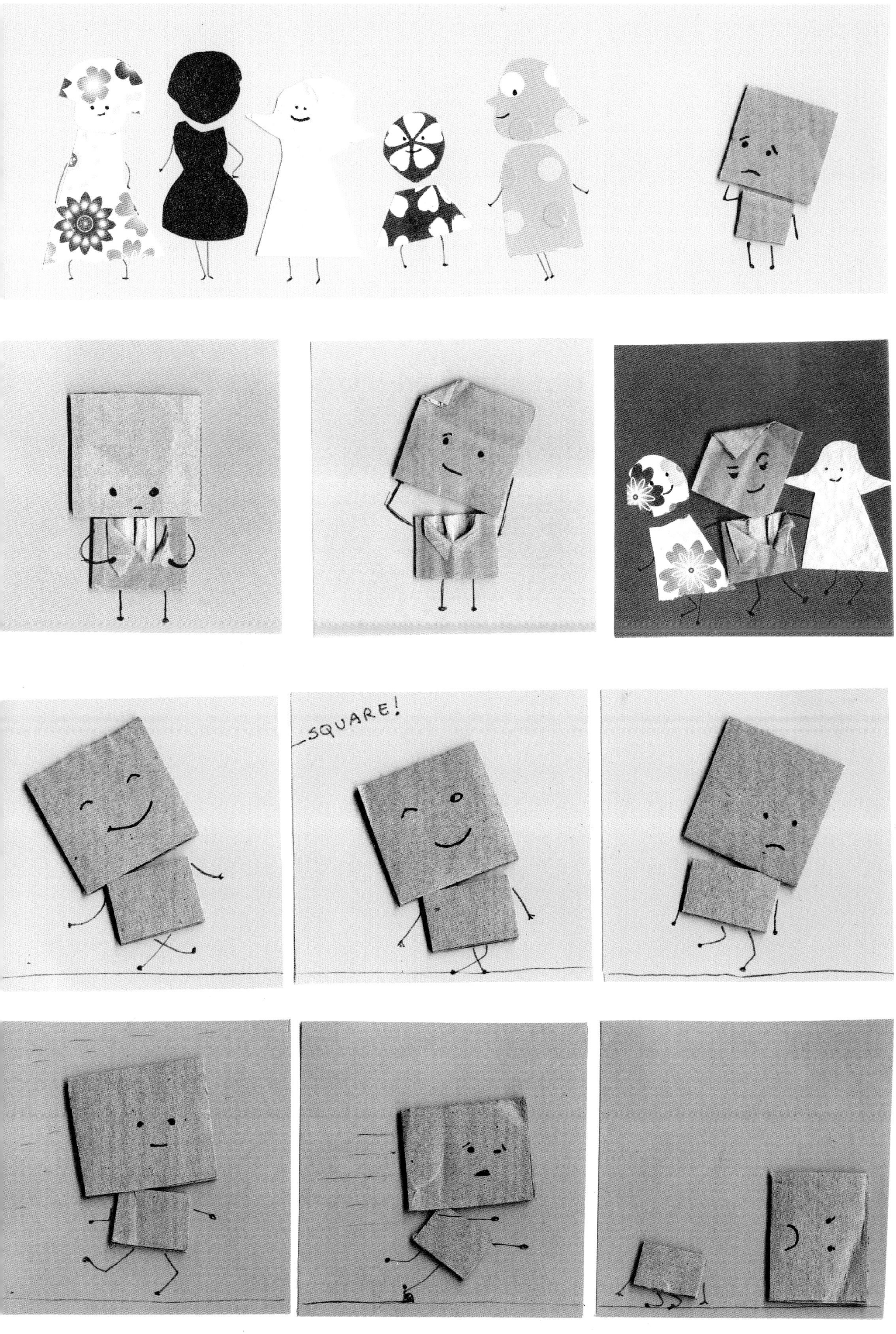
SQUARE!

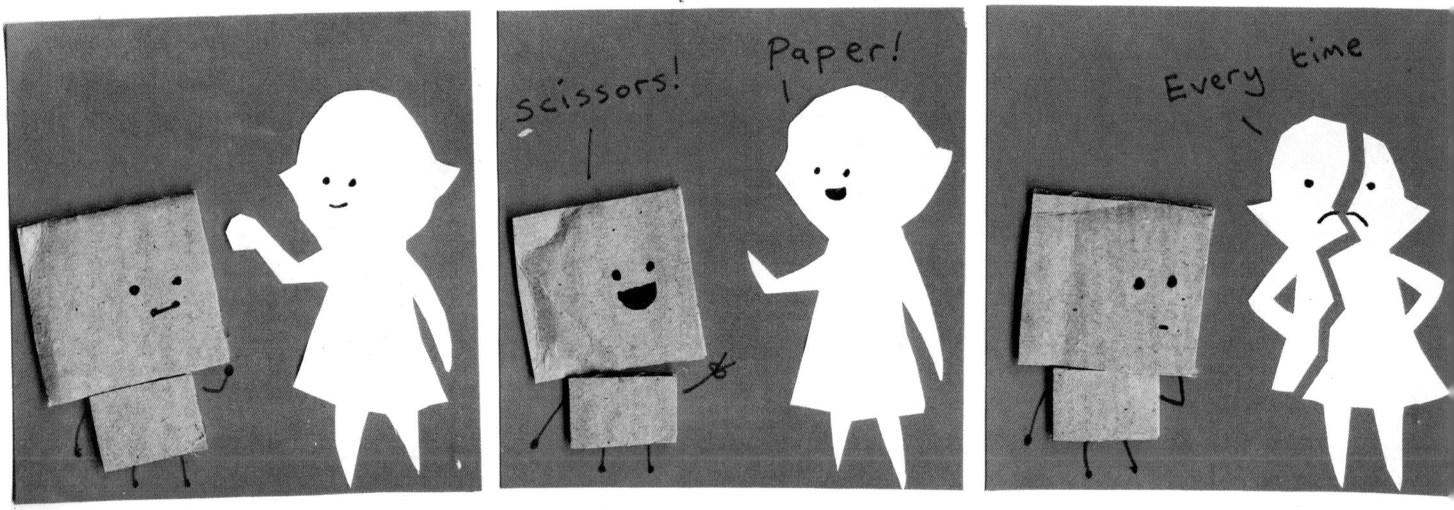
Scissors!
Paper!
Every time

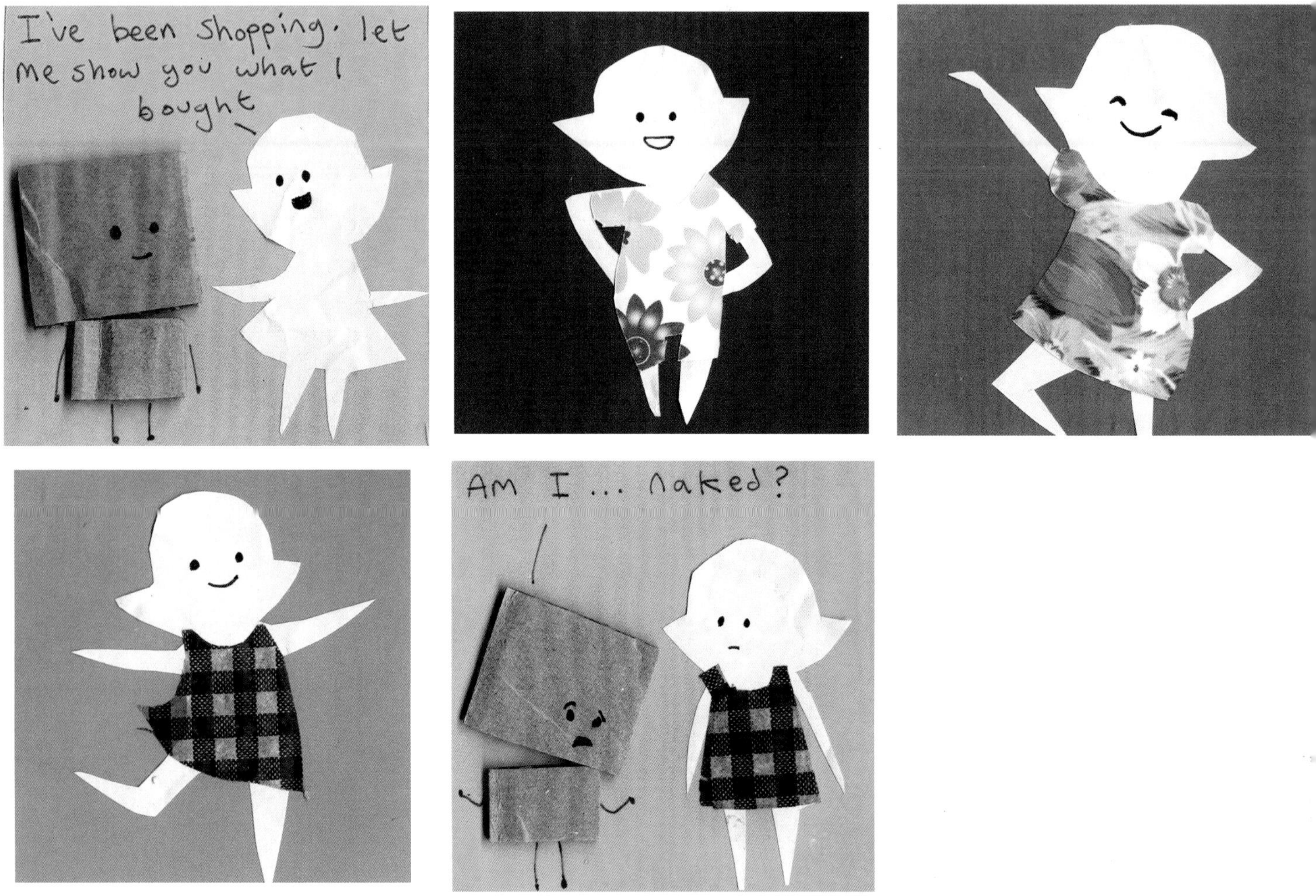
I've been shopping, let me show you what I bought
Am I ... naked?

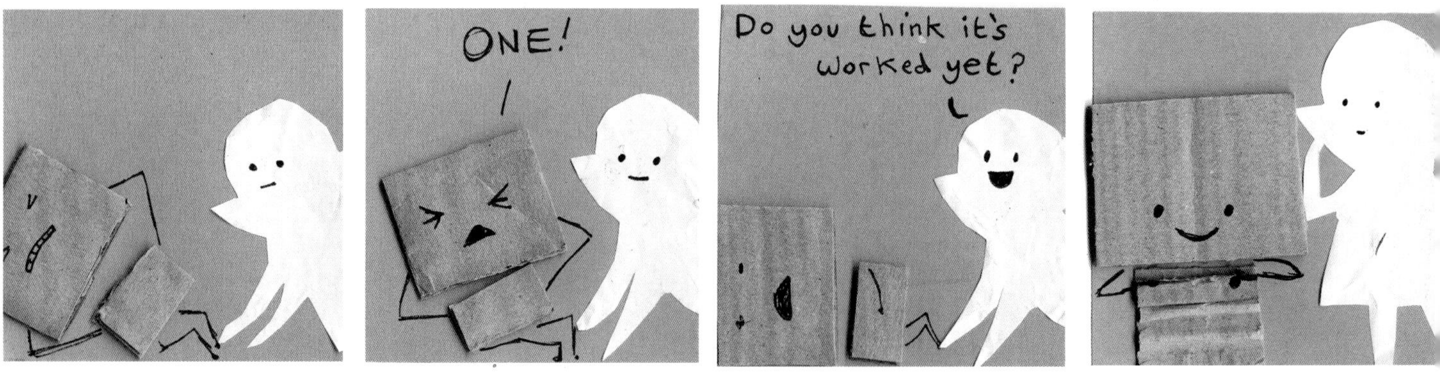
ONE!
Do you think it's worked yet?

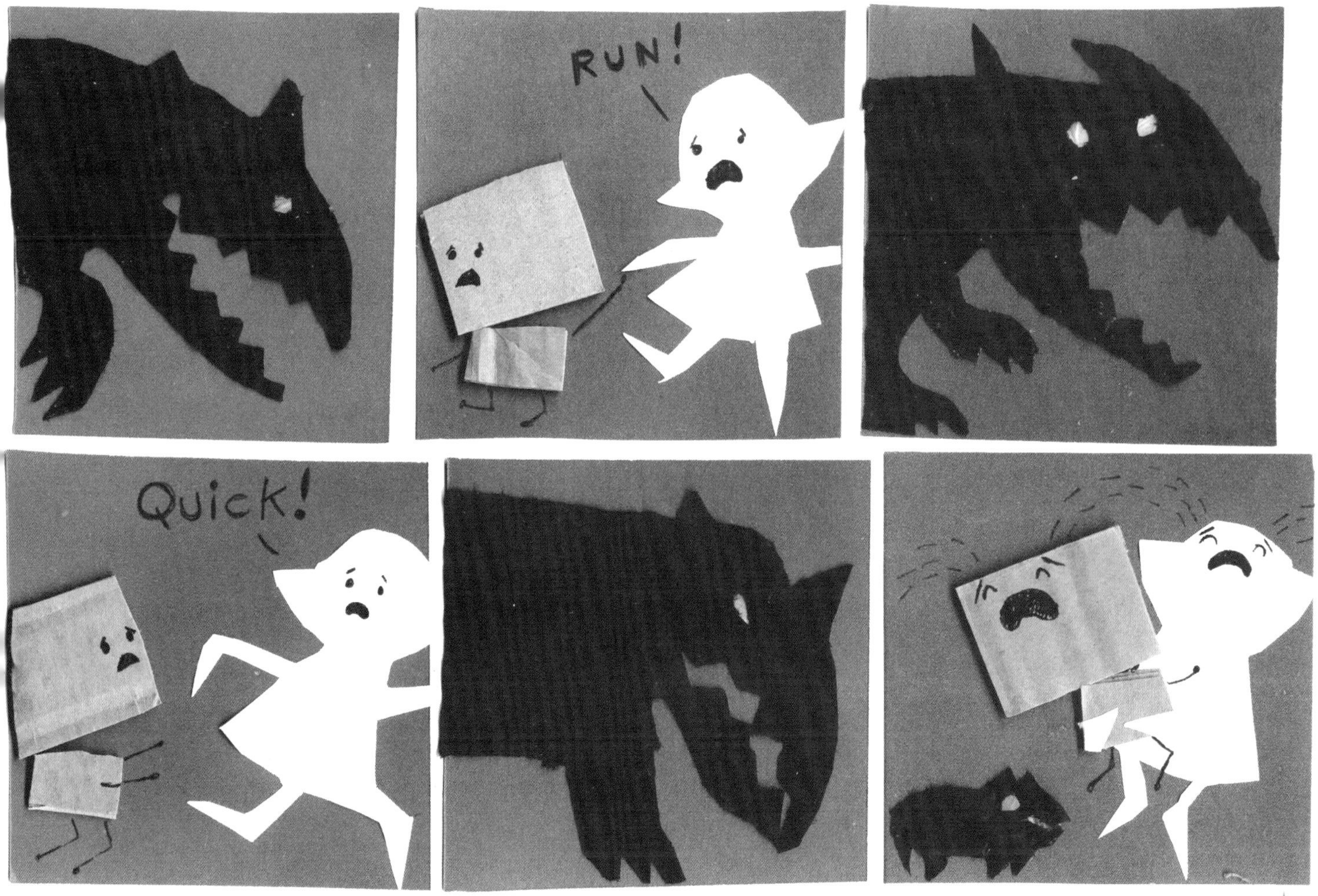
RUN!
Quick!

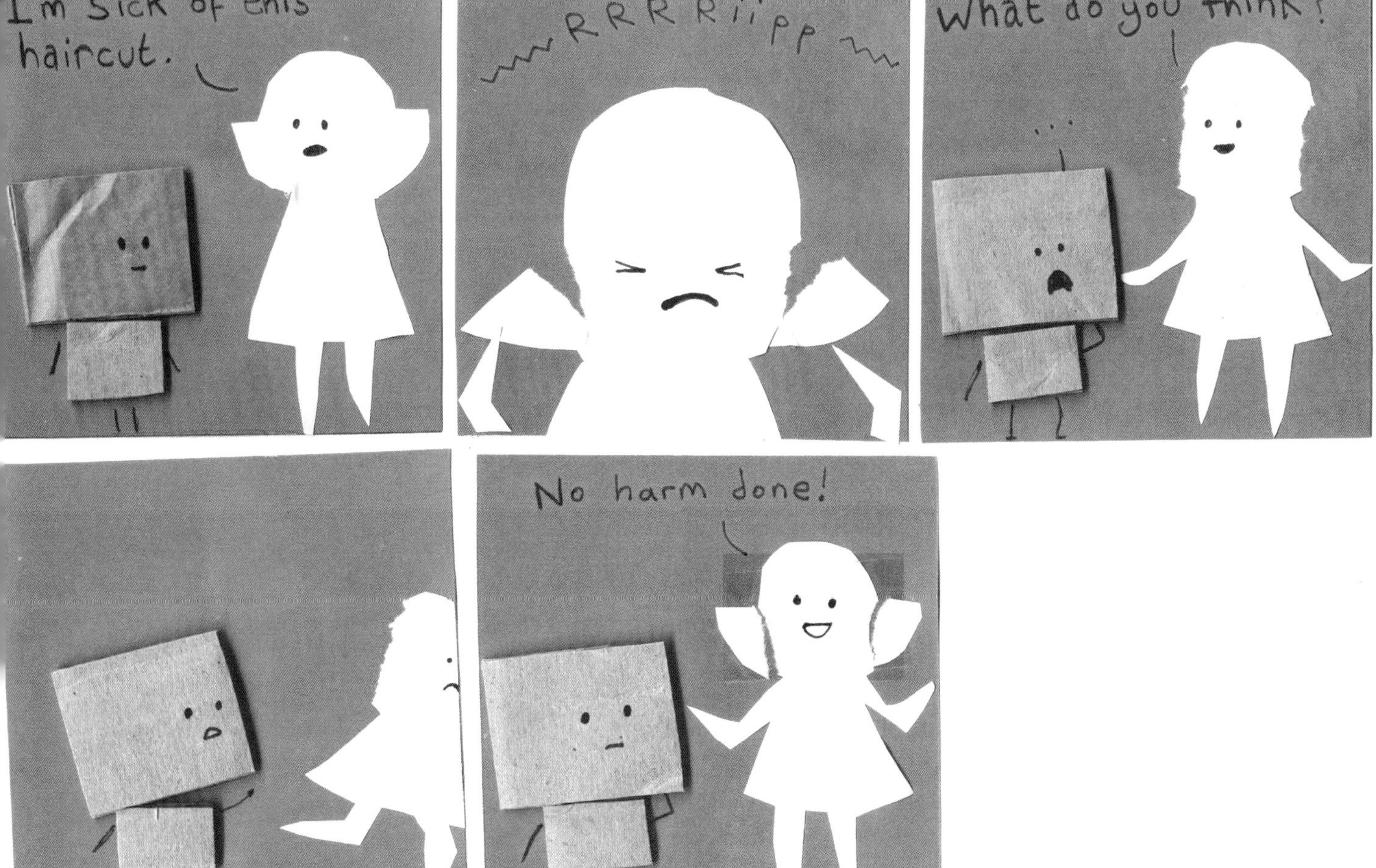
I'm sick of this haircut.
RRRRiipp
What do you think?
...
No harm done!

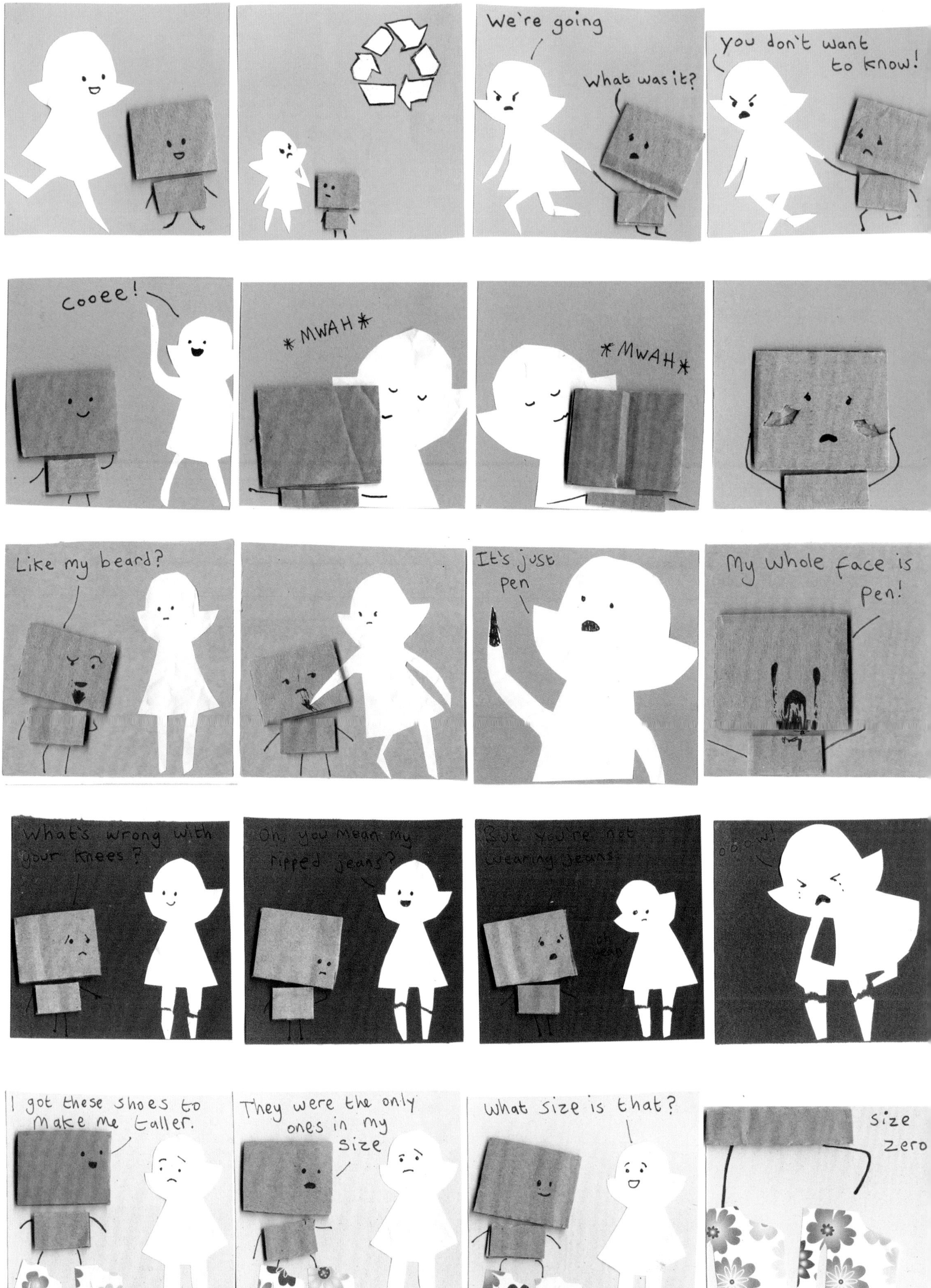
We're going
What was it?
you don't want to know!
cooee!
MWAH
MWAH
Like my beard?
It's just pen
My whole face is pen!
What's wrong with your knees?
Oh, you mean my ripped jeans?
But you're not wearing jeans.
oh yeah
Ooow!
I got these shoes to make me taller.
They were the only ones in my size
What size is that?
size zero

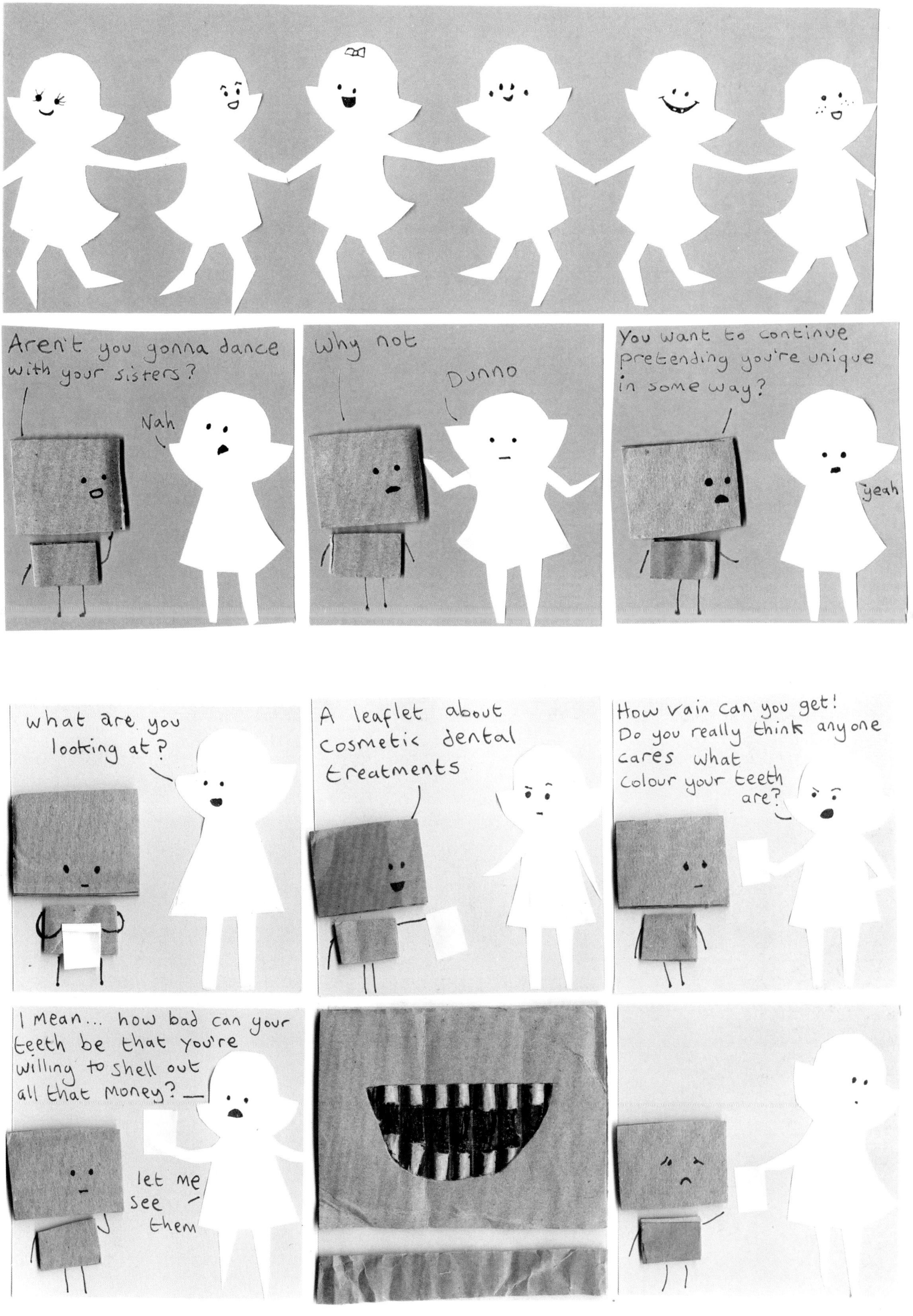

Aren't you gonna dance with your sisters?
Nah
Why not
Dunno
You want to continue pretending you're unique in some way?
yeah
What are you looking at?
A leaflet about cosmetic dental treatments
How vain can you get! Do you really think anyone cares what colour your teeth are?
I mean... how bad can your teeth be that you're willing to shell out all that money?
let me see them

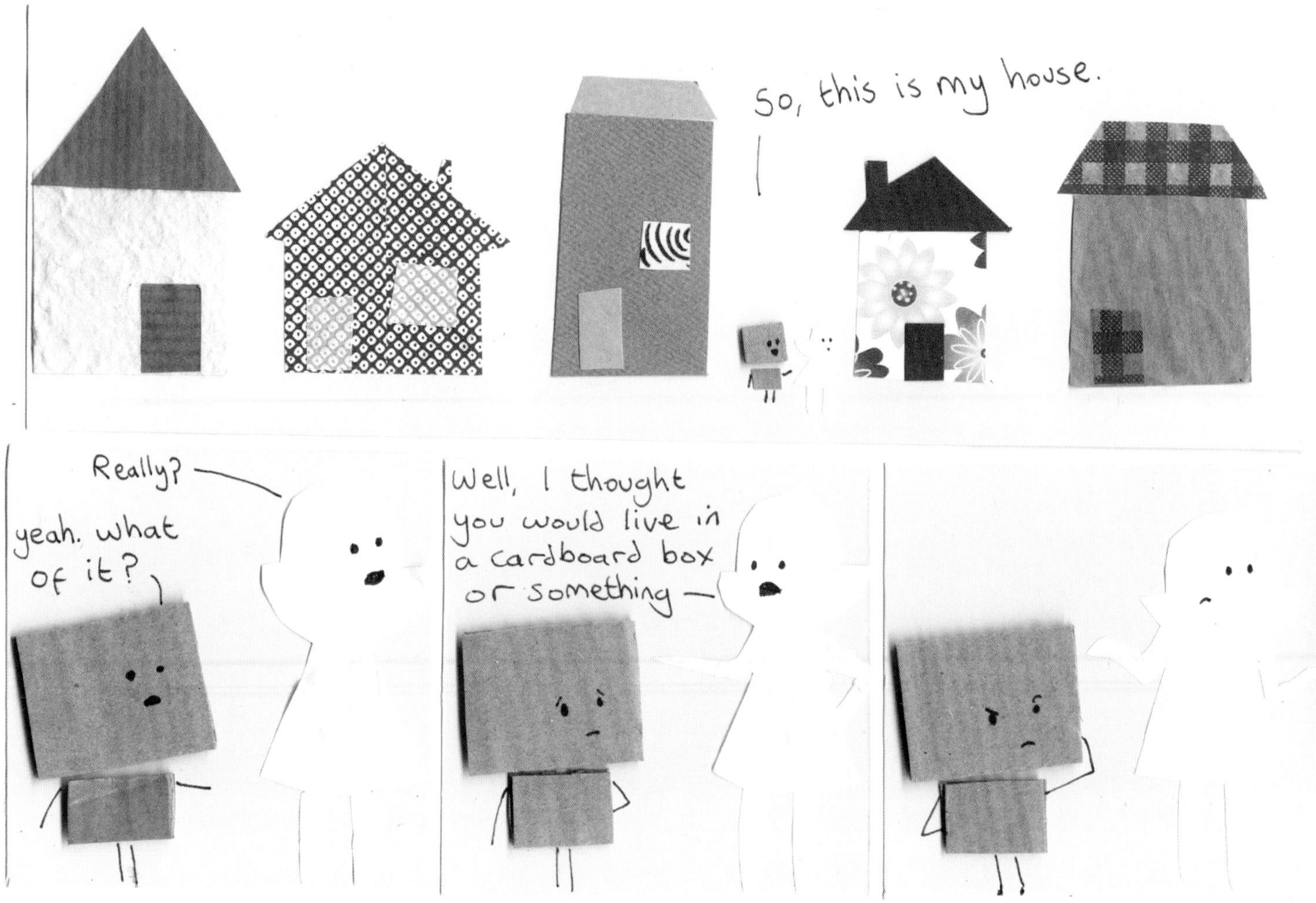
So, this is my house.
Really?
yeah. what of it?
Well, I thought you would live in a cardboard box or something

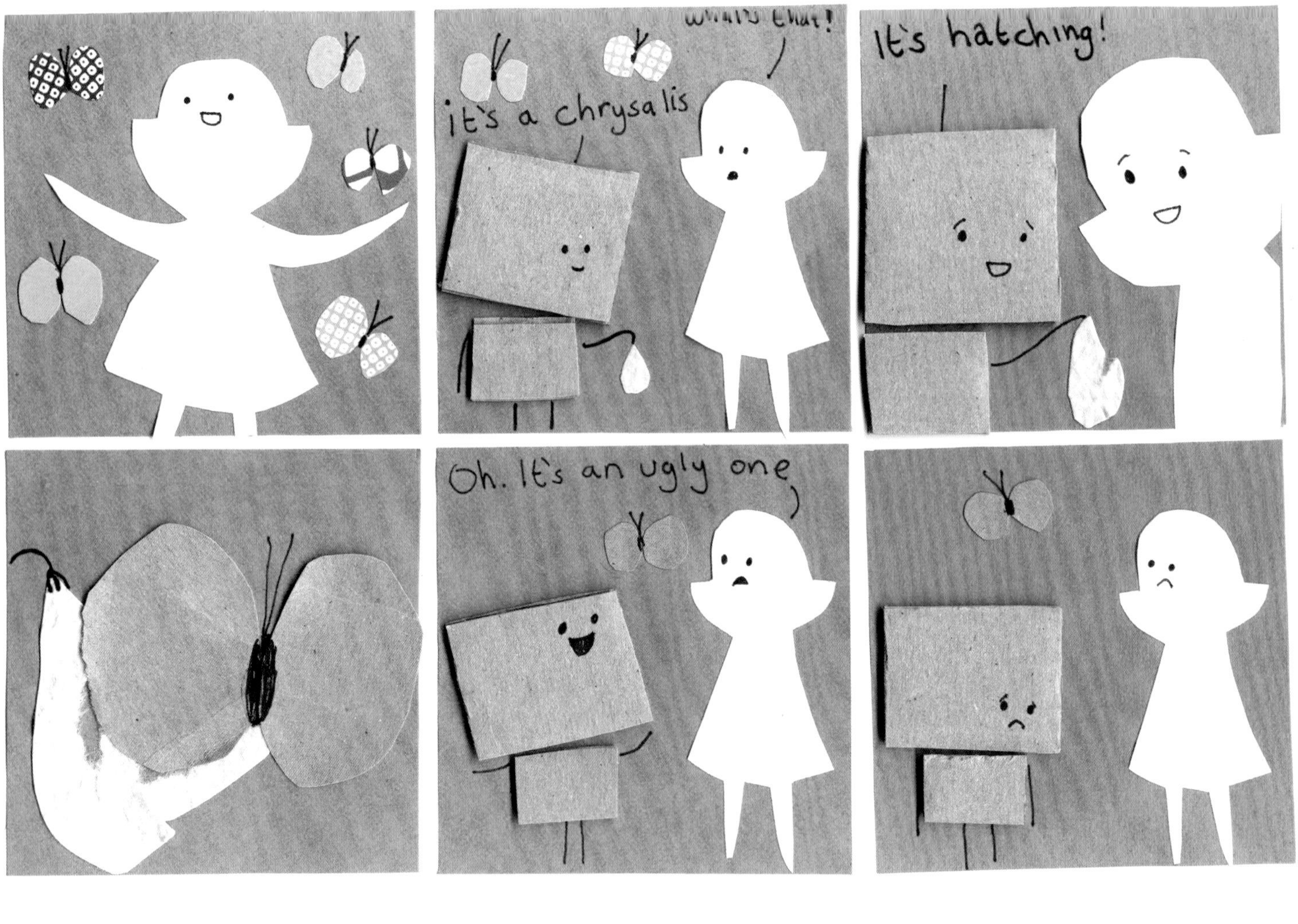
it's a chrysalis
It's hatching!
Oh. It's an ugly one

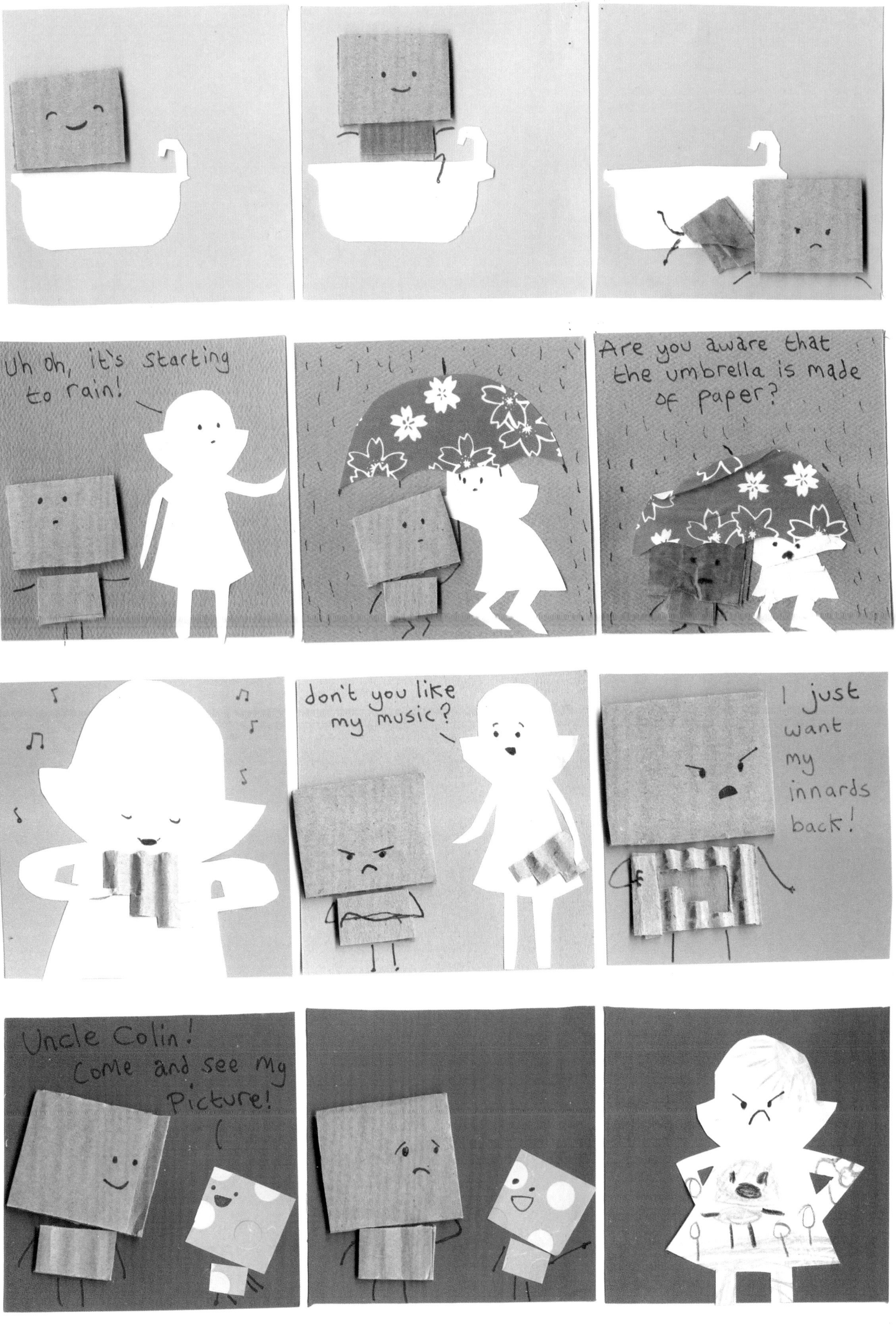
Uh oh, it's starting to rain!
Are you aware that the umbrella is made of paper?
don't you like my music?
I just want my innards back!
Uncle Colin! Come and see my Picture!

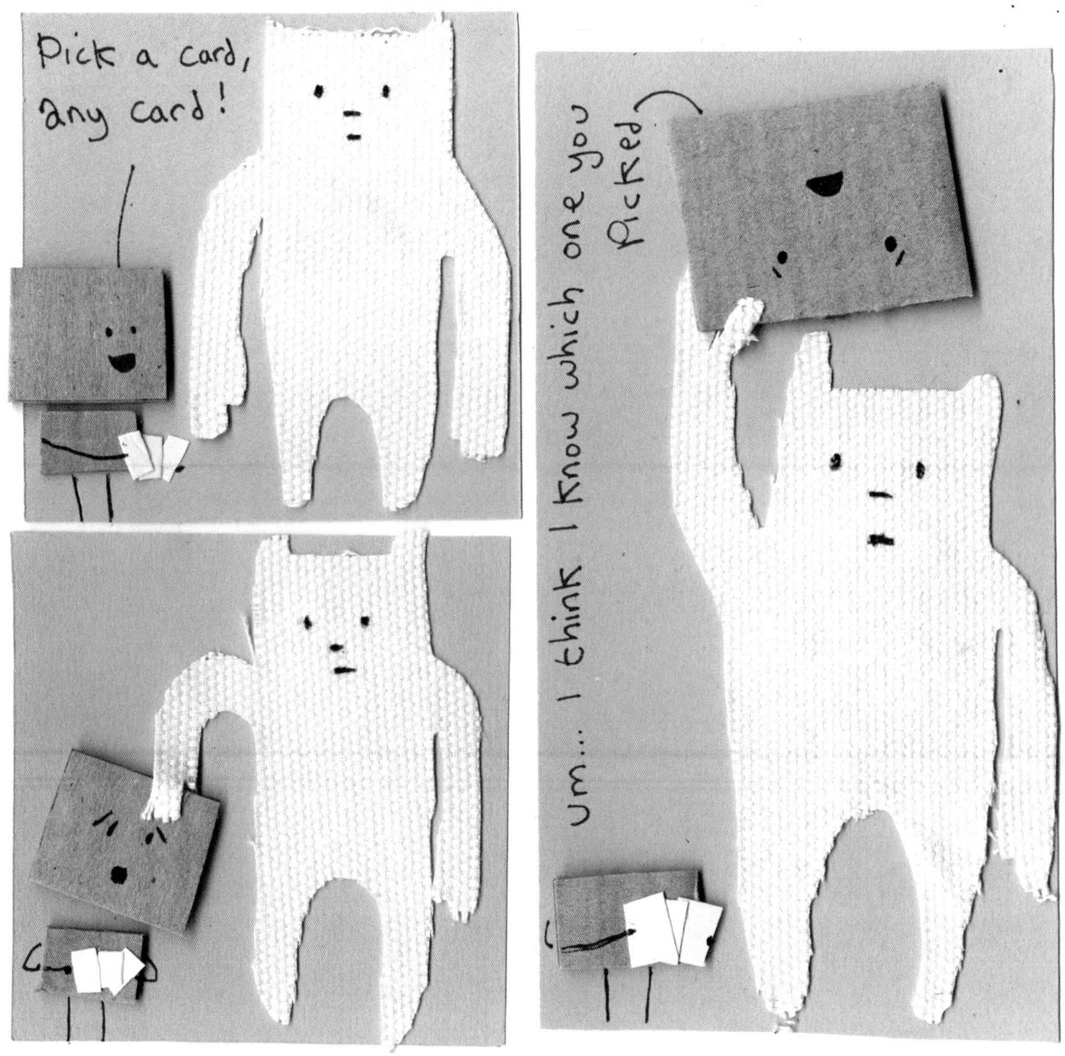
Pick a card, any card!
Um... I think I know which one you picked

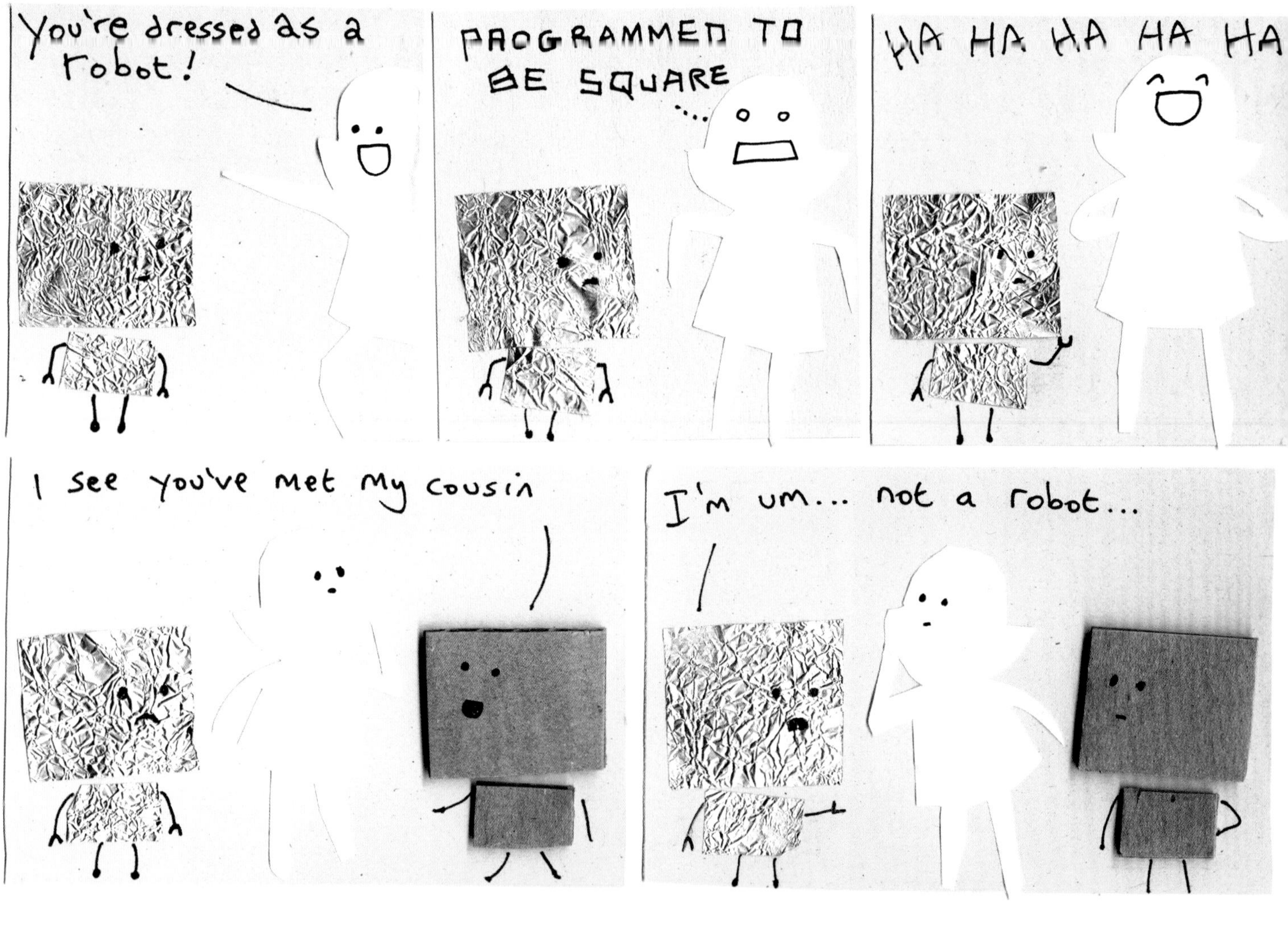
You're dressed as a robot!
PROGRAMMED TO BE SQUARE
HA HA HA HA HA
I see you've met my cousin
I'm um... not a robot...

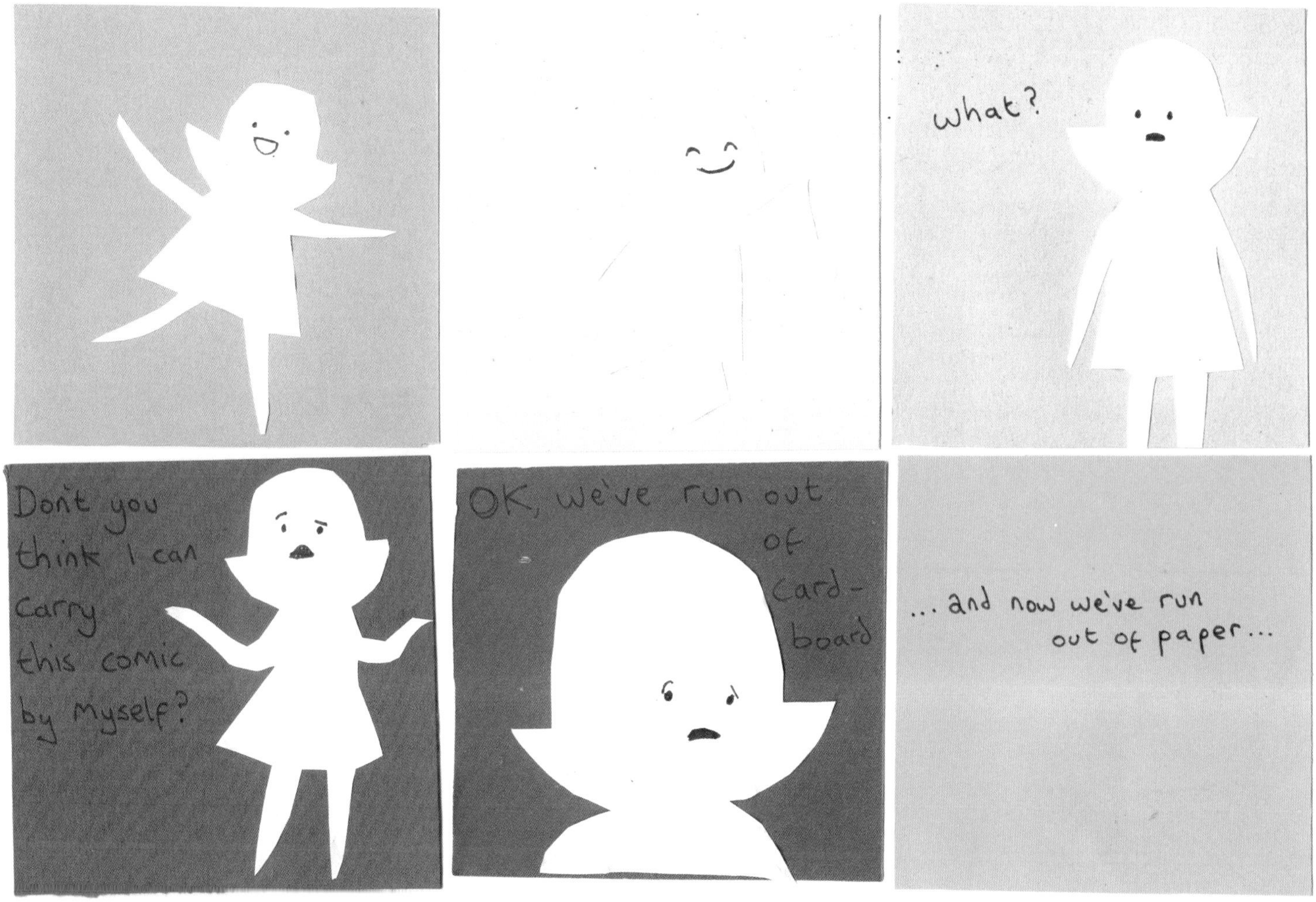
what?
Don't you think I can carry this comic by myself?
OK, we've run out of card-board
... and now we've run out of paper...

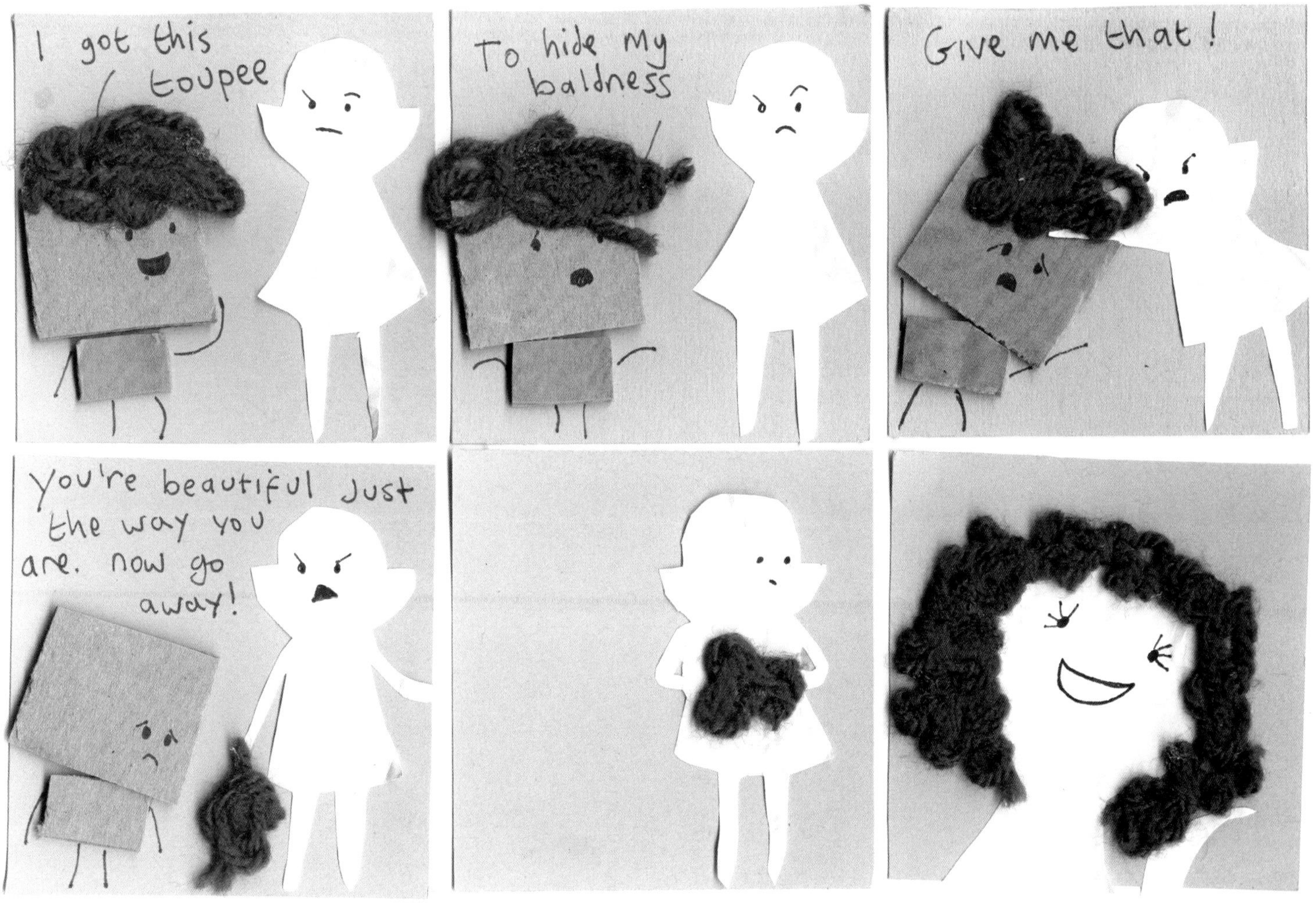
I got this toupee
To hide my baldness
Give me that!
you're beautiful just the way you are. now go away!

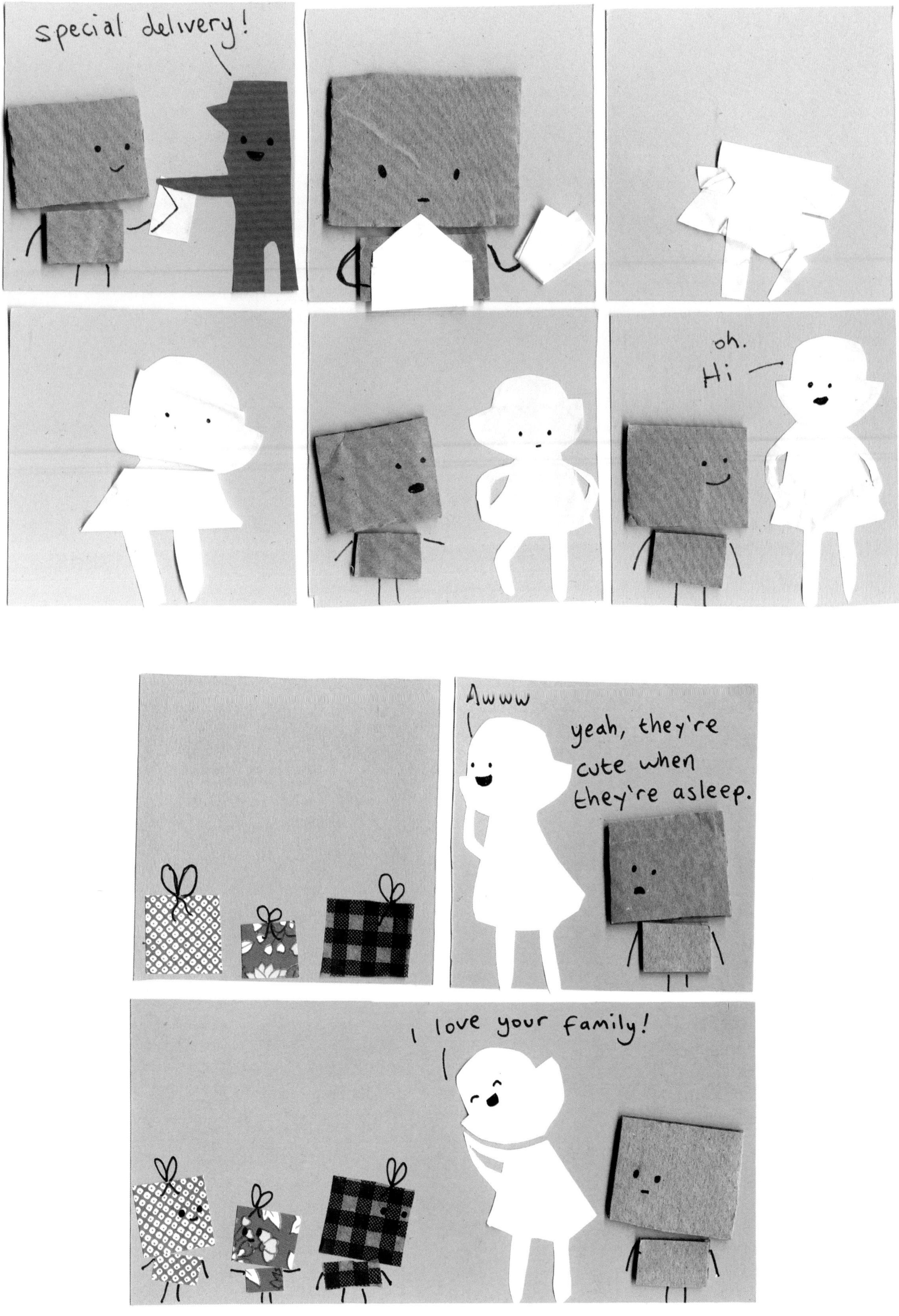
special delivery!
oh.
Hi
Awww
yeah, they're cute when they're asleep.
I love your family!

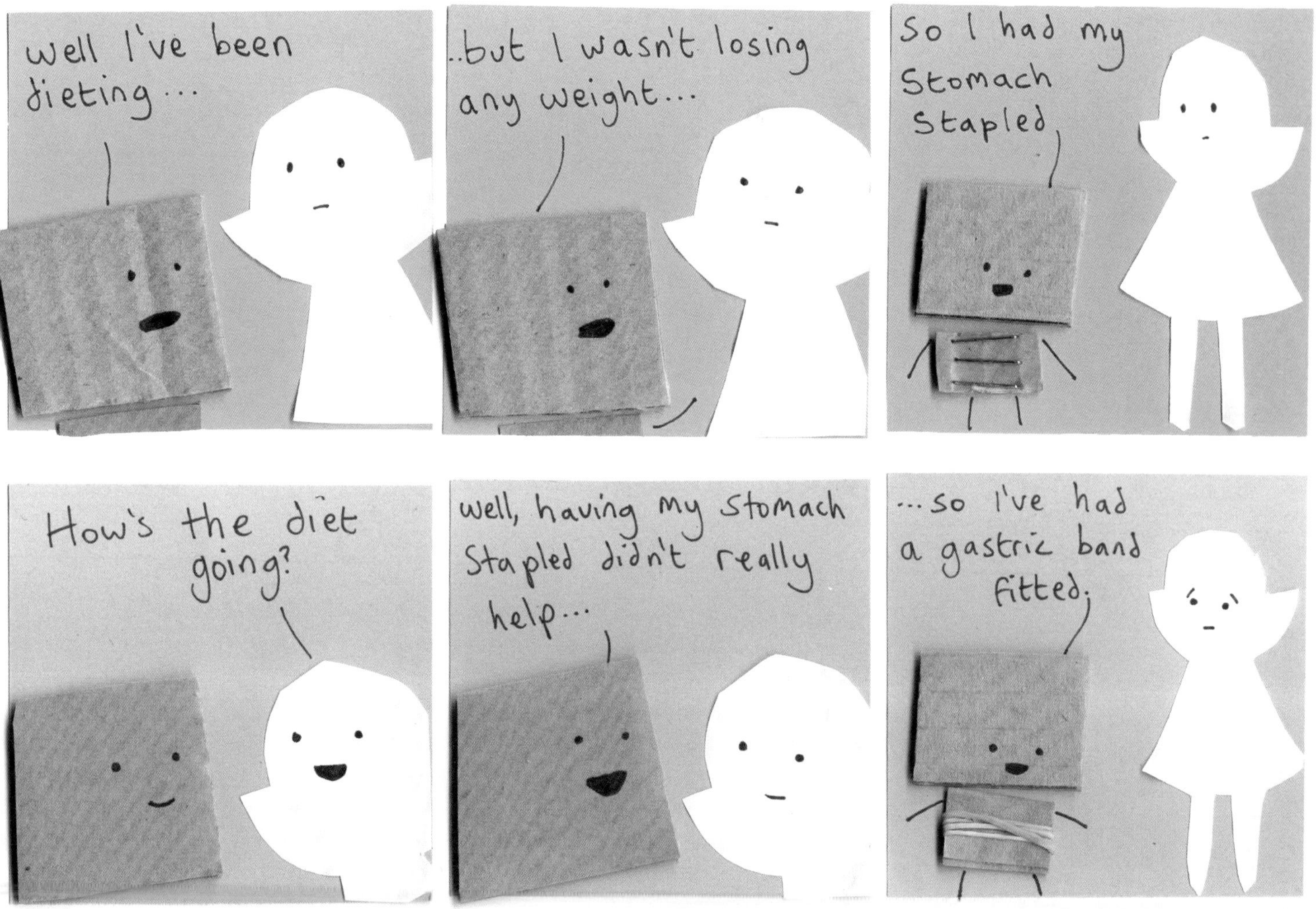
well I've been dieting...
..but I wasn't losing any weight...
So I had my Stomach Stapled
How's the diet going?
well, having my Stomach Stapled didn't really help...
...so I've had a gastric band fitted.

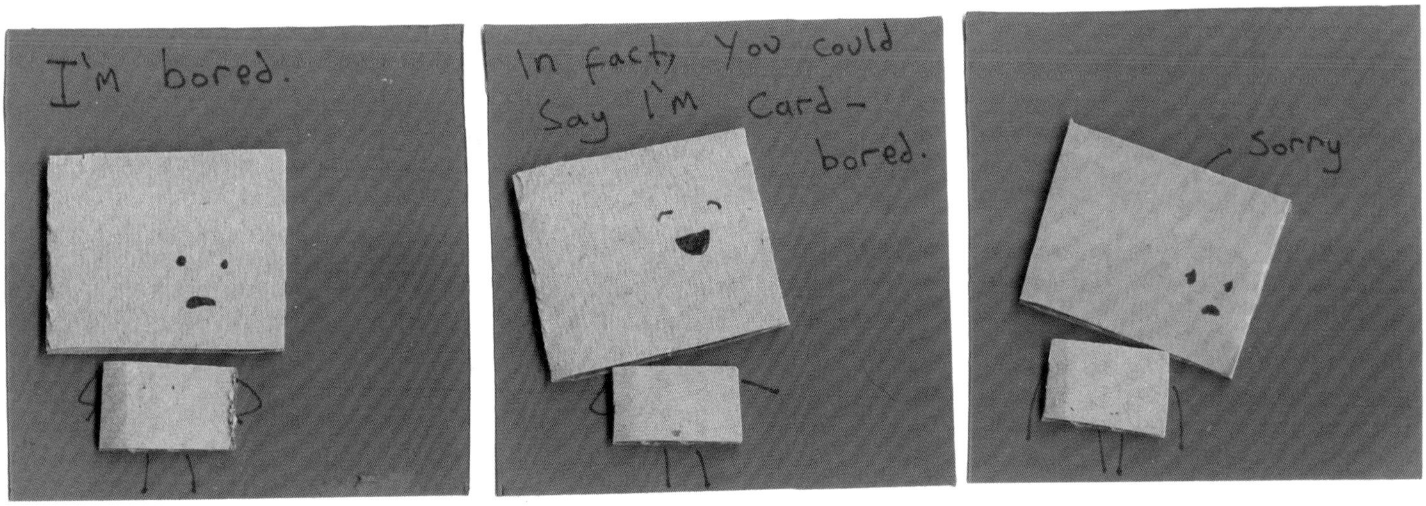
I'm bored.
In fact, You could Say I'm Card-bored.
Sorry

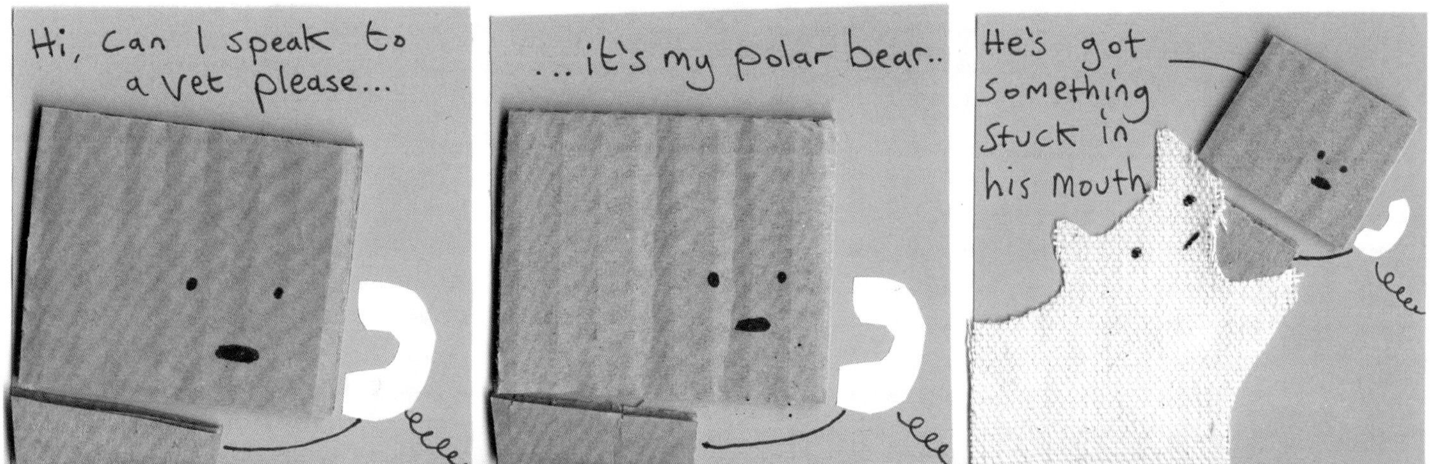
Hi, Can I speak to a vet please...
...it's my polar bear..
He's got something stuck in his mouth

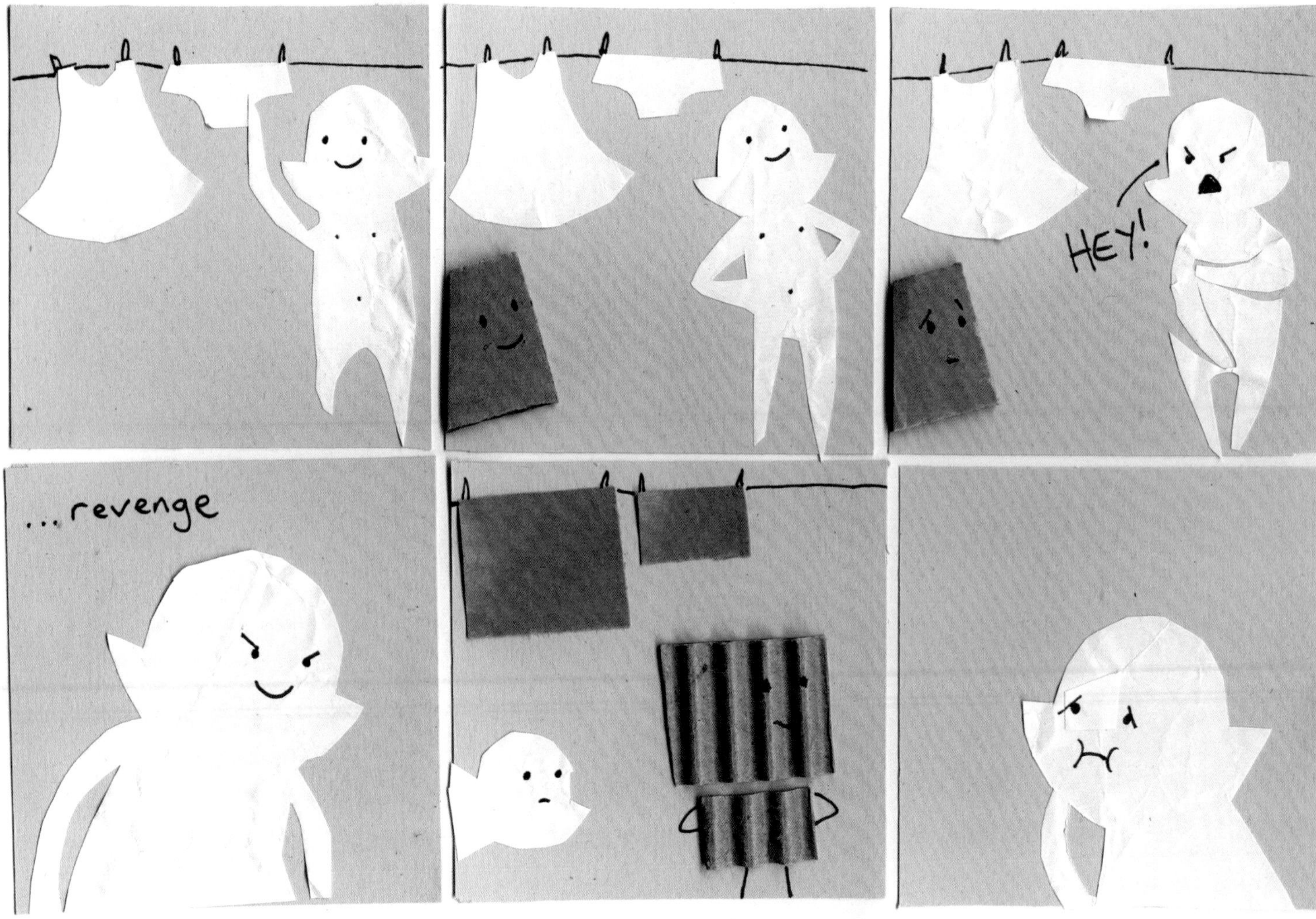
HEY!
...revenge

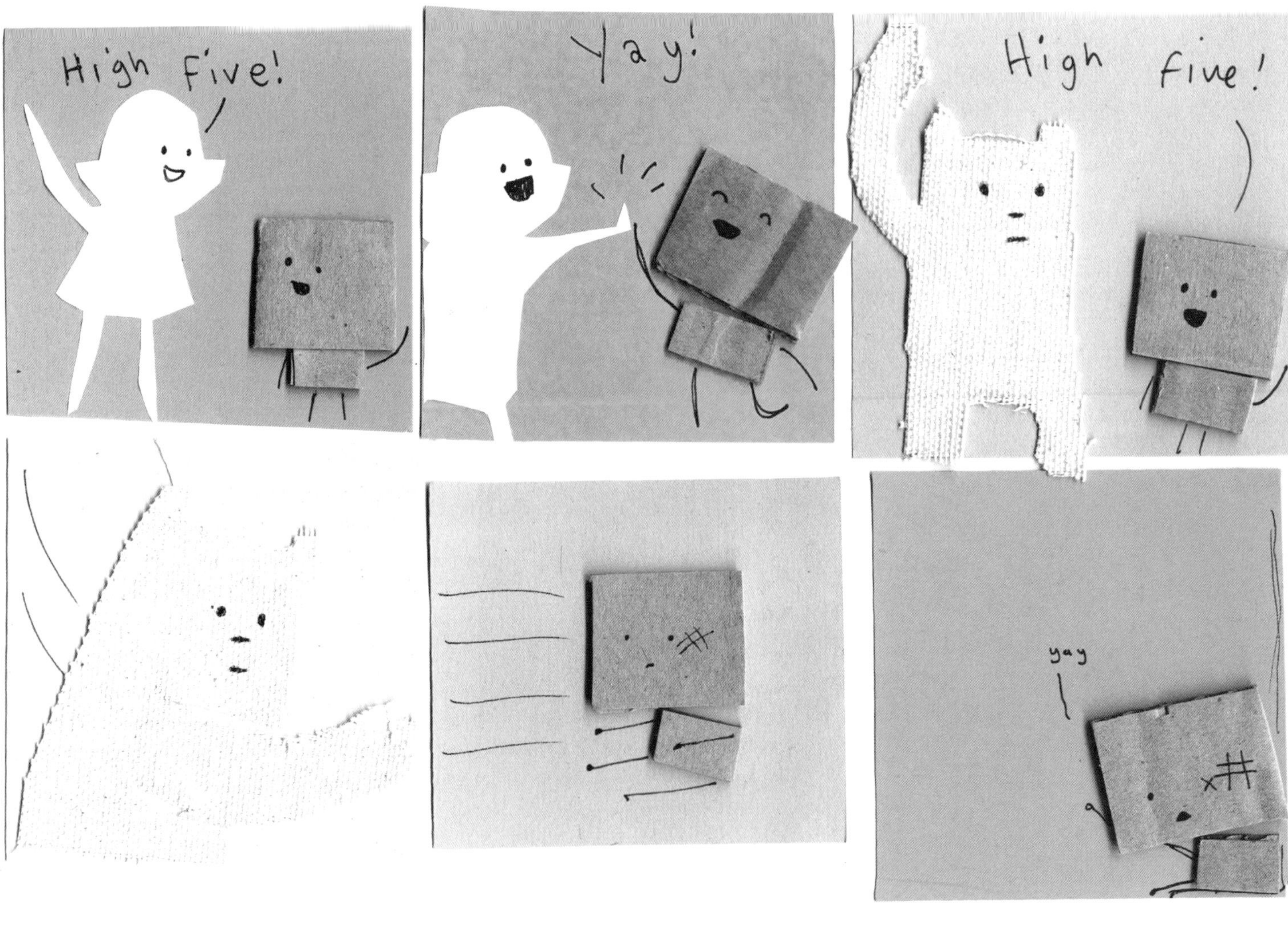
High five!
Yay!
High five!
yay

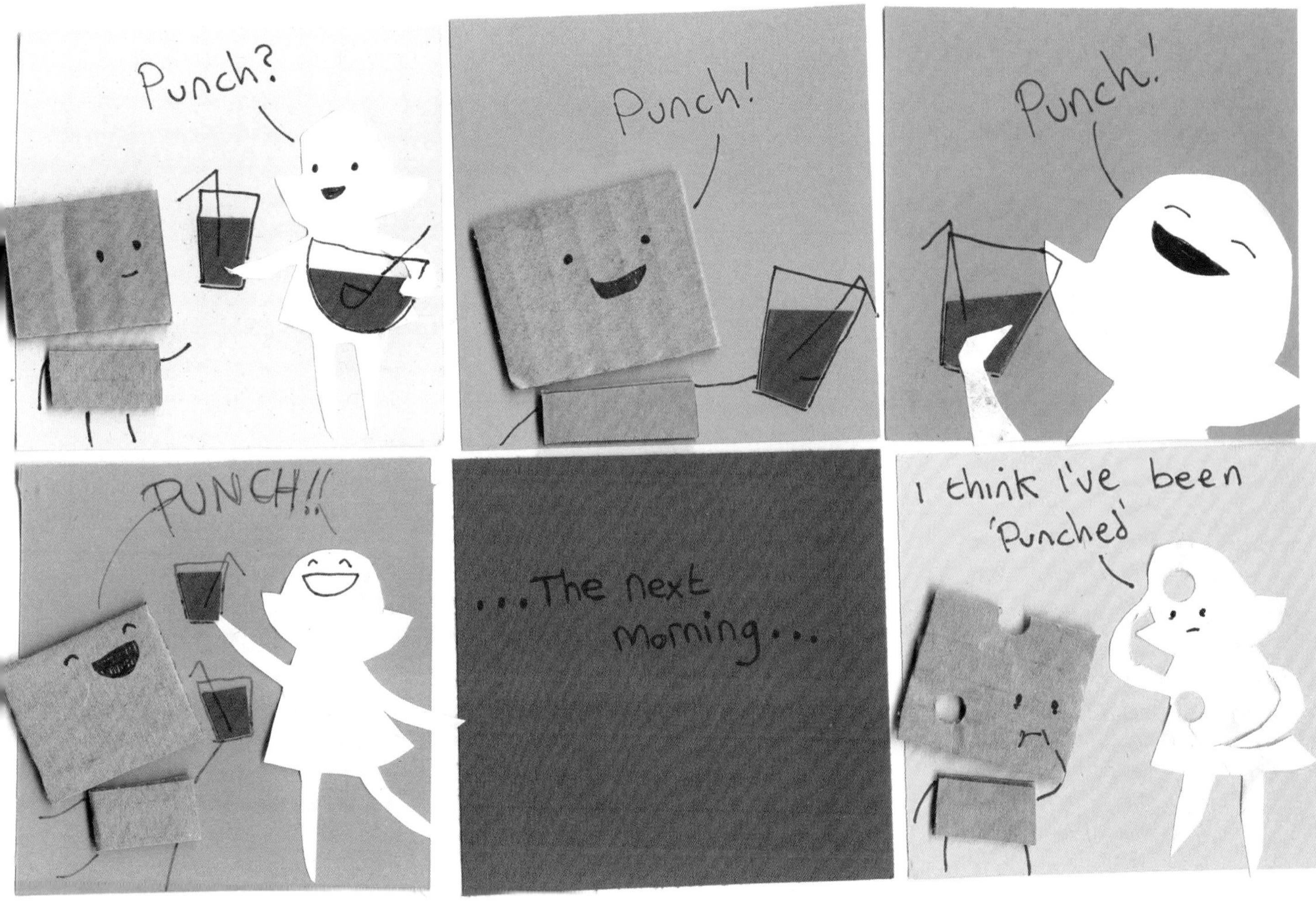
Punch?
Punch!
Punch!
PUNCH!!
...The next morning...
I think I've been 'Punched'

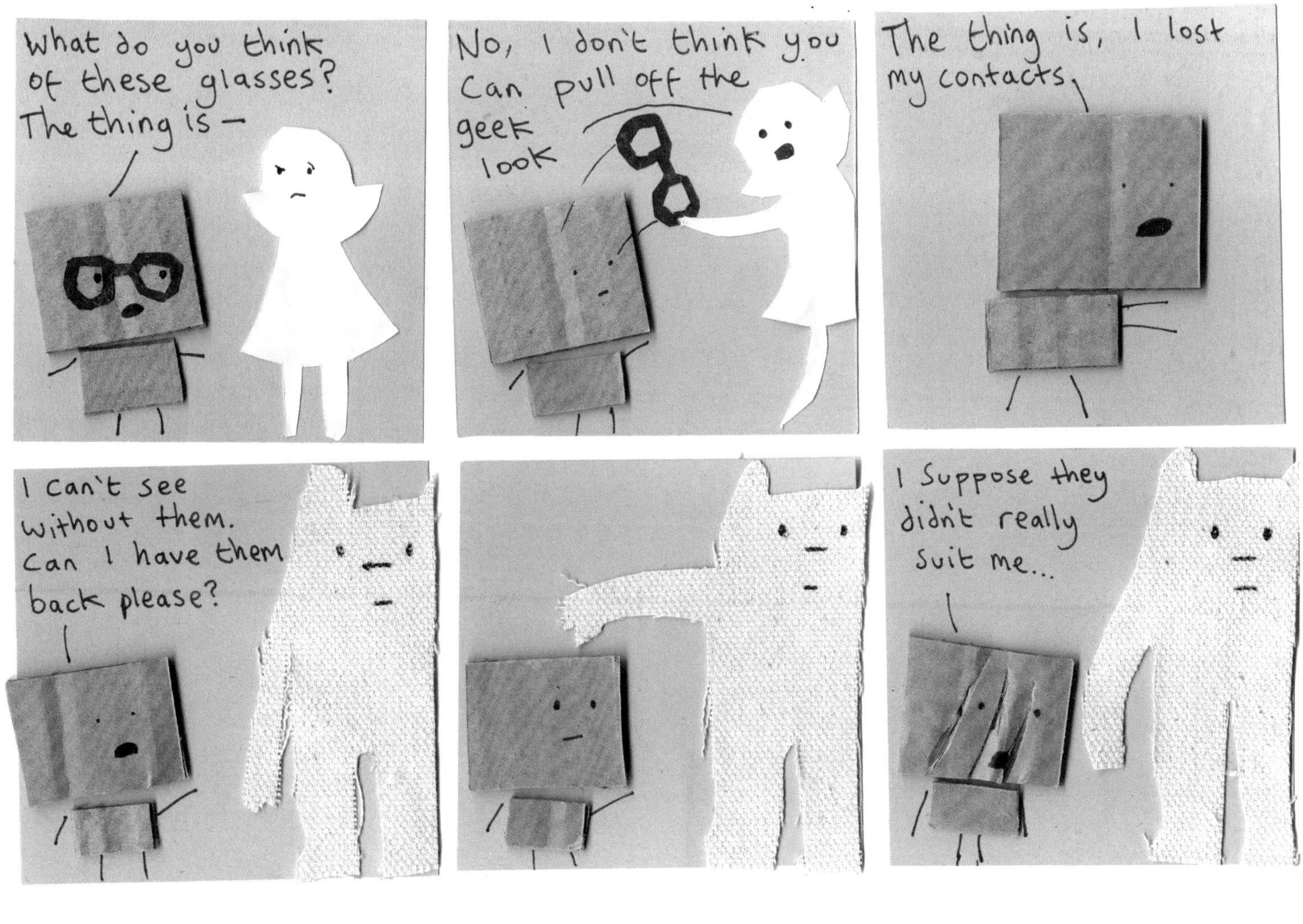
What do you think of these glasses? The thing is -
No, I don't think you can pull off the geek look
The thing is, I lost my contacts
I can't see without them. Can I have them back please?
I suppose they didn't really suit me...

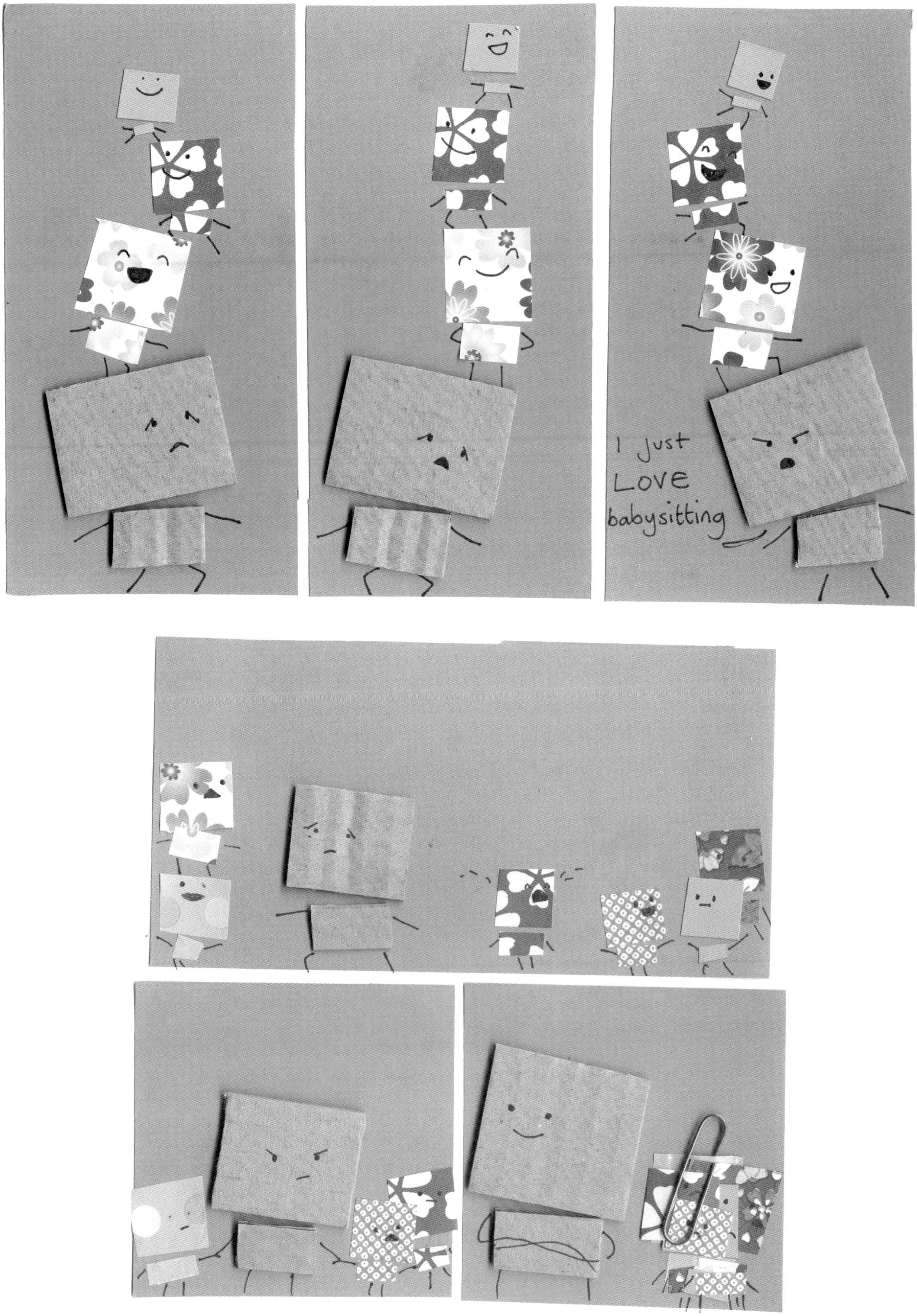
I just LOVE babysitting

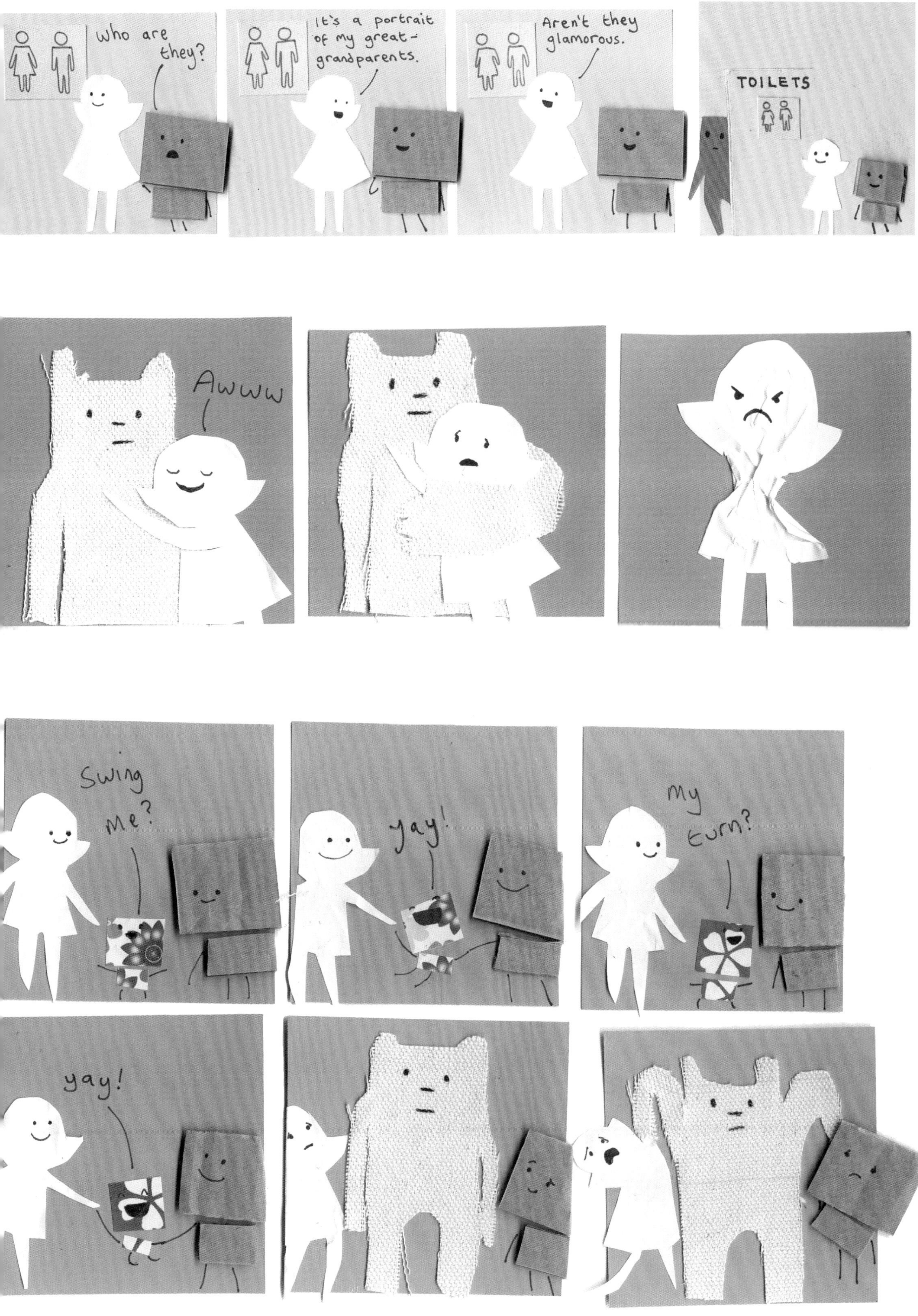
who are they?
It's a portrait of my great-grandparents.
Aren't they glamorous.
TOILETS
Awww
Swing me?
yay!
my turn?
yay!

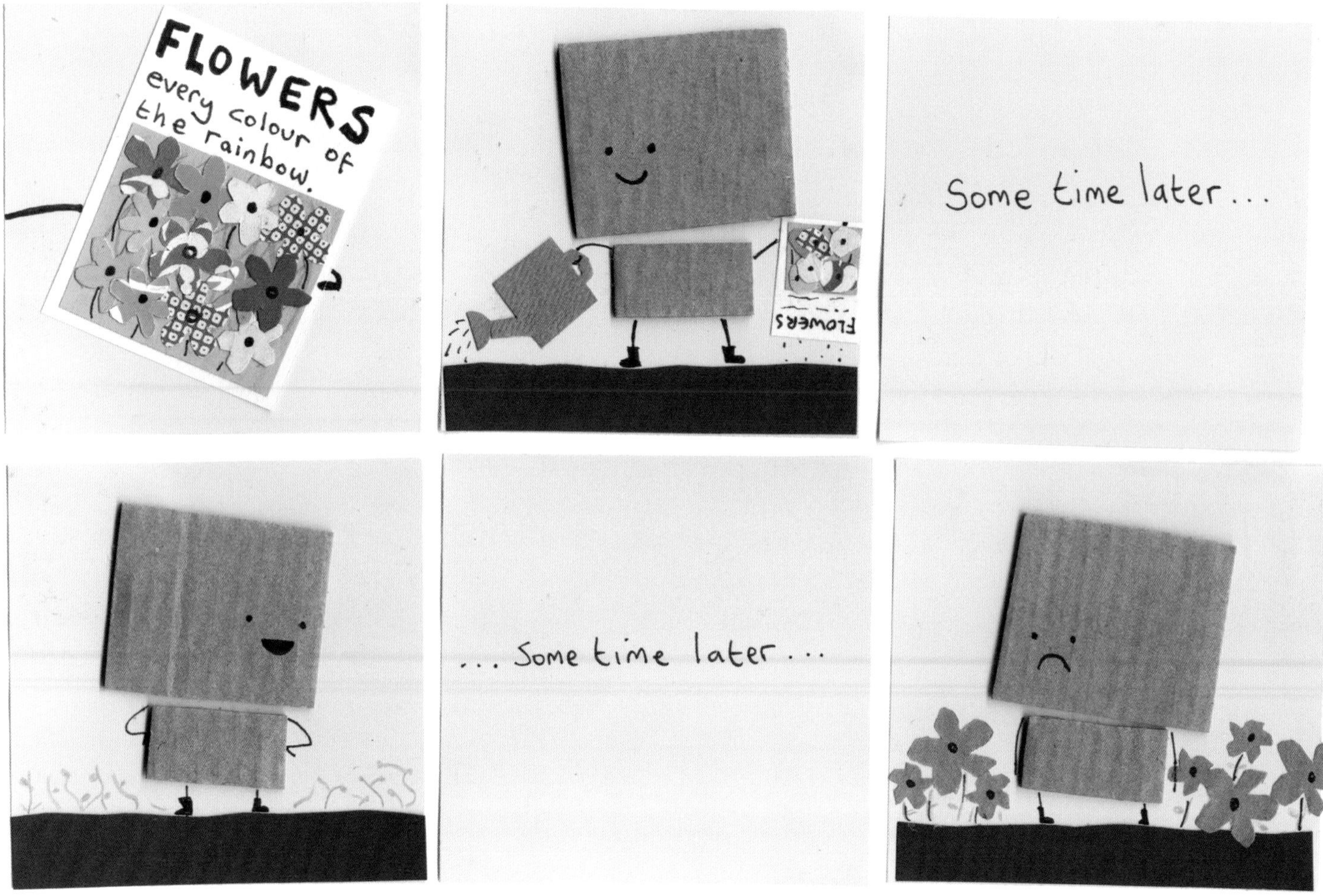
FLOWERS
every colour of the rainbow.
FLOWERS
Some time later...
... Some time later...

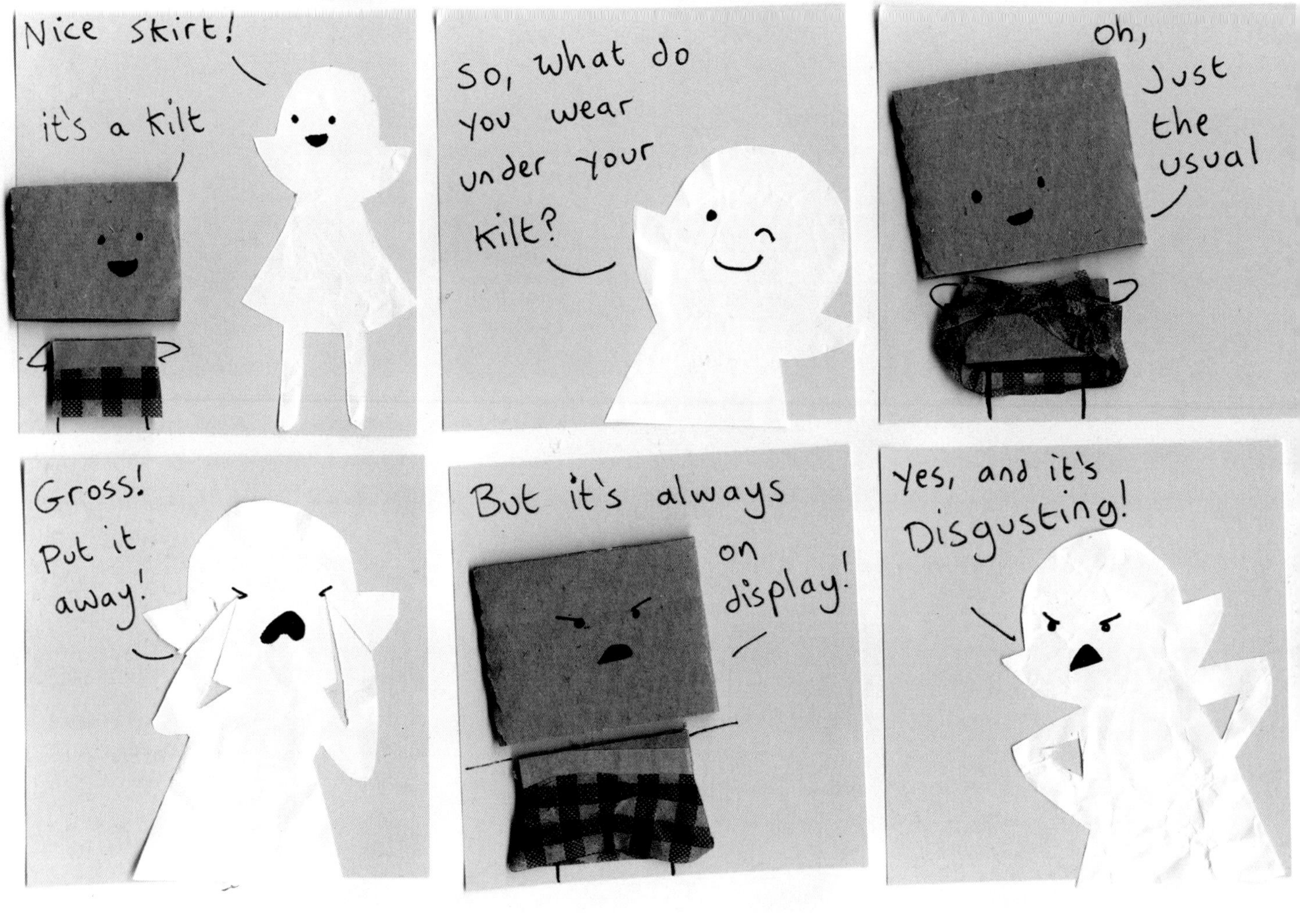
Nice Skirt!
it's a Kilt
So, what do you wear under your Kilt?
Oh, Just the usual
Gross! Put it away!
But it's always on display!
Yes, and it's Disgusting!

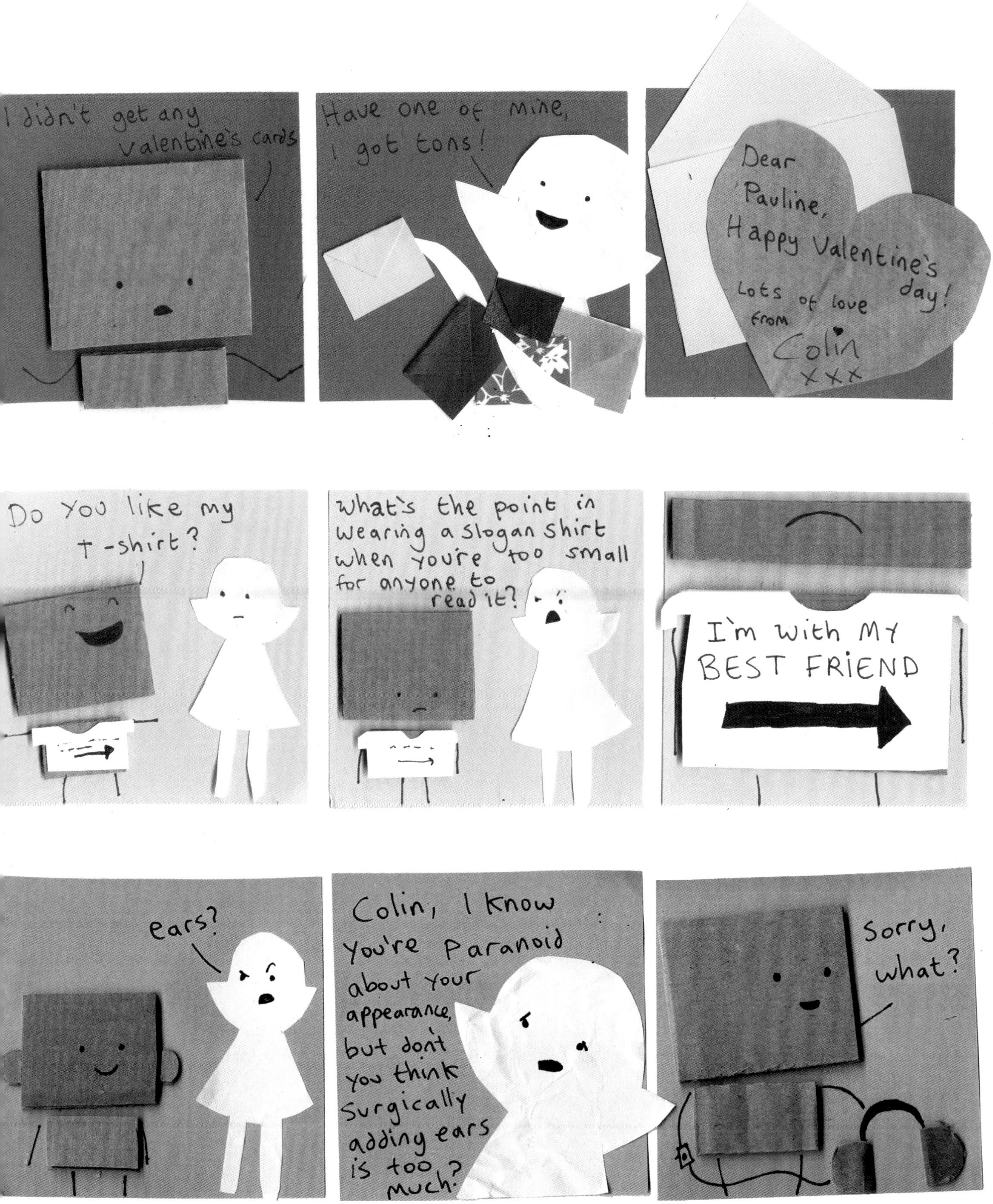
I didn't get any valentine's cards
Have one of mine, I got tons!
Dear Pauline, Happy Valentine's day! Lots of love from Colin xxx
Do you like my t-shirt?
what's the point in wearing a slogan shirt when you're too small for anyone to read it?
I'm with MY BEST FRIEND
ears?
Colin, I know you're paranoid about your appearance, but don't you think surgically adding ears is too much?
Sorry, what?

Uncle Colin! We did a picture for you.
in LOVE
paulin
colin
Like my new earrings?
Ears? I thought that was your Hair!
The ears are underneath the hair

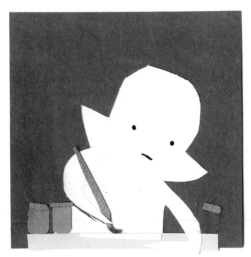

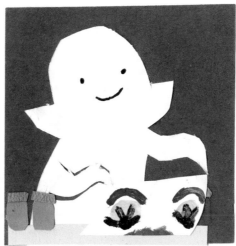

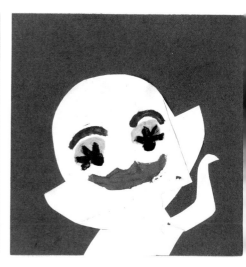

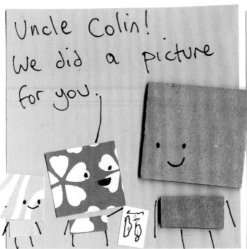

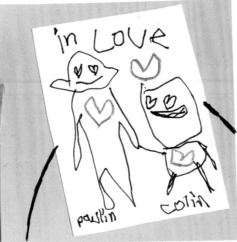

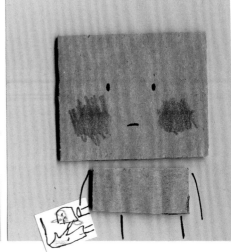

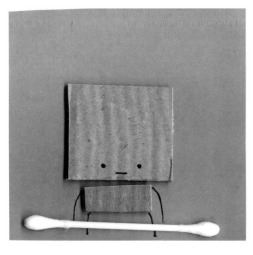

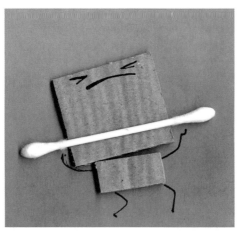

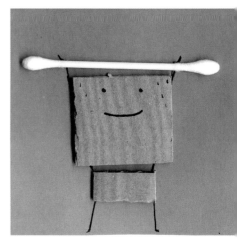

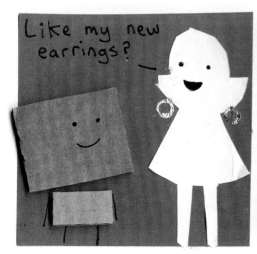

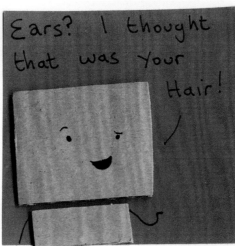

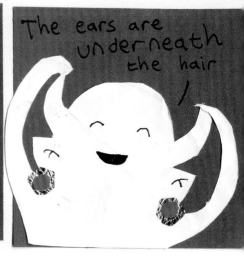

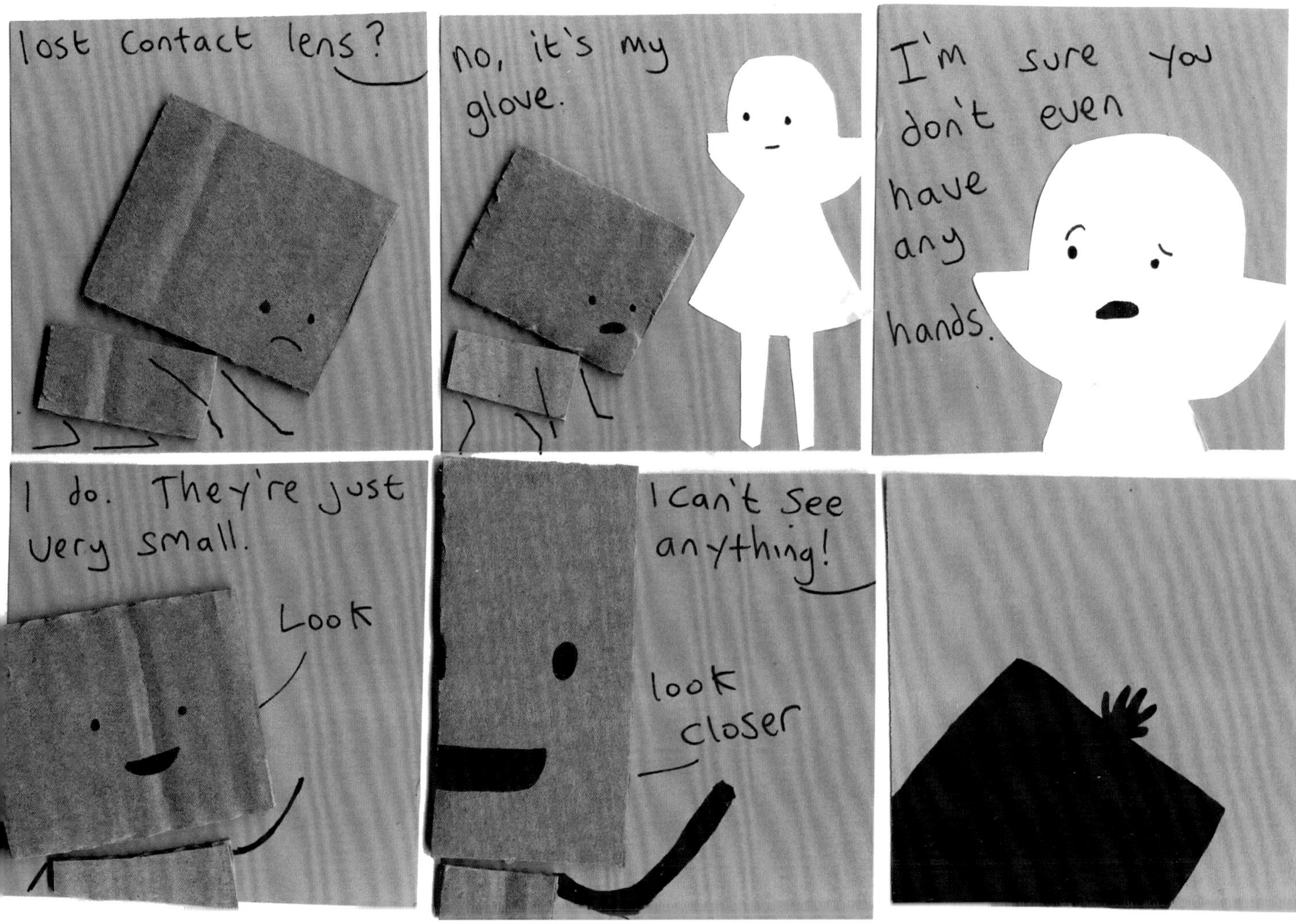
lost contact lens?
no, it's my glove.
I'm sure you don't even have any hands.
I do. They're just very small.
Look
I can't see anything!
look closer

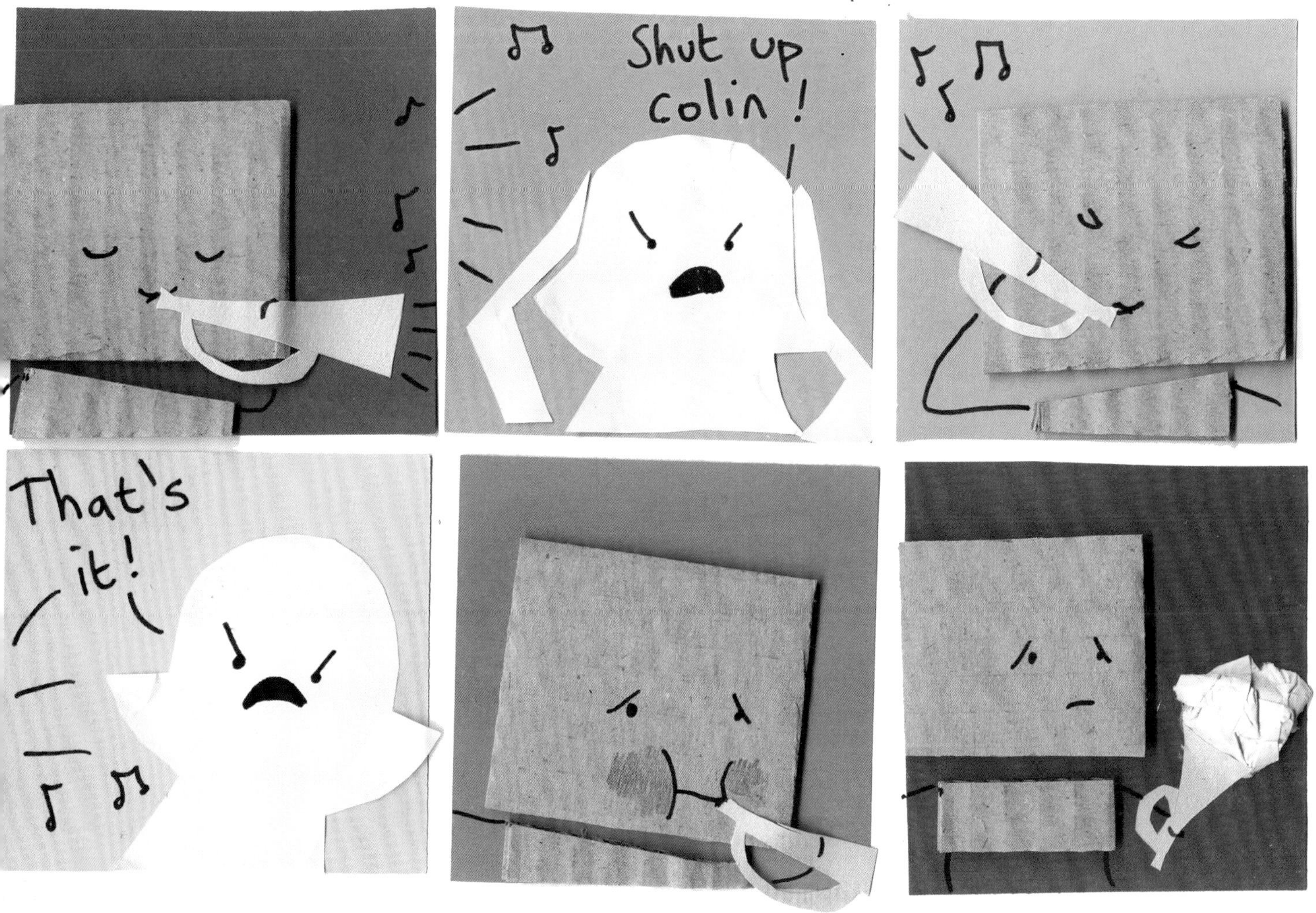
Shut up colin!
That's it!

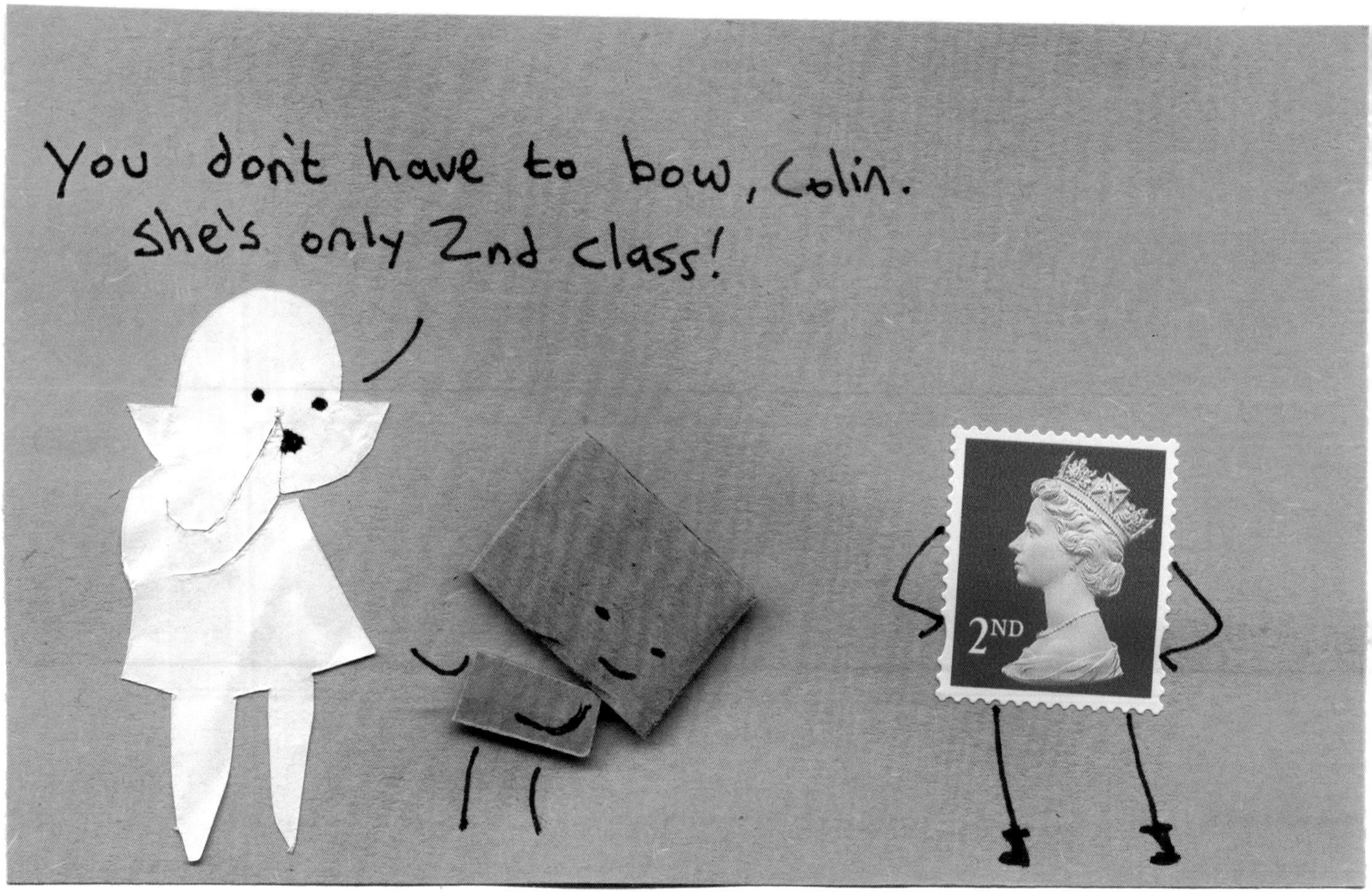
You don't have to bow, Colin. she's only 2nd class!
2ND

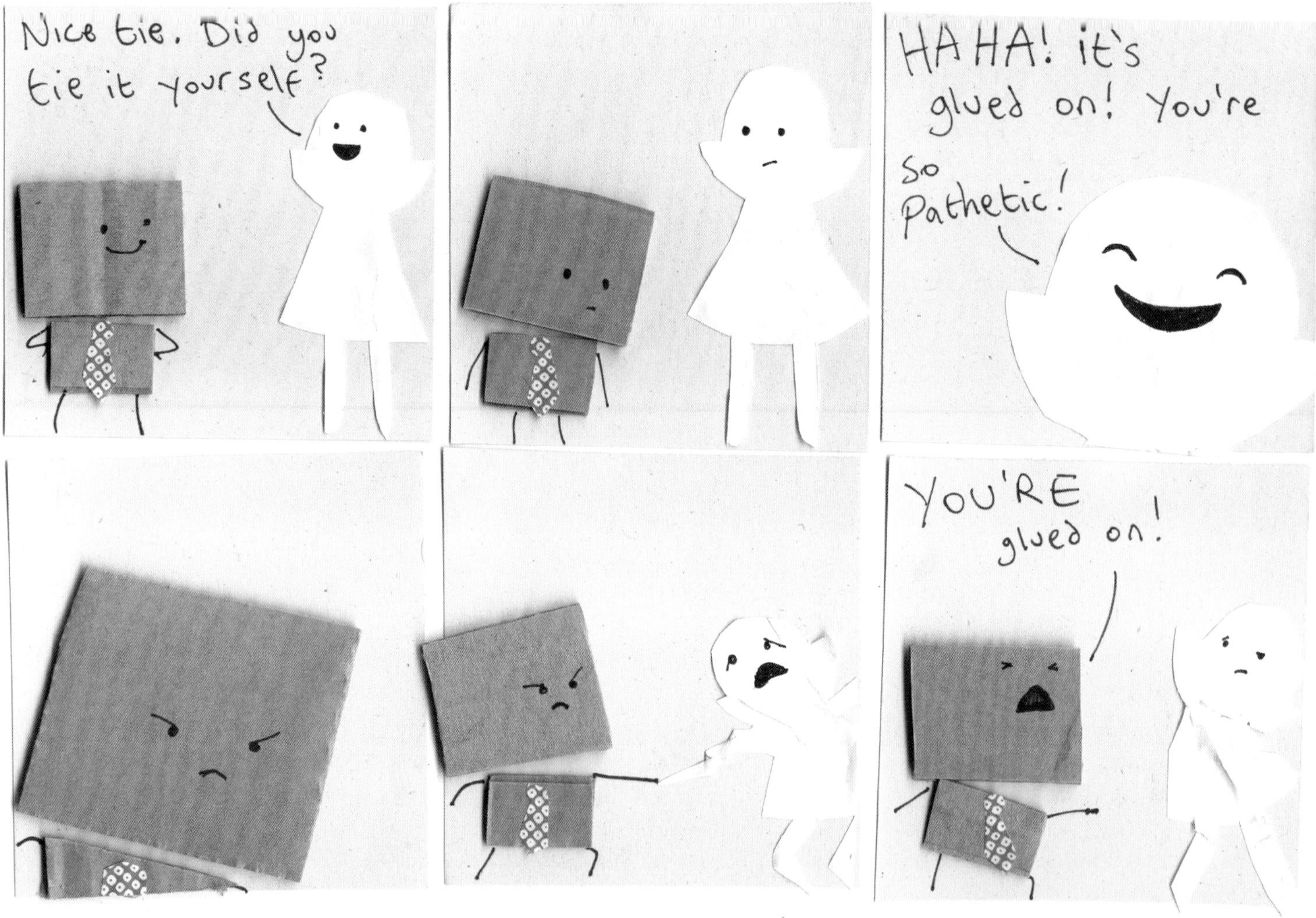
Nice tie. Did you tie it yourself?
HA HA! it's glued on! You're so Pathetic!
YOU'RE glued on!

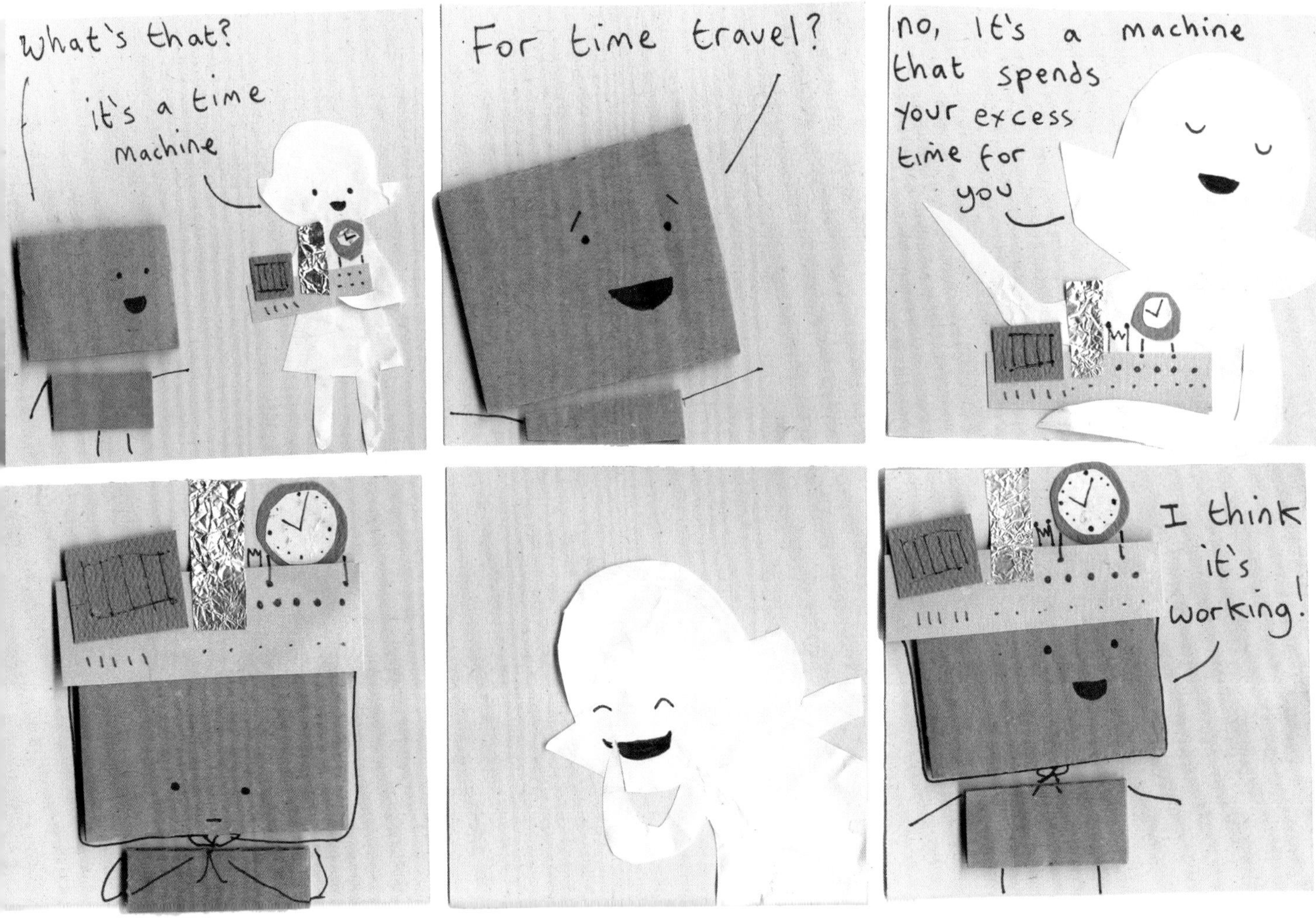
What's that?
it's a time machine
For time travel?
no, it's a machine that spends your excess time for you
I think it's working!

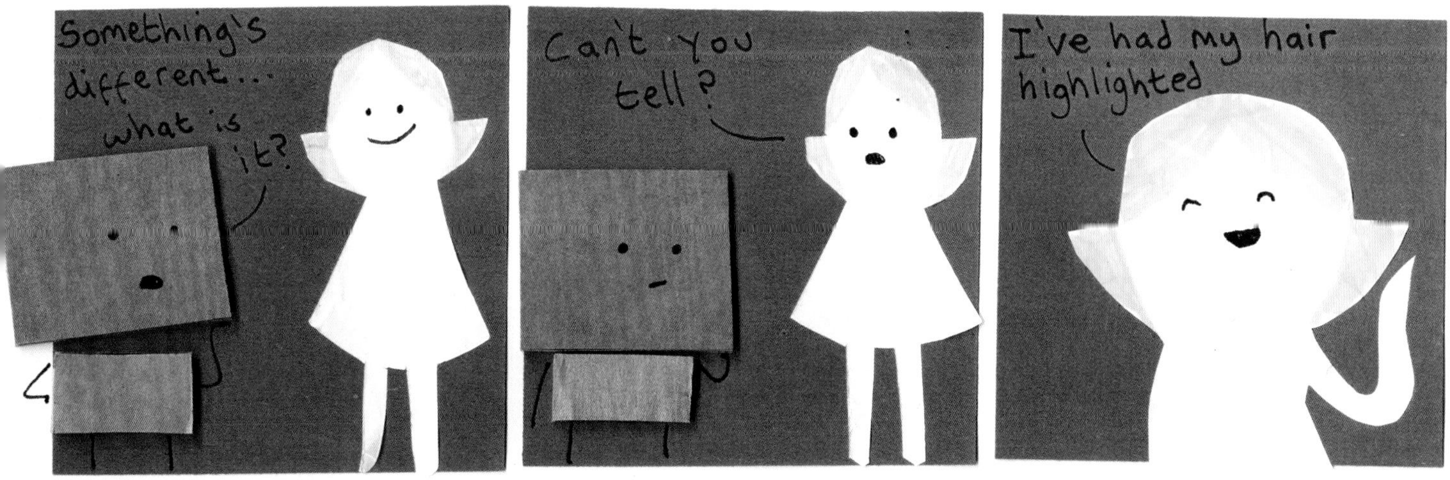
Something's different... what is it?
Can't you tell?
I've had my hair highlighted

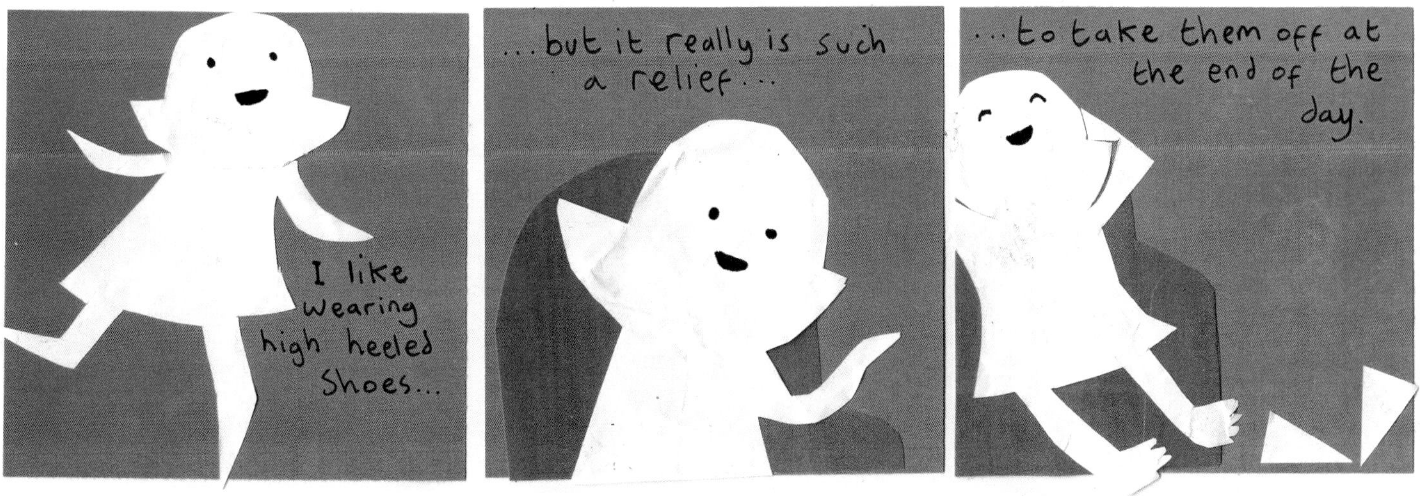
I like wearing high heeled shoes...
...but it really is such a relief...
...to take them off at the end of the day.

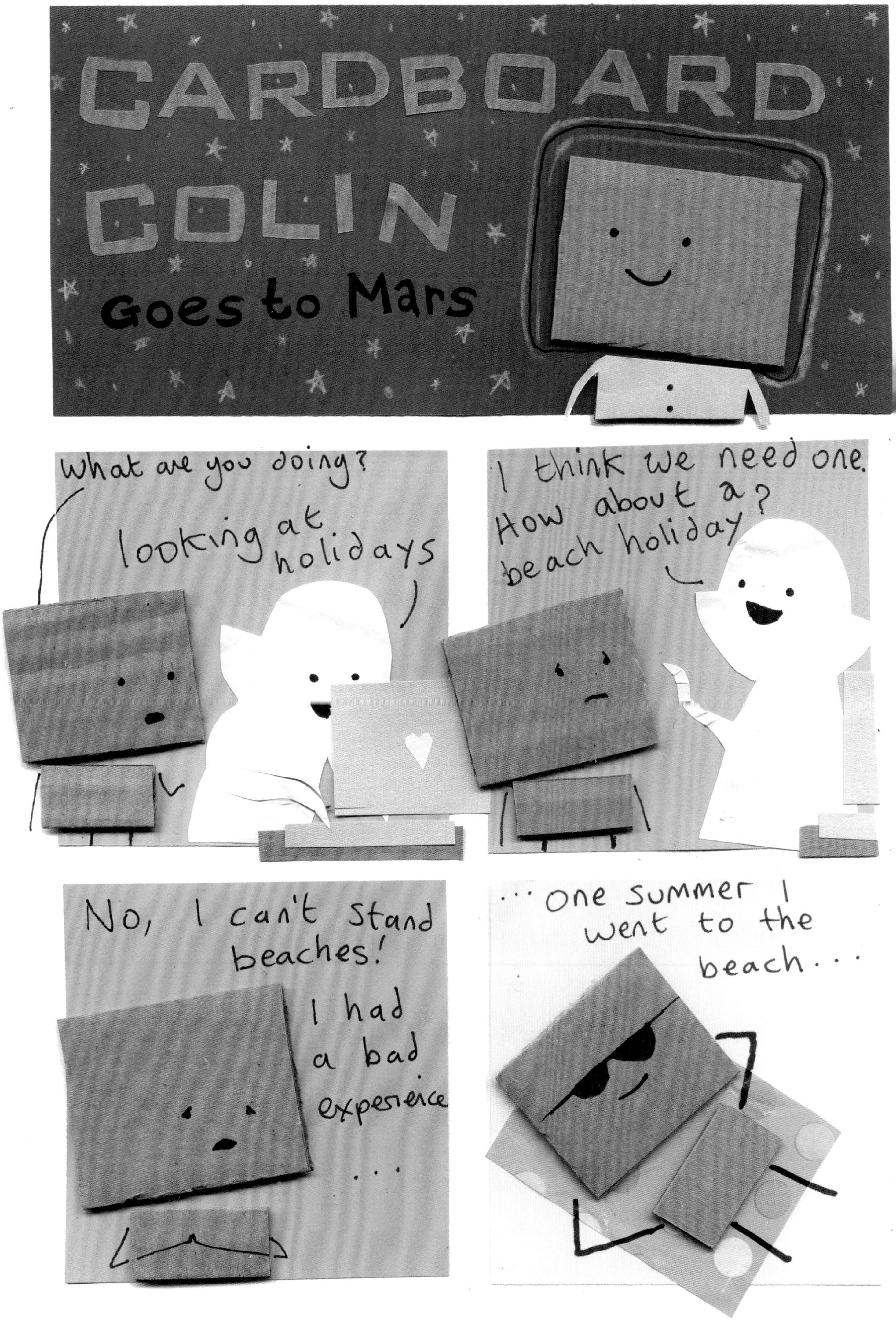
CARDBOARD COLIN
Goes to Mars
What are you doing?
looking at holidays
I think we need one. How about a beach holiday?
No, I can't stand beaches!
I had a bad experience
...
...One summer I went to the beach...

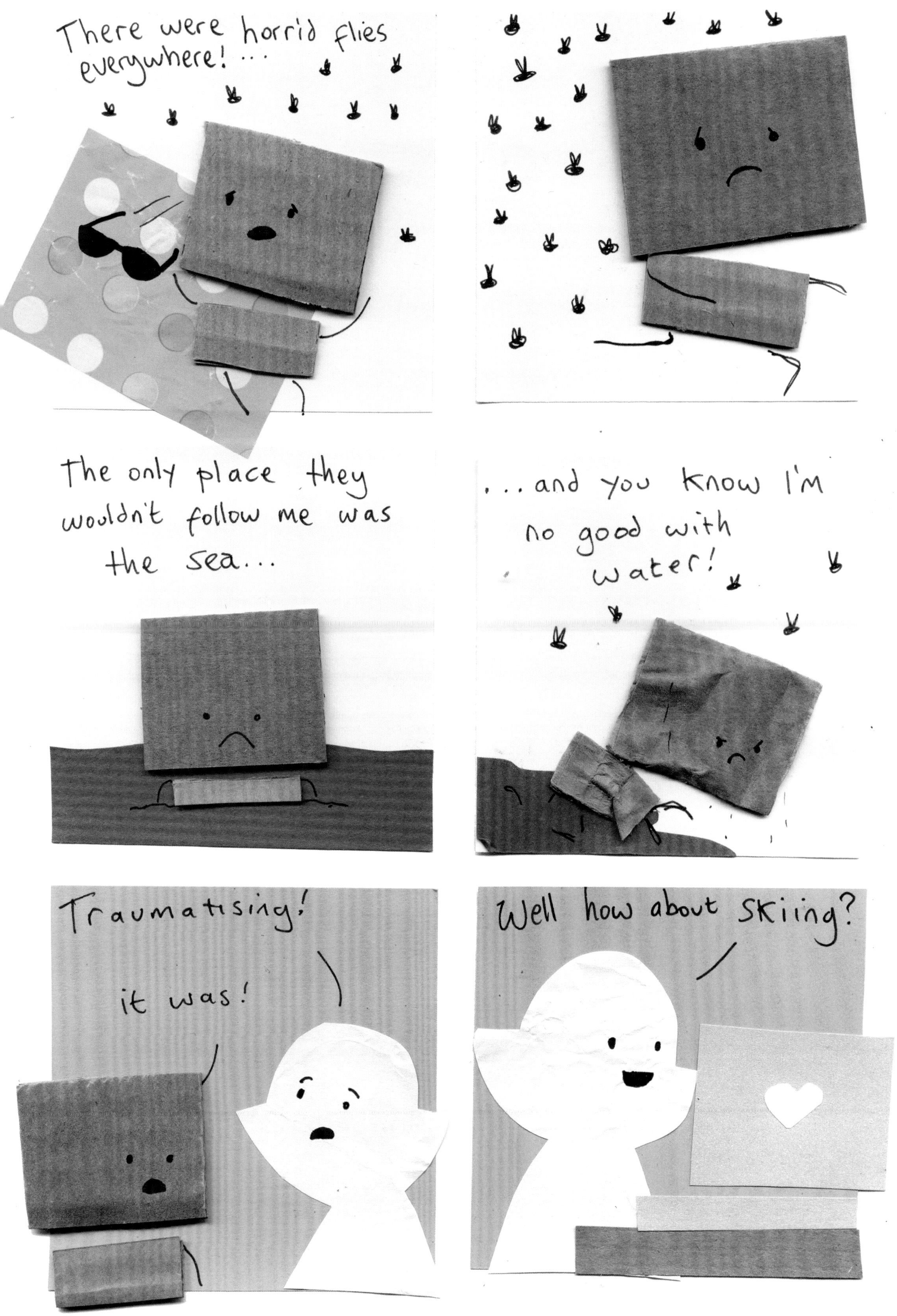

There were horrid flies everywhere! ...
The only place they wouldn't follow me was the sea...
... and you know I'm no good with water!
Traumatising!
it was!
Well how about skiing?

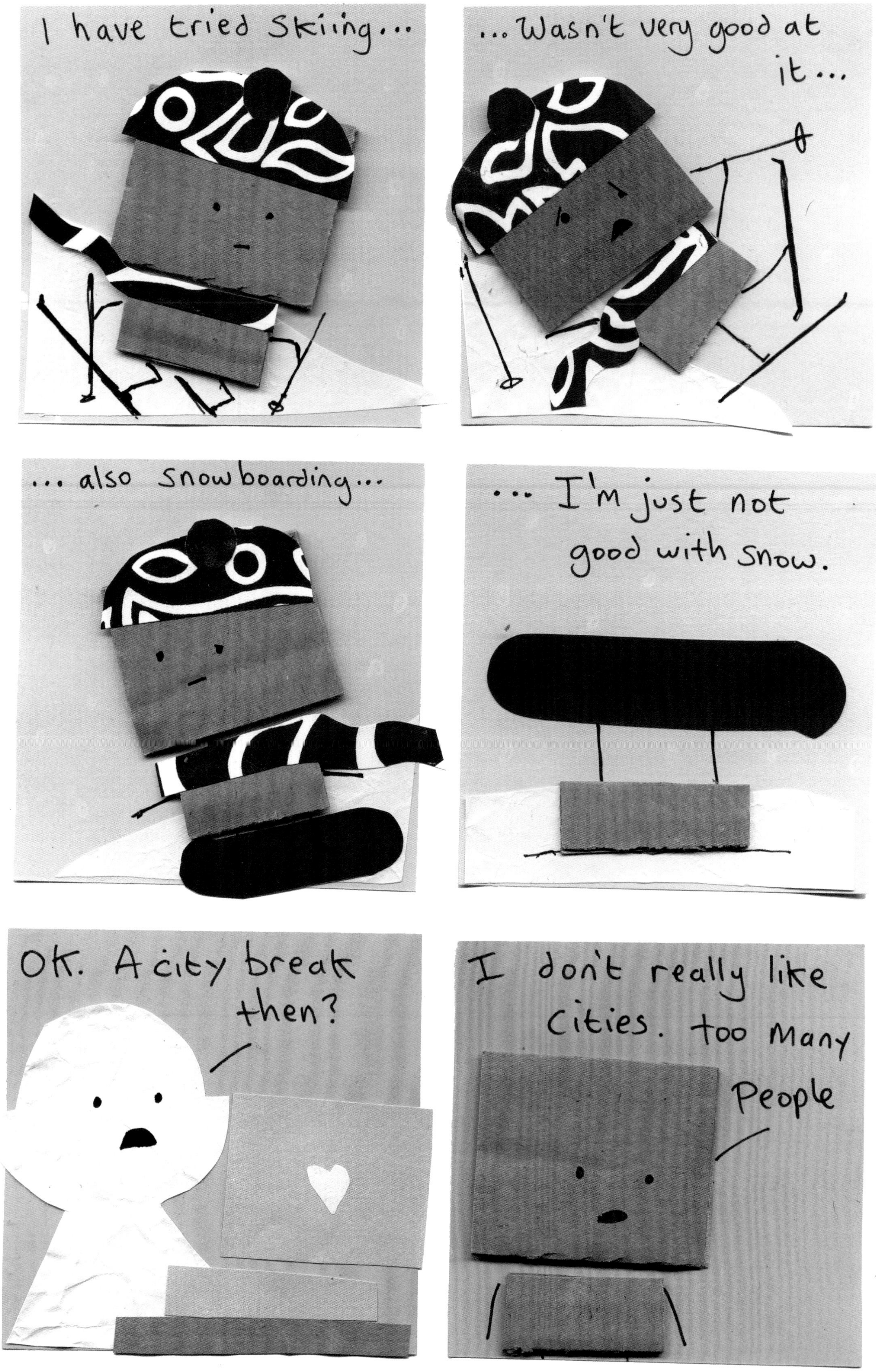
I have tried Skiing...
...Wasn't very good at it...
...also snowboarding...
...I'm just not good with snow.
OK. A city break then?
I don't really like Cities. too Many People

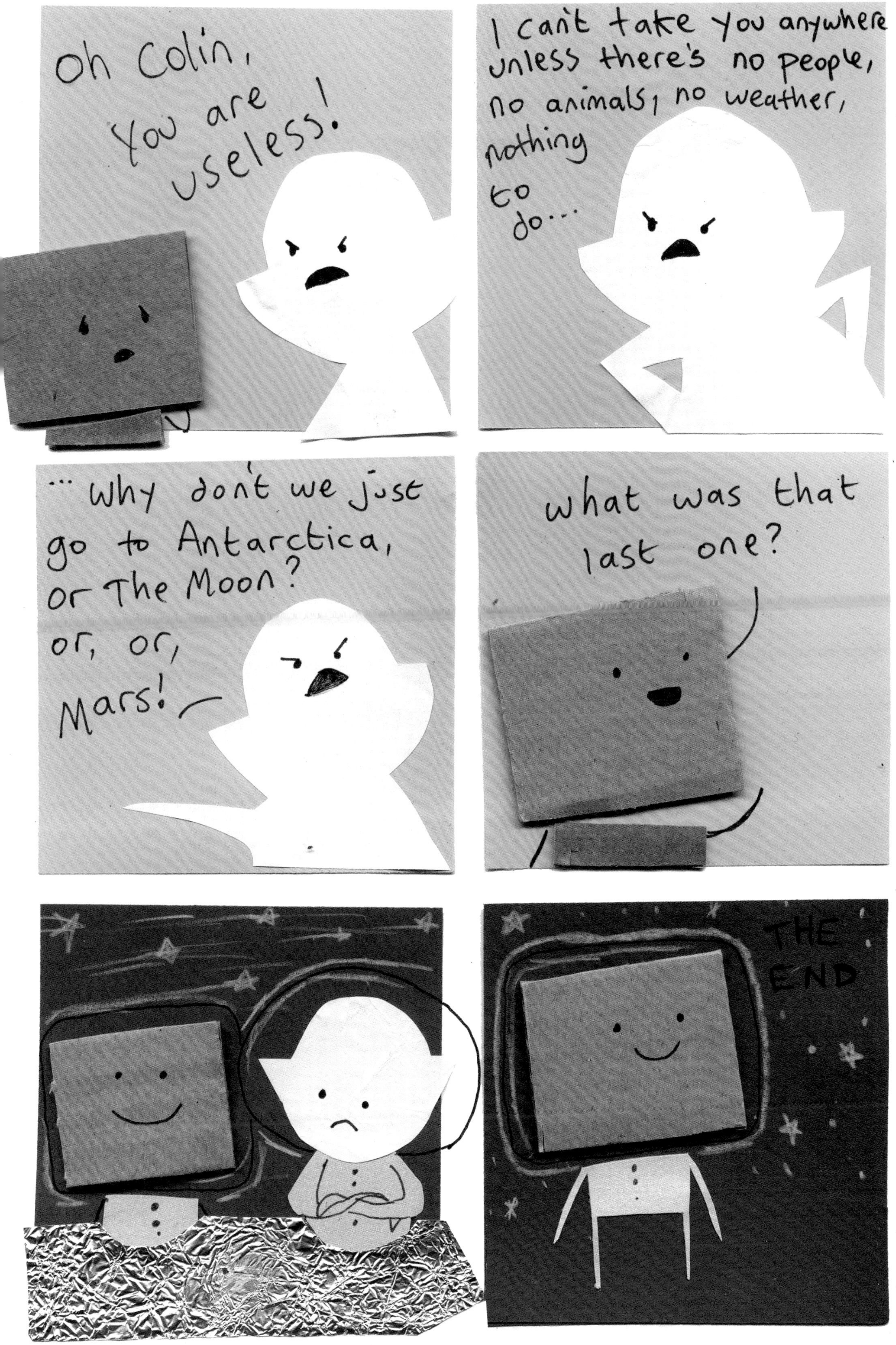
Oh Colin, You are useless!
I can't take you anywhere unless there's no people, no animals, no weather, nothing to do...
...why don't we just go to Antarctica, or The Moon? or, or, Mars!
what was that last one?
THE END

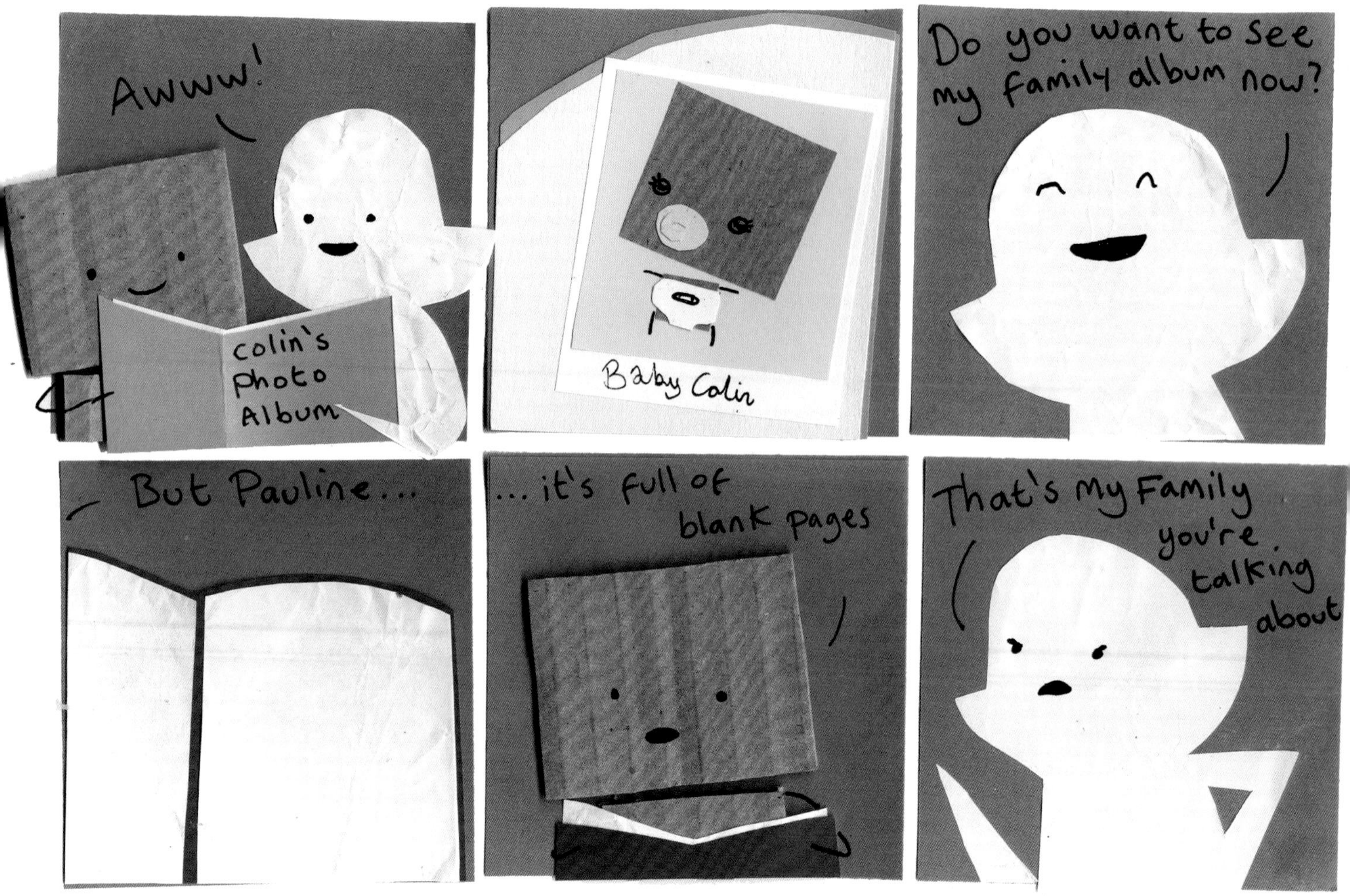
Awww!
Colin's Photo Album
Baby Colin
Do you want to see my family album now?
But Pauline...
... it's full of blank pages
That's my Family you're talking about

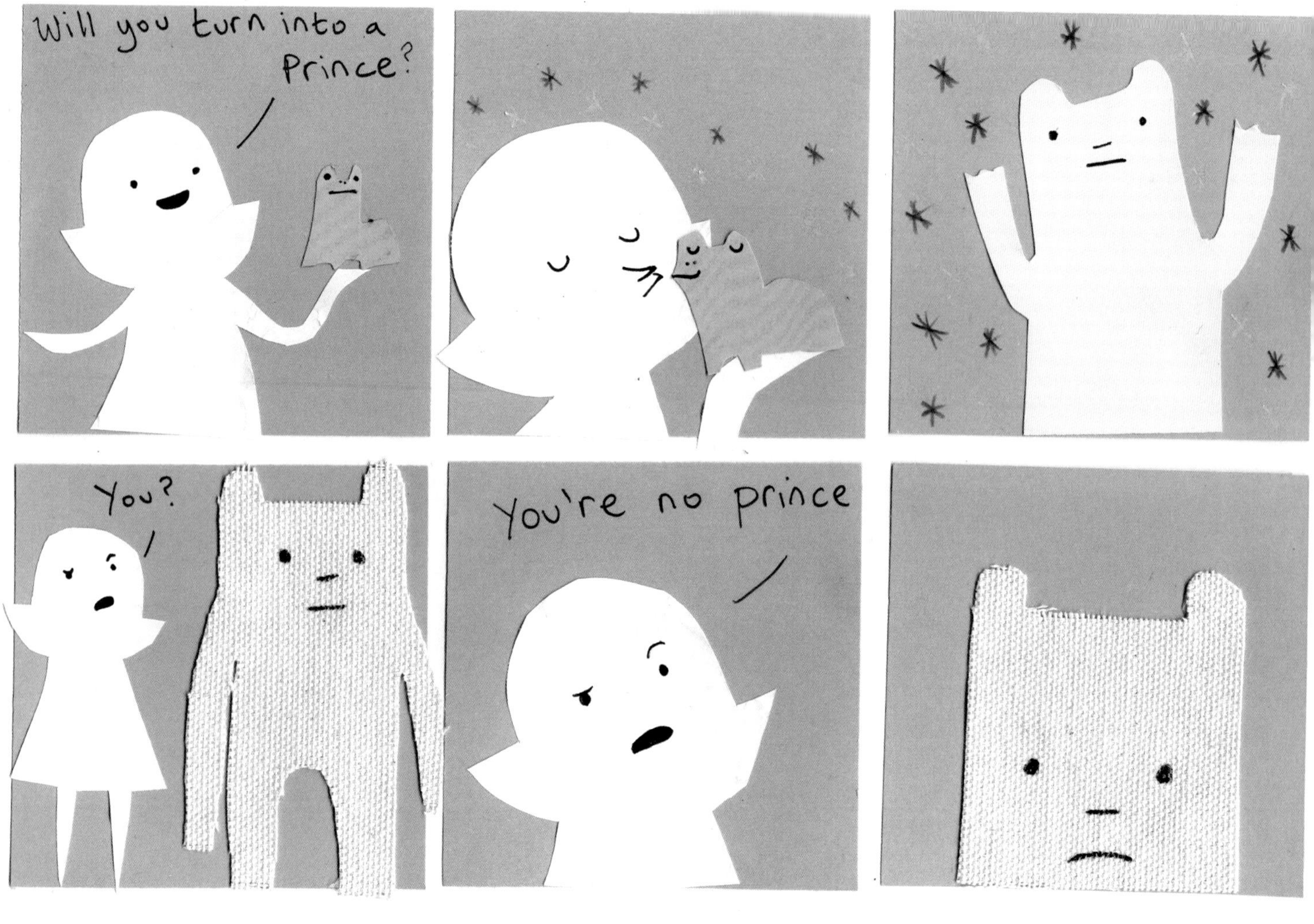
Will you turn into a Prince?
You?
You're no prince

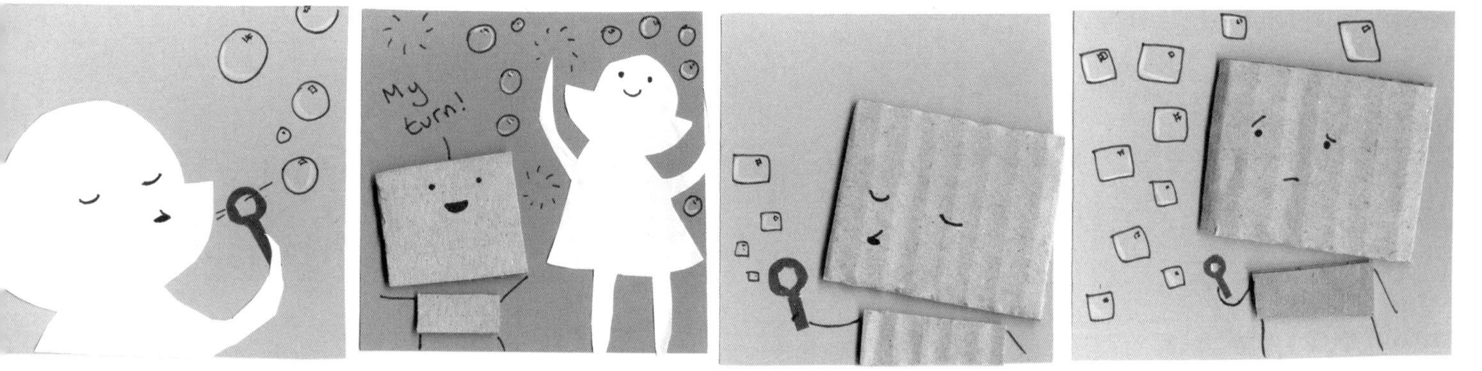
My turn!

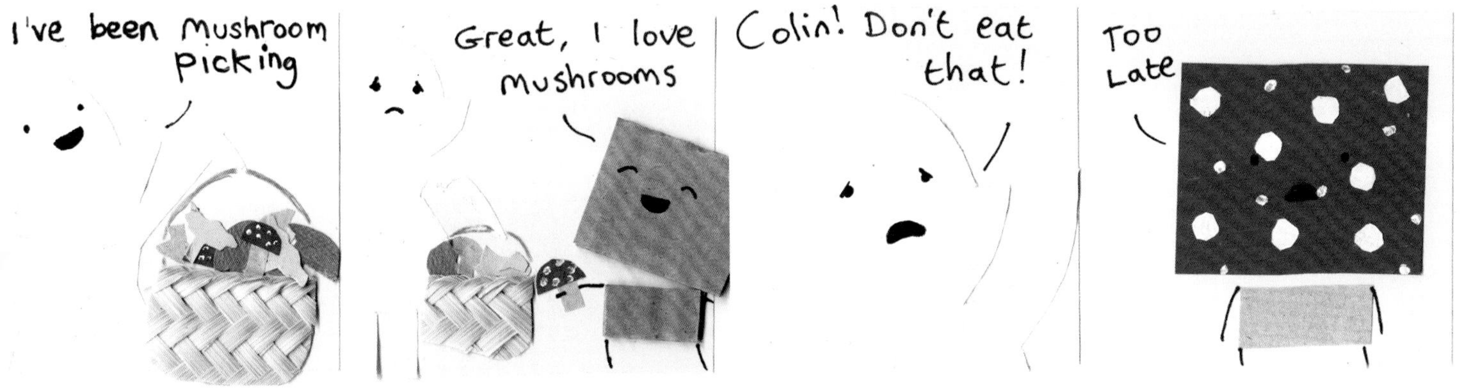
I've been mushroom picking
Great, I love mushrooms
Colin! Don't eat that!
Too Late

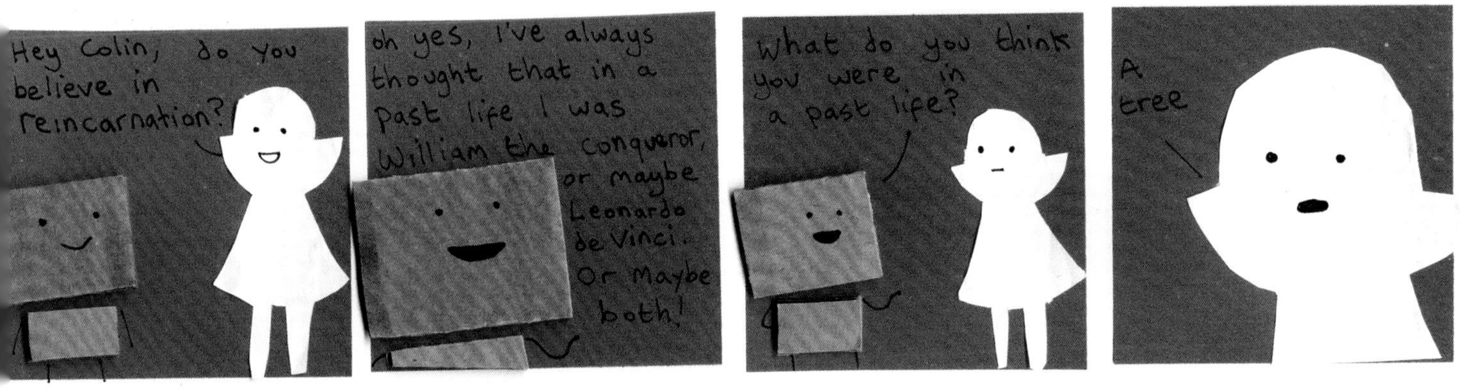
Hey Colin, do you believe in reincarnation?
oh yes, I've always thought that in a past life I was William the conqueror, or maybe Leonardo de Vinci. Or maybe both!
What do you think you were in a past life?
A tree

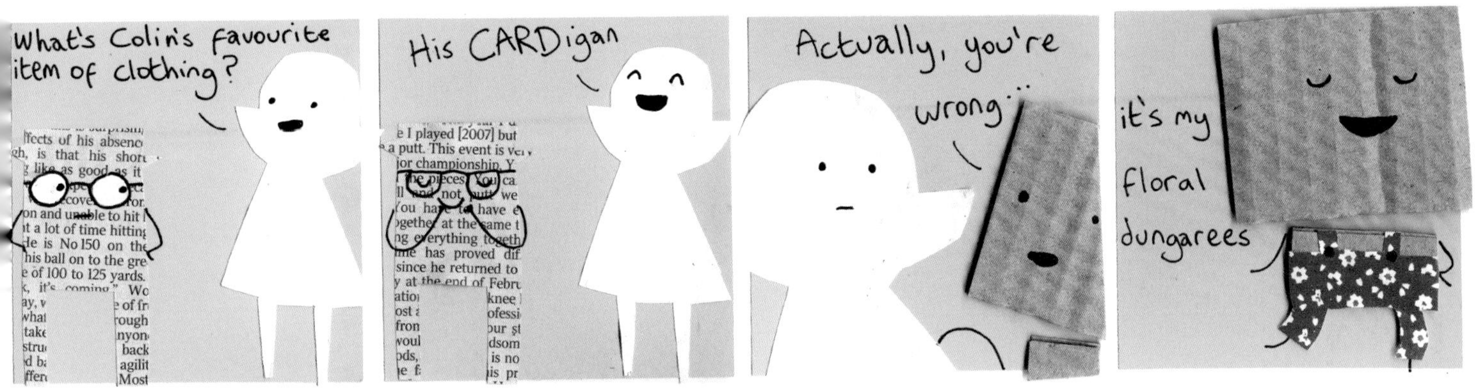
What's Colin's favourite item of clothing?
His CARDigan
Actually, you're wrong...
it's my floral dungarees

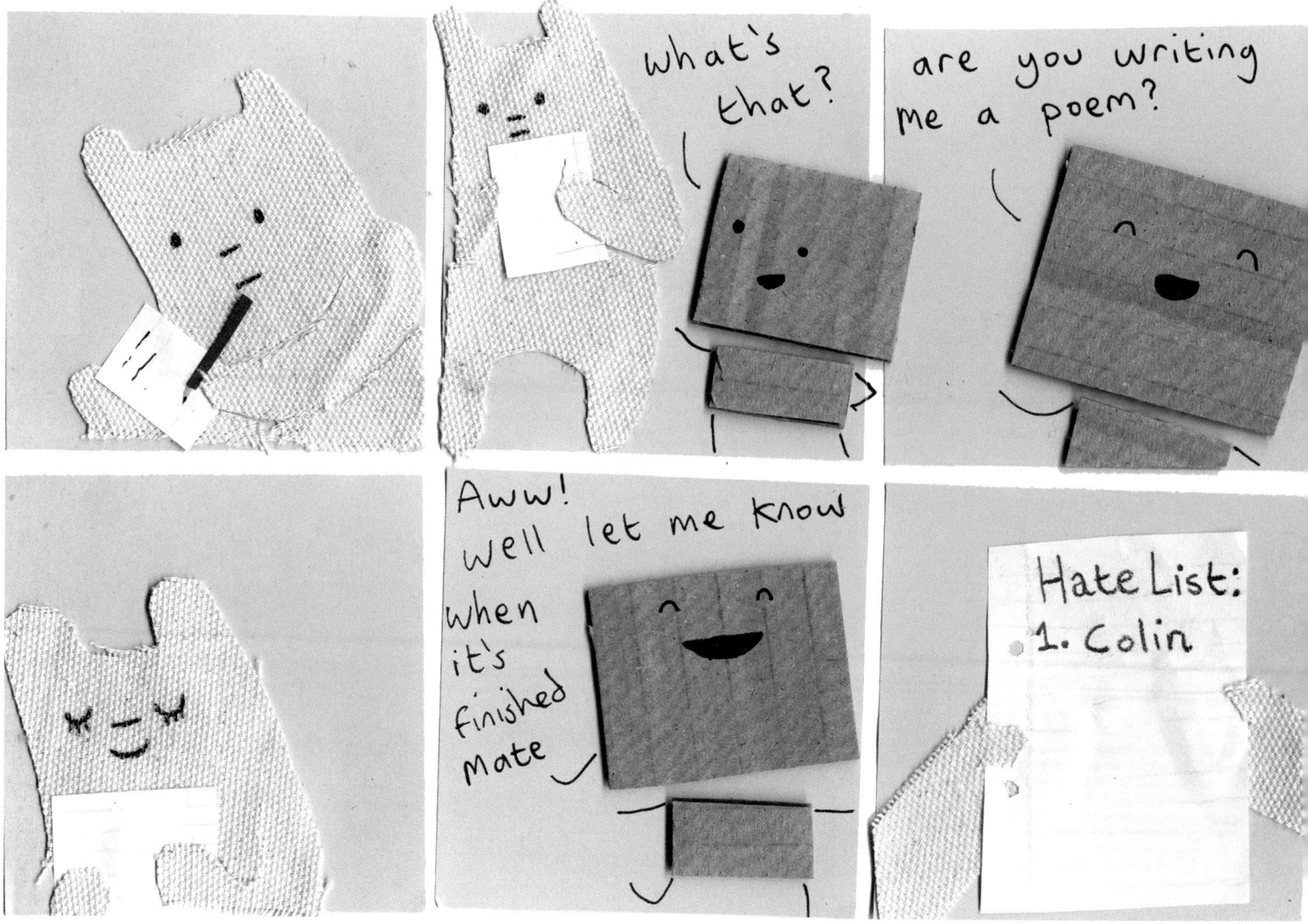
what's that?
are you writing me a poem?
Aww! well let me know when it's finished mate
Hate List:
1. Colin

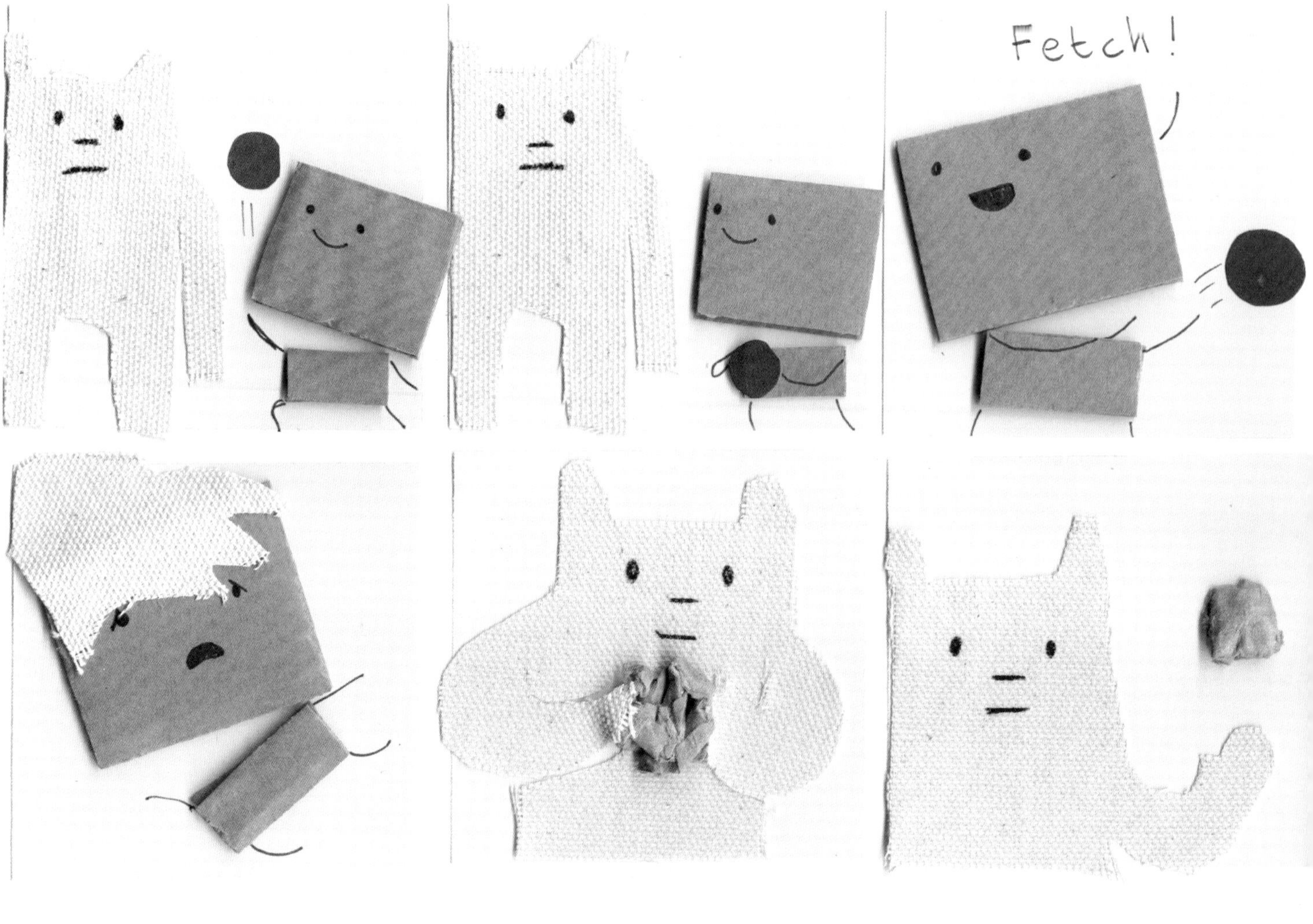
Fetch!

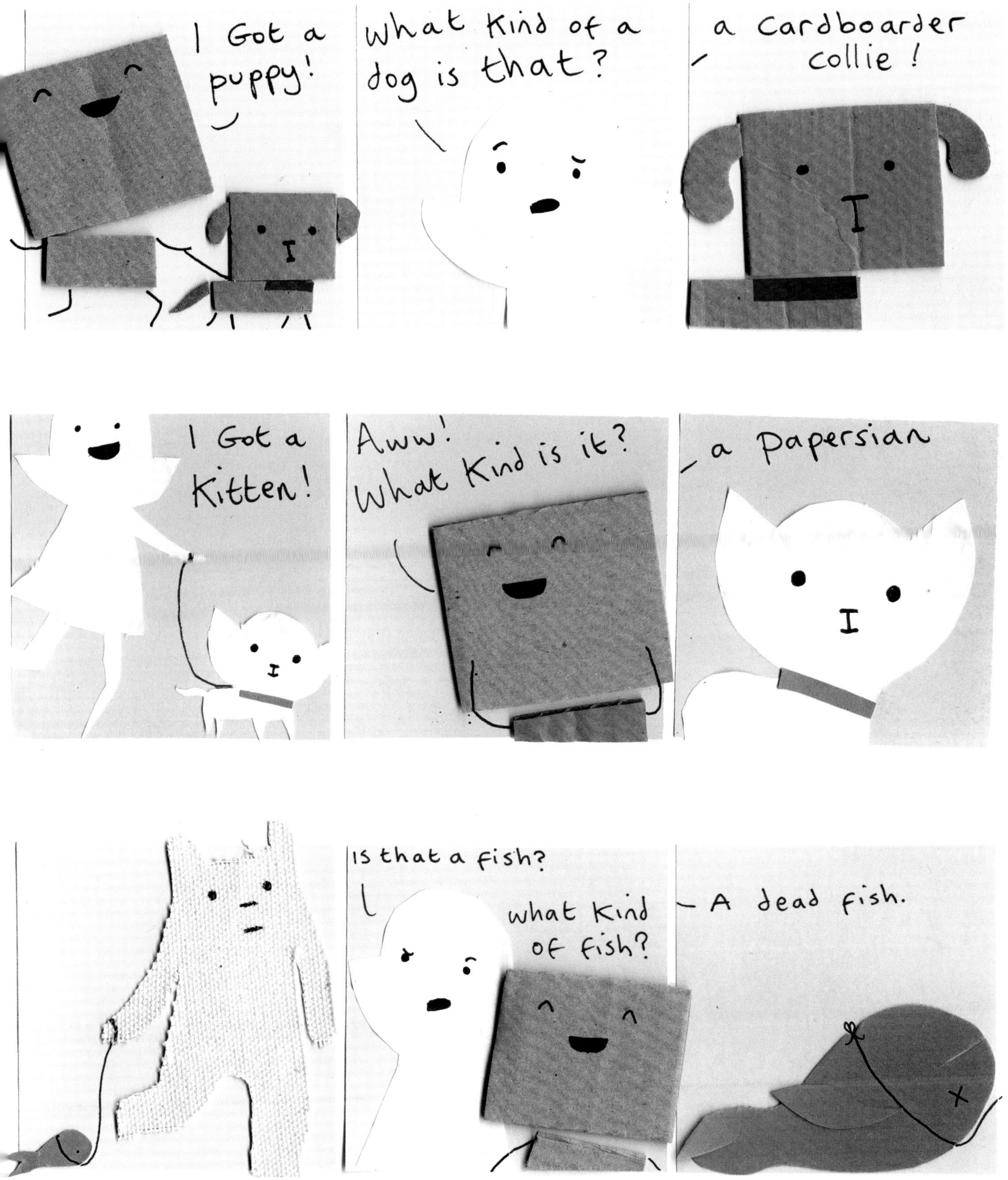
I Got a puppy!
What Kind of a dog is that?
a Cardboarder collie!
I Got a Kitten!
Aww! What Kind is it?
a Papersian
Is that a fish?
what Kind of fish?
A dead fish.

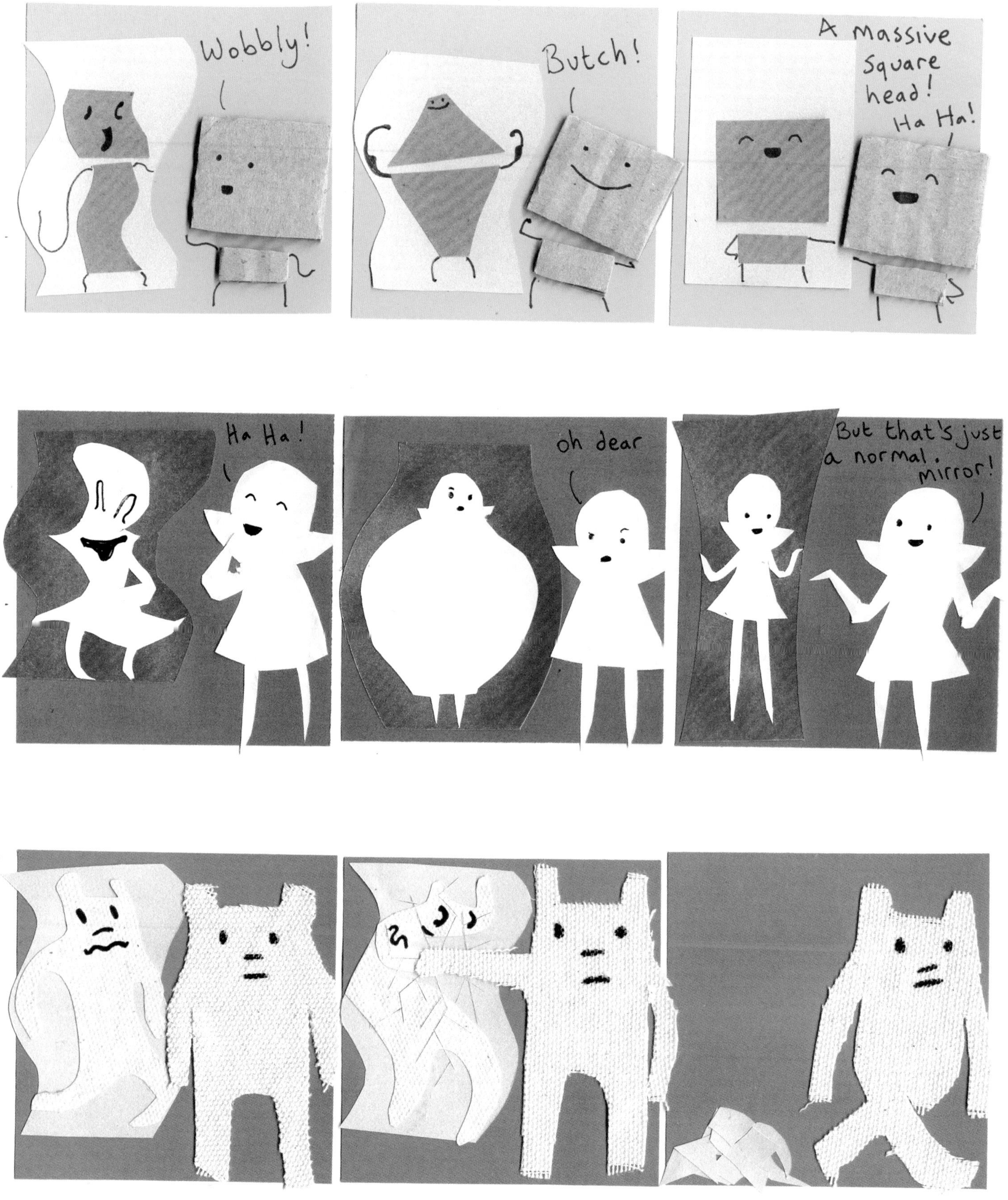
Wobbly!
Butch!
A massive square head!
Ha Ha!
Ha Ha!
oh dear
But that's just a normal mirror!

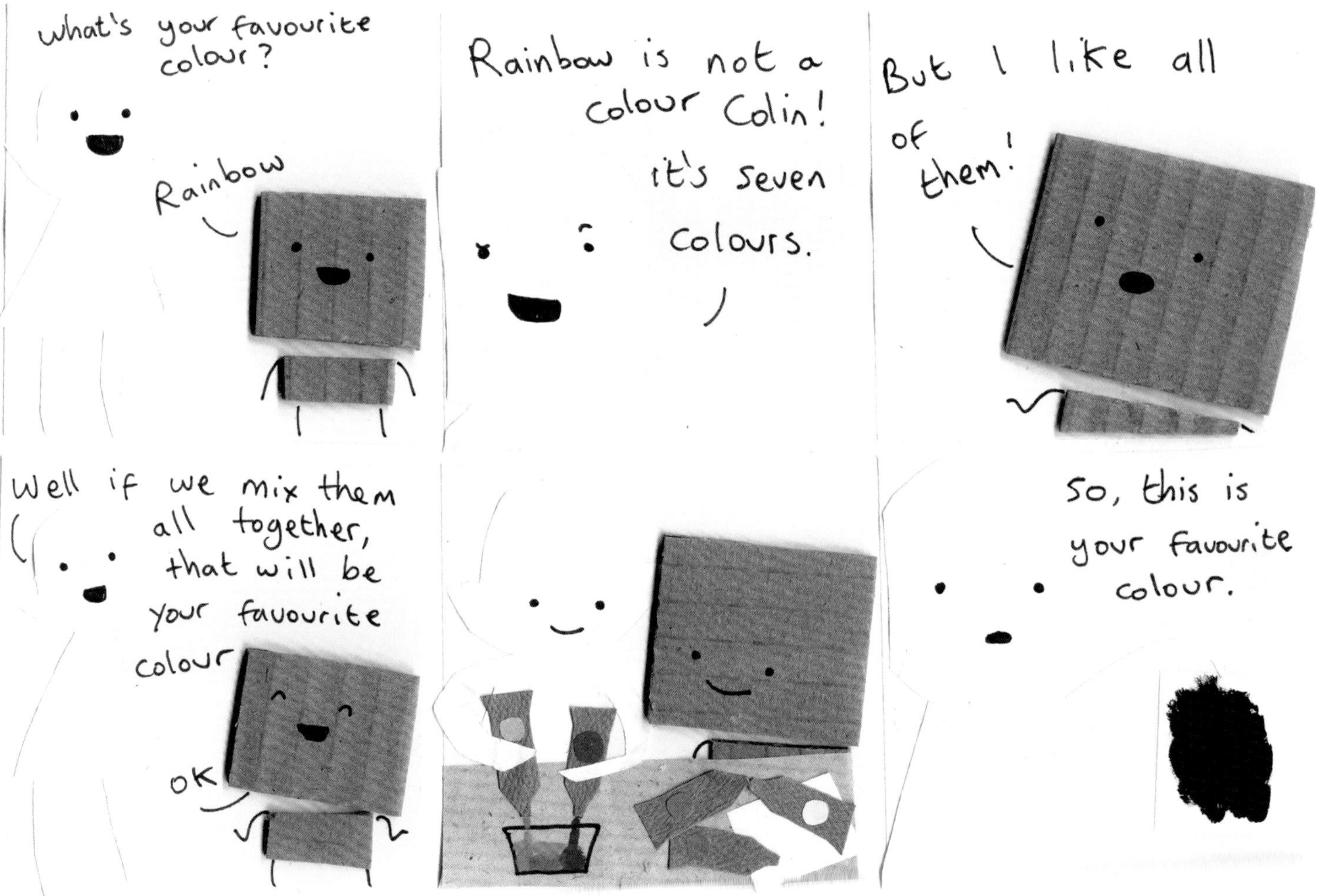
what's your favourite colour?
Rainbow
Rainbow is not a colour Colin!
it's seven colours.
But I like all of them!
Well if we mix them all together, that will be your favourite colour
OK
So, this is your favourite colour.

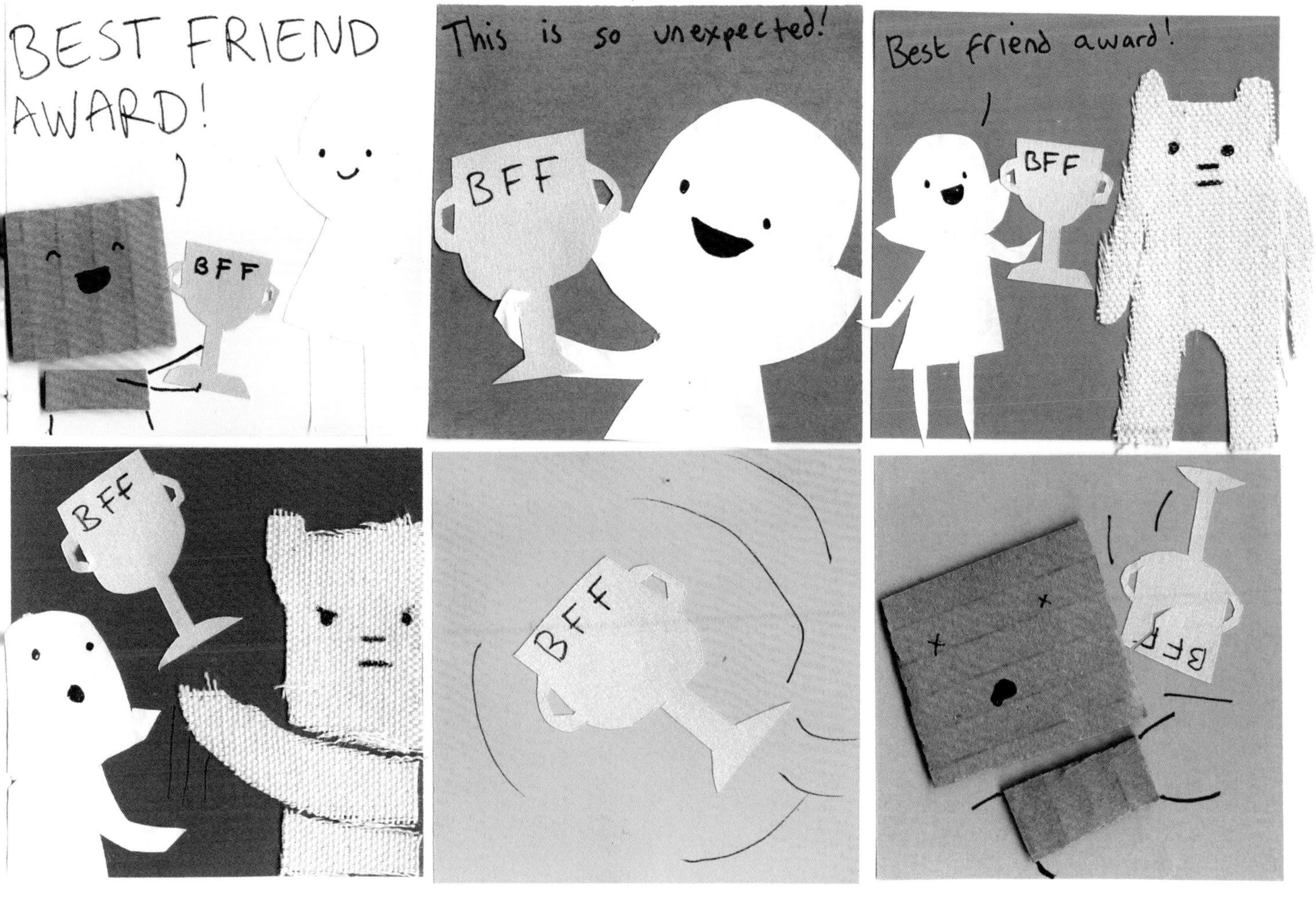
BEST FRIEND AWARD!
BFF
This is so unexpected!
BFF
Best friend award!
BFF
BFF
BFF
BFF

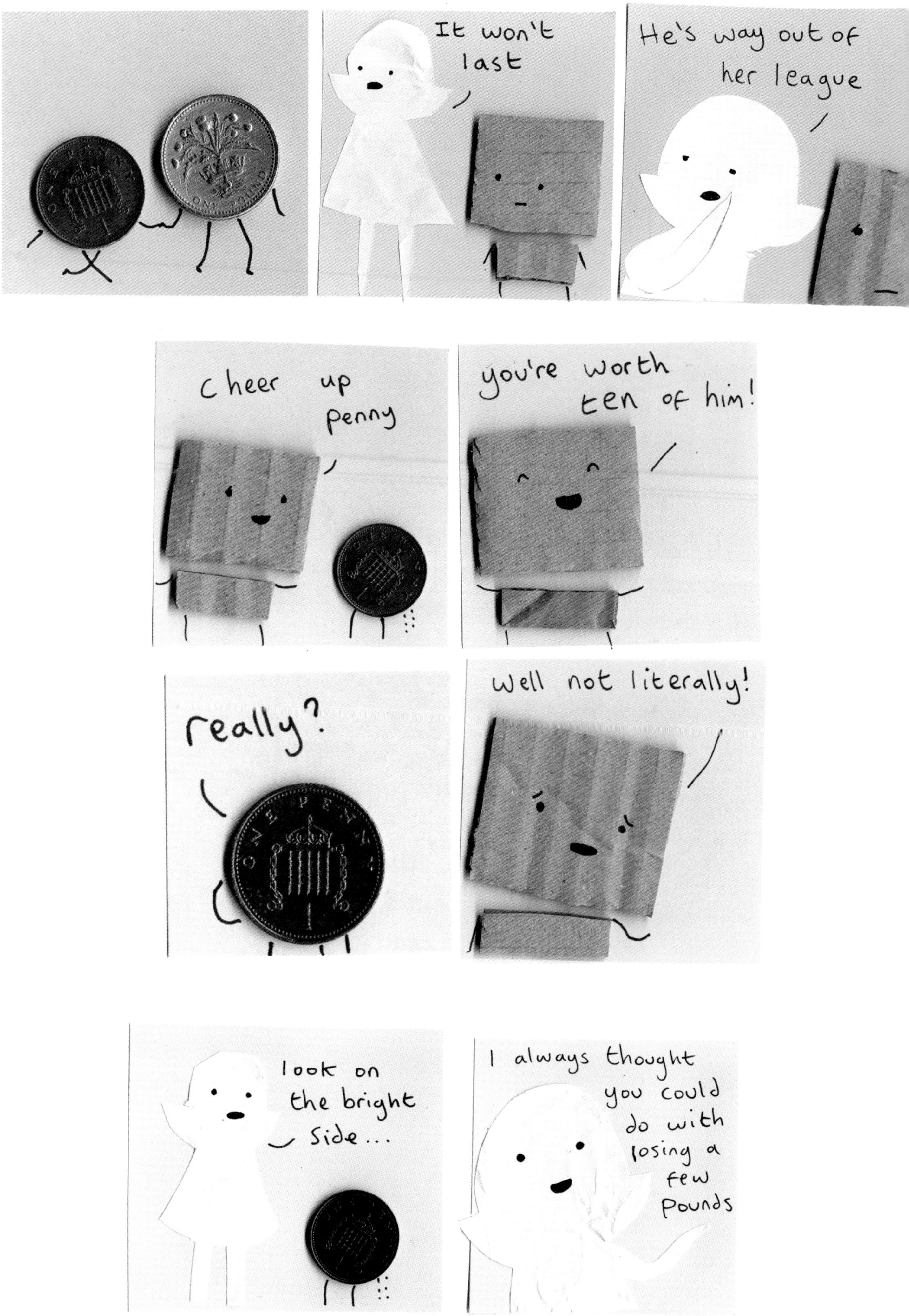
It won't last
He's way out of her league
Cheer up penny
you're worth ten of him!
really?
ONE PENNY
Well not literally!
look on the bright side...
I always thought you could do with losing a few pounds

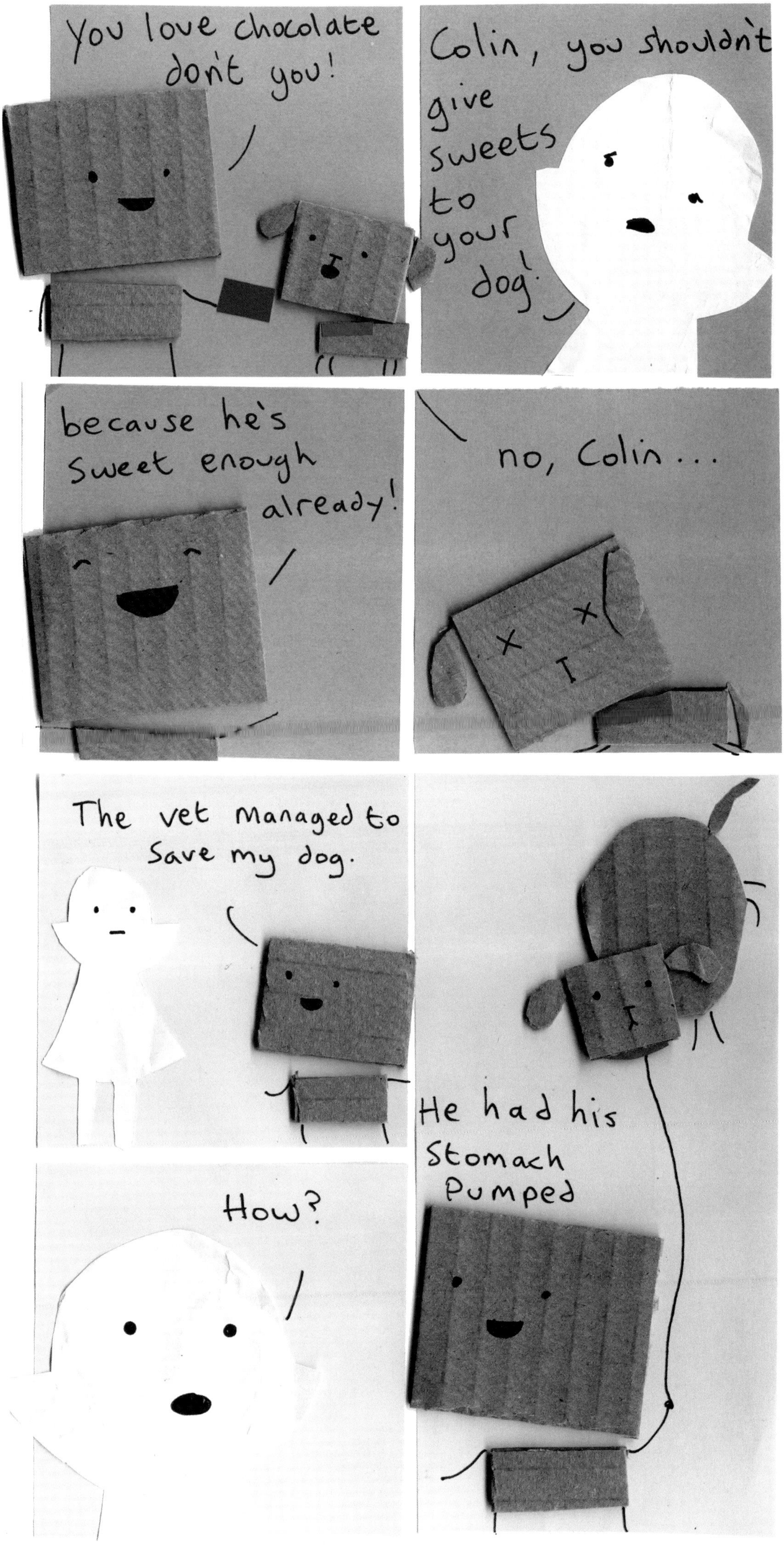

You love chocolate don't you!
Colin, you shouldn't give sweets to your dog!
because he's sweet enough already!
no, Colin...
The vet managed to save my dog.
How?
He had his stomach pumped

Super Colin

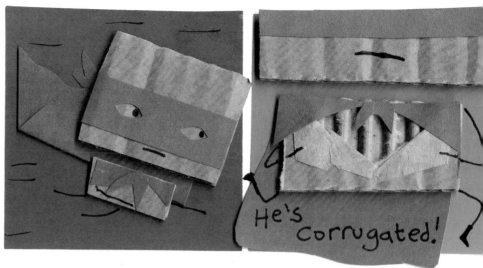

He's corrugated!

Power Pauline

Paper cut!

The Polar King

YAWN

He's charismatic!

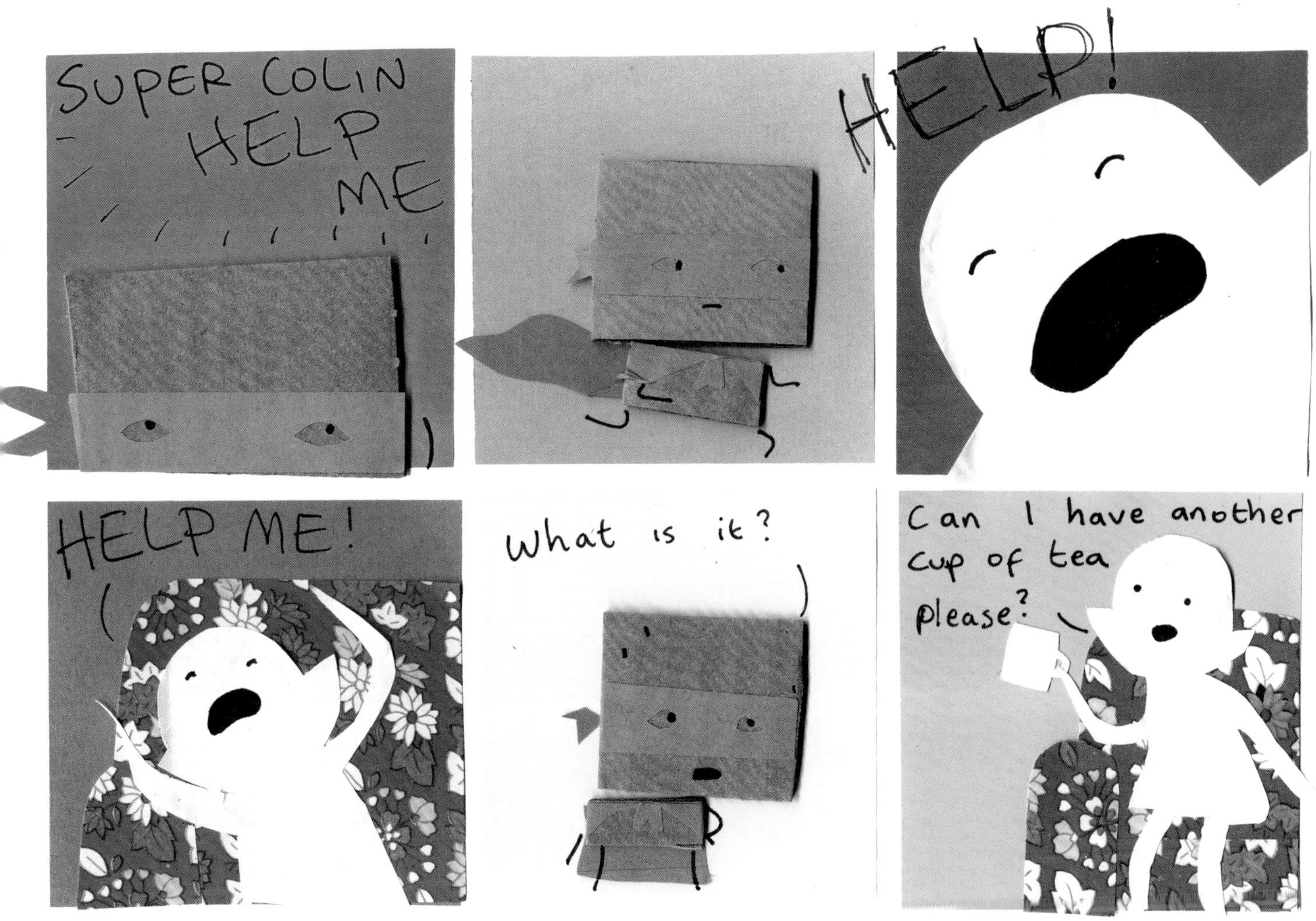
SUPER COLIN HELP ME
HELP!
HELP ME!
What is it?
Can I have another cup of tea please?

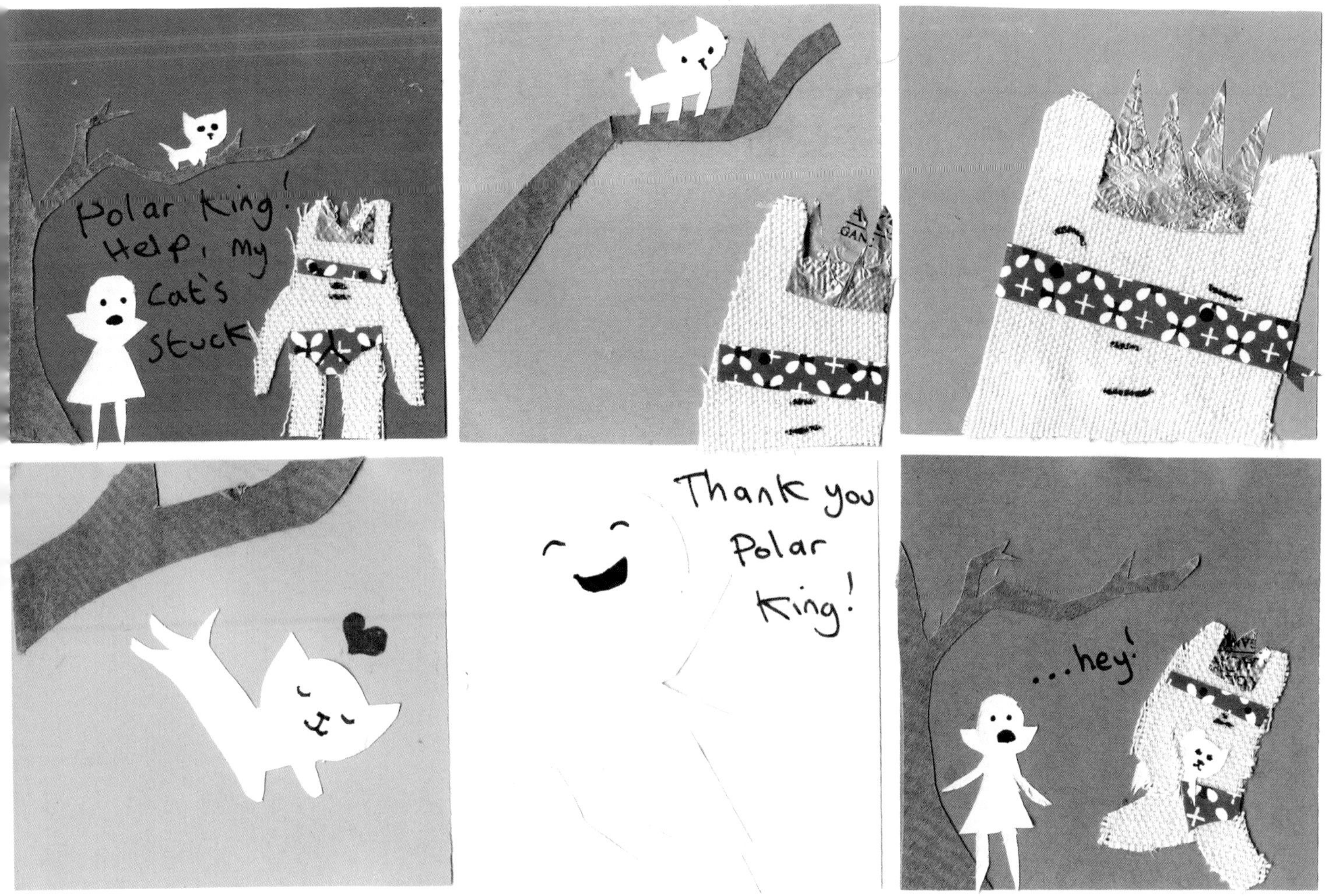
Polar King! Help, my cat's stuck
Thank you Polar King!
...hey!

POWER PAULINE'S POWERS

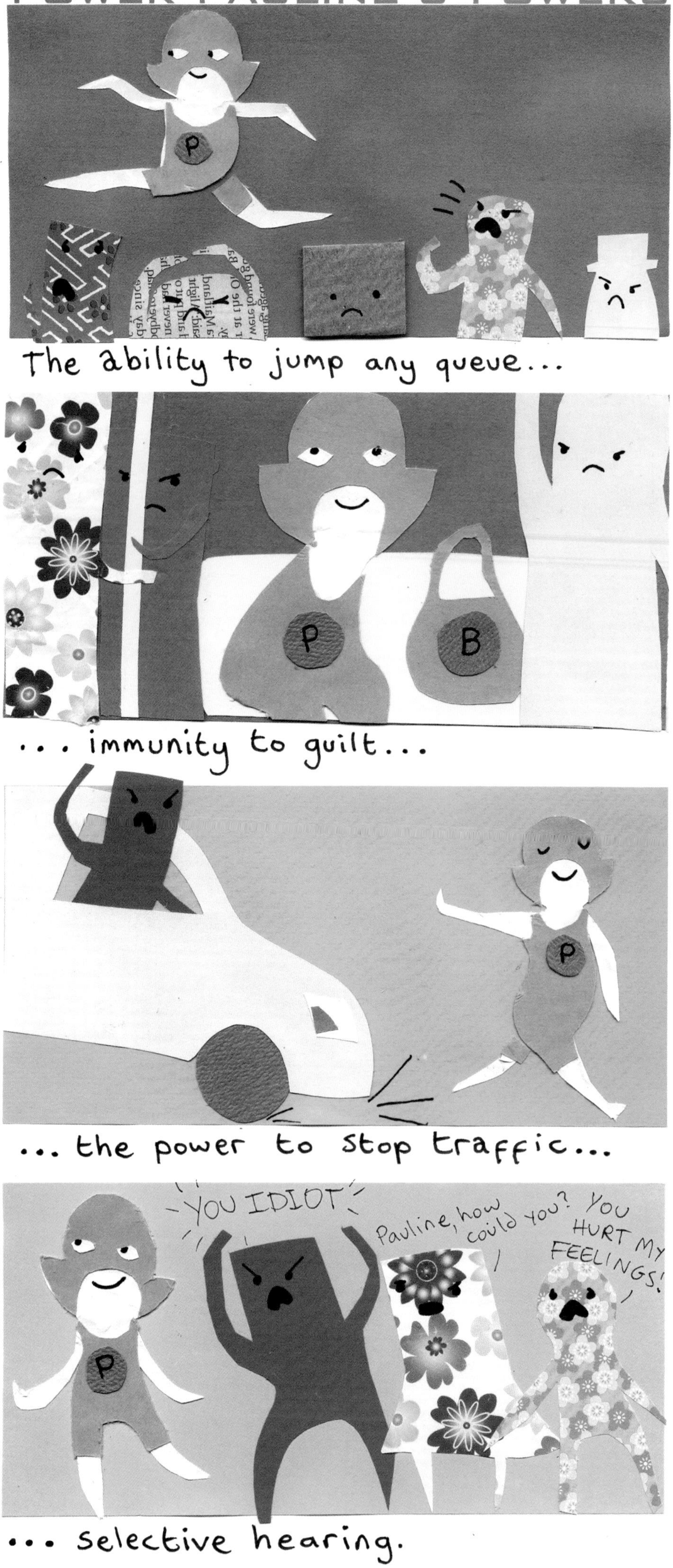

The ability to jump any queue...
P
P
B
... immunity to guilt...
P
... the power to stop traffic...
YOU IDIOT
Pauline, how could you?
YOU HURT MY FEELINGS!
P
... selective hearing.

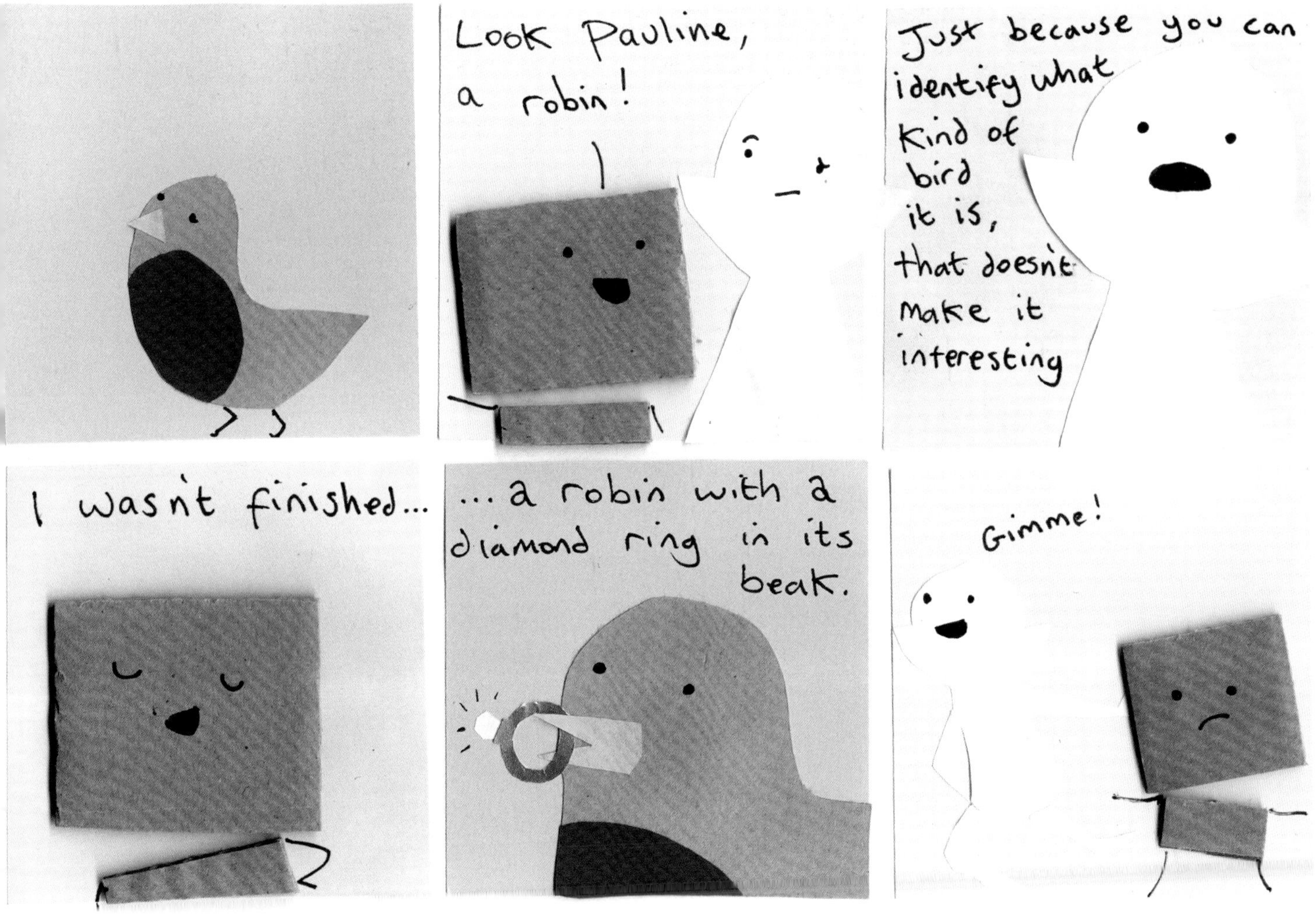
Look Pauline,
a robin!
Just because you can identify what kind of bird it is, that doesn't make it interesting
I wasn't finished...
...a robin with a diamond ring in its beak.
Gimme!

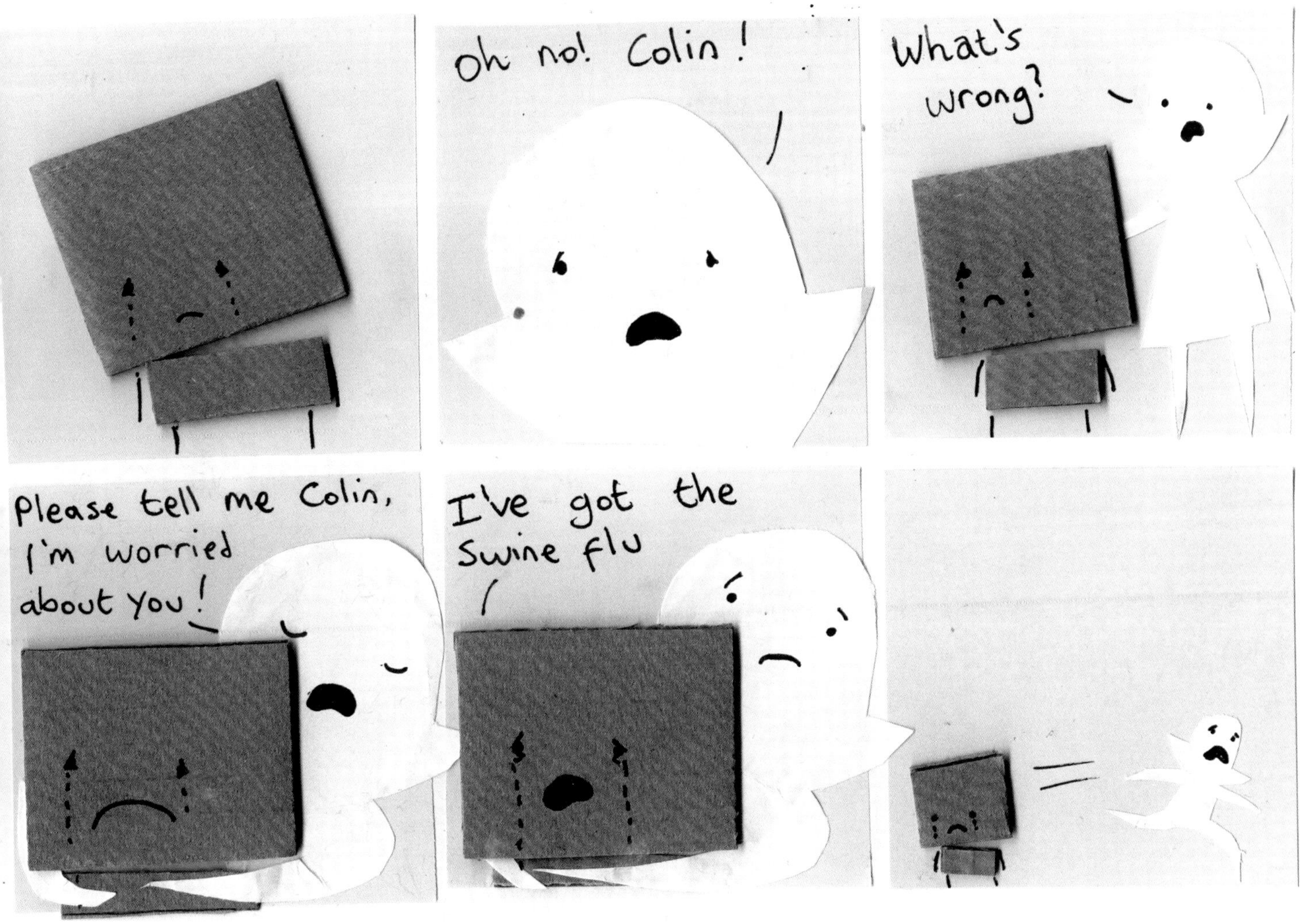
Oh no! Colin!
What's wrong?
Please tell me Colin, I'm worried about you!
I've got the Swine flu

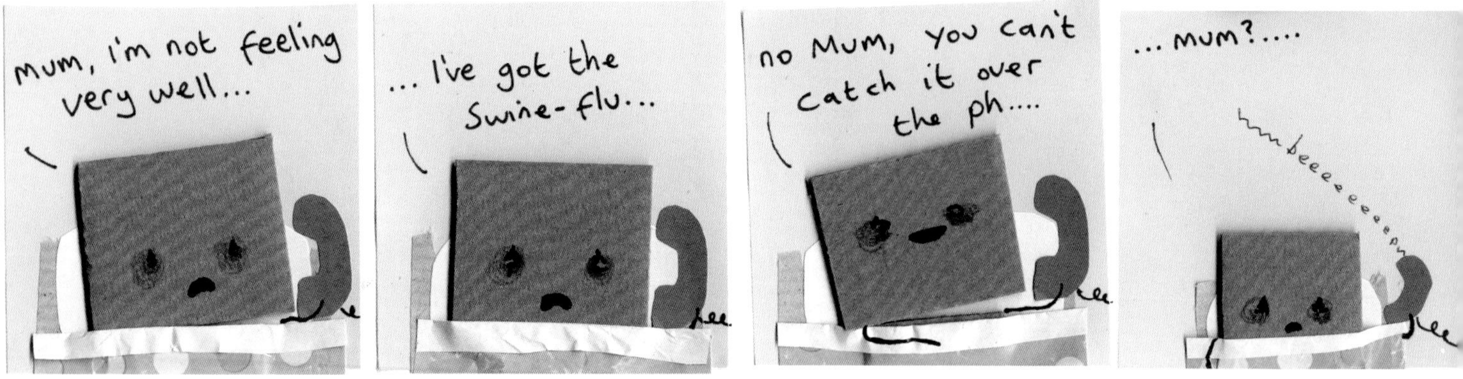
Mum, I'm not feeling very well...
... I've got the Swine-flu...
no Mum, you can't catch it over the ph....
... mum?....

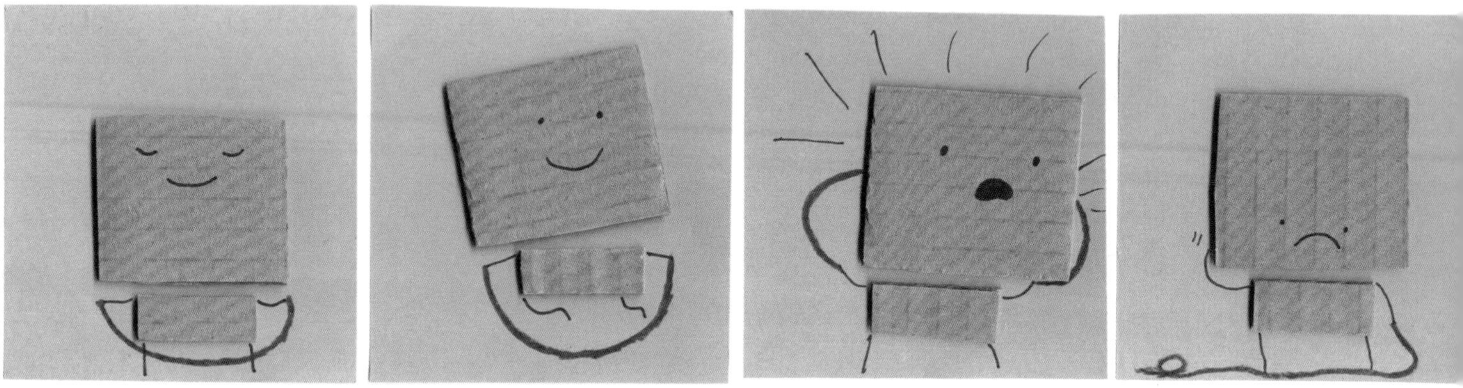

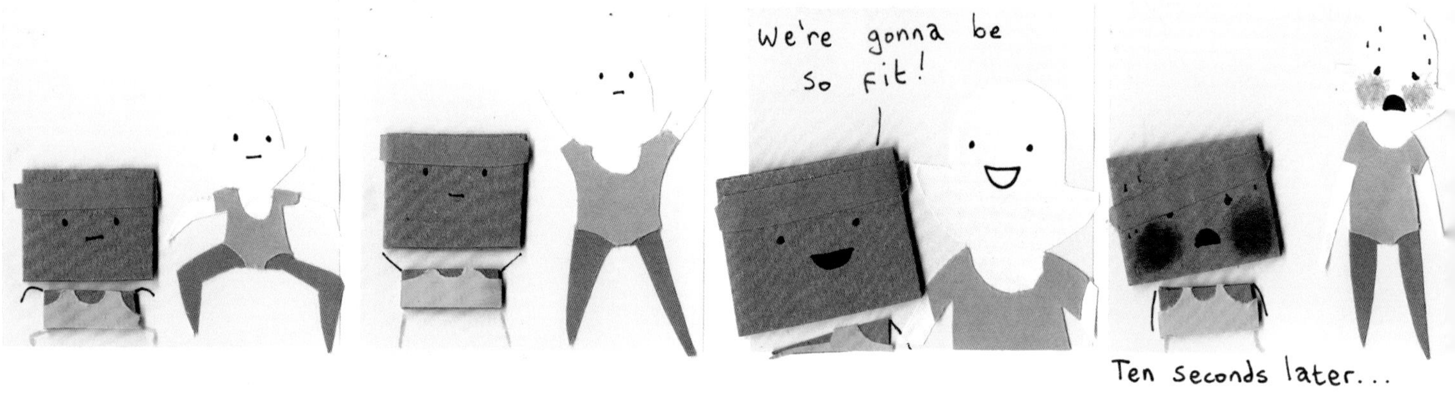
We're gonna be so fit!
Ten seconds later...

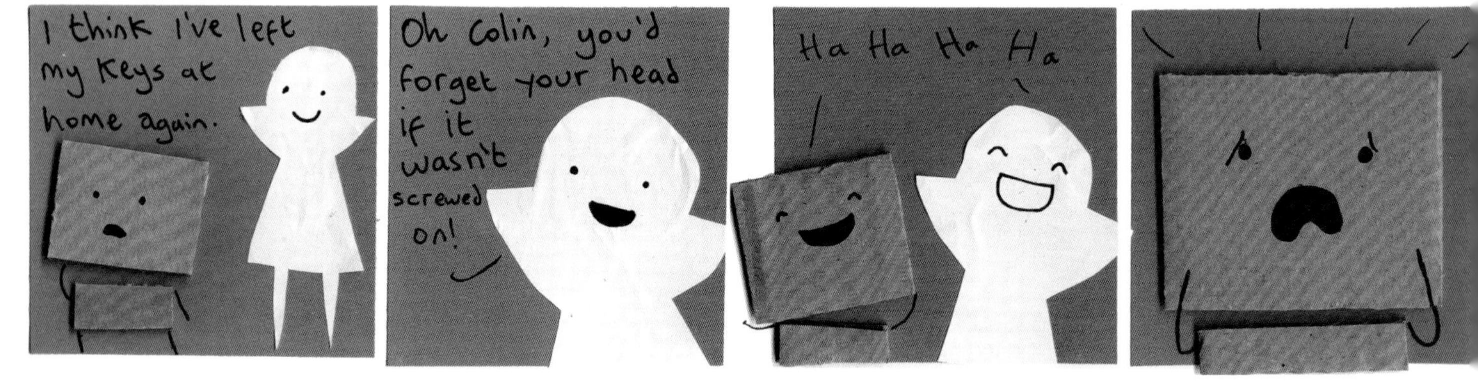
I think I've left my keys at home again.
Oh Colin, you'd forget your head if it wasn't screwed on!
Ha Ha Ha Ha

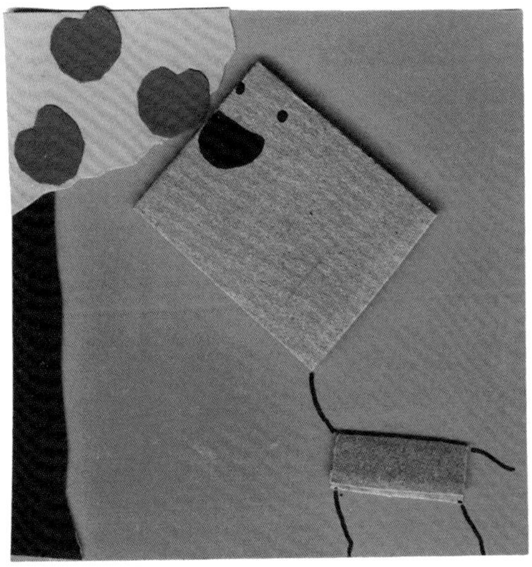
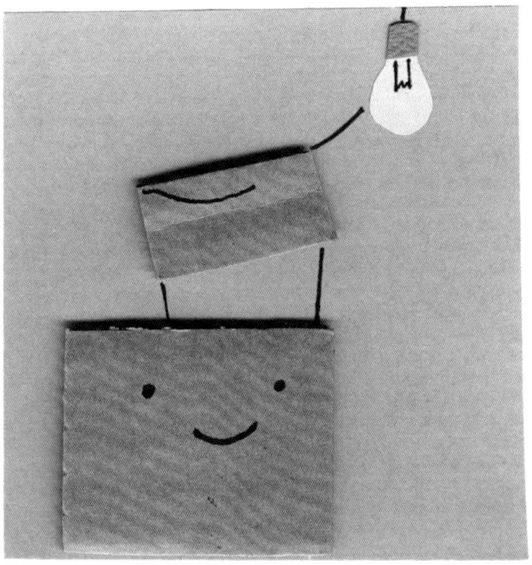
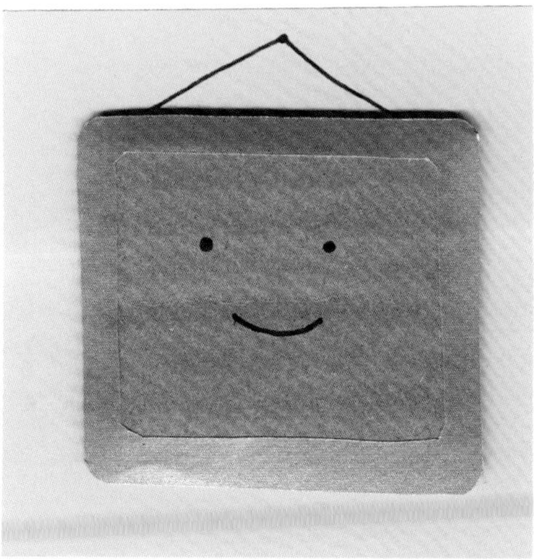
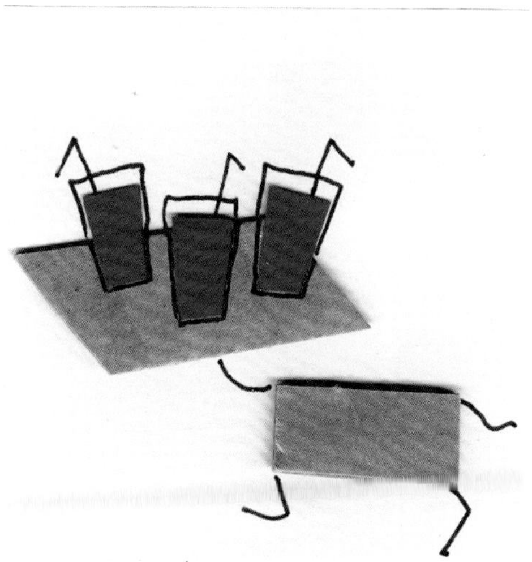
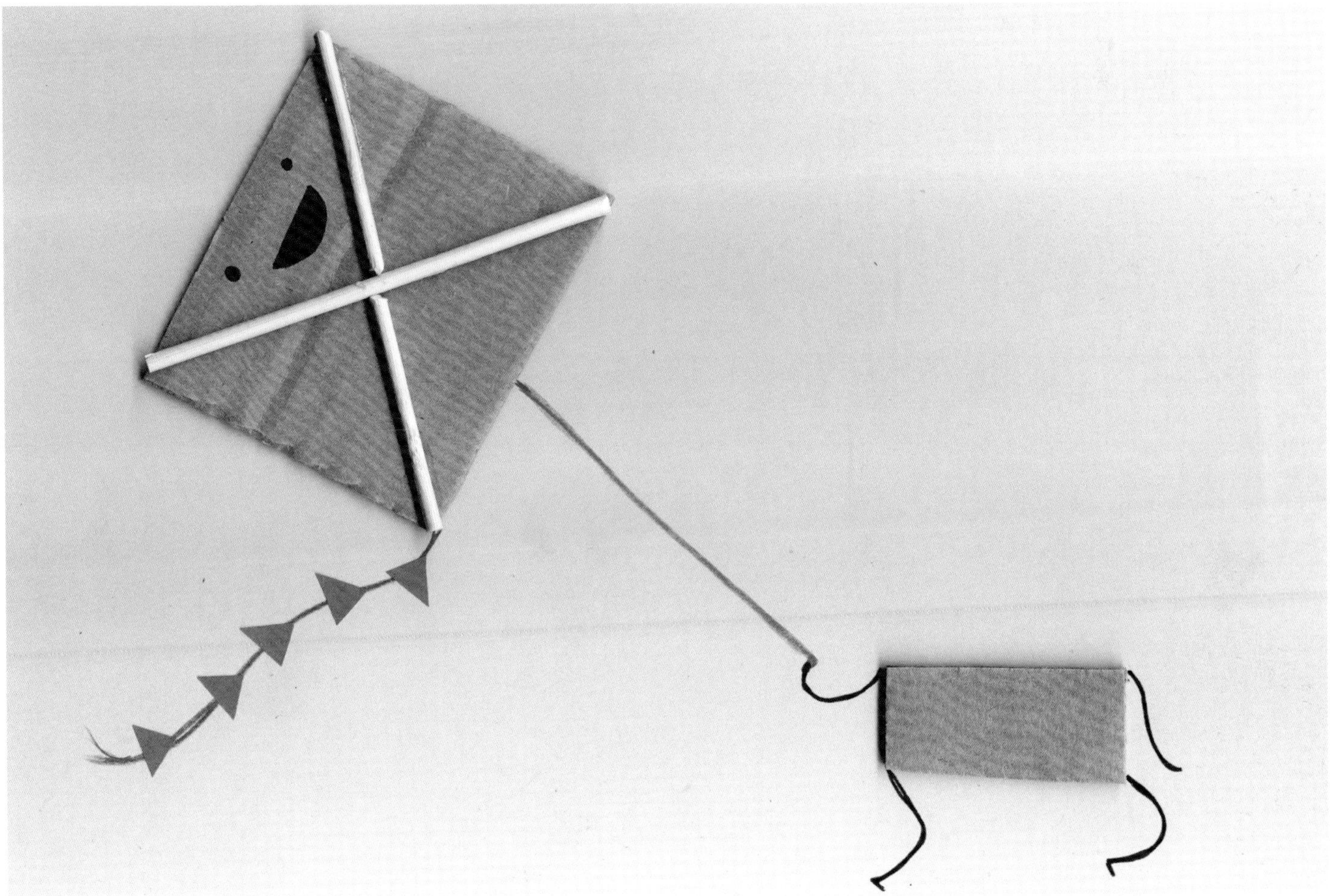

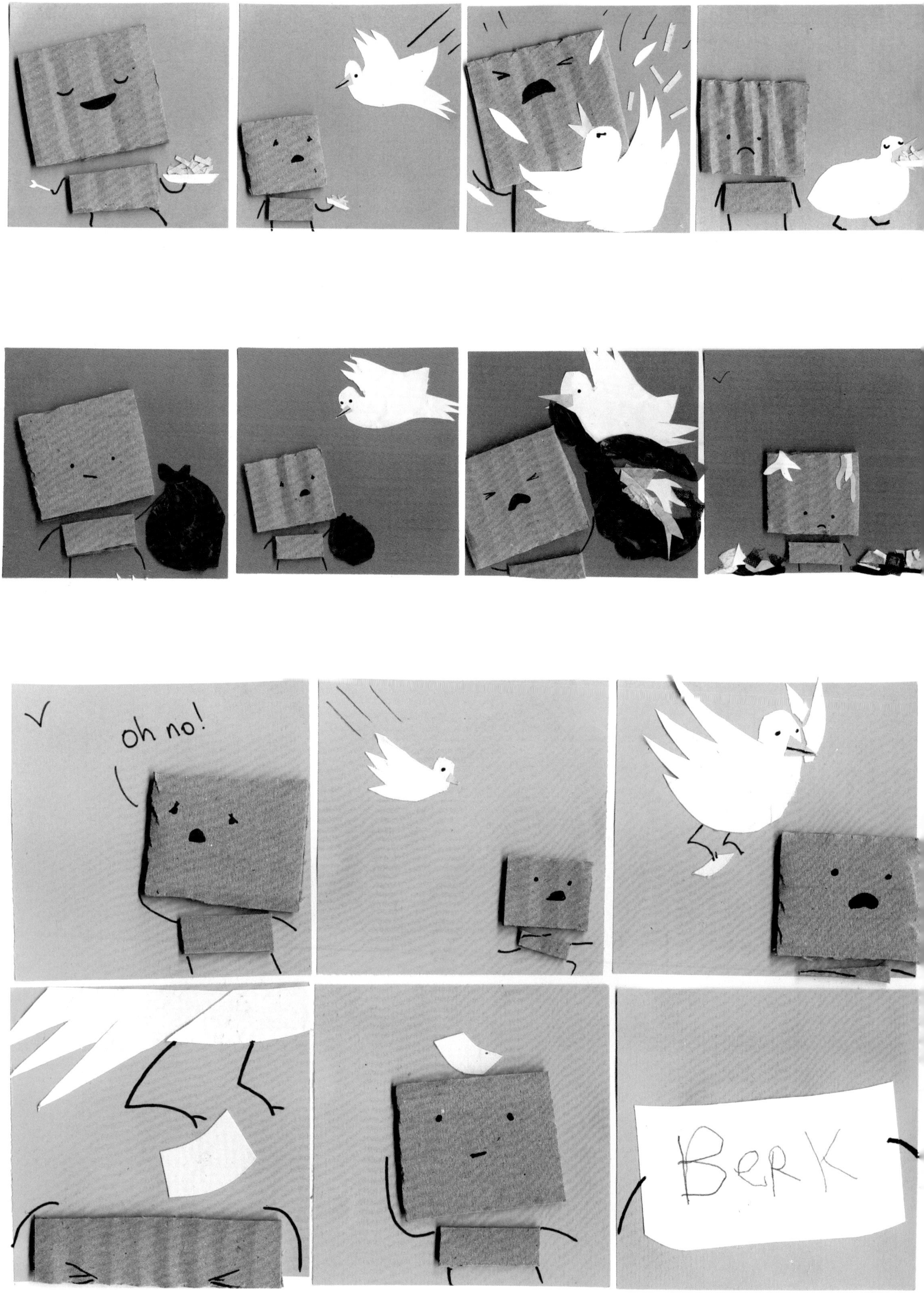
oh no!
BeRK

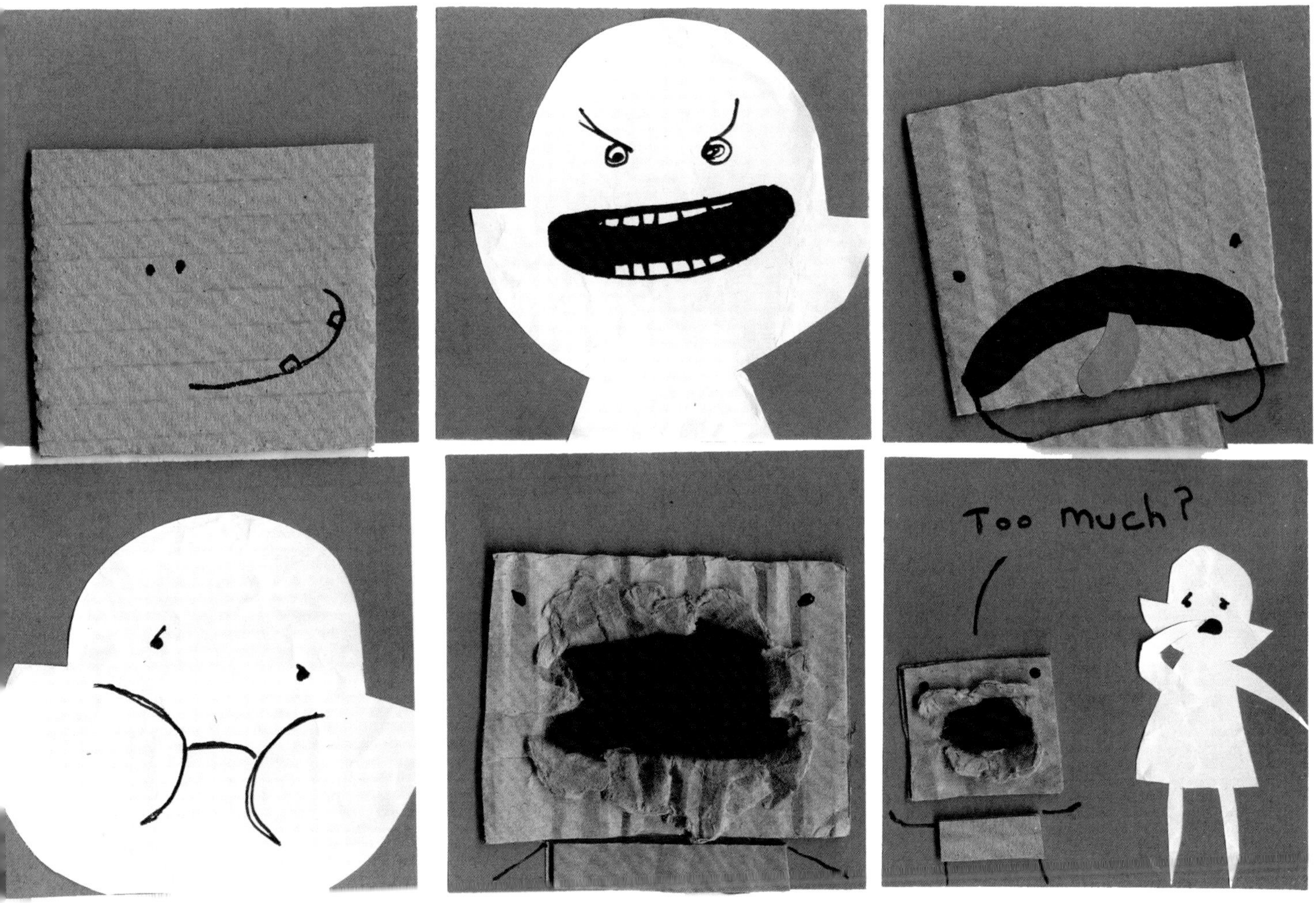
Too much?

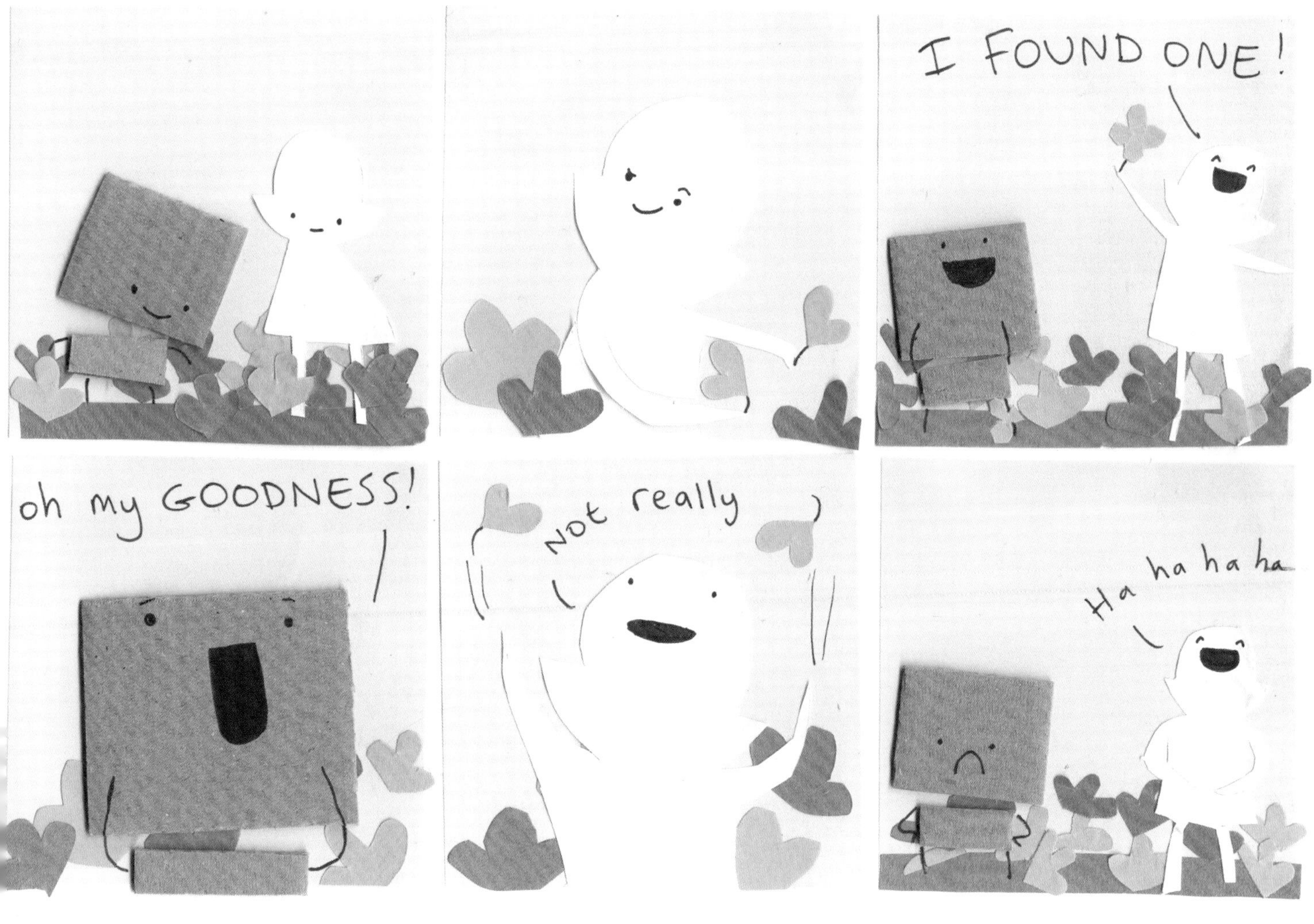
I FOUND ONE!
oh my GOODNESS!
not really
Ha ha ha ha ha

This wine's really nice. What is it?

Cardbordeaux

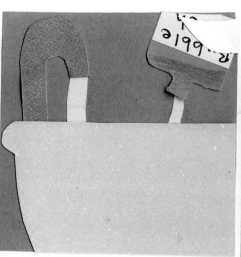

Dear Secret Diary, it's been a good day so far...

Colin, you're so stupid. It's not going to be secret if you read it out loud as you write it! You dunce!

Dear Secret Diary, Pauline has really hurt my feelings yet again!

Uncle Colin, can we give you a makeover?

OK

How do I look?

hopping onions always makes me cry.
what are you crying about this time?
it's the o...
Oh boo hoo, there's always Something isn't there. why don't you grow up Colin!
Well now I'm double-crying
A cup of tea in my own Personalised Mug!
colin
I'll just get the milk...
colin
colin
boring
A penny saved is a penny earned.
I've "earned" a lot of money by not having a car...
...and when you consider how much I've "earned" by not having a mansion, or a helicopter, or a pony or kids, not to mention designer Clothes....
... I'm a bloomin' Millionaire!
Come and see this new dessert I've invented
oh my goodness! what's in it?
Well... there's Some Paper, a bit of glue, Card, Some Paint, ink, felt-tippen
More paint, a bit of selotape, colouring pencils...

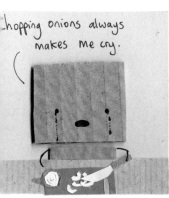

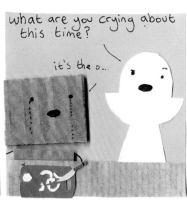

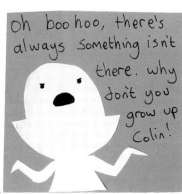

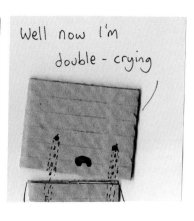

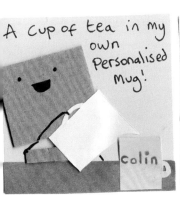

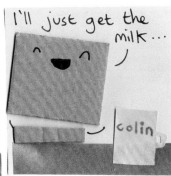

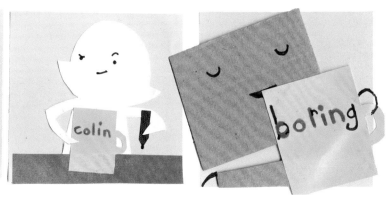

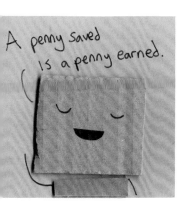

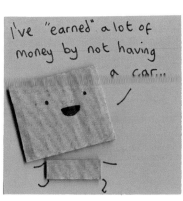

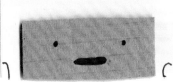

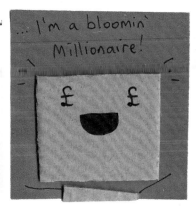

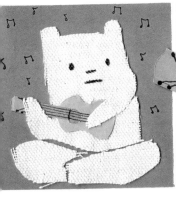

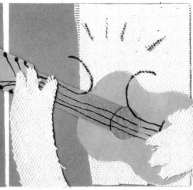

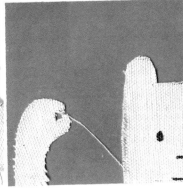

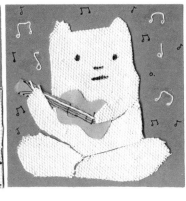

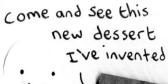

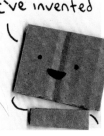

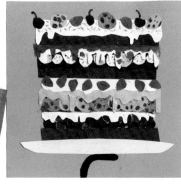

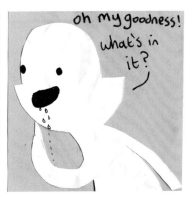

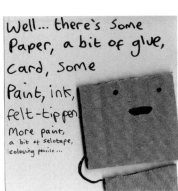

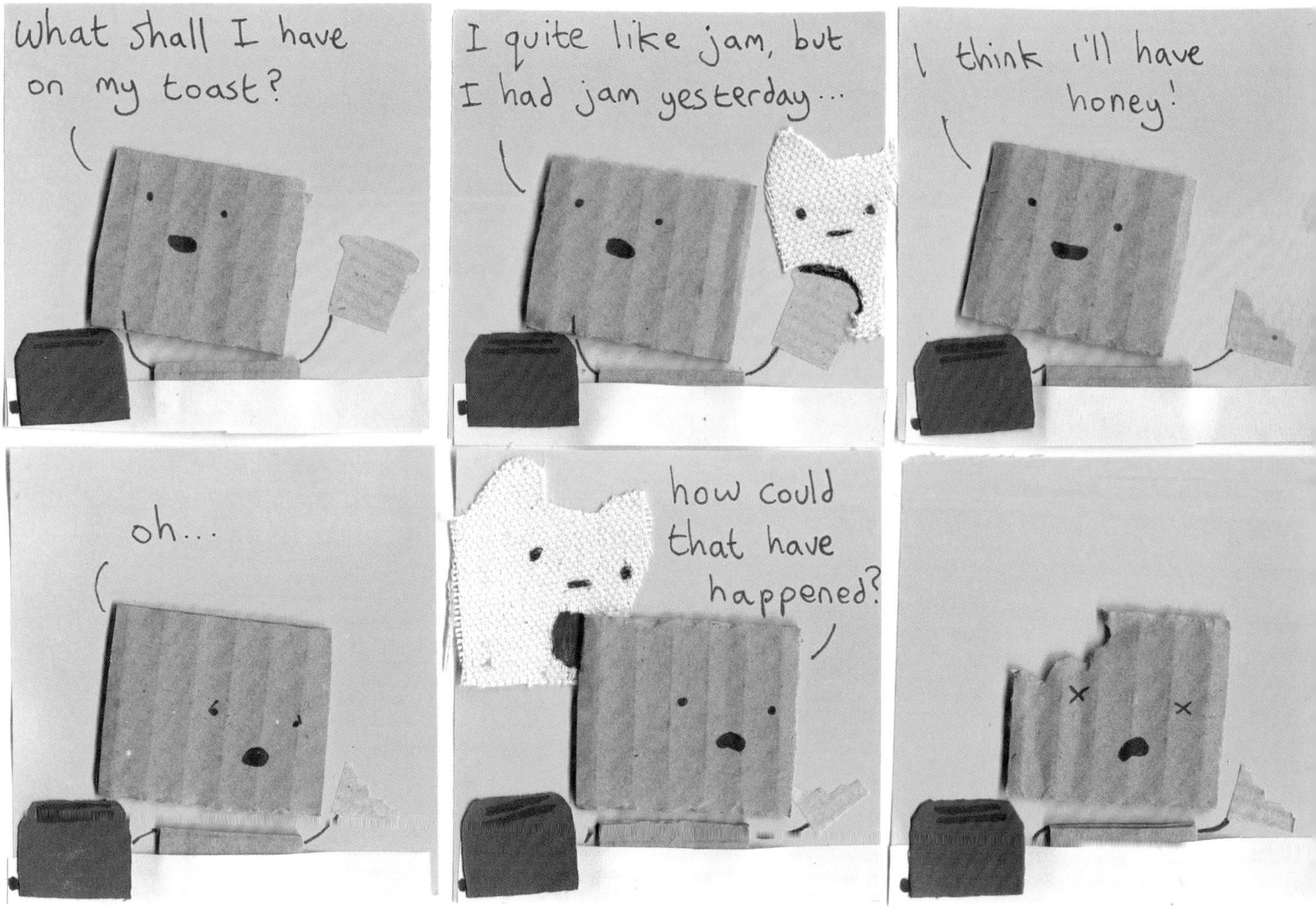
What shall I have on my toast?
I quite like jam, but I had jam yesterday...
I think I'll have honey!
oh...
how could that have happened?

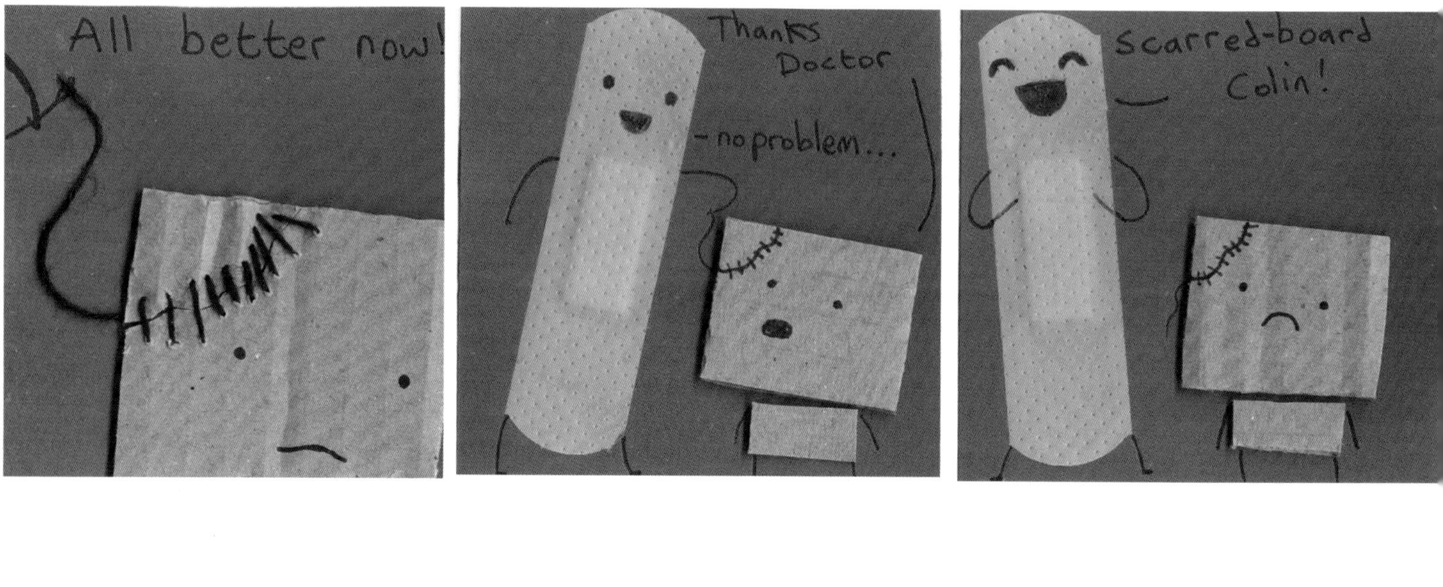
All better now!
Thanks Doctor
- no problem...
Scarred-board Colin!

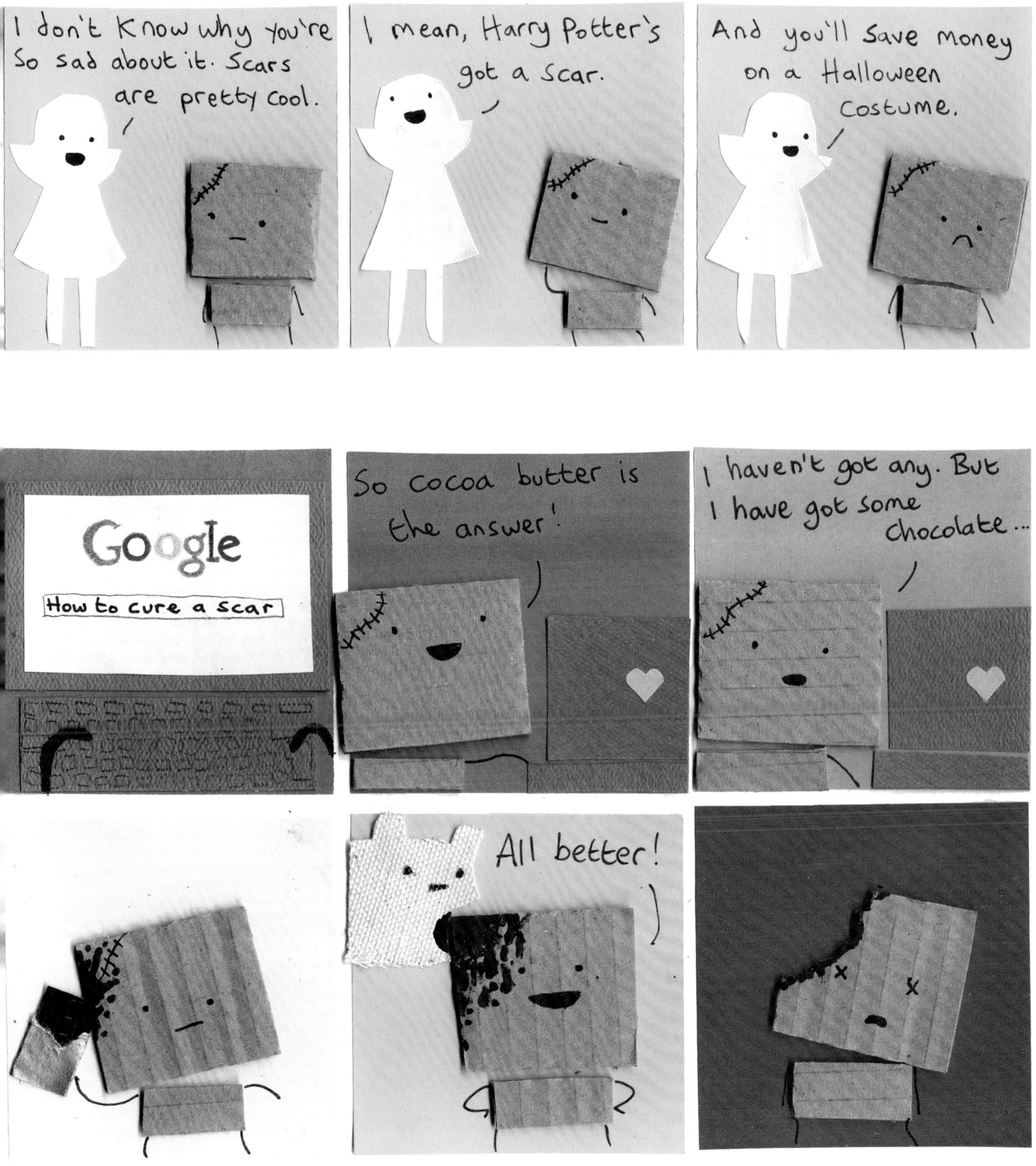
I don't Know why you're So sad about it. Scars are pretty cool.
I mean, Harry Potter's got a Scar.
And you'll save money on a Halloween Costume.
Google
How to cure a scar
So cocoa butter is the answer!
I haven't got any. But I have got some chocolate...
All better!

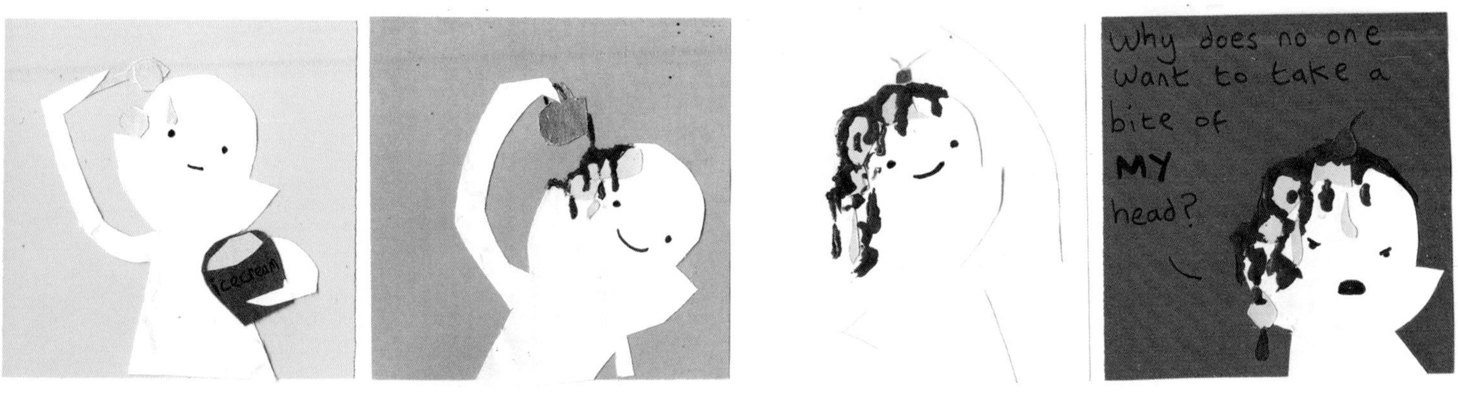
Why does no one want to take a bite of MY head?

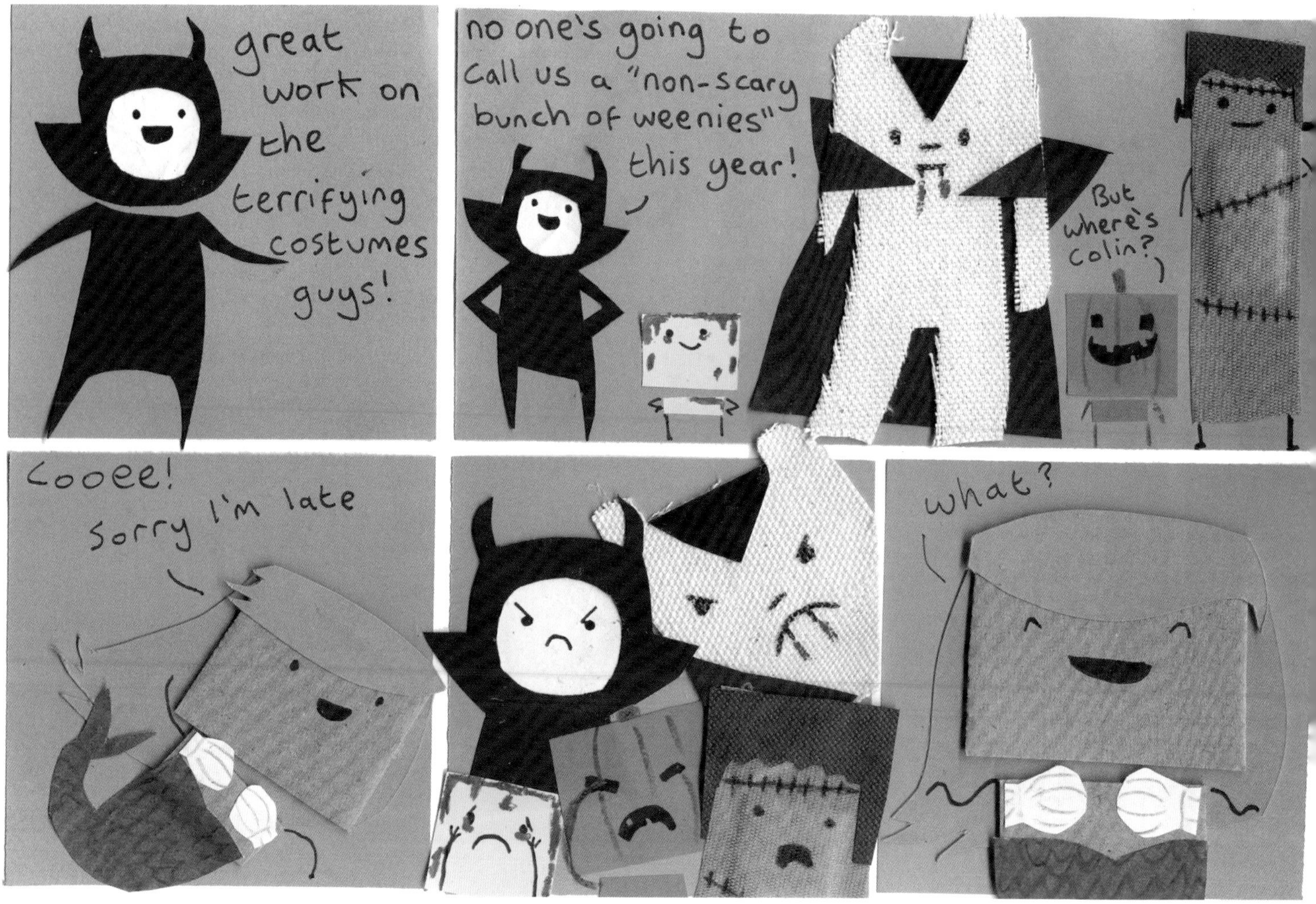
great work on the terrifying costumes guys!
no one's going to call us a "non-scary bunch of weenies" this year!
But where's colin?
Cooee! Sorry I'm late
what?

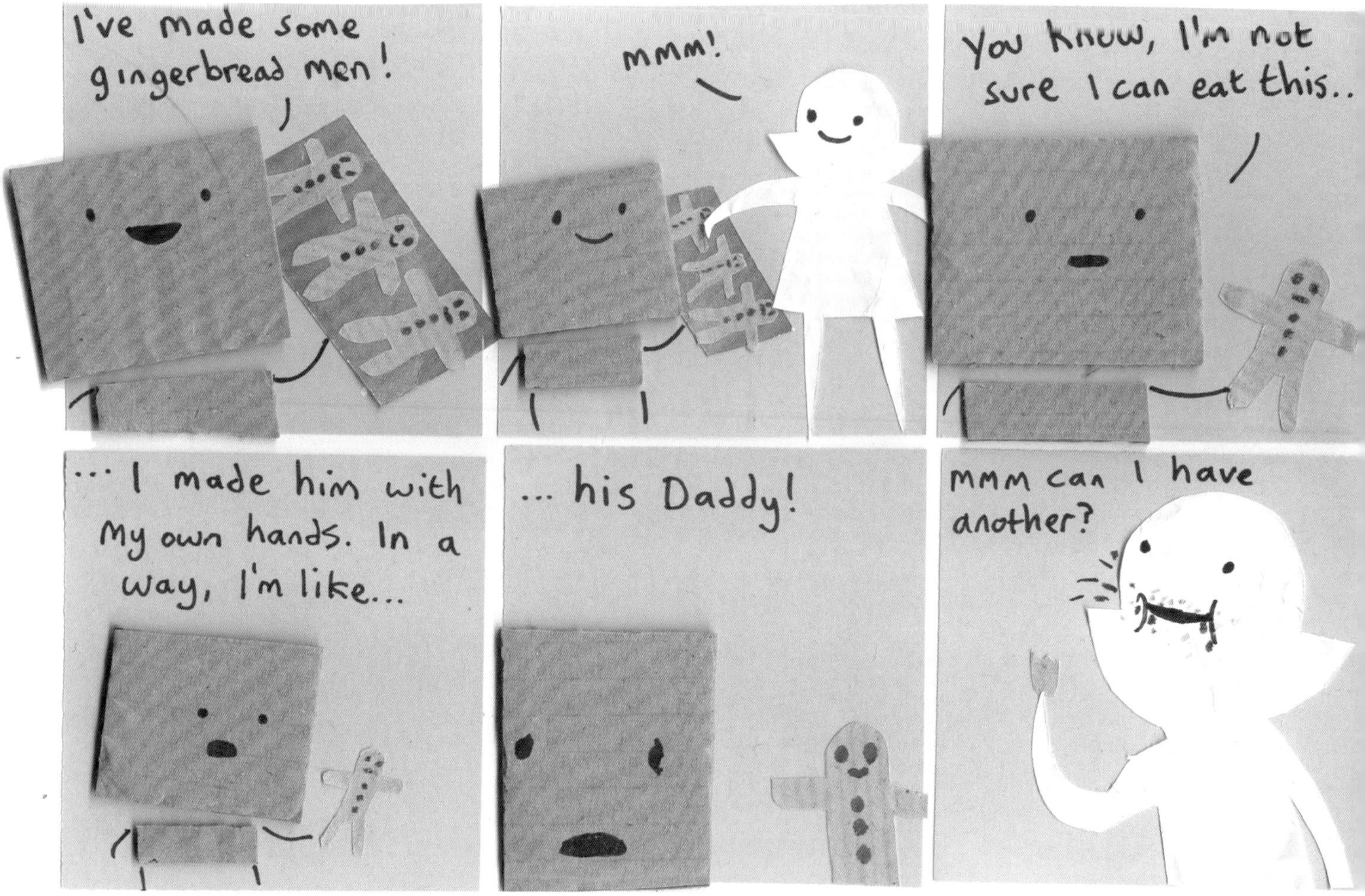
I've made some gingerbread men!
mmm!
You know, I'm not sure I can eat this..
... I made him with my own hands. In a way, I'm like...
... his Daddy!
mmm can I have another?

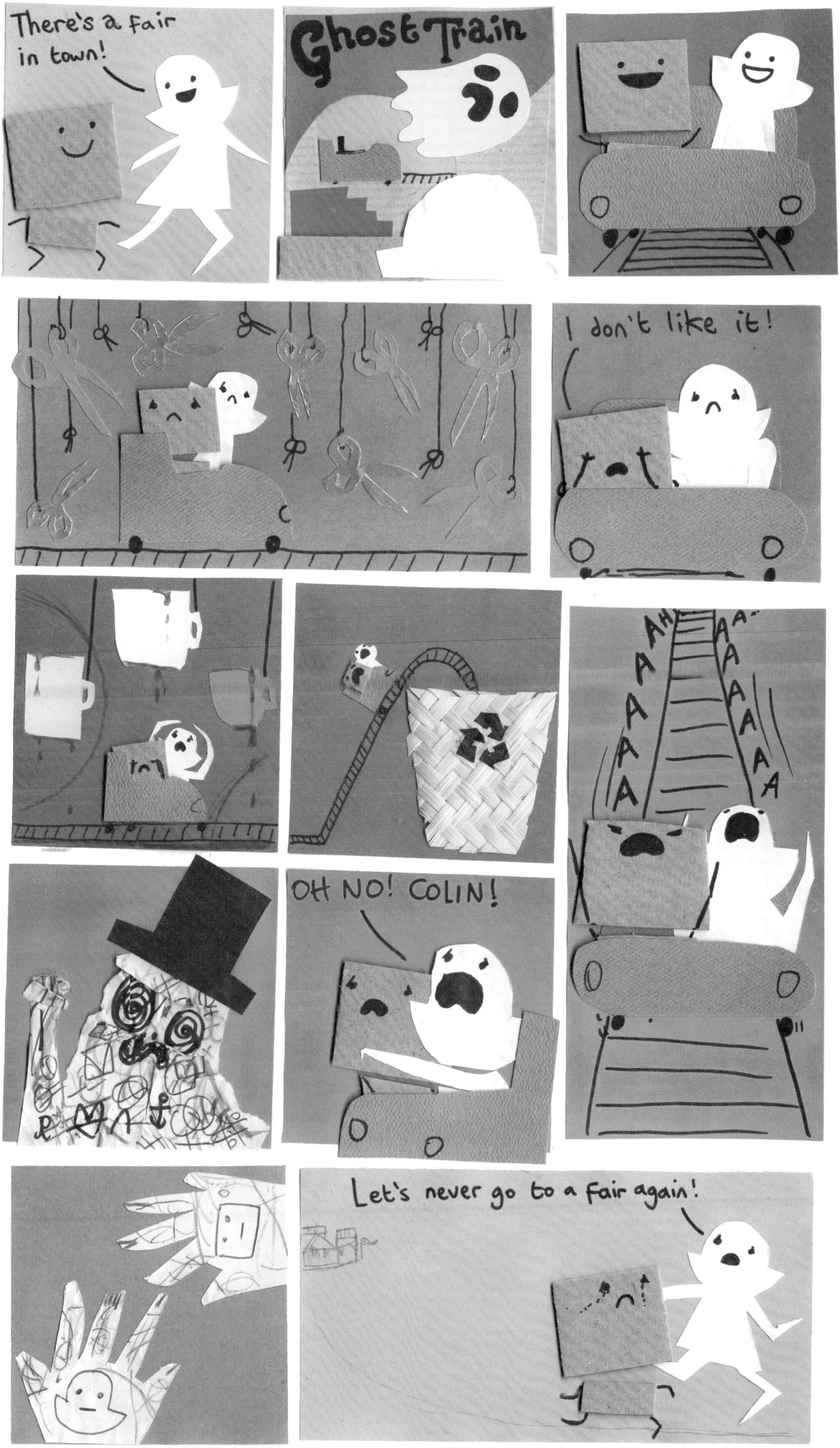

There's a Fair in town!
Ghost Train
I don't like it!
AAAAAAAAH
AAAAAAAAAA
OH NO! COLIN!
Let's never go to a Fair again!

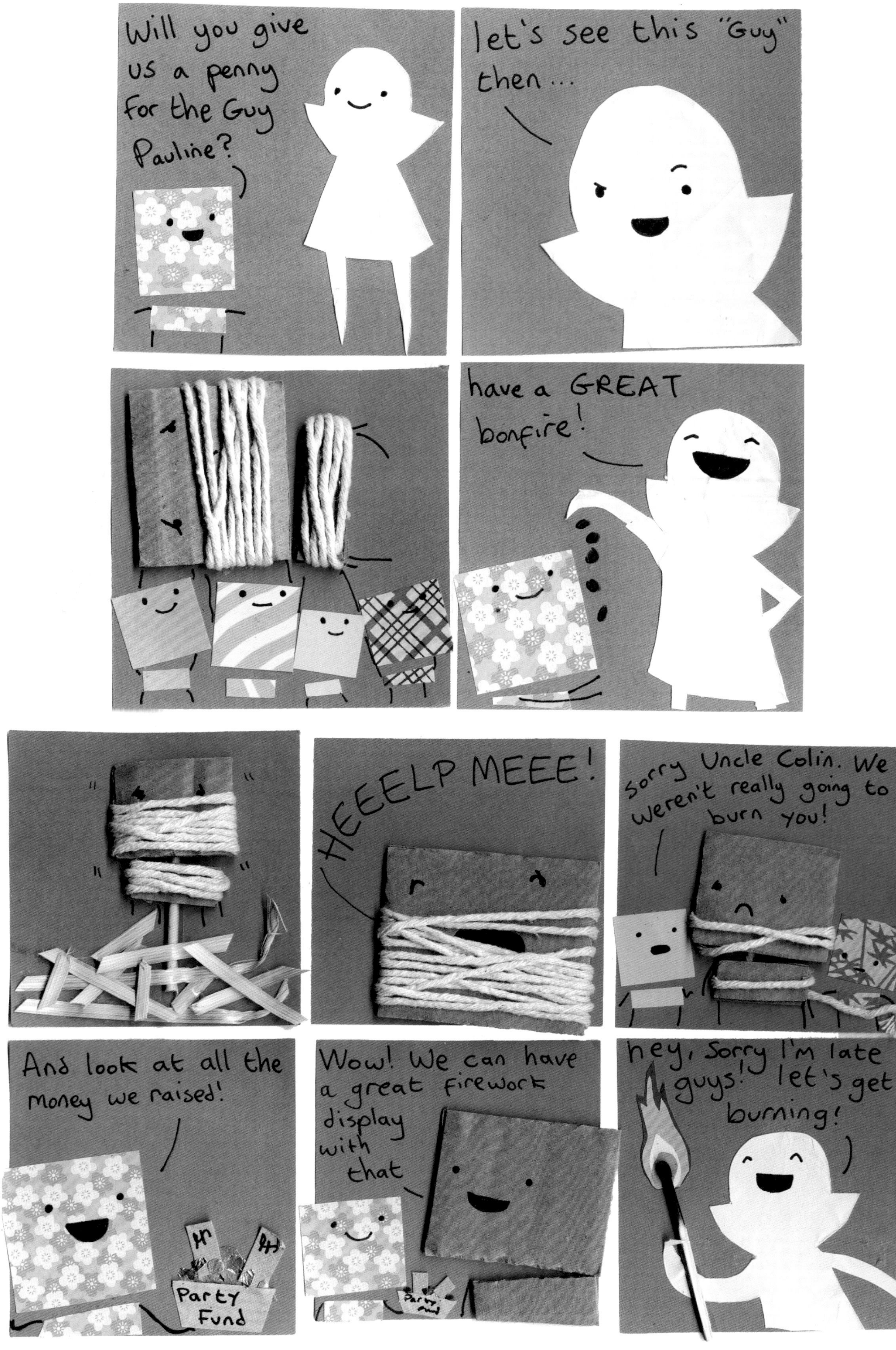
Will you give us a penny for the Guy Pauline?
let's see this "Guy" then...
have a GREAT bonfire!
HEEELP MEEE!
sorry Uncle Colin. We weren't really going to burn you!
And look at all the money we raised!
Party Fund
Wow! We can have a great firework display with that
hey, Sorry I'm late guys! let's get burning!

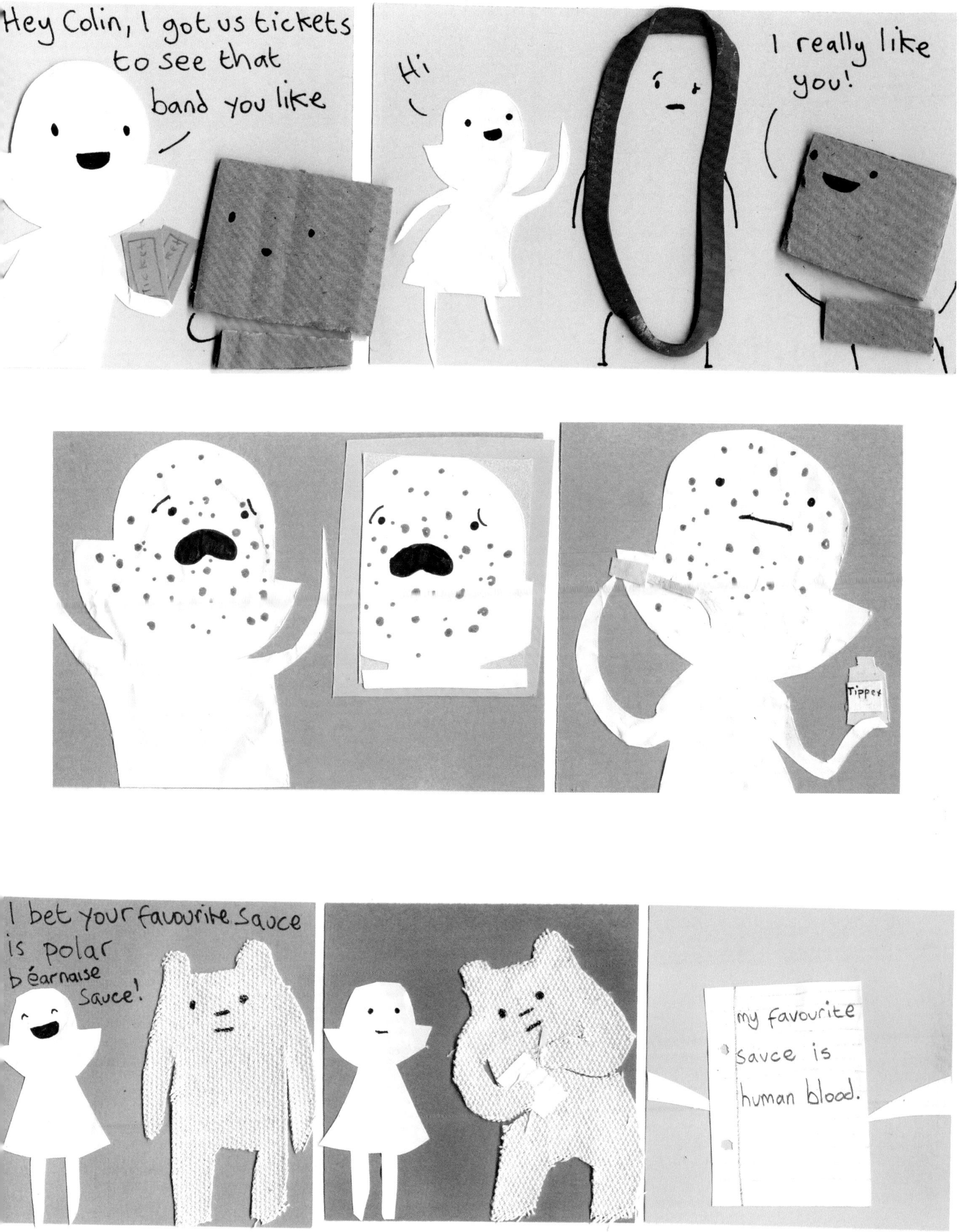
Hey Colin, I got us tickets to see that band you like
Hi
I really like you!
Tippex
I bet your favourite sauce is polar béarnaise sauce!
my favourite sauce is human blood.

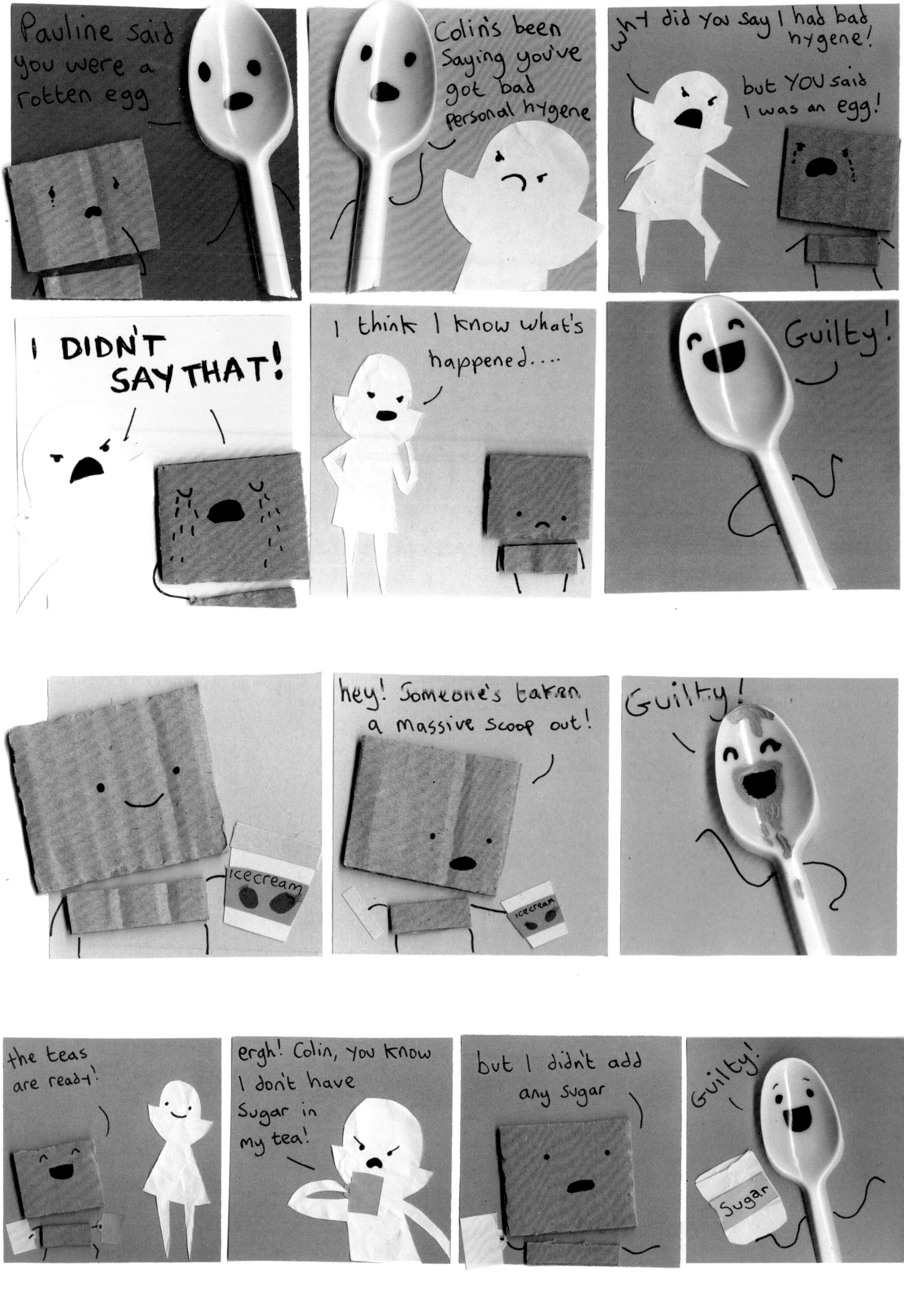
Pauline said you were a rotten egg
Colin's been saying you've got bad personal hygene
why did you say I had bad hygene!
but YOU said I was an egg!
I DIDN'T SAY THAT!
I think I know what's happened....
Guilty!
icecream
hey! Someone's taken a massive scoop out!
icecream
Guilty!
the teas are ready!
ergh! Colin, you know I don't have sugar in my tea!
but I didn't add any sugar
Guilty!
Sugar

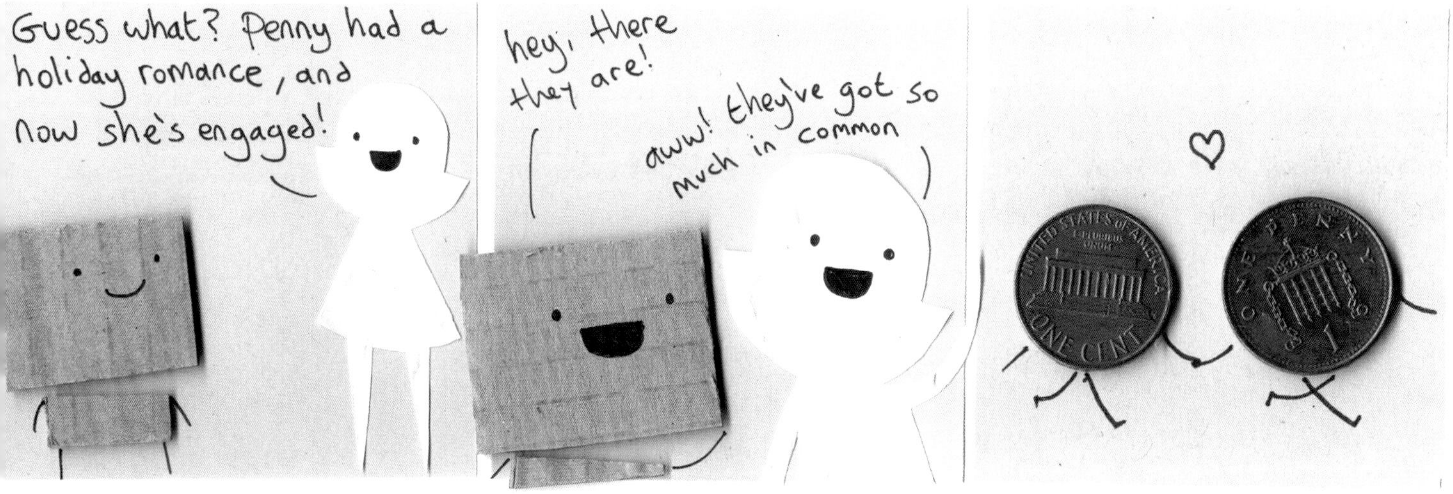
Guess what? Penny had a holiday romance, and now she's engaged!
hey, there they are!
aww! they've got so much in common

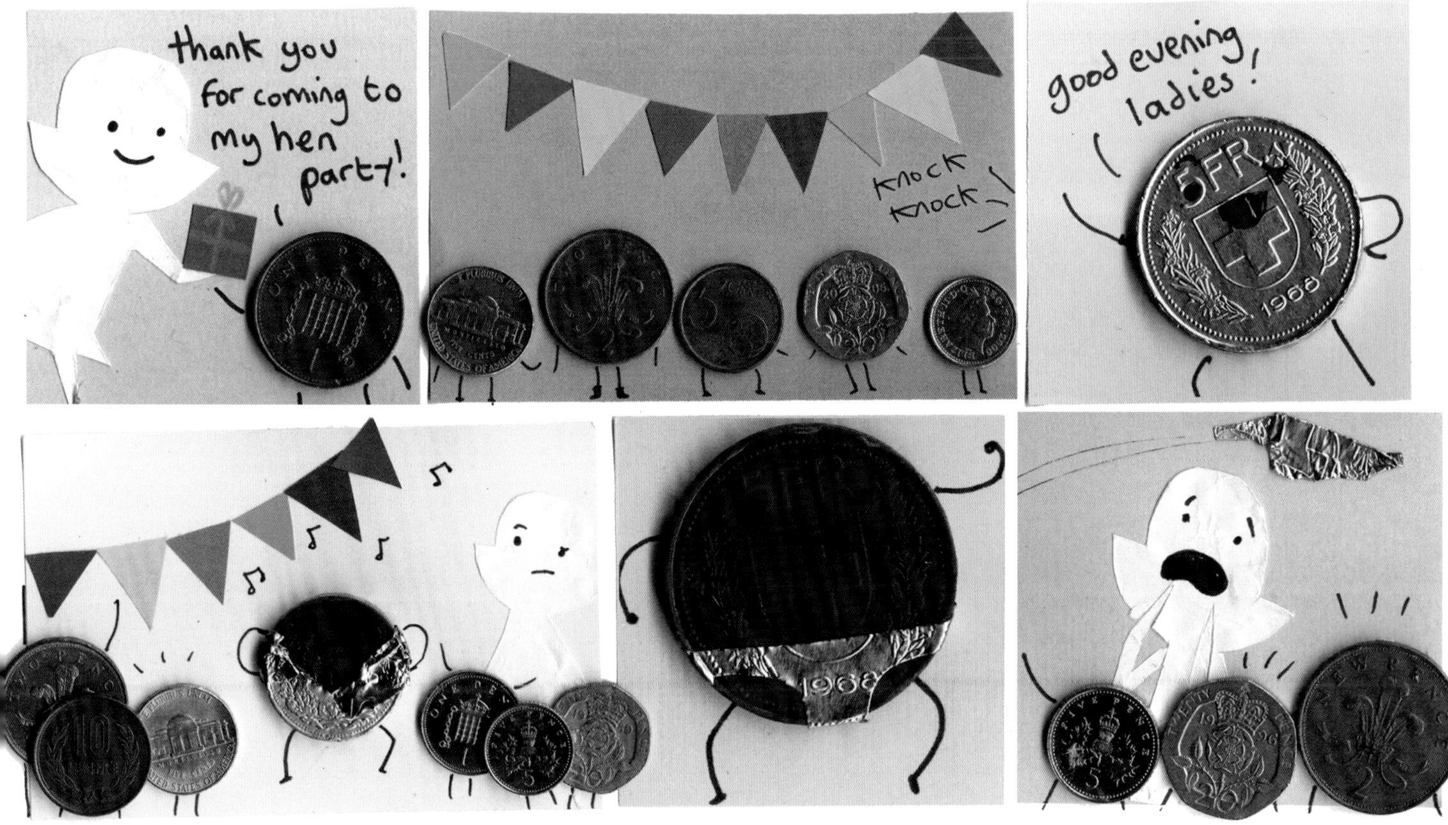
thank you for coming to my hen party!
knock knock
good evening ladies!

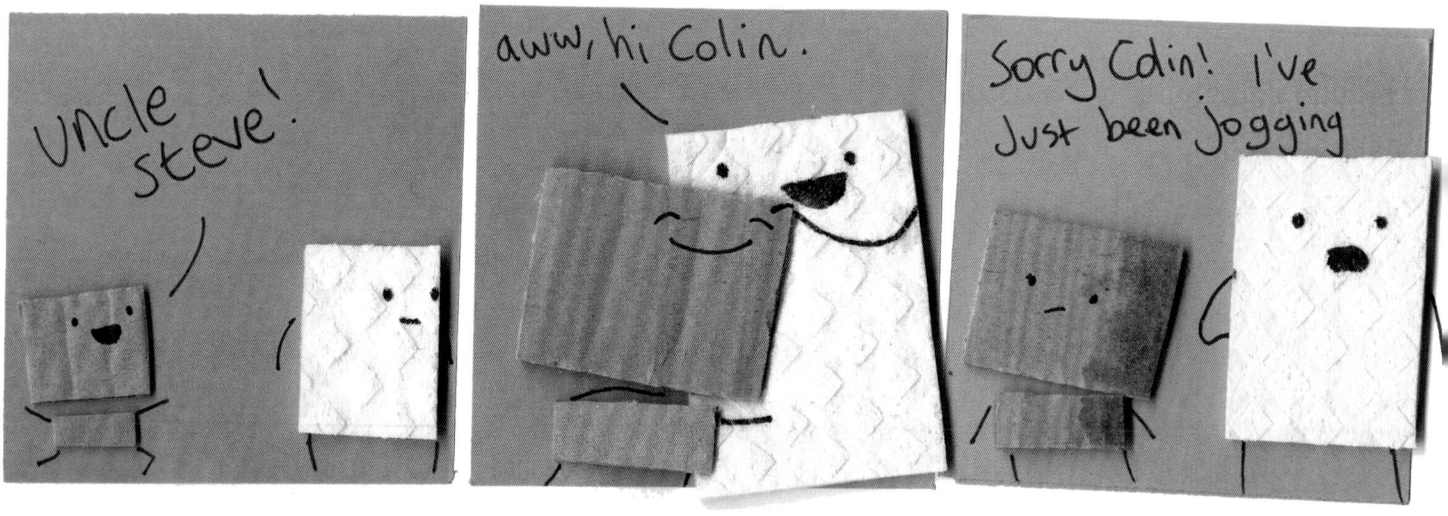
Uncle Steve!
aww, hi Colin.
Sorry Colin! I've Just been jogging

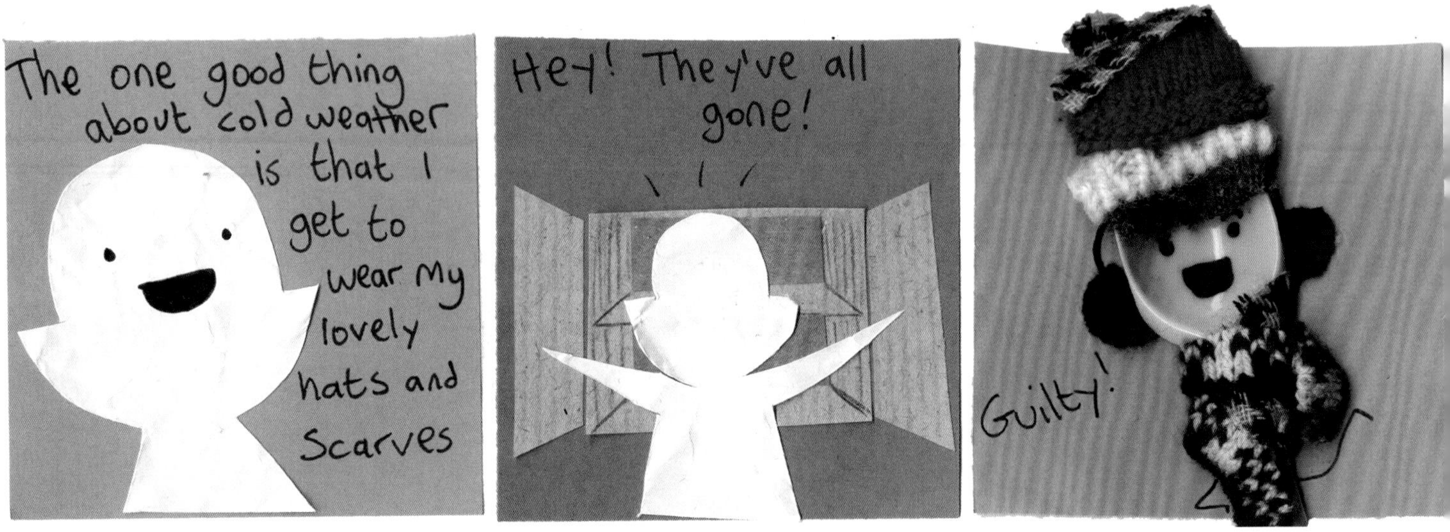
The one good thing about cold weather is that I get to wear my lovely hats and scarves
Hey! They've all gone!
Guilty!

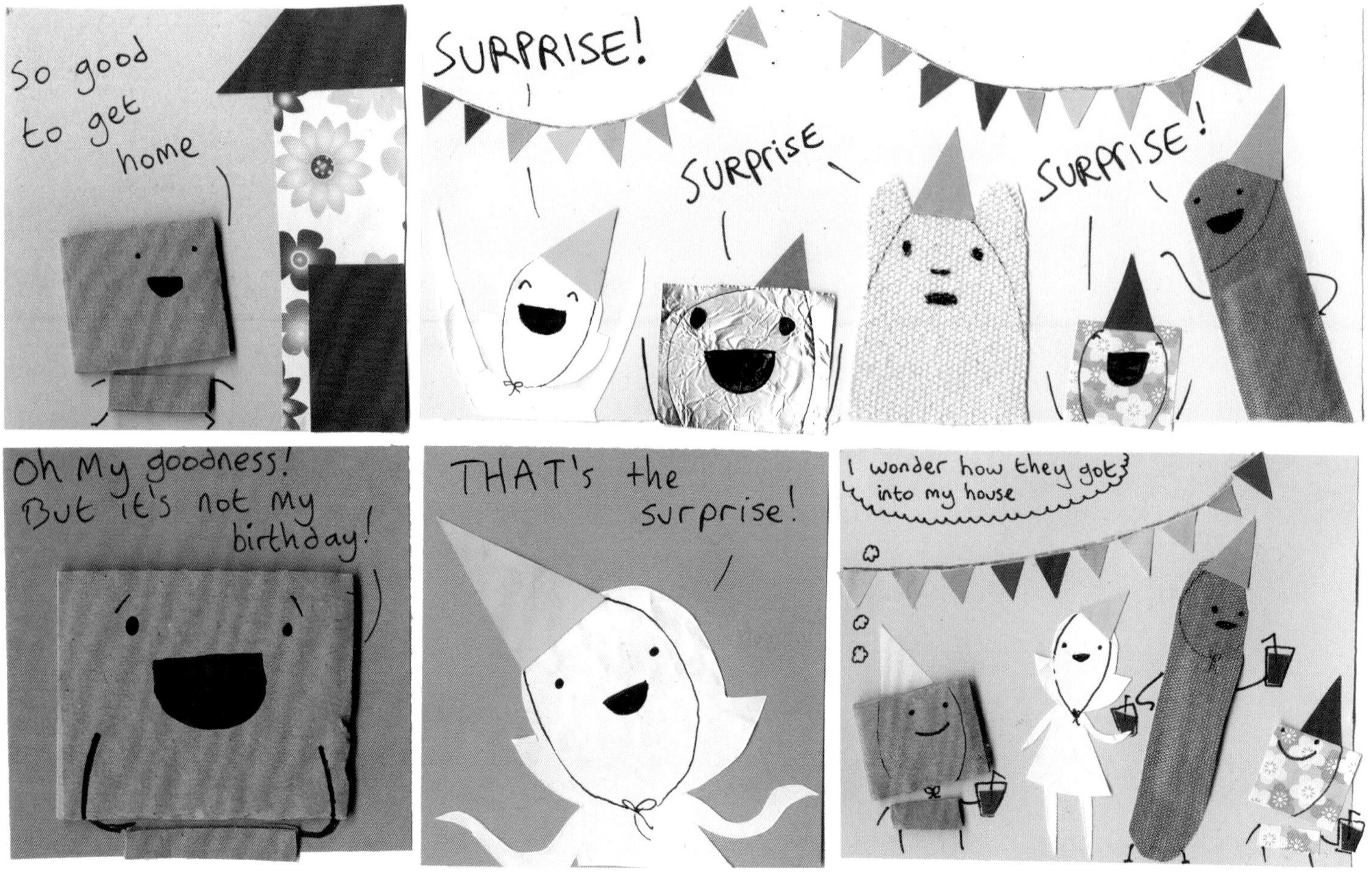
So good to get home
SURPRISE!
SURPRISE
SURPRISE!
Oh My goodness! But it's not my birthday!
THAT's the surprise!
I wonder how they got into my house

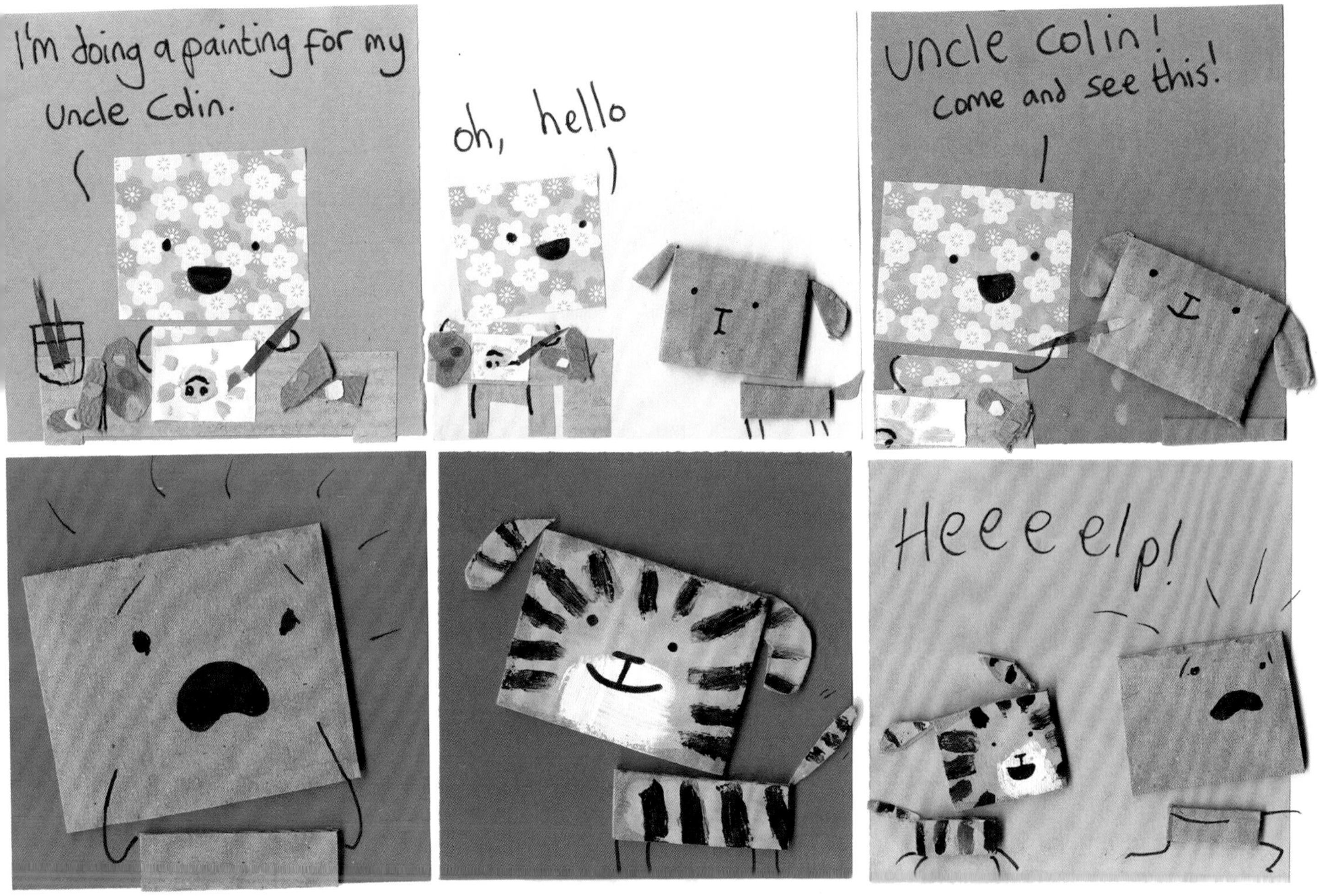
I'm doing a painting for my uncle Colin.
oh, hello
Uncle Colin! come and see this!
Heeeelp!

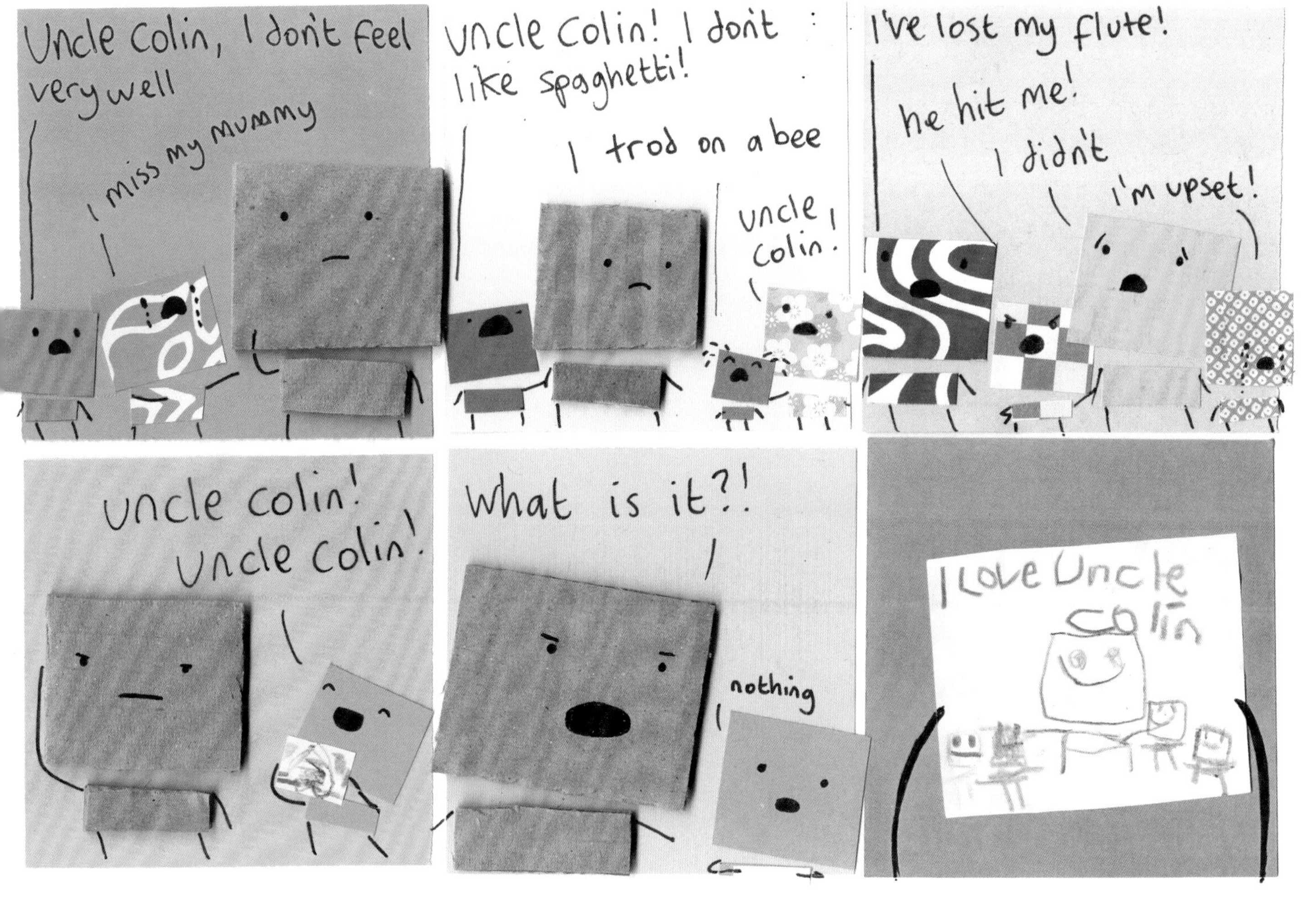
Uncle Colin, I don't feel very well
I miss my mummy
Uncle Colin! I don't like spaghetti!
I trod on a bee
uncle Colin!
I've lost my flute!
he hit me!
I didn't
I'm upset!
uncle colin! Uncle Colin!
What is it?!
nothing
I Love Uncle Colin

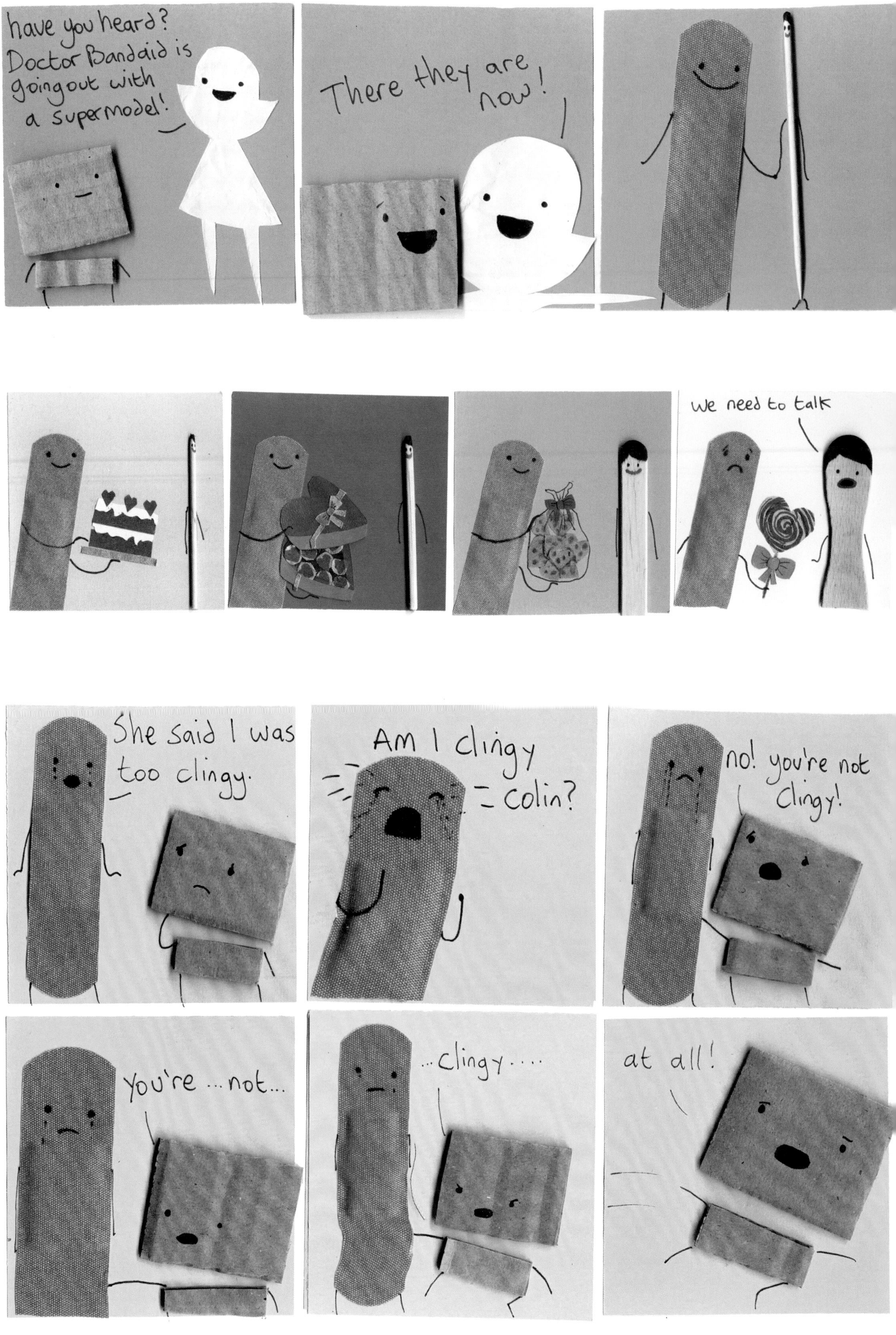
have you heard? Doctor Bandaid is goingout with a supermodel!
There they are now!
we need to talk
She said I was too clingy.
Am I clingy colin?
no! you're not clingy!
you're ...not...
...clingy....
at all!

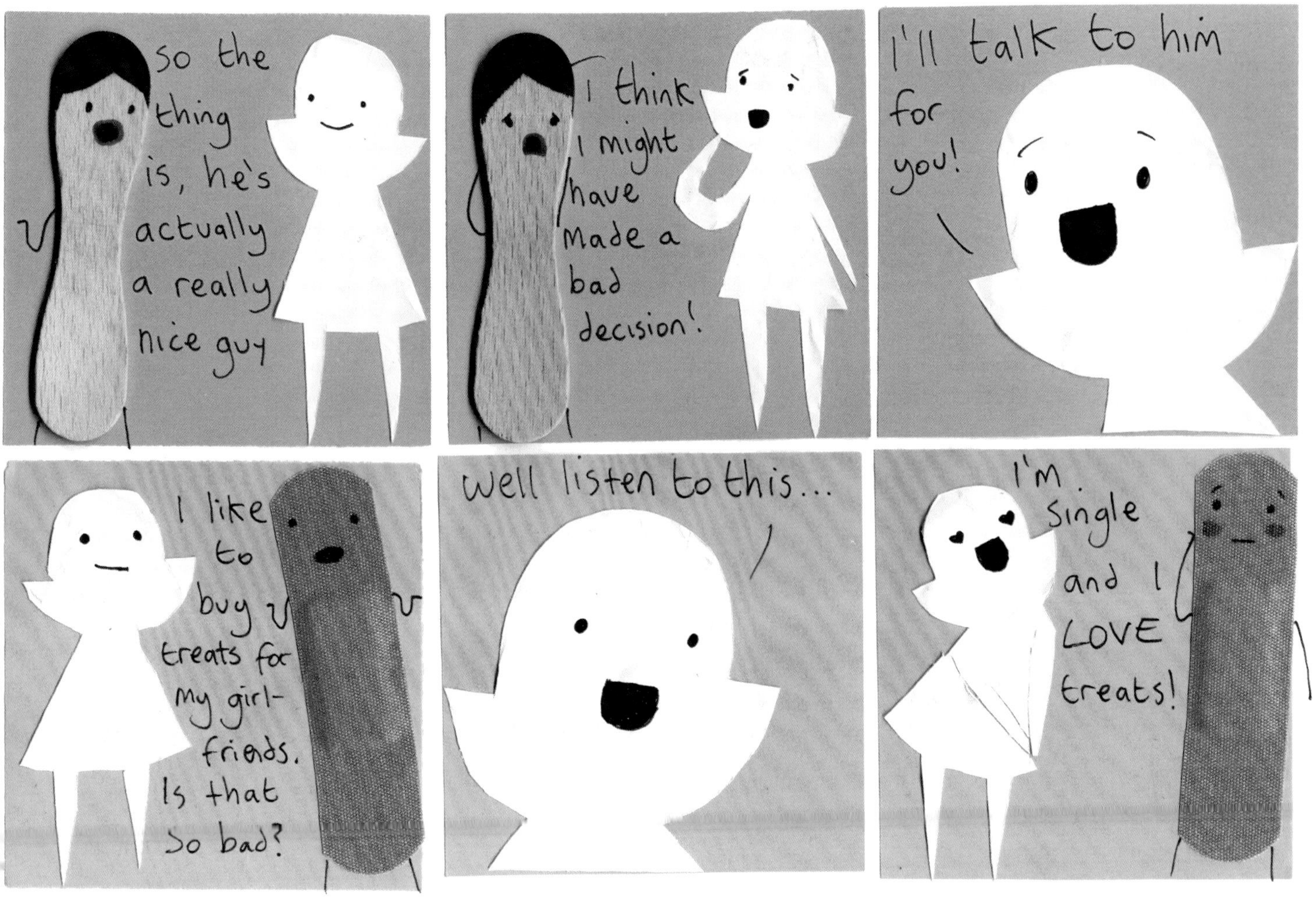
So the thing is, he's actually a really nice guy
I think I might have made a bad decision!
I'll talk to him for you!
I like to buy treats for my girl-friends. Is that so bad?
well listen to this...
I'm single and I LOVE treats!

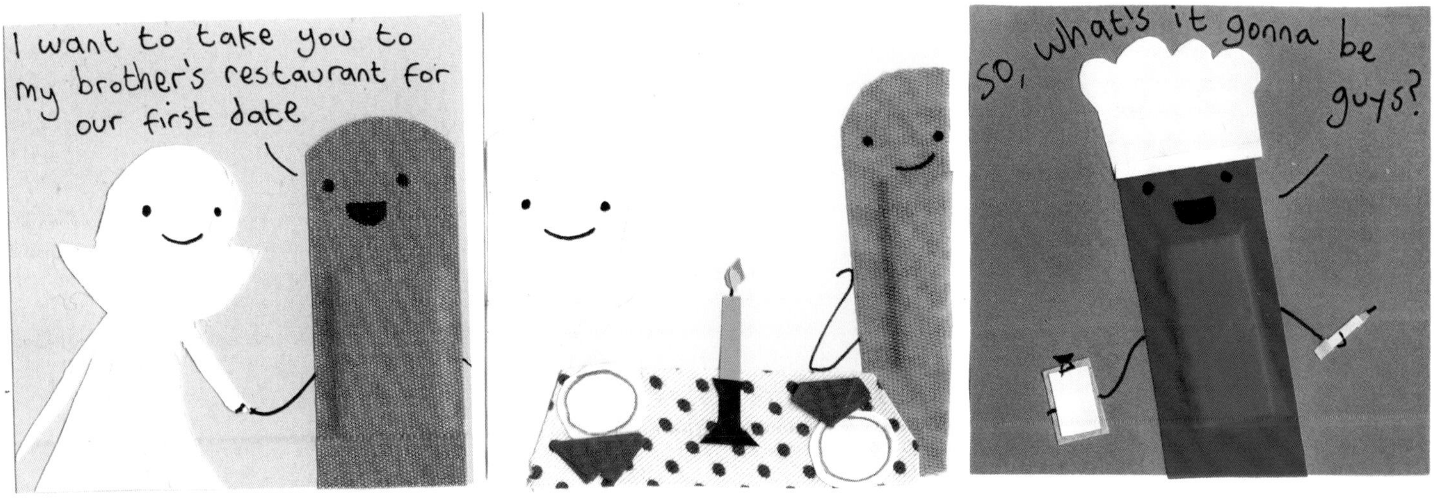
I want to take you to my brother's restaurant for our first date
So, what's it gonna be guys?

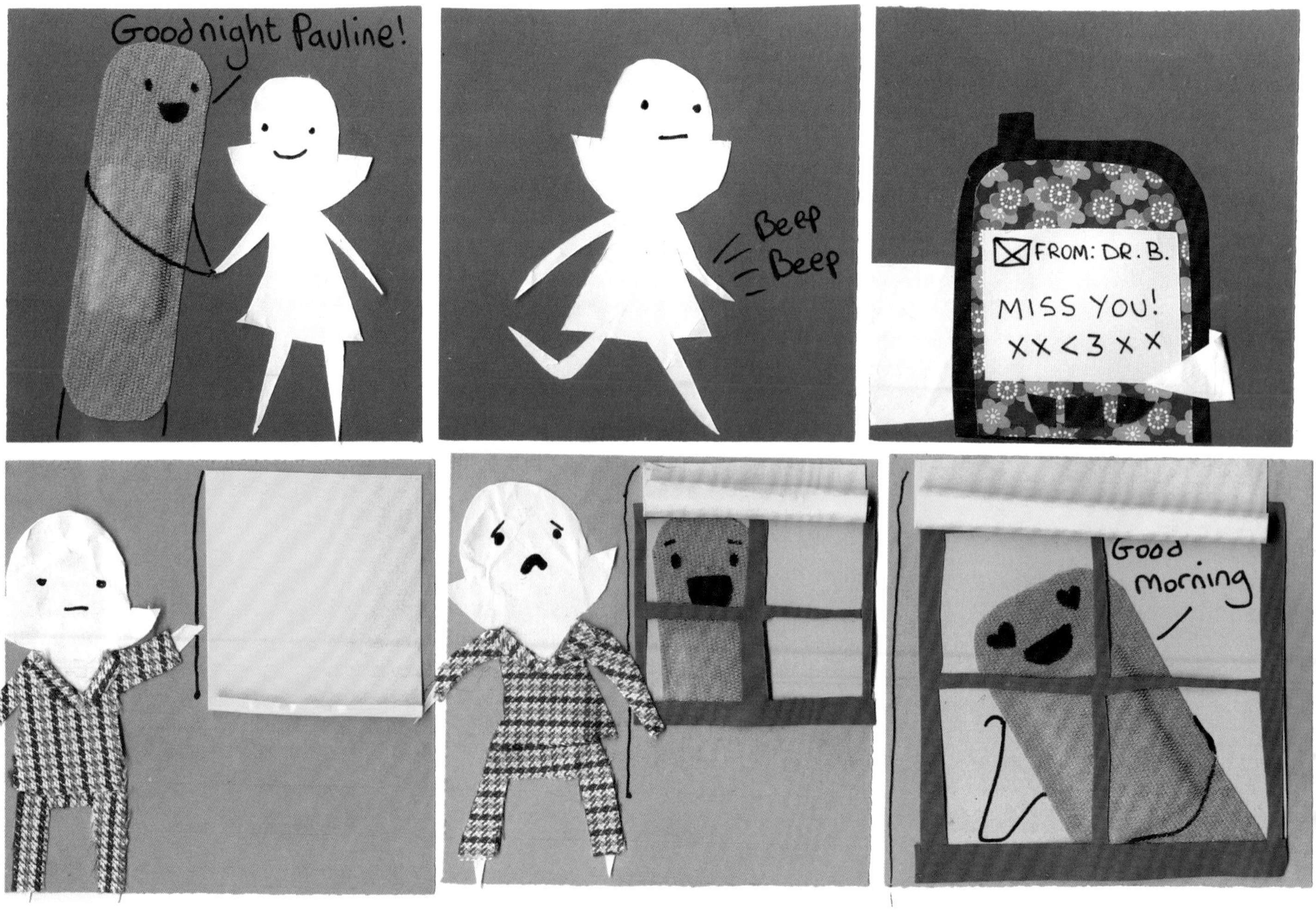
Goodnight Pauline!
Beep Beep
FROM: DR. B.
MISS YOU!
XX <3 XX
Good morning

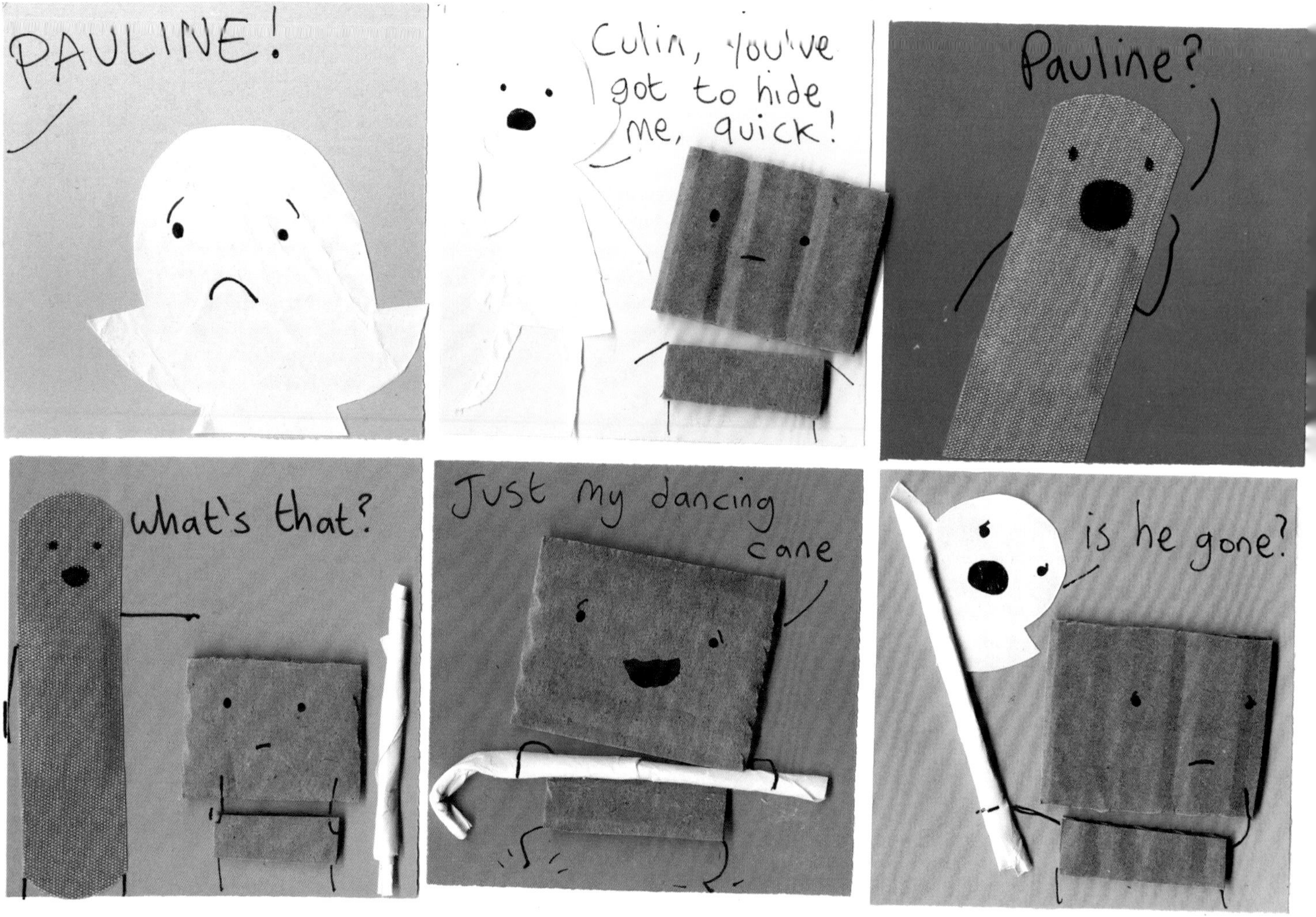
PAULINE!
Culin, you've got to hide me, quick!
Pauline?
what's that?
Just my dancing cane
is he gone?

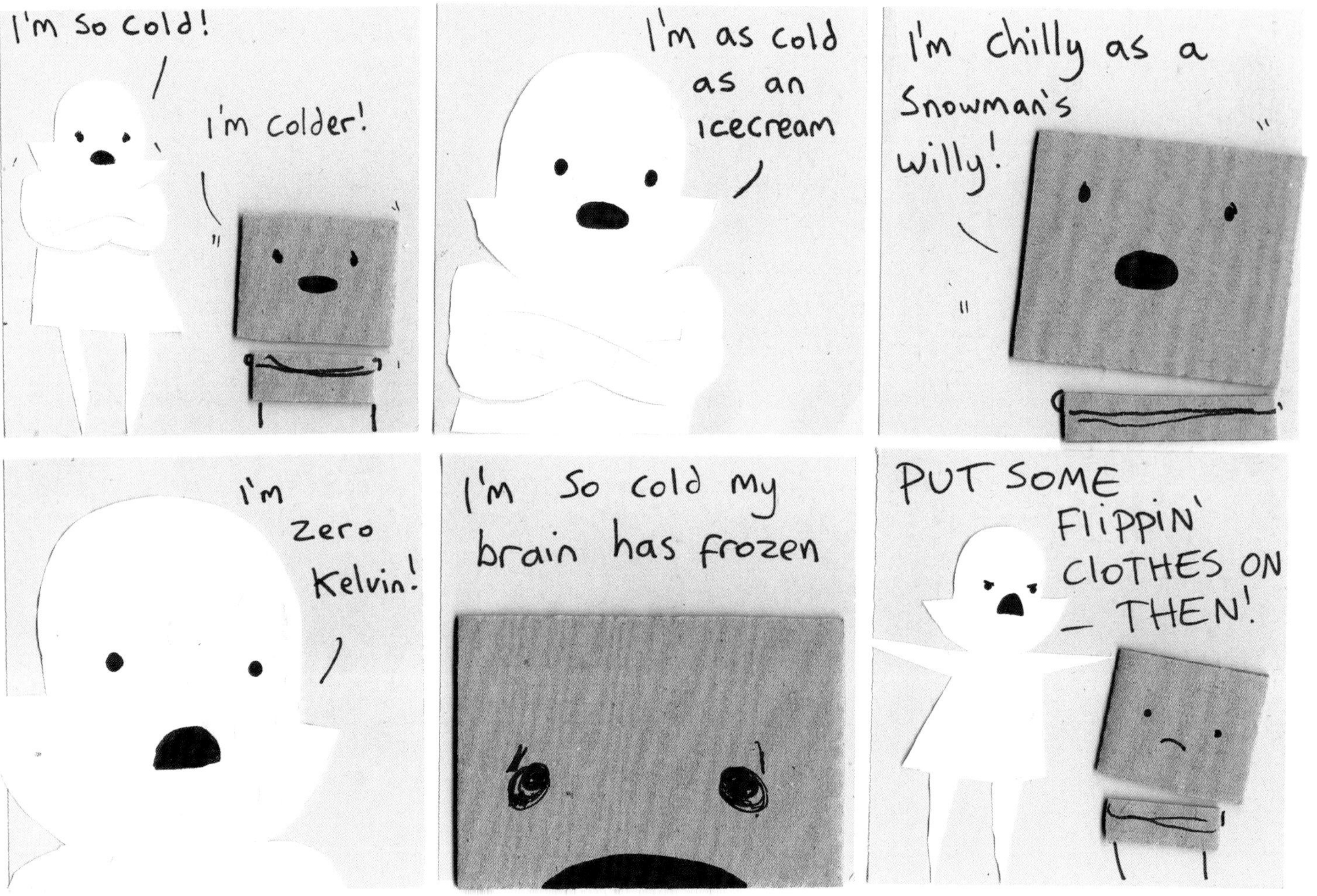
I'm so cold!
i'm colder!
I'm as cold as an icecream
I'm chilly as a snowman's willy!
i'm zero Kelvin!
I'm so cold my brain has frozen
PUT SOME FLIPPIN' CLOTHES ON THEN!

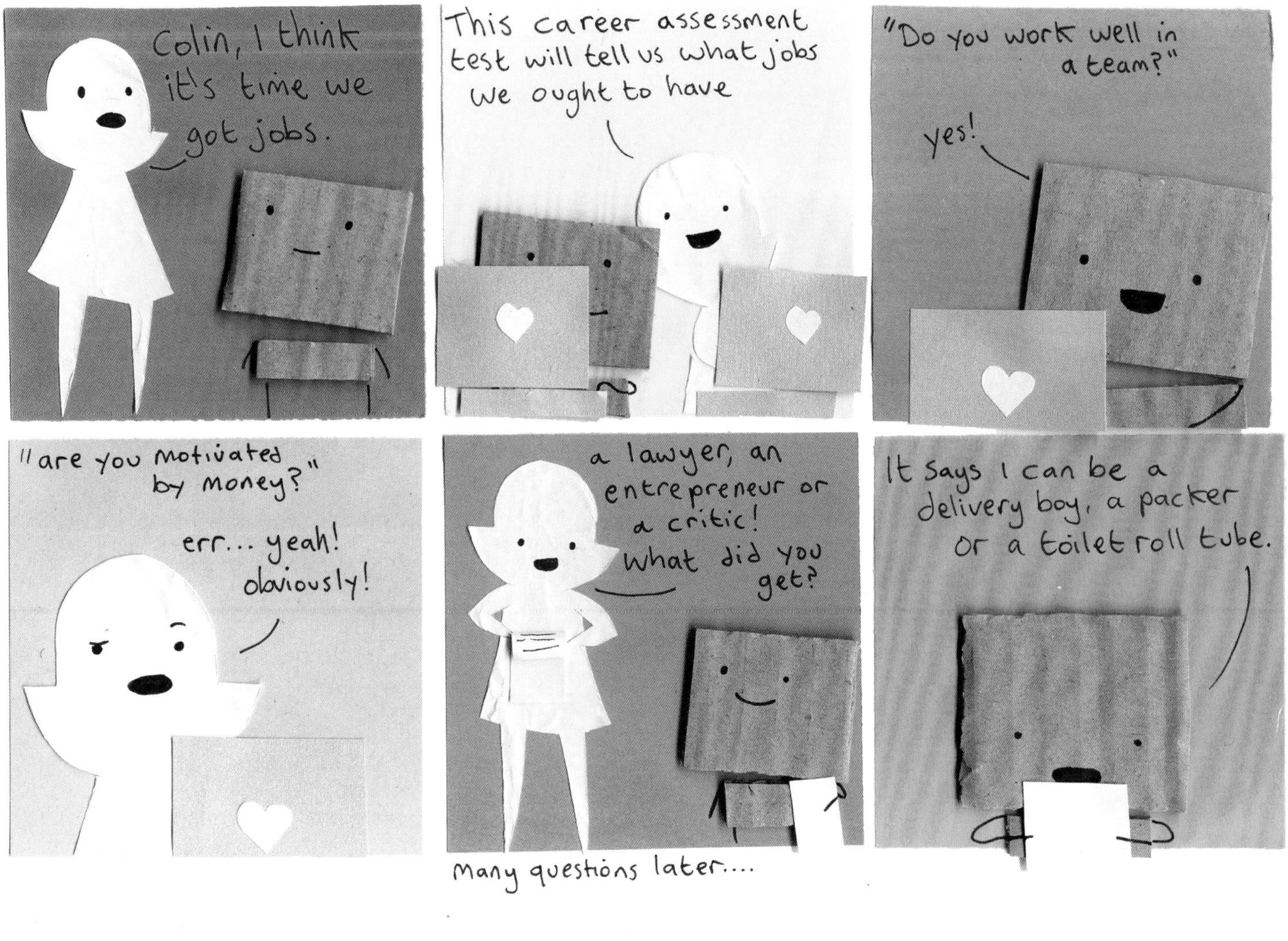
Colin, I think it's time we got jobs.
This career assessment test will tell us what jobs we ought to have
"Do you work well in a team?"
yes!
"are you motivated by money?"
err... yeah! obviously!
Many questions later....
a lawyer, an entrepreneur or a critic! what did you get?
It says I can be a delivery boy, a packer or a toilet roll tube.

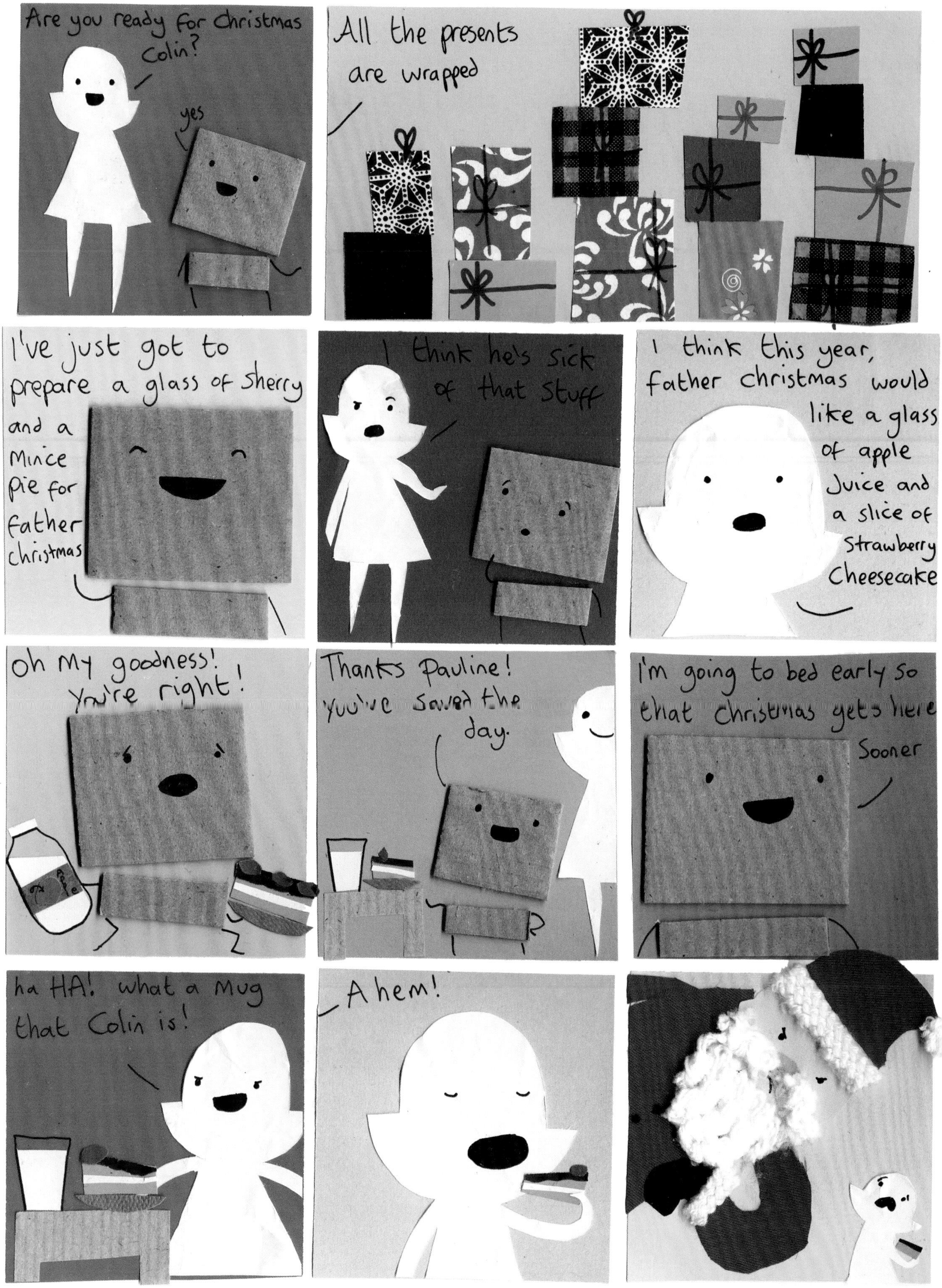
Are you ready for christmas Colin?
yes
All the presents are wrapped
I've just got to prepare a glass of sherry and a Mince pie for father christmas
I think he's sick of that stuff
I think this year, father christmas would like a glass of apple Juice and a slice of Strawberry Cheesecake
oh My goodness! You're right!
Thanks Pauline! you've saved the day.
I'm going to bed early so that christmas gets here sooner
ha HA! what a Mug that Colin is!
Ahem!

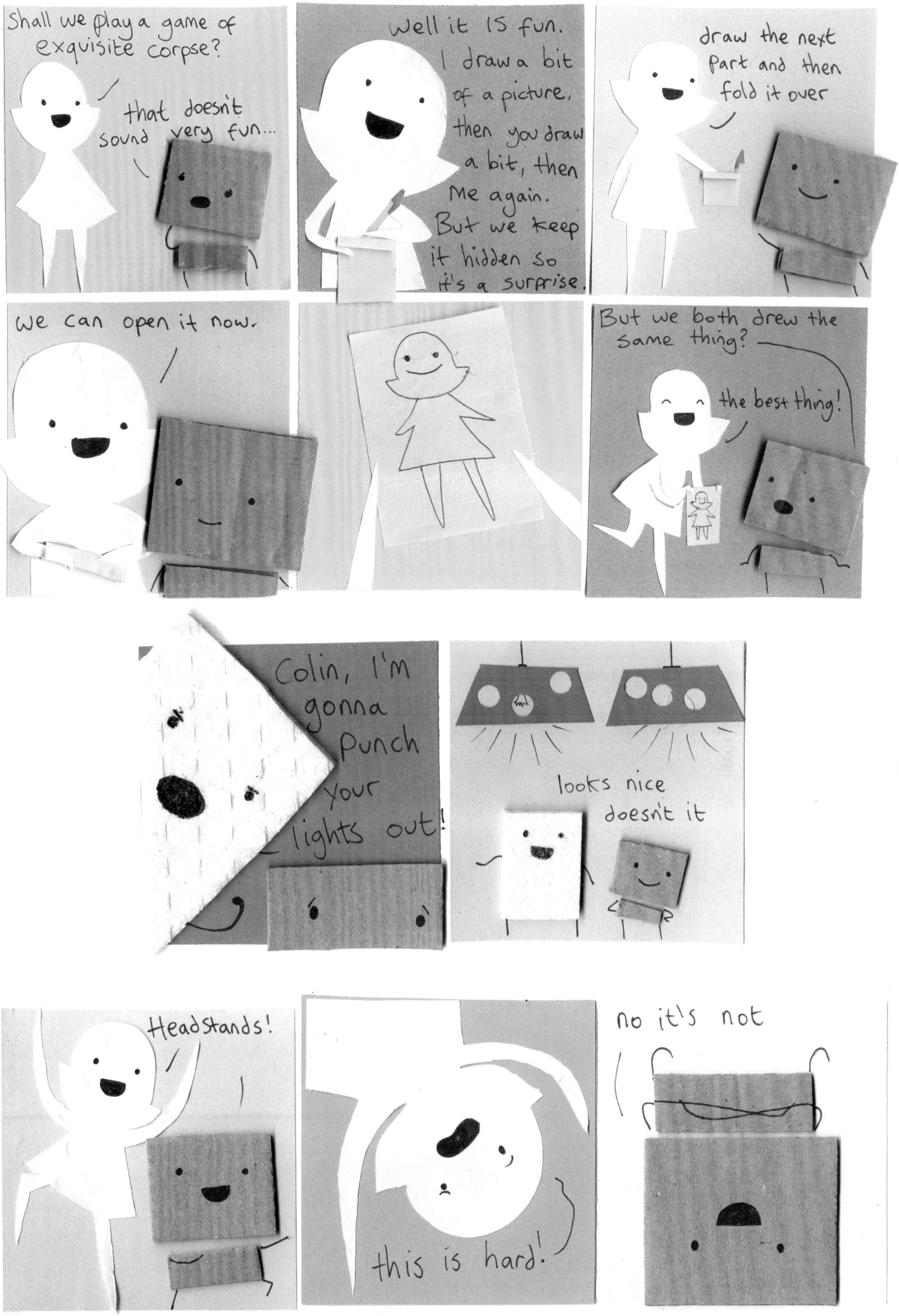

Shall we play a game of exquisite corpse?
that doesn't sound very fun...
Well it IS fun. I draw a bit of a picture, then you draw a bit, then me again. But we keep it hidden so it's a surprise.
draw the next part and then fold it over
we can open it now.
But we both drew the same thing?
the best thing!
Colin, I'm gonna punch your lights out!
looks nice doesn't it
Headstands!
this is hard!
no it's not

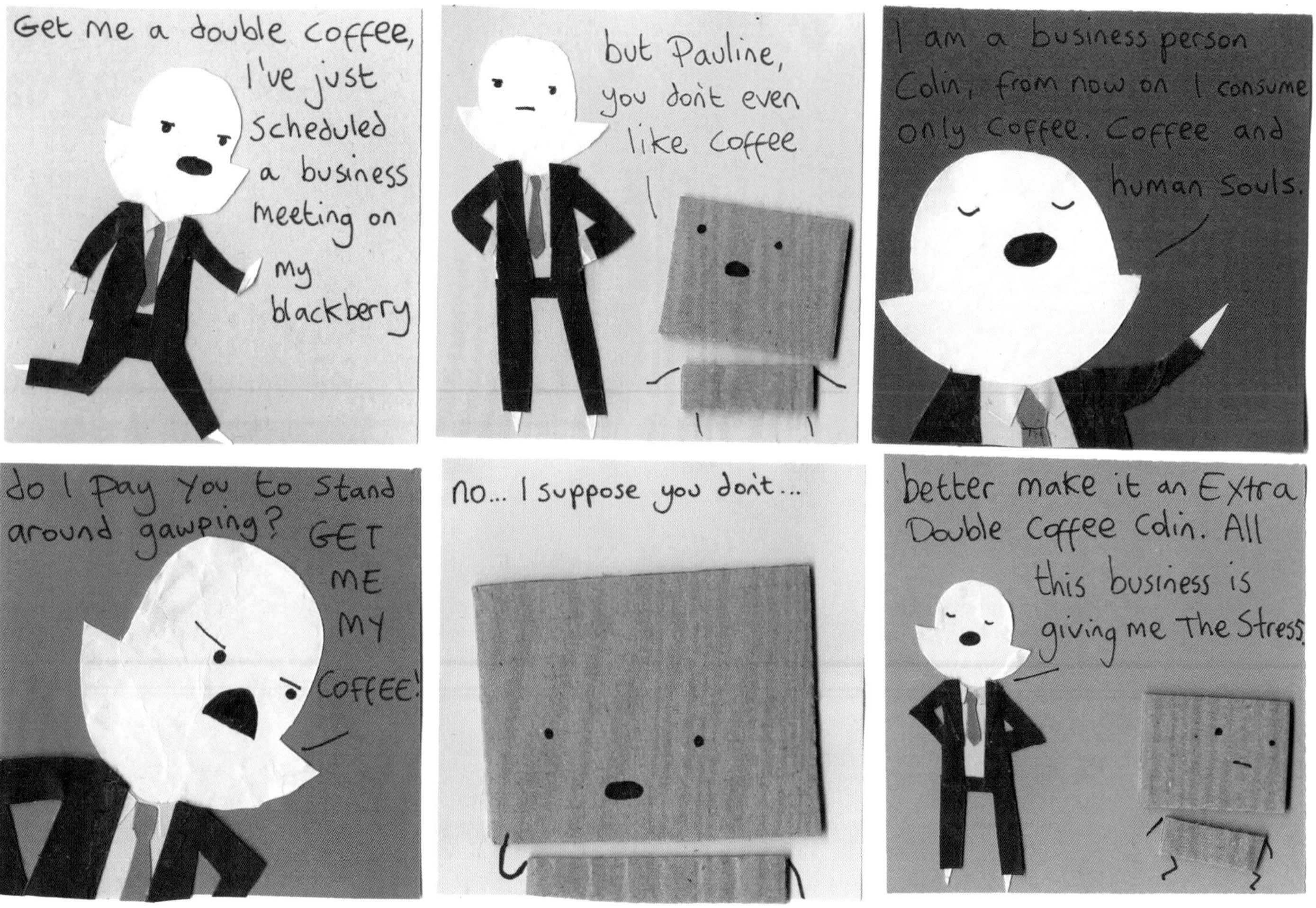
Get me a double coffee, I've just scheduled a business meeting on my blackberry
but Pauline, you don't even like coffee
I am a business person Colin, from now on I consume only coffee. Coffee and human souls.
do I pay you to stand around gawping? GET ME MY COFFEE!
no... I suppose you don't...
better make it an Extra Double Coffee Colin. All this business is giving me the stress.

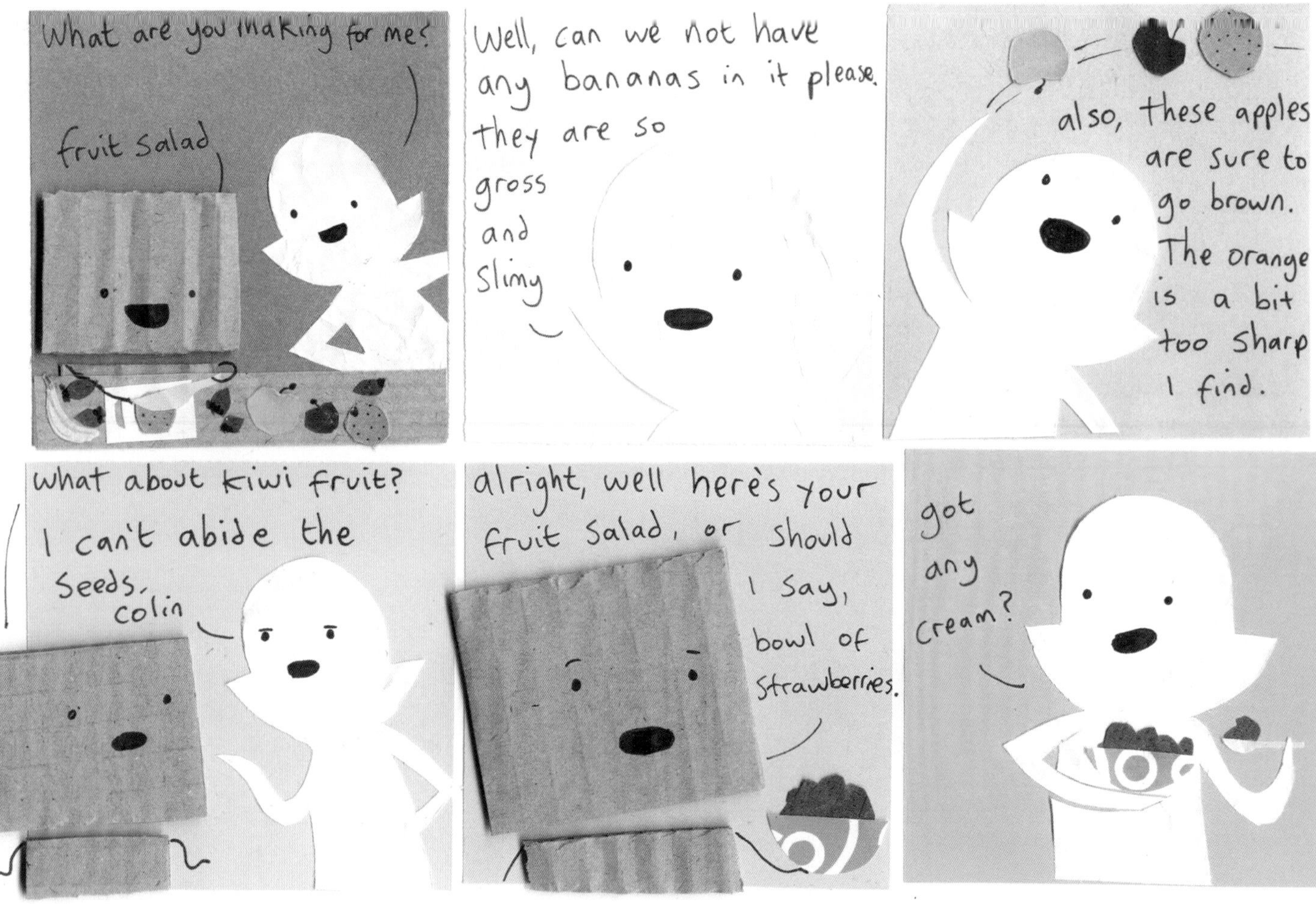
What are you making for me?
fruit salad
Well, can we not have any bananas in it please. they are so gross and slimy
also, these apples are sure to go brown. The orange is a bit too sharp I find.
what about kiwi fruit? I can't abide the seeds, colin
alright, well here's your fruit salad, or should I say, bowl of strawberries.
got any cream?

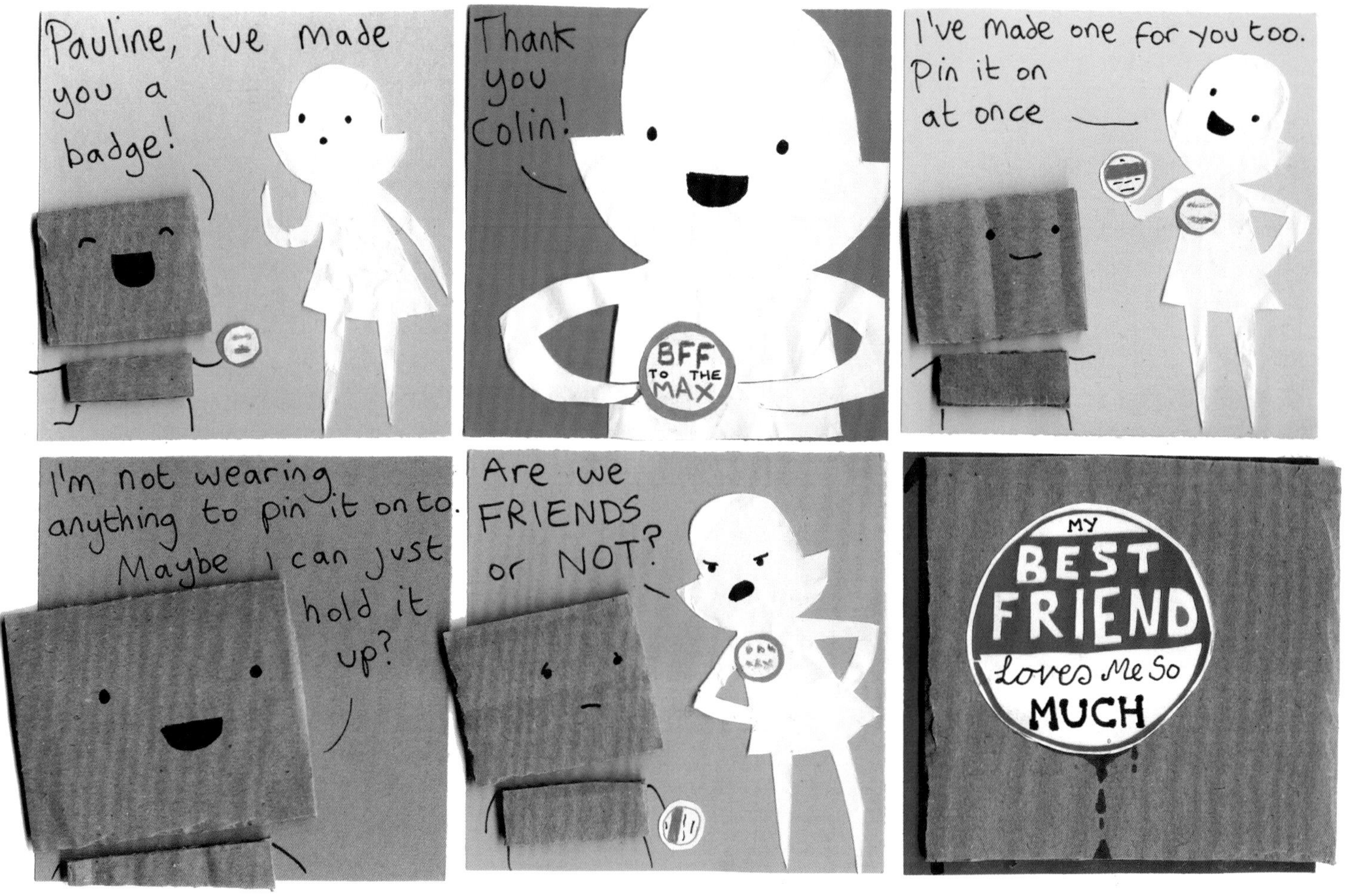
Pauline, I've made you a badge!
Thank you Colin!
BFF TO THE MAX
I've made one for you too. Pin it on at once
I'm not wearing anything to pin it on to. Maybe I can just hold it up?
Are we FRIENDS or NOT?
MY BEST FRIEND Loves Me So MUCH

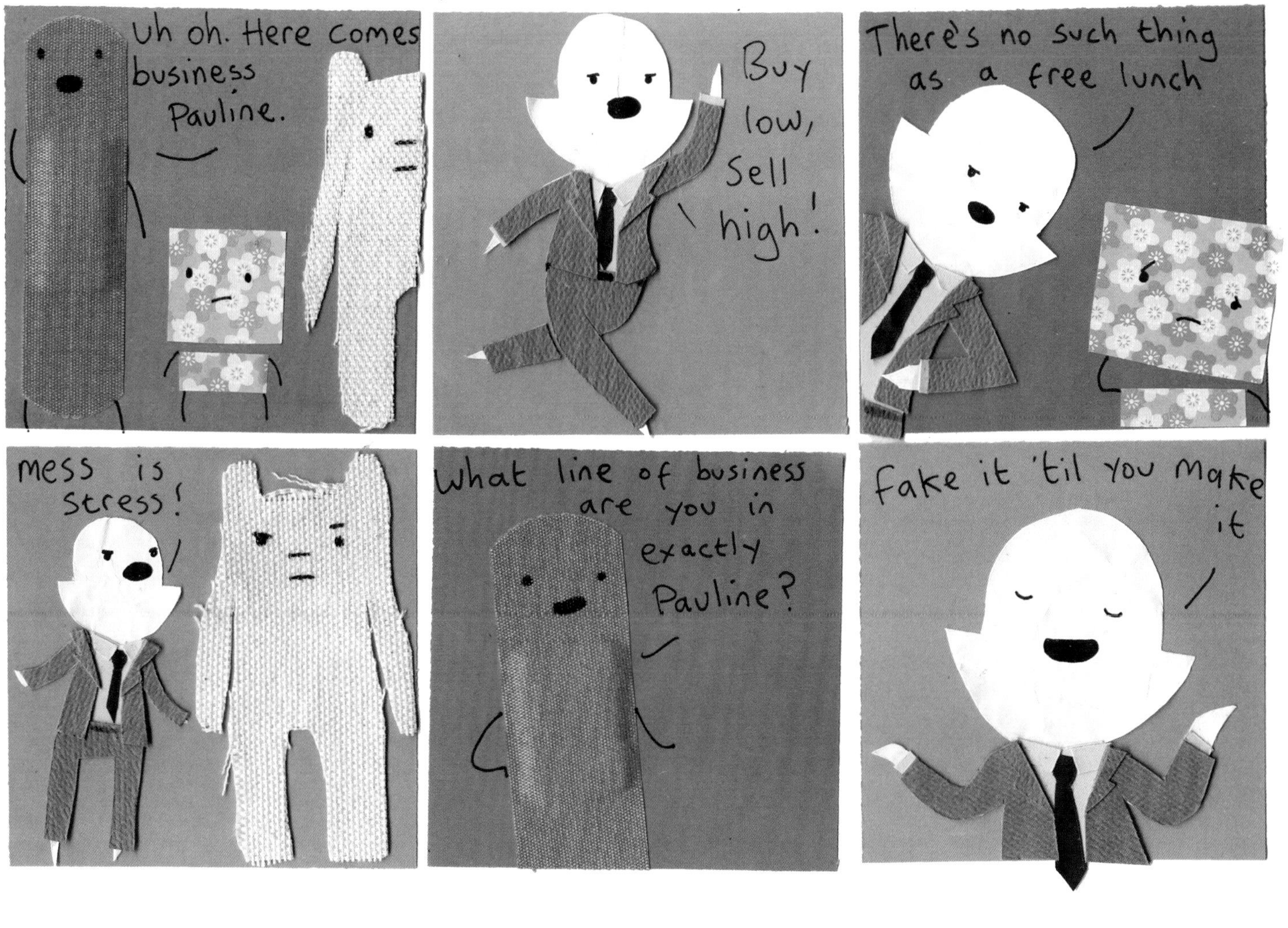
Uh oh. Here comes business Pauline.
Buy low, Sell high!
There's no such thing as a free lunch
mess is stress!
What line of business are you in exactly Pauline?
Fake it 'til you make it

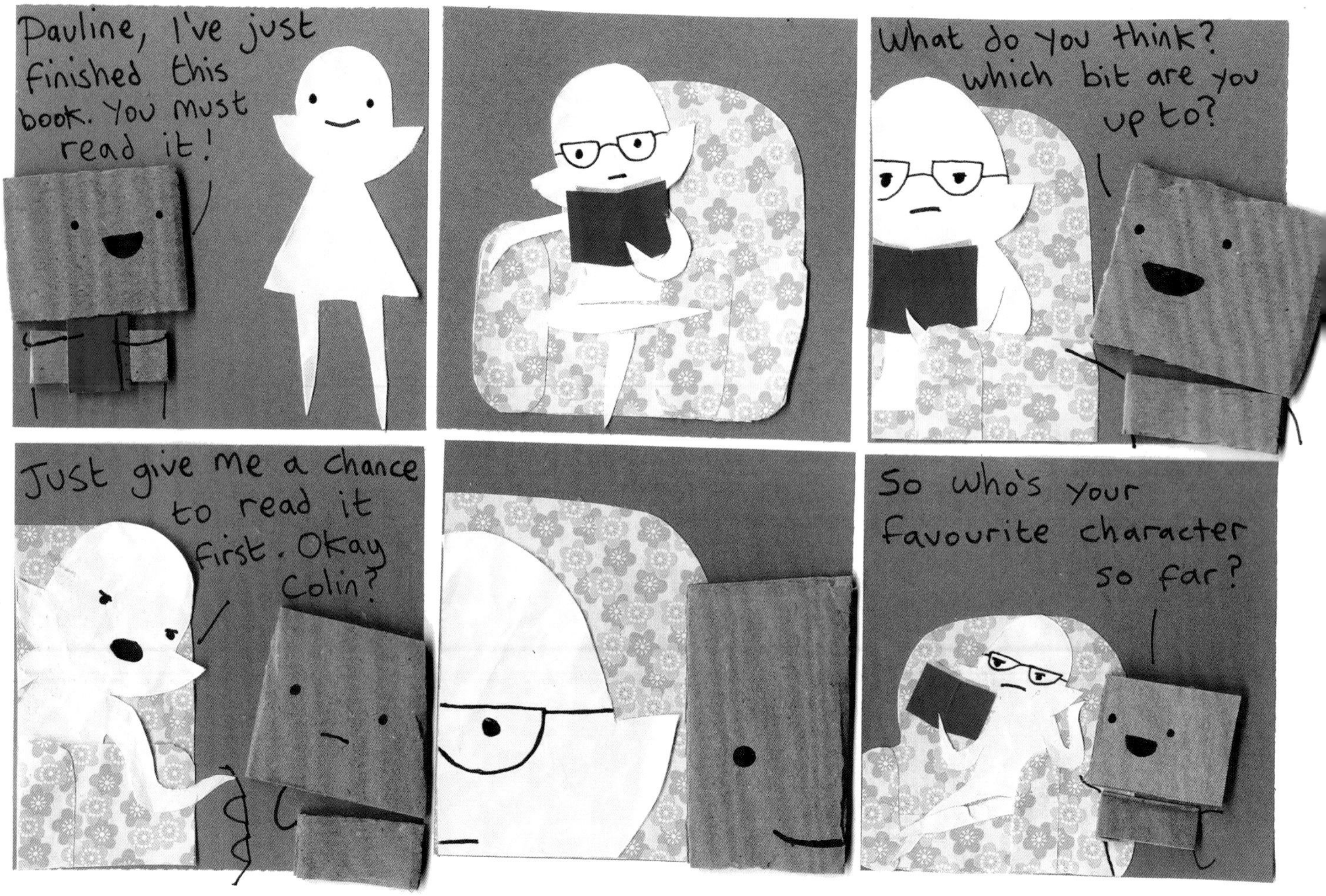
Pauline, I've just finished this book. You must read it!
What do you think? which bit are you up to?
Just give me a chance to read it first. Okay Colin?
So who's your favourite character so far?

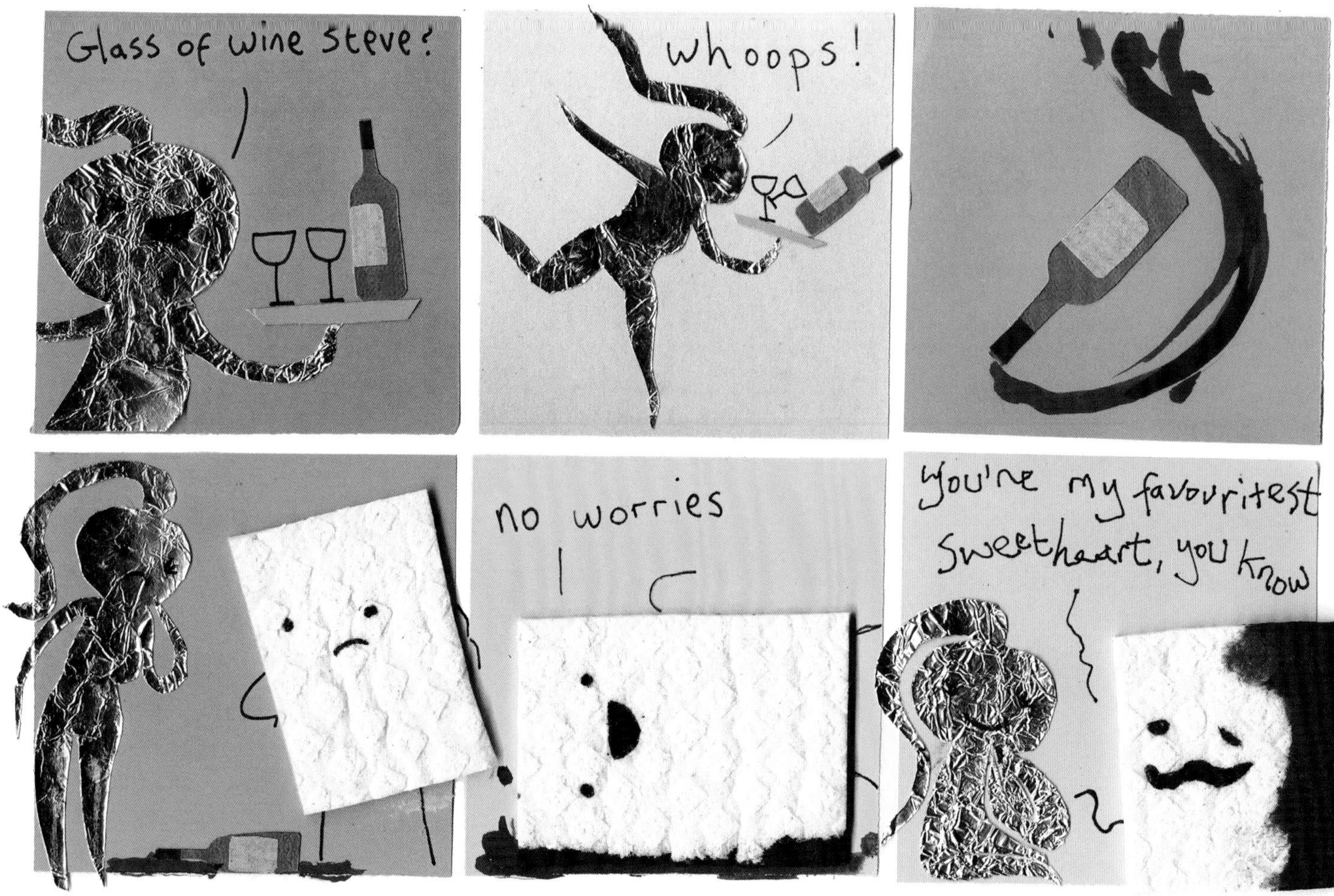
Glass of wine steve?
whoops!
no worries
You're my favouritest Sweetheart, you know

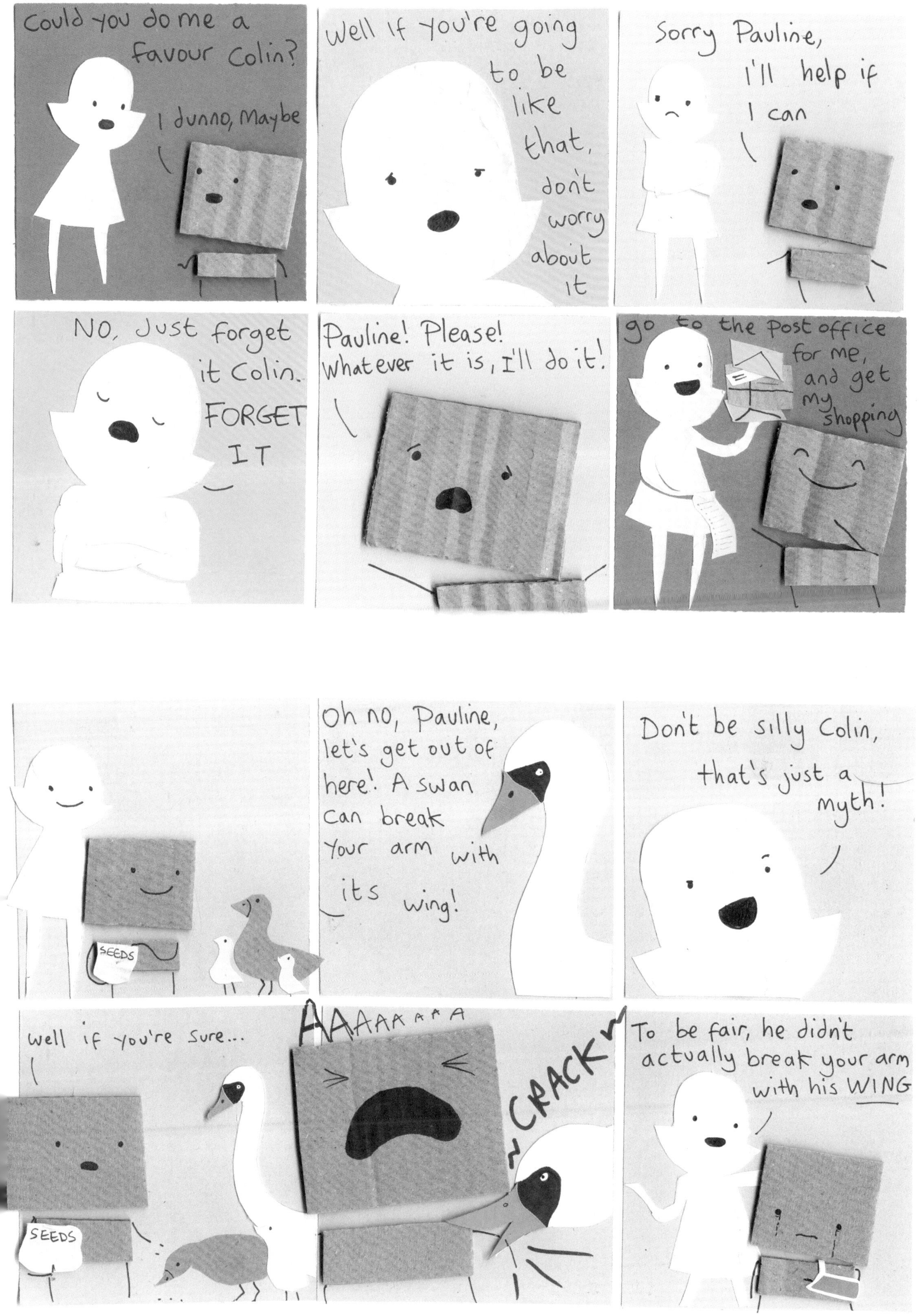

Could you do me a favour Colin?
I dunno, Maybe
Well if you're going to be like that, don't worry about it
Sorry Pauline, I'll help if I can
NO, Just forget it Colin. FORGET IT
Pauline! Please! Whatever it is, I'll do it!
go to the post office for me, and get my shopping
SEEDS
Oh no, Pauline, let's get out of here! A swan can break your arm with its wing!
Don't be silly Colin, that's just a myth!
well if you're sure...
SEEDS
AAAAAAAA
CRACK
To be fair, he didn't actually break your arm with his WING

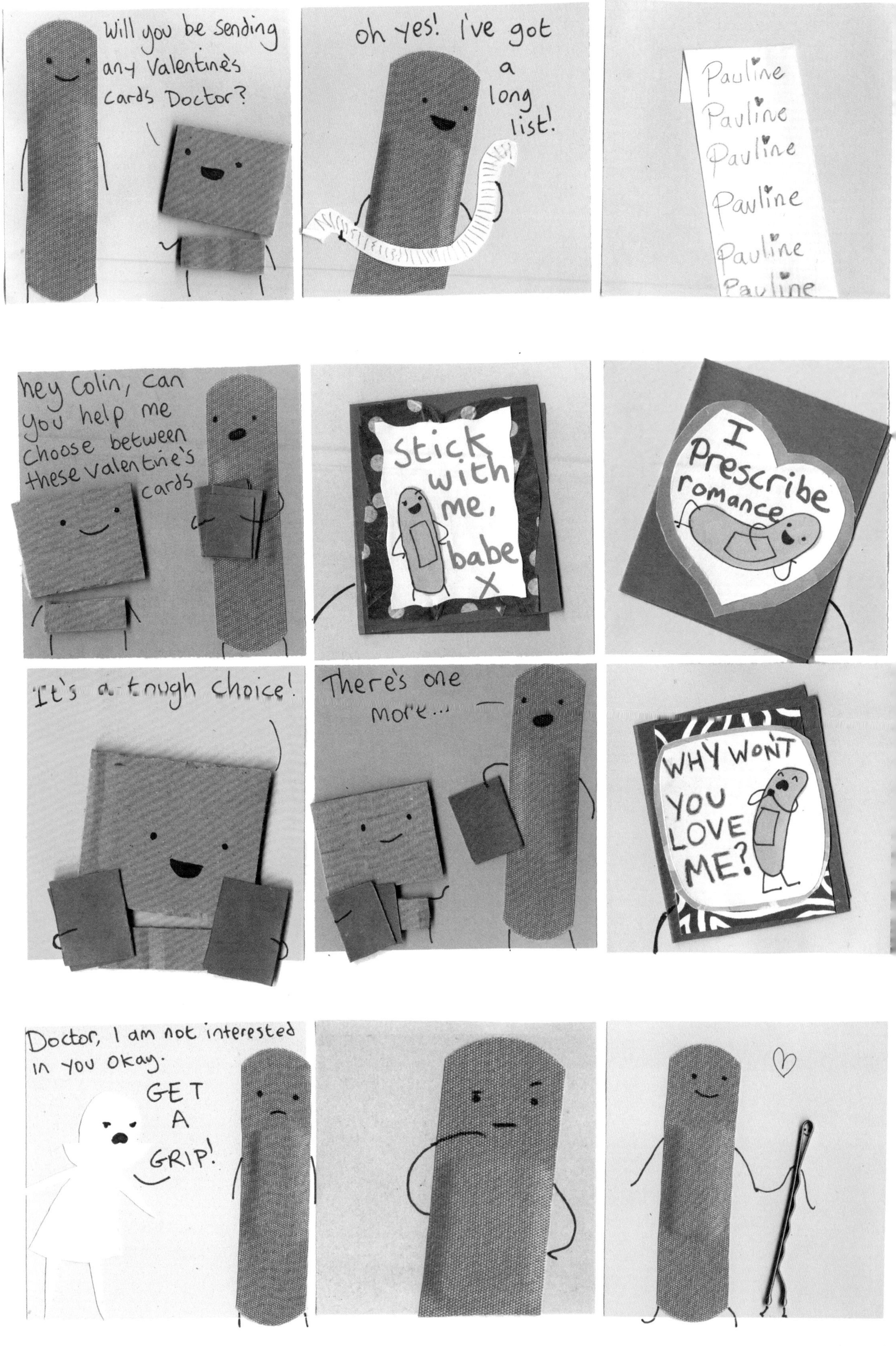

Will you be sending any Valentine's cards Doctor?
oh yes! I've got a long list!
Pauline
Pauline
Pauline
Pauline
Pauline
Pauline
Pauline
hey Colin, can you help me choose between these valentine's cards
Stick with me, babe x
I Prescribe romance
It's a tough choice!
There's one more...
WHY WON'T YOU LOVE ME?
Doctor, I am not interested in you okay.
GET A GRIP!

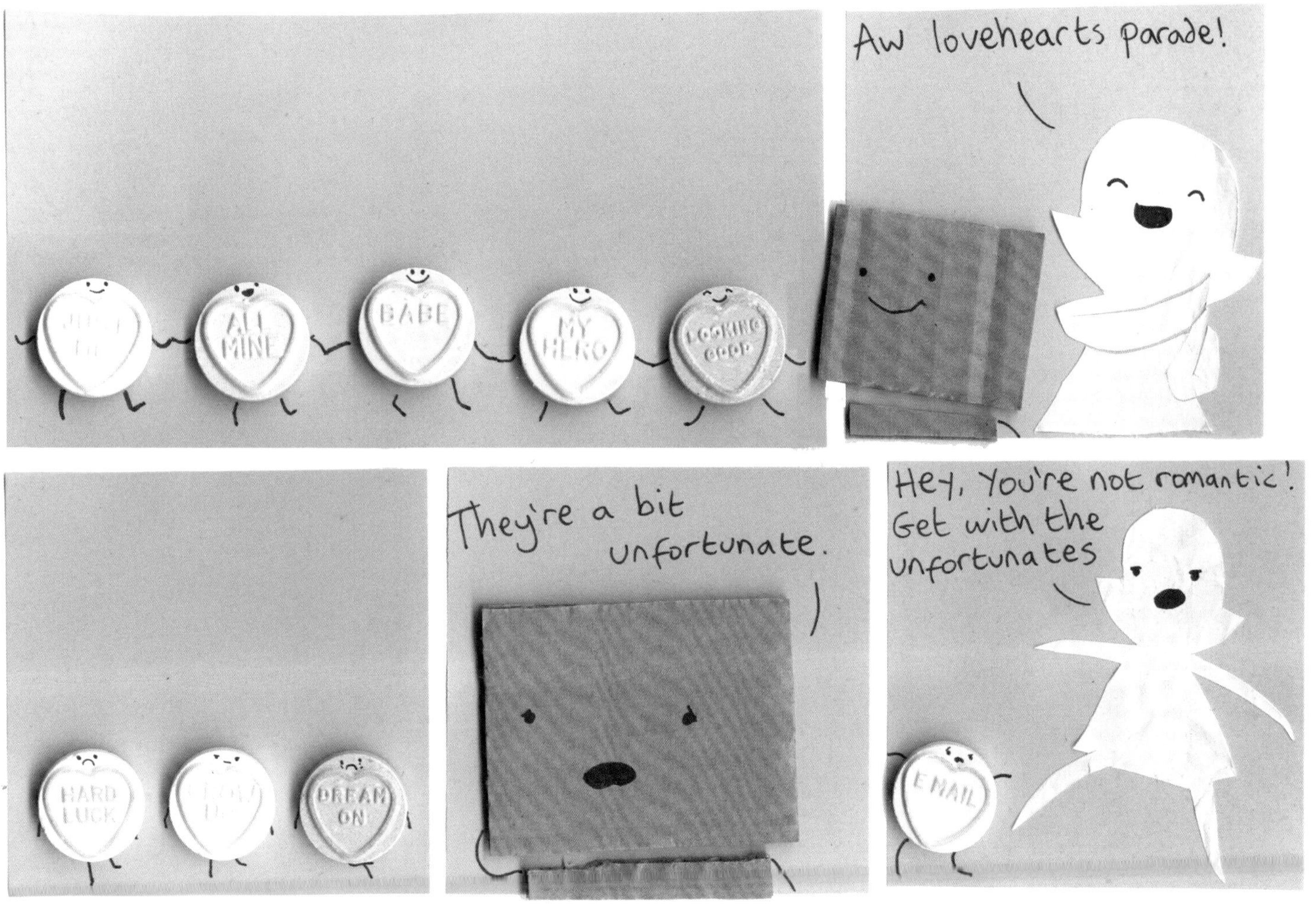
ALL MINE
BABE
MY HERO
LOOKING GOOD
Aw lovehearts parade!
HARD LUCK
DREAM ON
They're a bit unfortunate.
Hey, You're not romantic! Get with the unfortunates
EMAIL

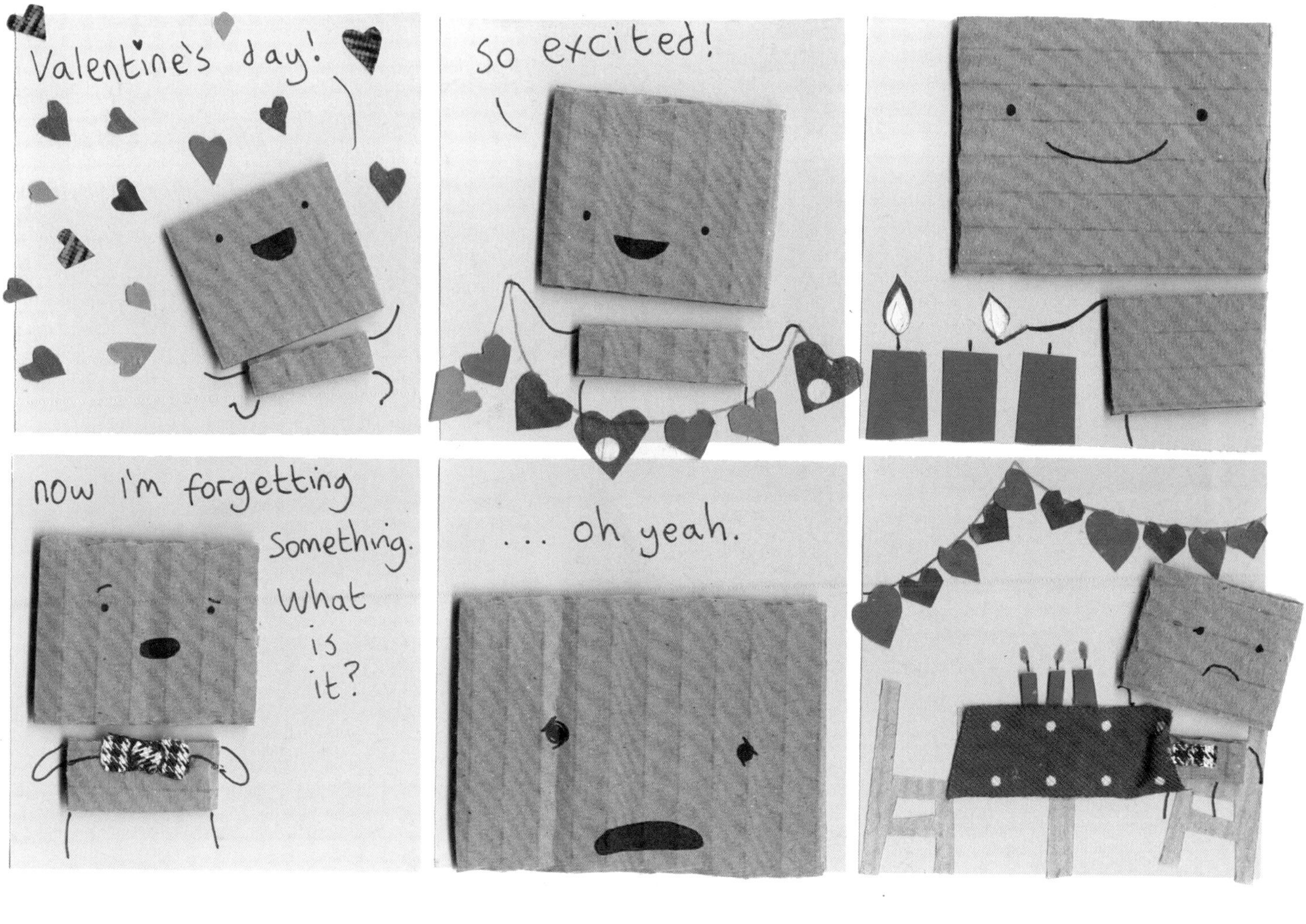
Valentine's day!
So excited!
now I'm forgetting Something. What is it?
... oh yeah.

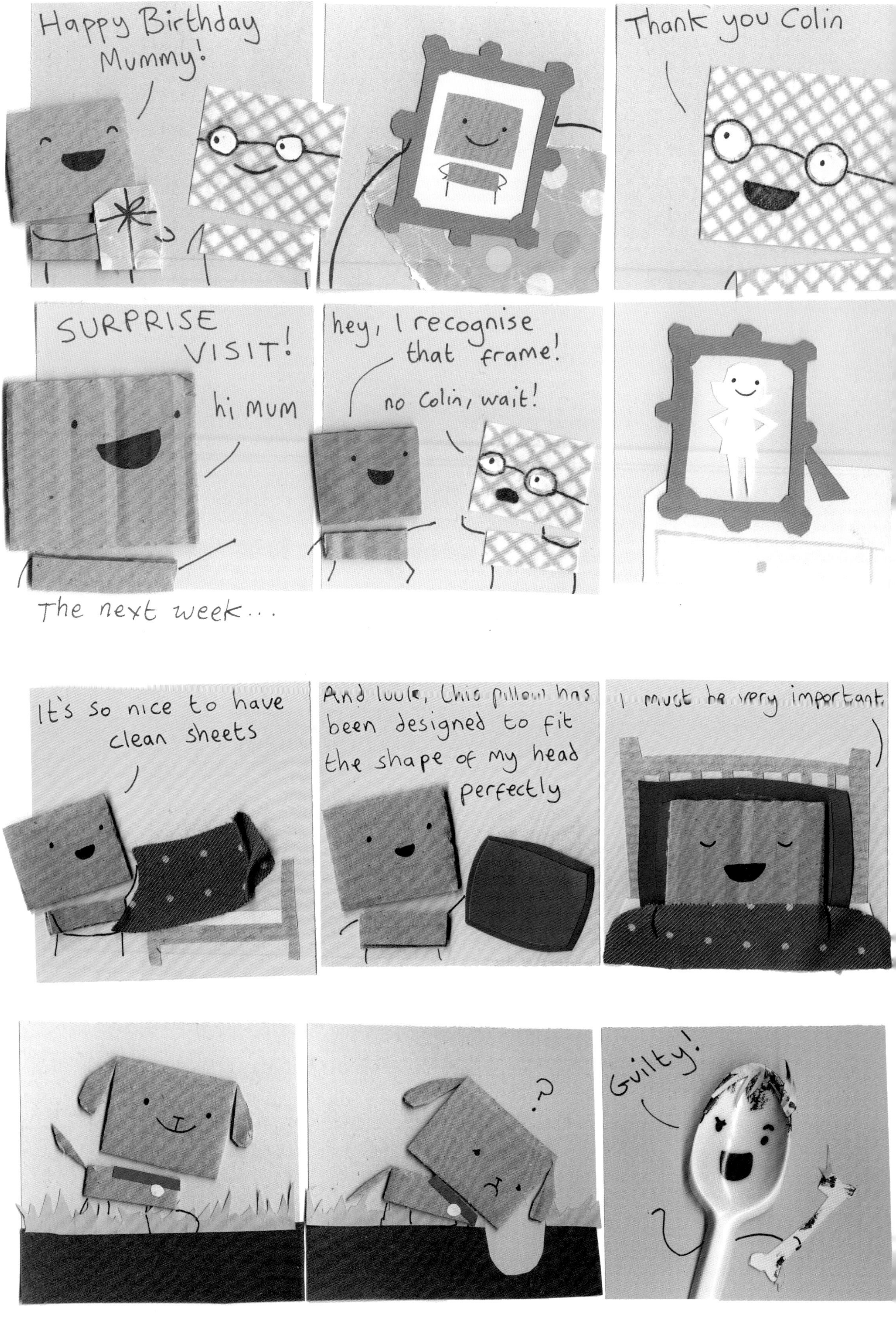
Happy Birthday Mummy!
Thank you Colin
SURPRISE VISIT!
hi MUM
hey, I recognise that frame!
no Colin, wait!
The next week...
It's so nice to have clean sheets
And look, this pillow has been designed to fit the shape of my head perfectly
I must be very important
?
Guilty!

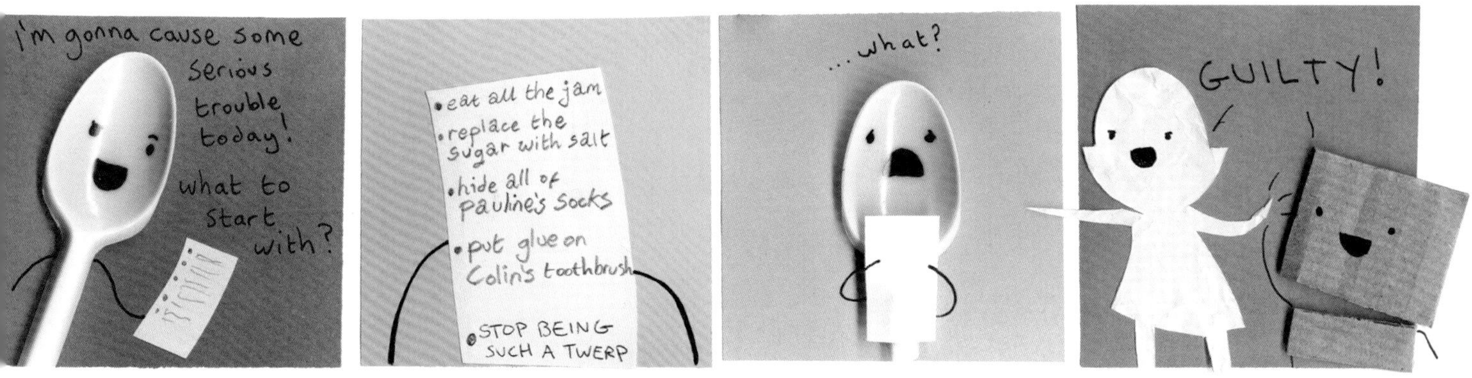
I'm gonna cause some serious trouble today! what to start with?
eat all the jam
replace the sugar with salt
hide all of Pauline's socks
put glue on Colin's toothbrush
STOP BEING SUCH A TWERP
...what?
GUILTY!

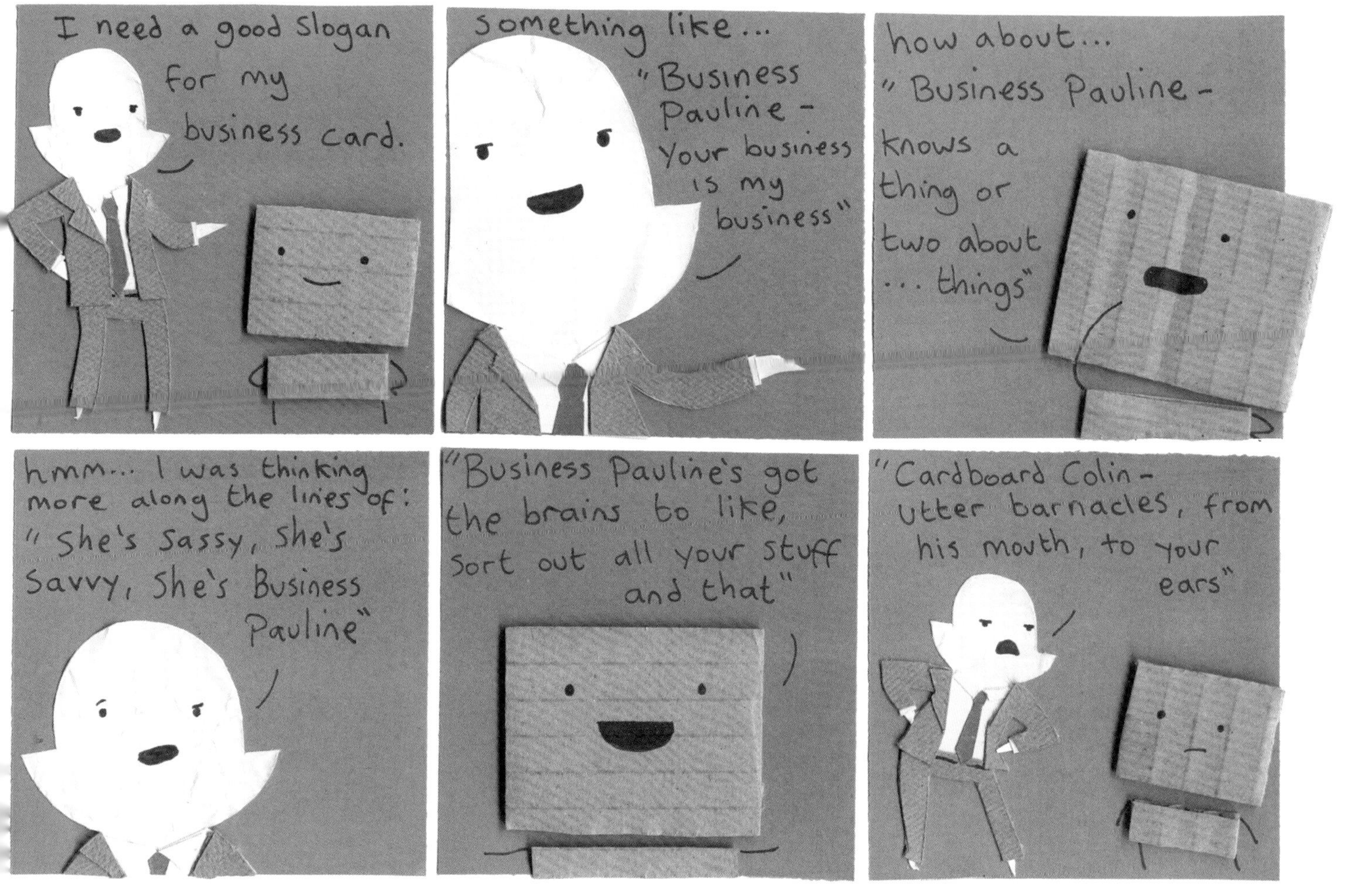
I need a good slogan for my business card.
something like... "Business Pauline - Your business is my business"
how about... "Business Pauline - knows a thing or two about ... things"
hmm... I was thinking more along the lines of: "She's sassy, she's savvy, she's Business Pauline"
"Business Pauline's got the brains to like, sort out all your stuff and that"
"Cardboard Colin - utter barnacles, from his mouth, to your ears"

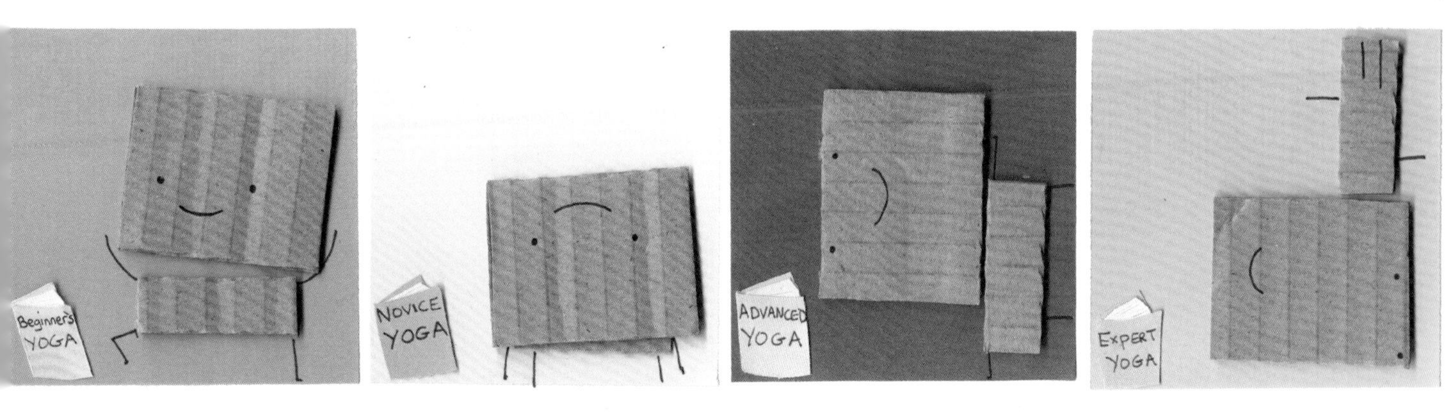
Beginner's YOGA
NOVICE YOGA
ADVANCED YOGA
EXPERT YOGA

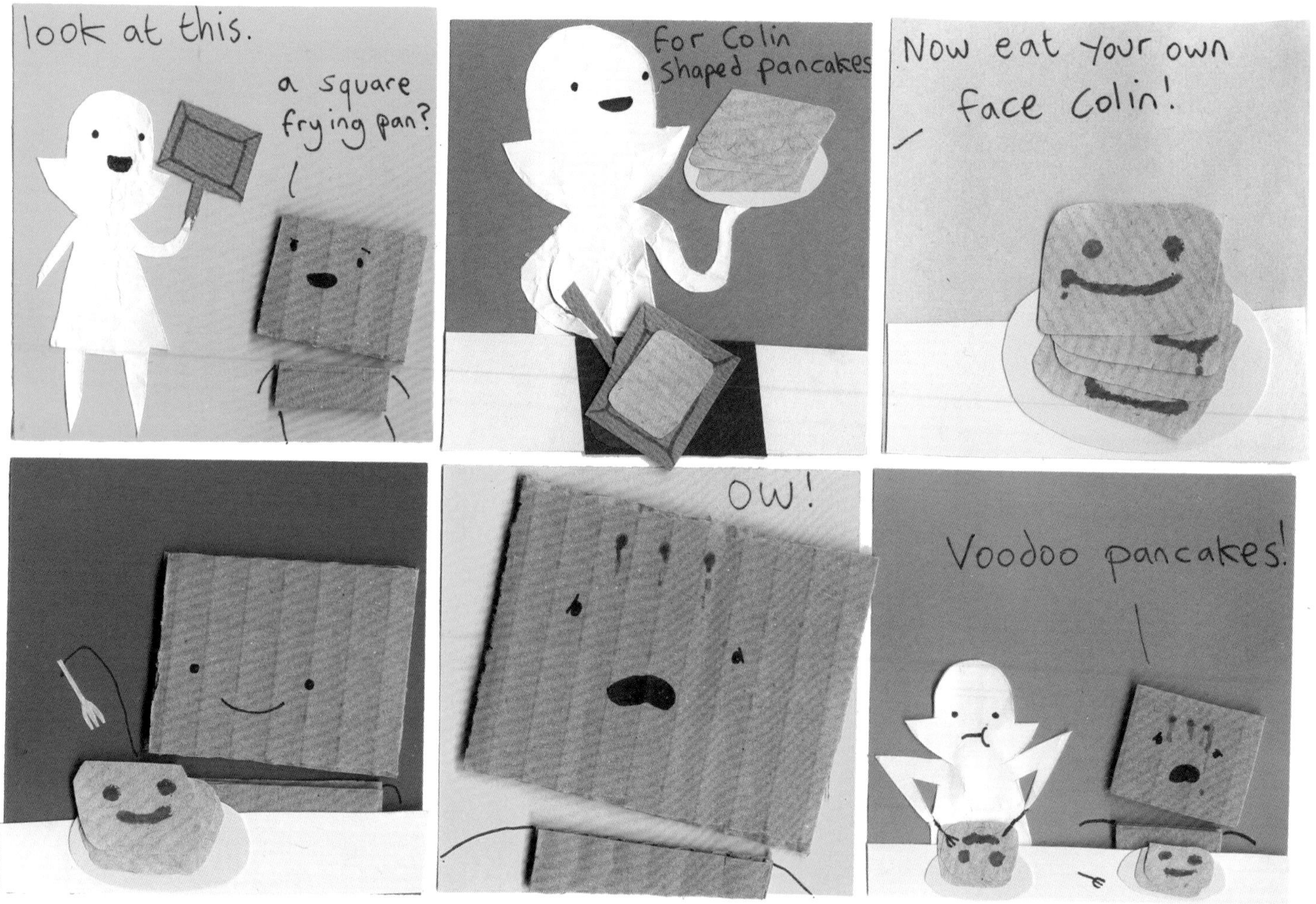
look at this.
a square frying pan?
For Colin shaped pancakes
Now eat your own face Colin!
OW!
Voodoo pancakes!

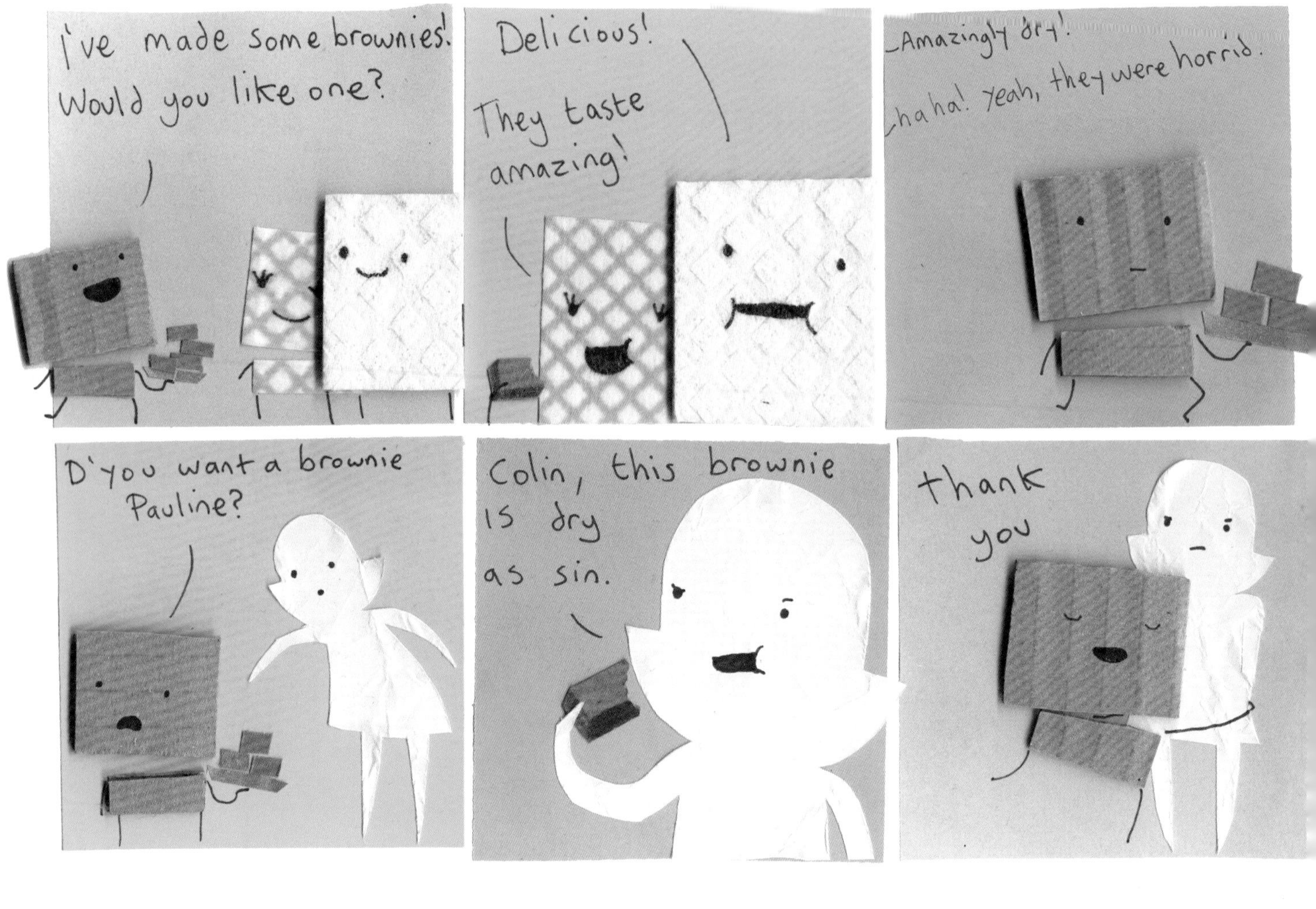
I've made some brownies! Would you like one?
Delicious!
They taste amazing!
Amazingly dry!
haha! Yeah, they were horrid.
D'you want a brownie Pauline?
Colin, this brownie is dry as sin.
thank you

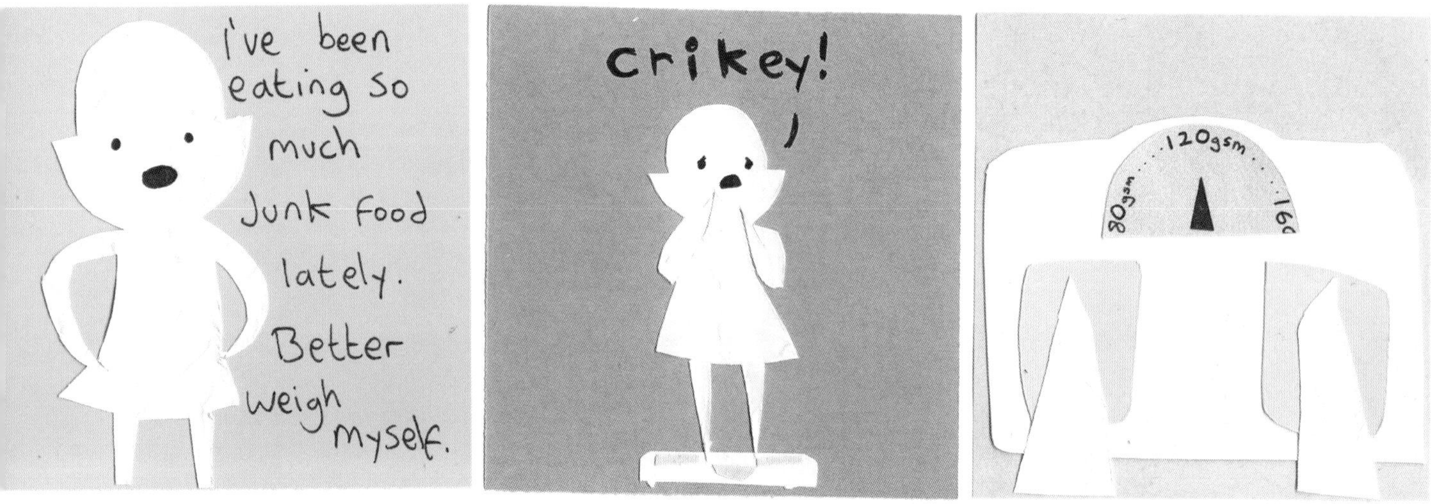
I've been eating so much Junk food lately. Better weigh myself.
Crikey!
80gsm
120gsm

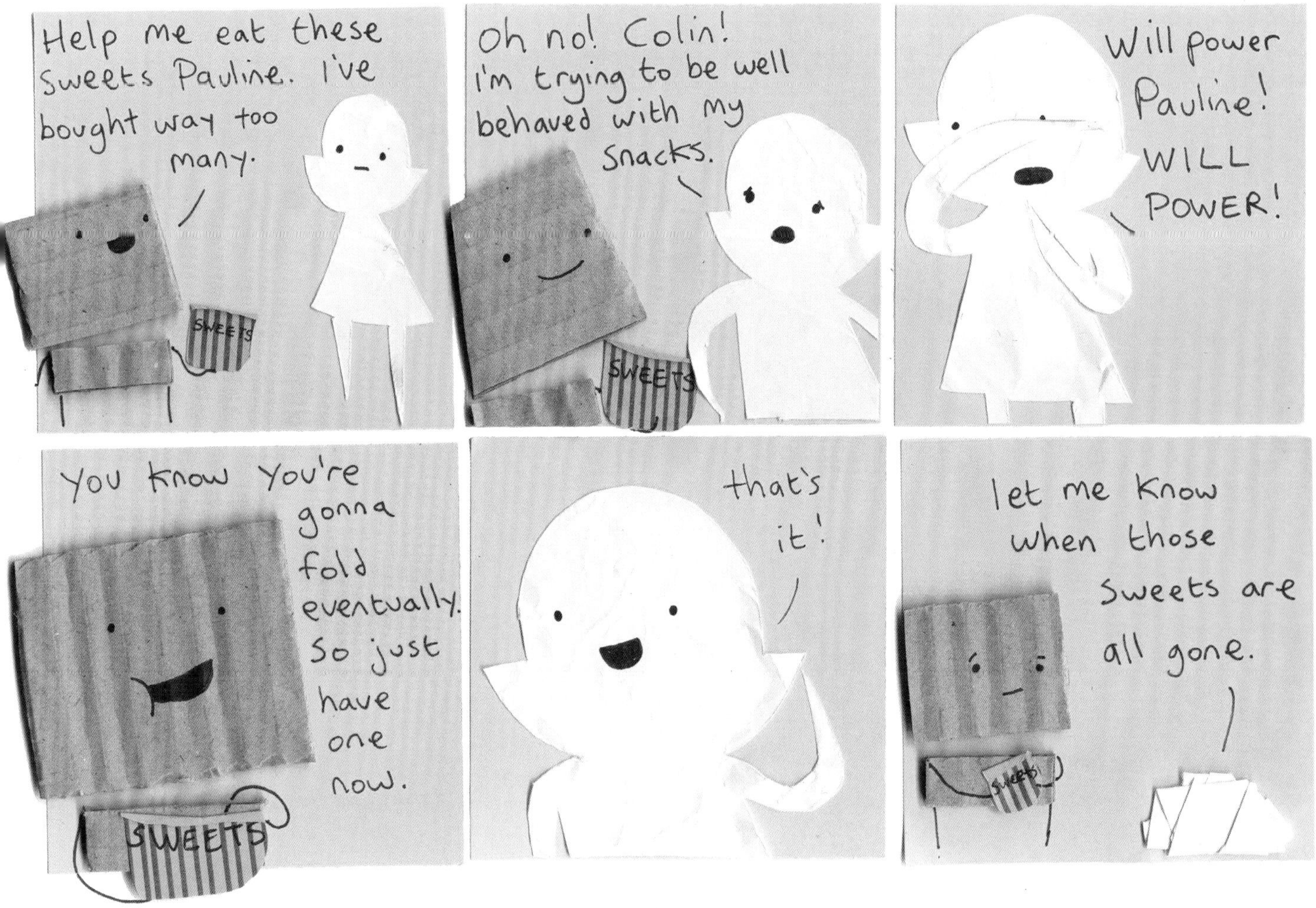
Help me eat these sweets Pauline. I've bought way too many.
SWEETS
Oh no! Colin! I'm trying to be well behaved with my snacks.
SWEETS
Will power Pauline! WILL POWER!
You know you're gonna fold eventually. So just have one now.
SWEETS
that's it!
let me know when those sweets are all gone.

CARDBOARD COLIN & Tim Foil

walk their dogs in the park

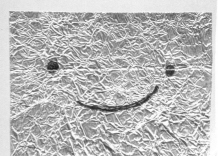

Cousin Colin! I got a dog!

Yay! Let's walk our dogs in the park

Walkies!

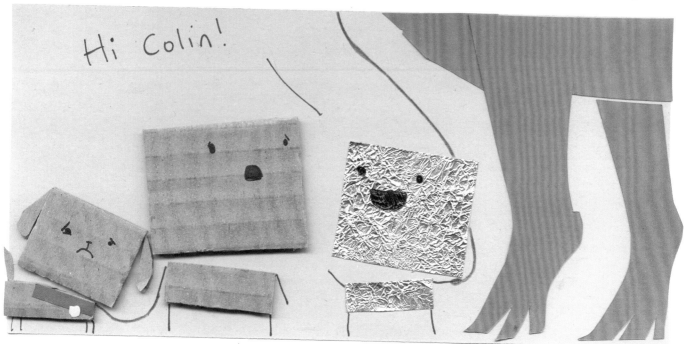

Hi Colin!

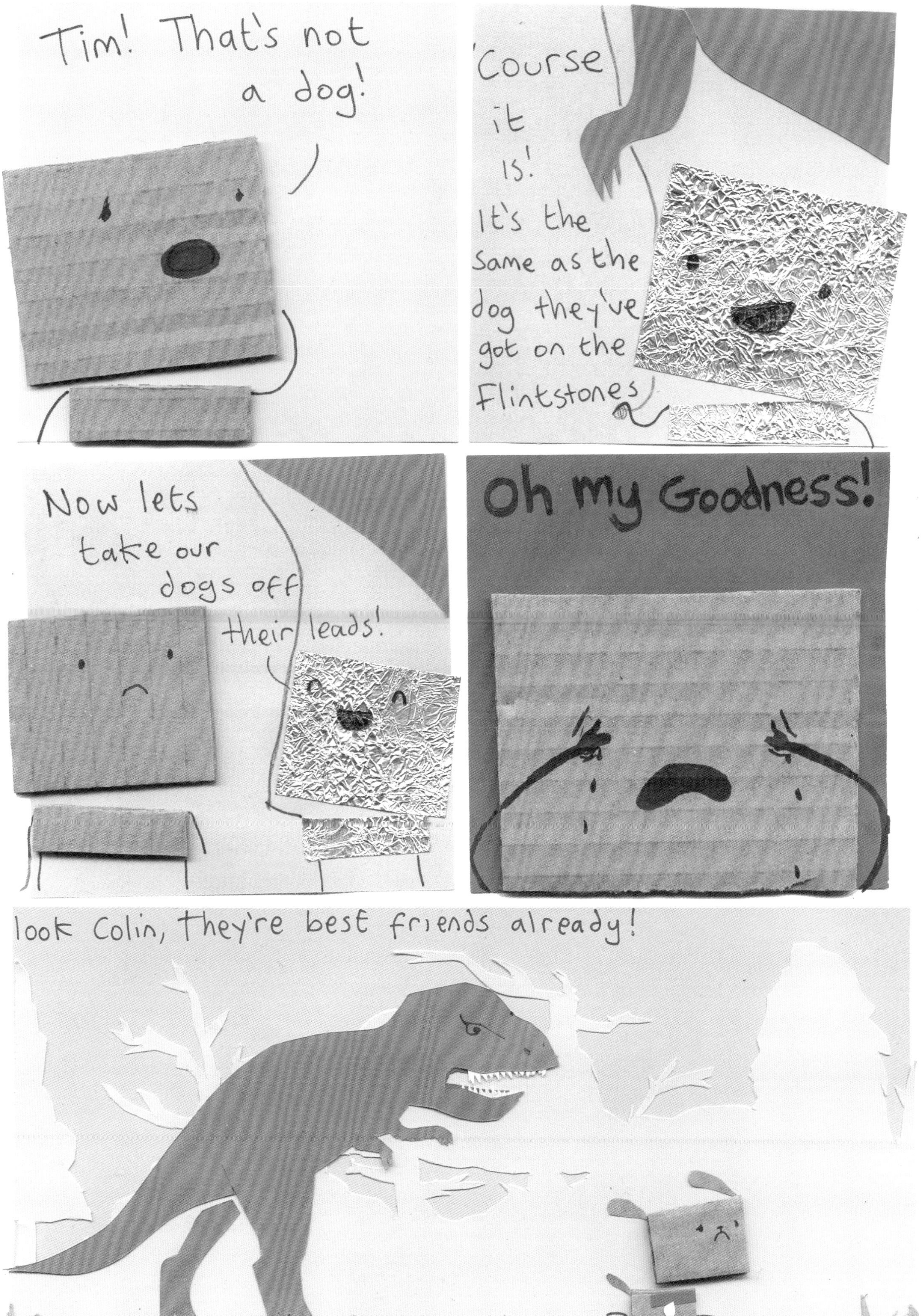
Tim! That's not a dog!
'Course it is! It's the same as the dog they've got on the Flintstones
Now lets take our dogs off their leads!
Oh my Goodness!
look Colin, they're best friends already!

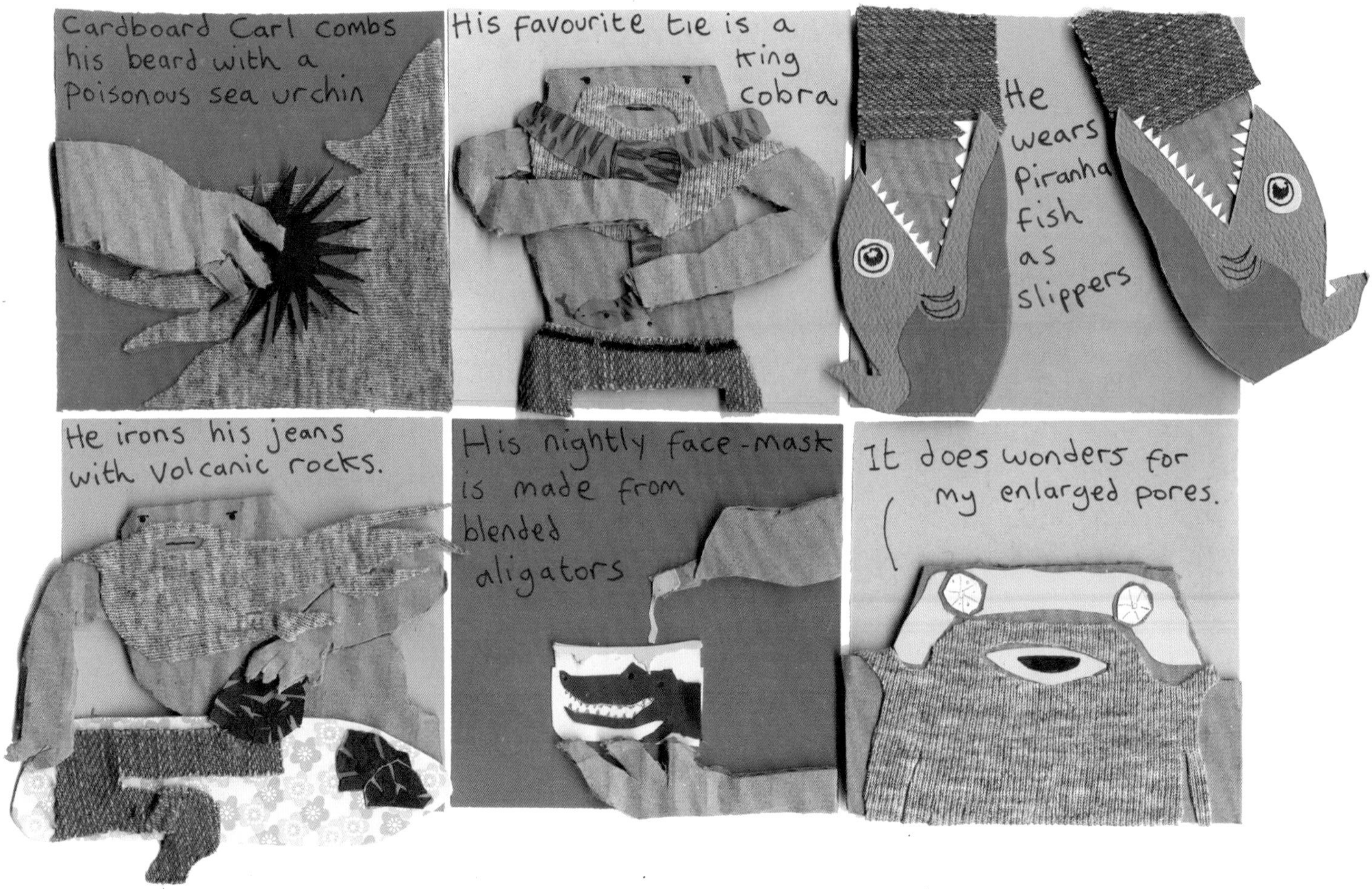
Cardboard Carl combs his beard with a poisonous sea urchin
His favourite tie is a king cobra
He wears piranha fish as slippers
He irons his jeans with volcanic rocks.
His nightly face-mask is made from blended aligators
It does wonders for my enlarged pores.

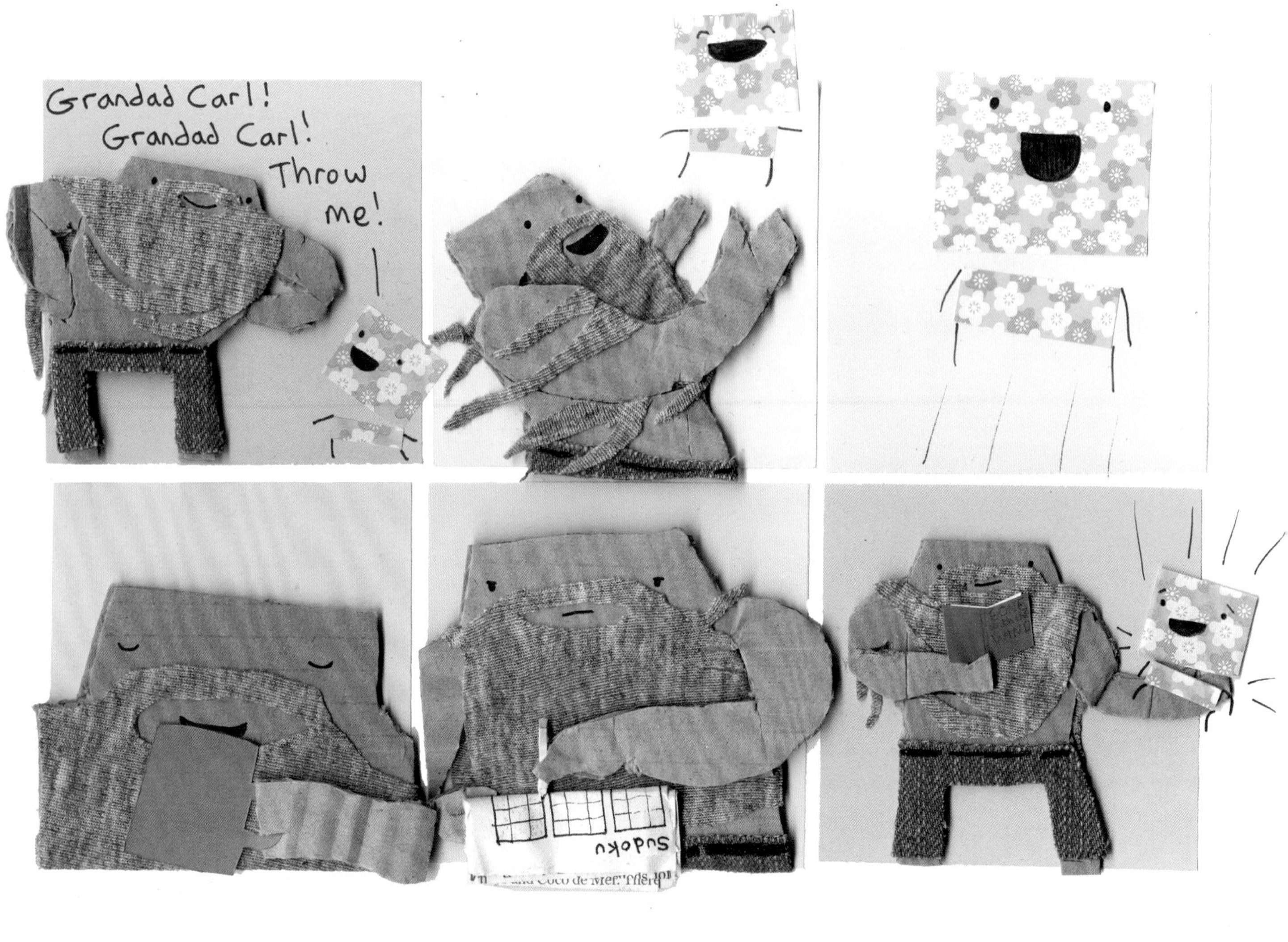
Grandad Carl! Grandad Carl! Throw me!
Sudoku

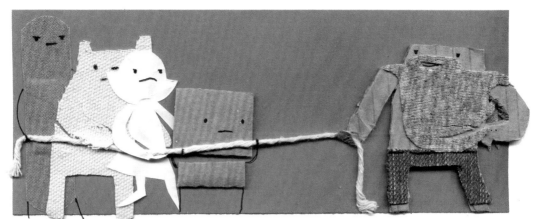

AH HA HA HA

¡COLIN LIKES TO DRESS IN DRAG!

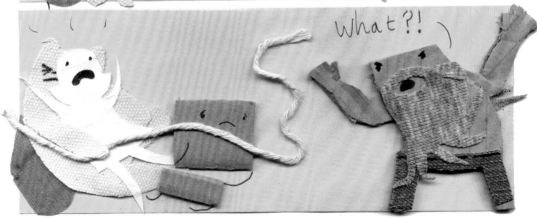

What?!

So, where do you get your wigs made?

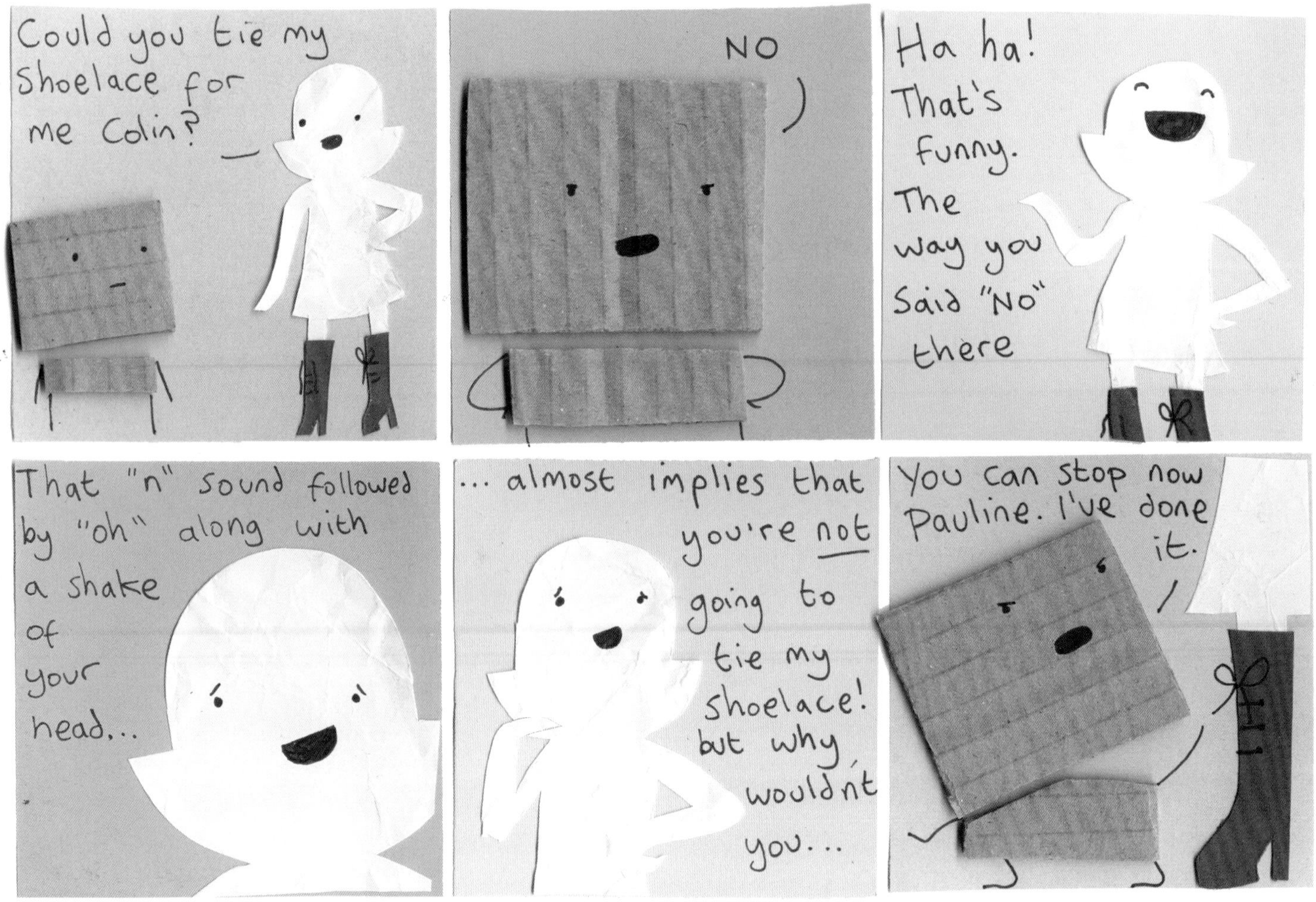
Could you tie my Shoelace for me Colin?
NO
Ha ha! That's funny. The way you Said "No" there
That "n" sound followed by "oh" along with a shake of your head...
... almost implies that you're not going to tie my shoelace! but why wouldn't you...
You can stop now Pauline. I've done it.

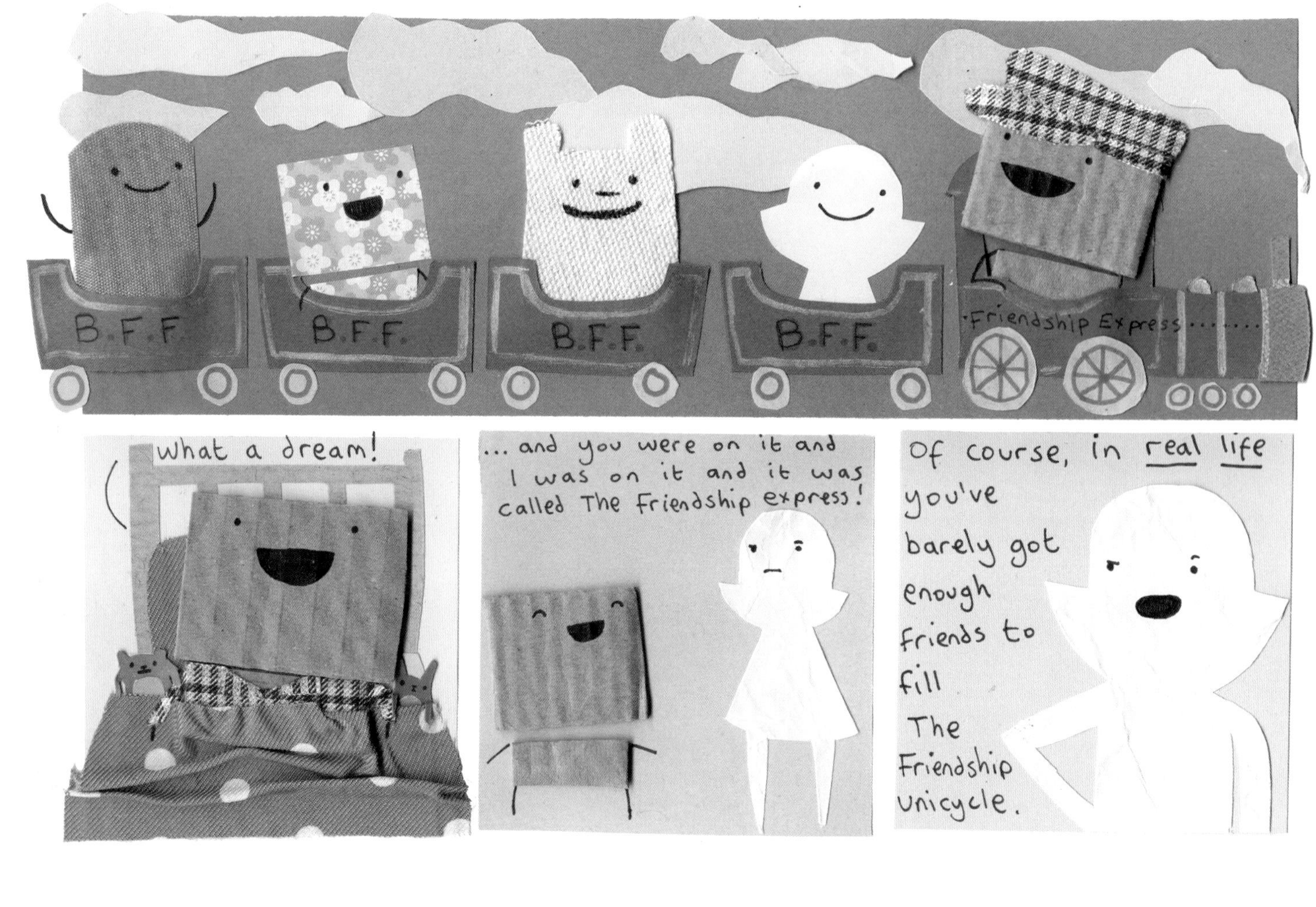
B.F.F.
B.F.F.
B.F.F.
B.F.F.
Friendship Express
what a dream!
... and you were on it and I was on it and it was called The Friendship express!
Of course, in real life you've barely got enough friends to fill The Friendship unicycle.

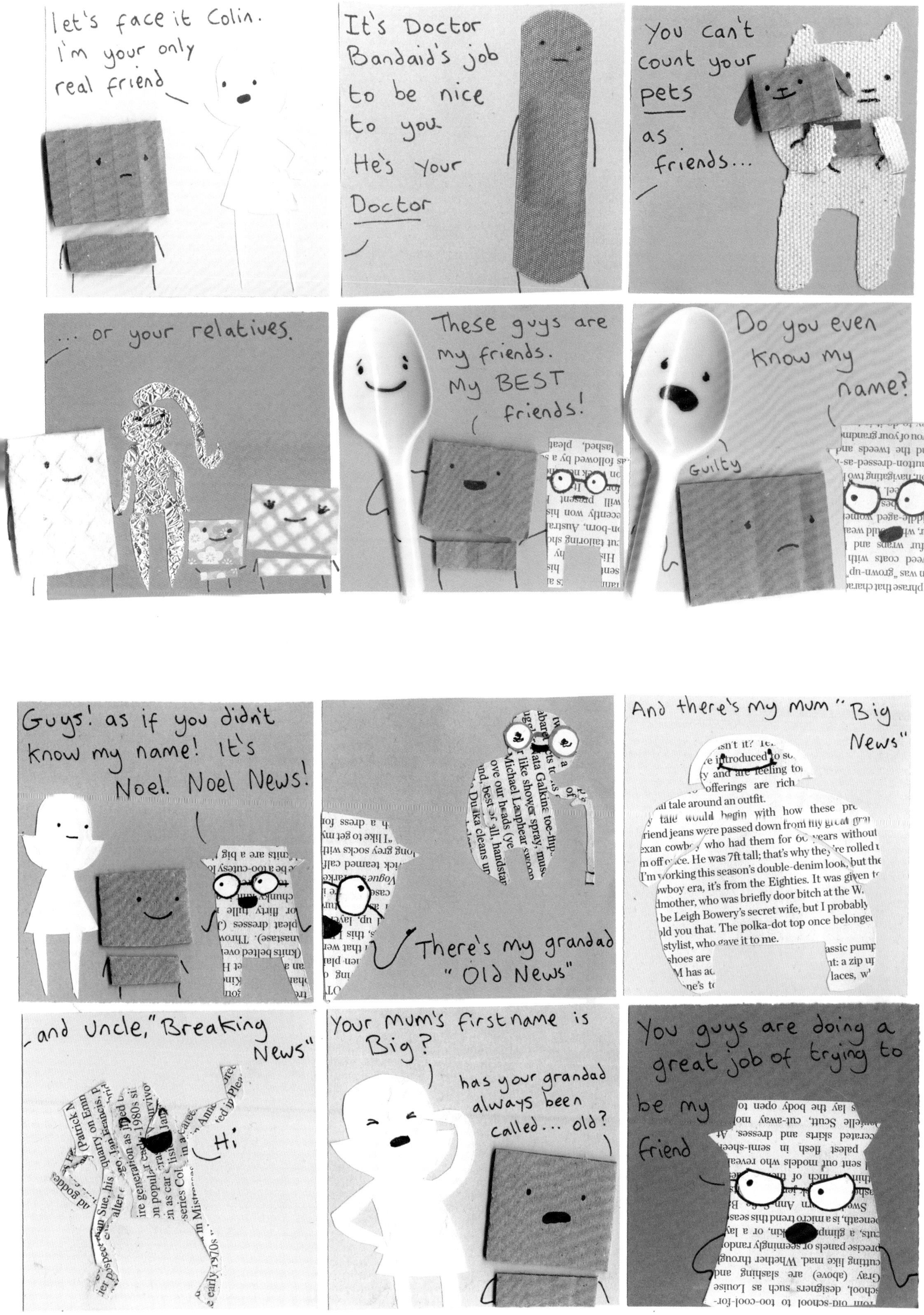
let's face it Colin. I'm your only real friend
It's Doctor Bandaid's job to be nice to you He's your Doctor
You can't count your pets as friends...
... or your relatives.
These guys are my friends. My BEST friends!
Do you even know my name?
Guilty
Guys! as if you didn't know my name! It's Noel. Noel News!
There's my grandad "Old News"
And there's my mum "Big News"
and Uncle, "Breaking News"
Hi
Your Mum's first name is Big?
has your grandad always been called... old?
You guys are doing a great job of trying to be my friend

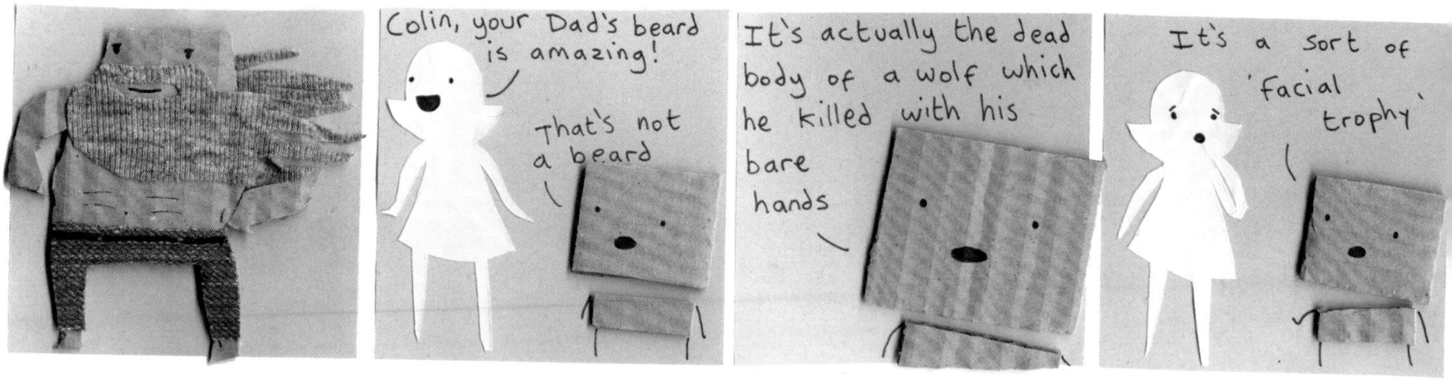
Colin, your Dad's beard is amazing!
That's not a beard
It's actually the dead body of a wolf which he killed with his bare hands
It's a sort of 'facial trophy'

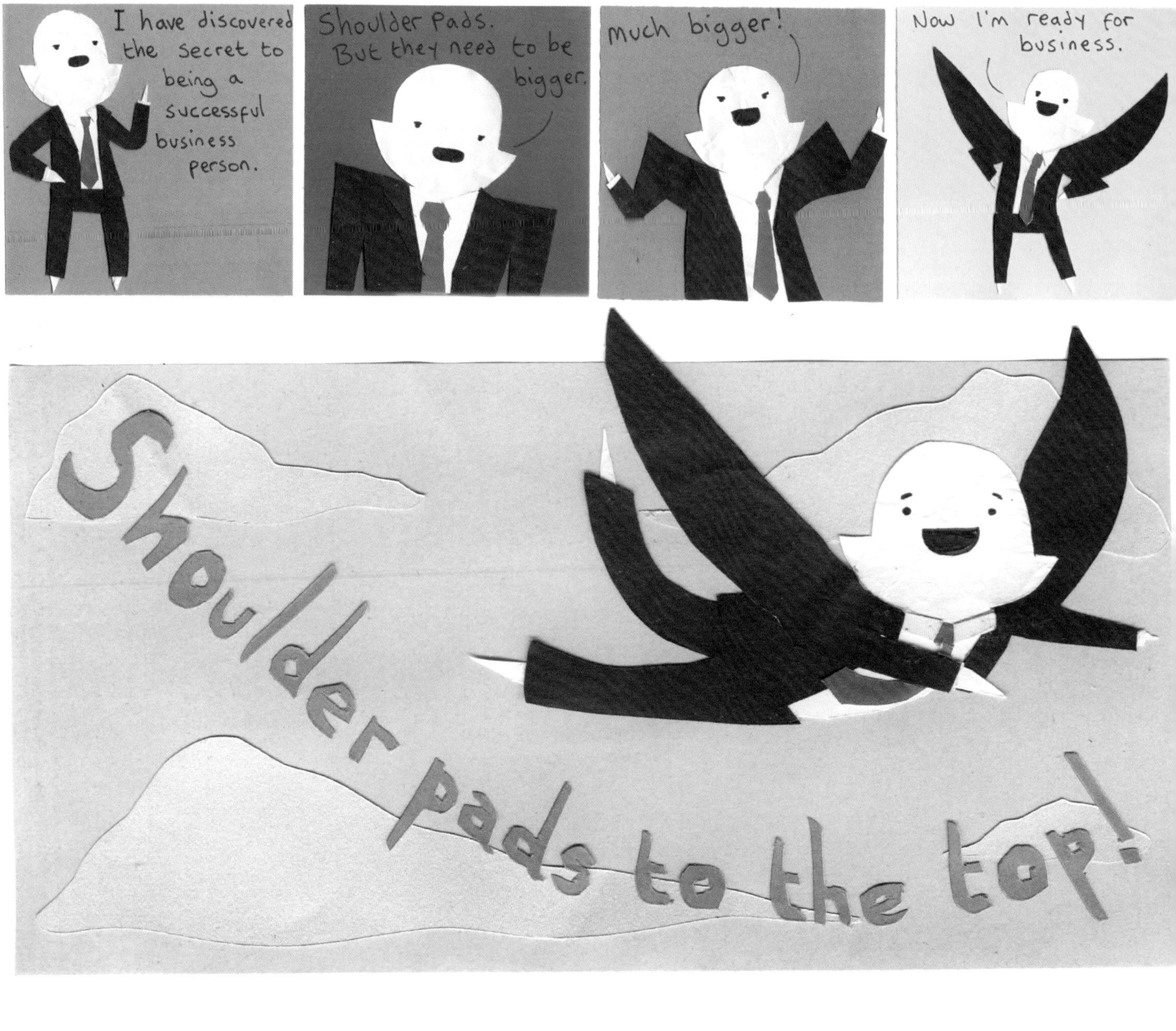
I have discovered the secret to being a successful business person.
Shoulder pads. But they need to be bigger.
much bigger!
Now I'm ready for business.
Shoulder pads to the top!

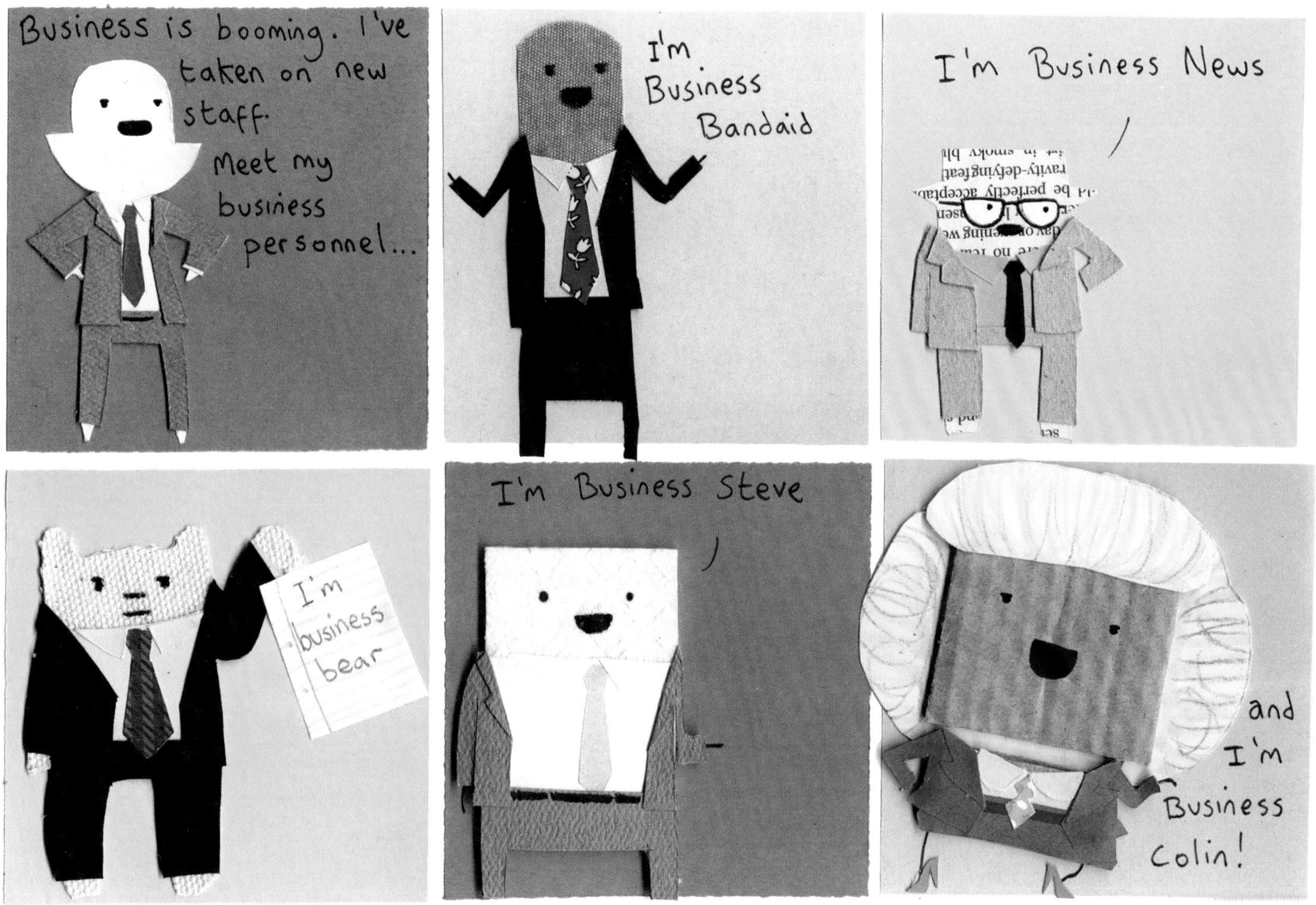
Business is booming. I've taken on new staff.
Meet my business personnel...
I'm Business Bandaid
I'm Business News
I'm business bear
I'm Business Steve
and I'm Business Colin!

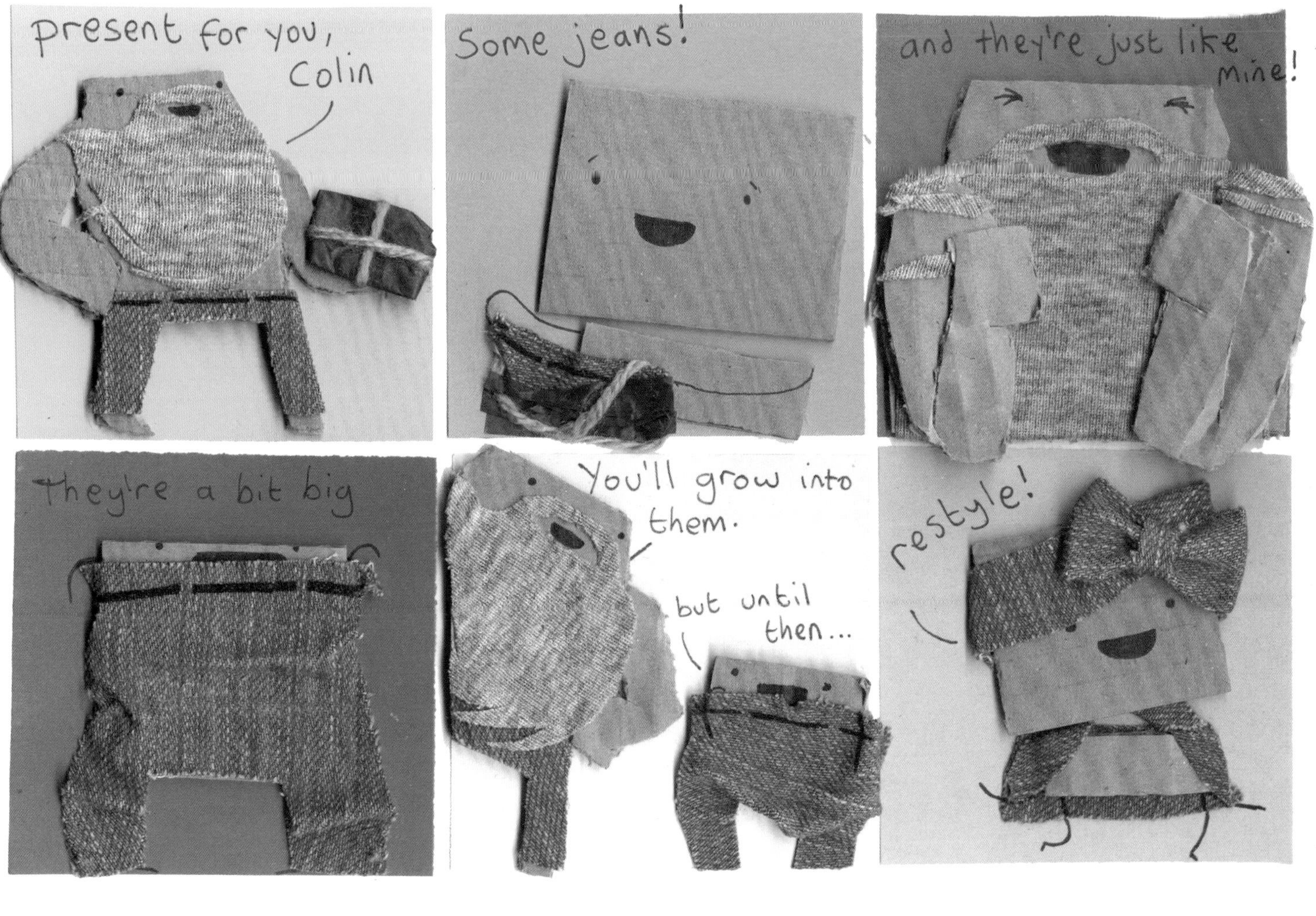
present for you, Colin
Some jeans!
and they're just like mine!
they're a bit big
You'll grow into them.
but until then...
restyle!

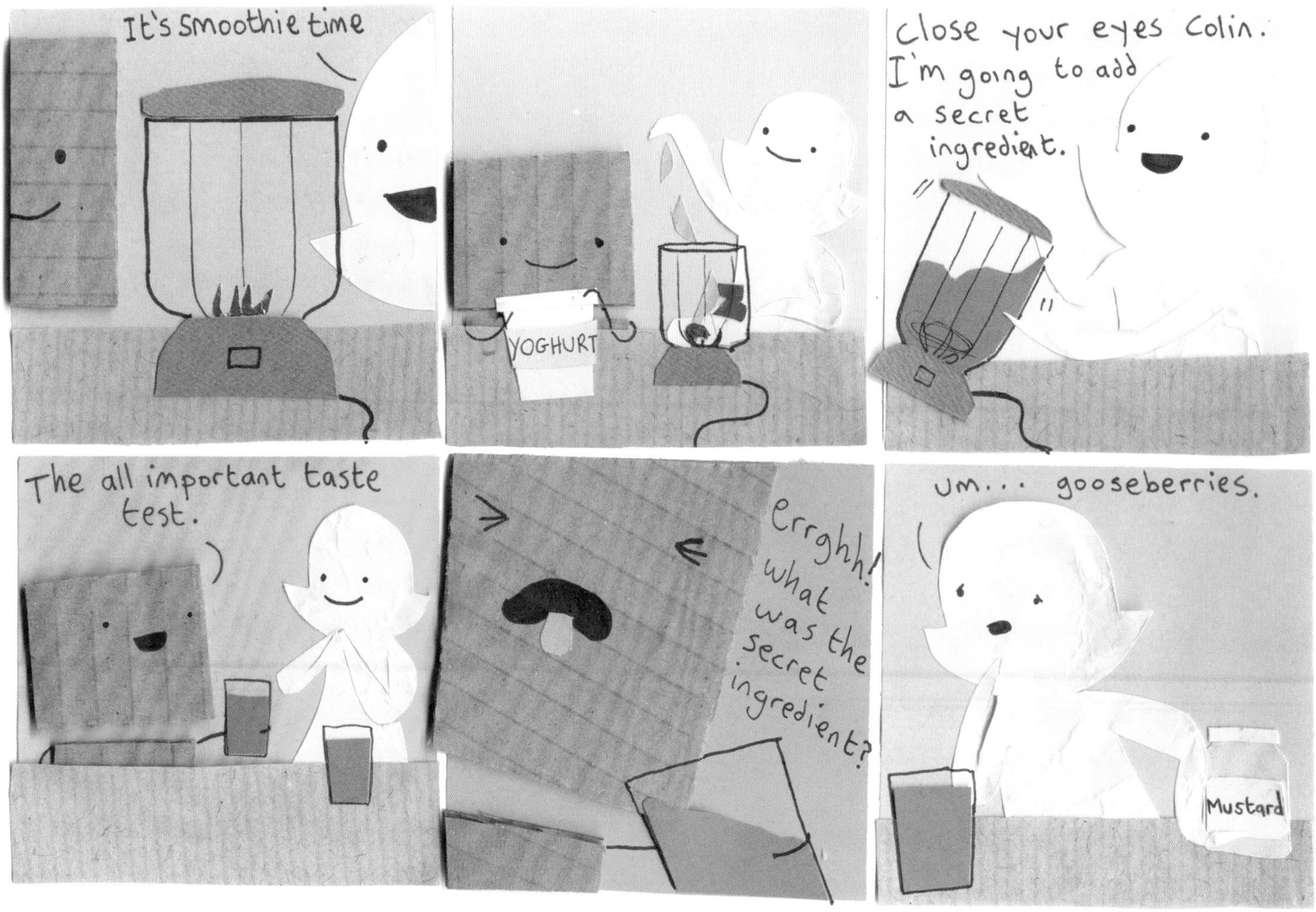
It's smoothie time
YOGHURT
Close your eyes Colin. I'm going to add a secret ingredient.
The all important taste test.
Errghh! what was the secret ingredient?
um... gooseberries.
Mustard

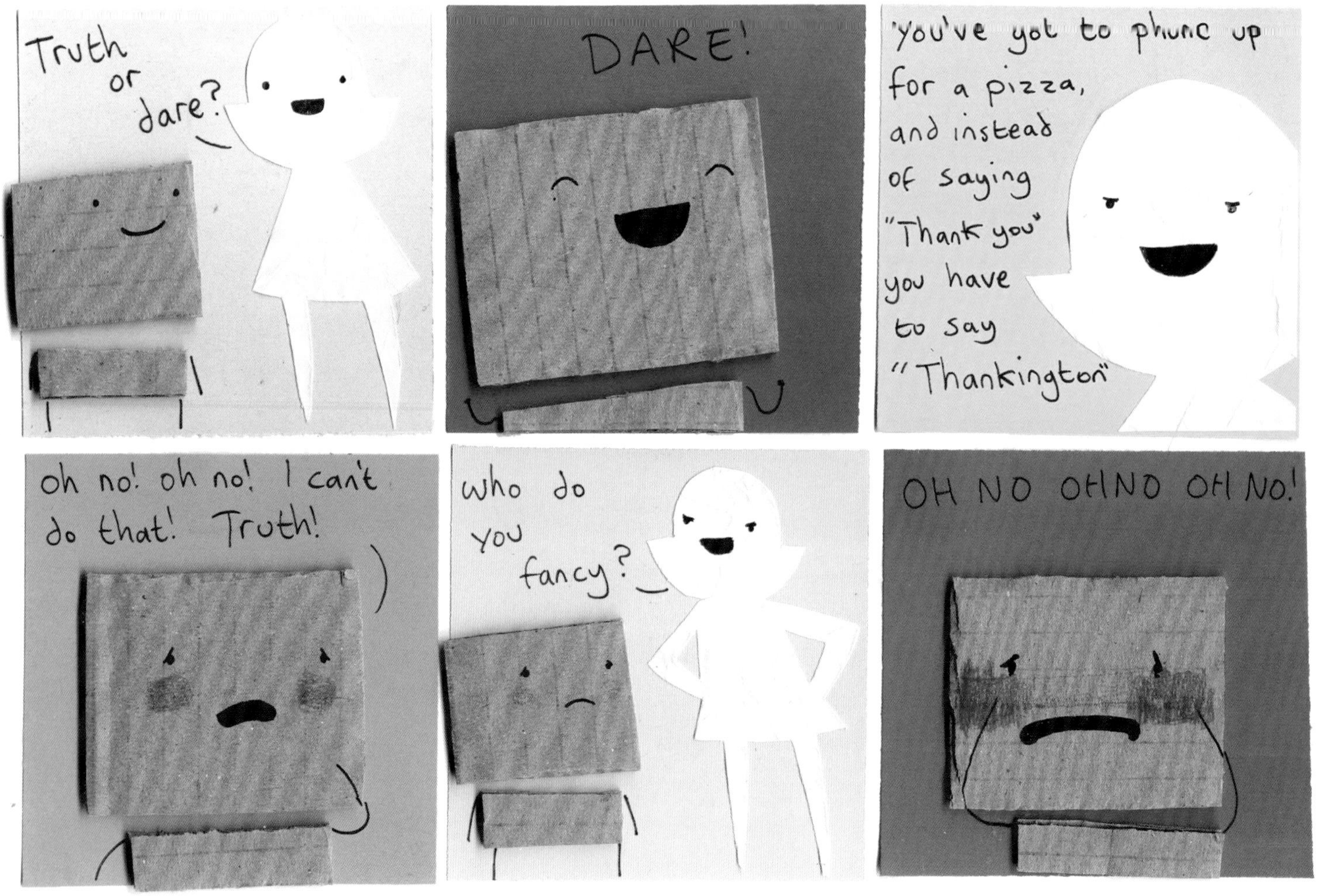
Truth or dare?
DARE!
You've got to phone up for a pizza, and instead of saying "Thank you" you have to say "Thankington"
oh no! oh no! I can't do that! Truth!
who do you fancy?
OH NO OH NO OH NO!

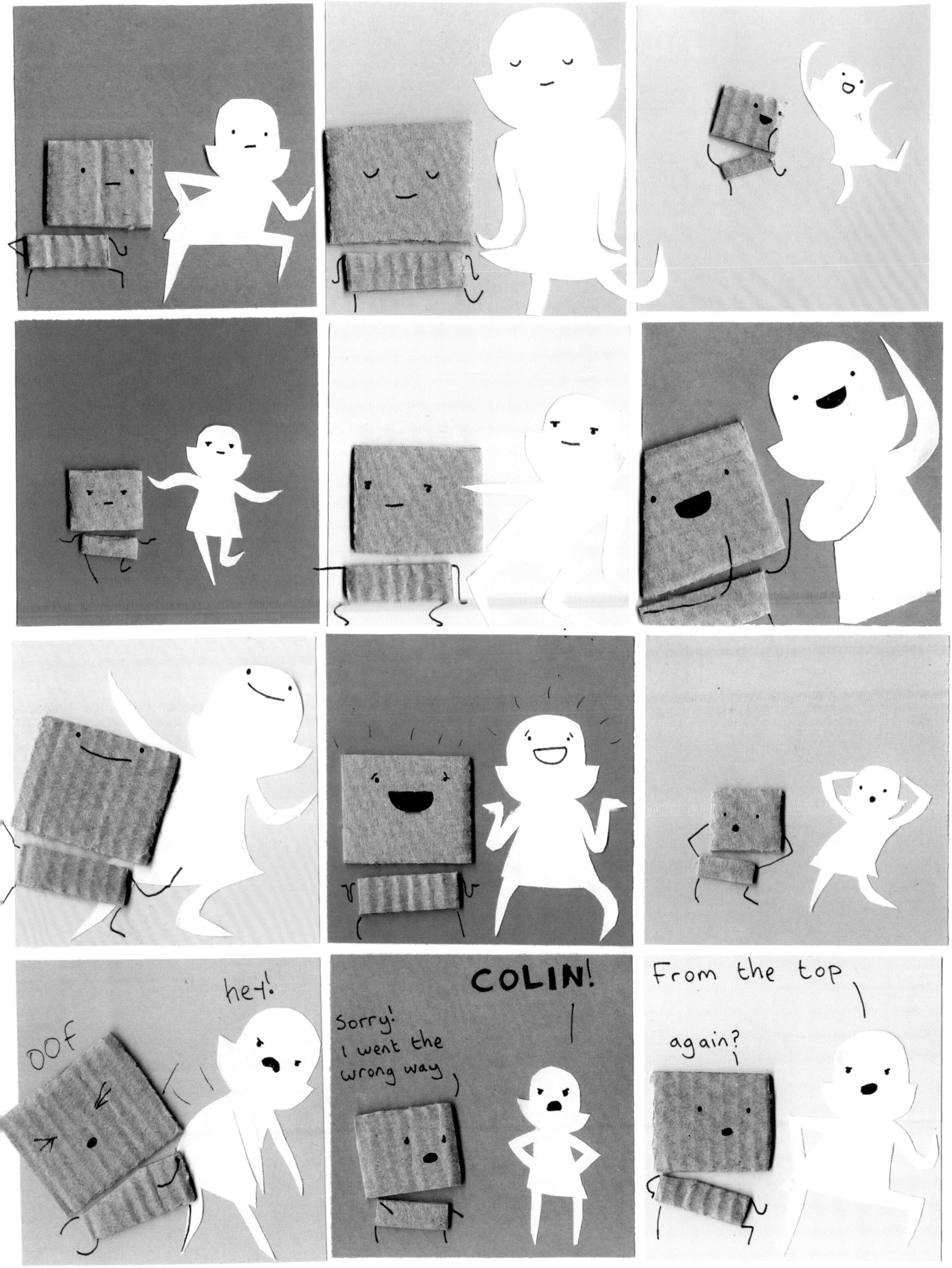
OOF
hey!
Sorry!
I went the
wrong way
COLIN!
From the top
again?

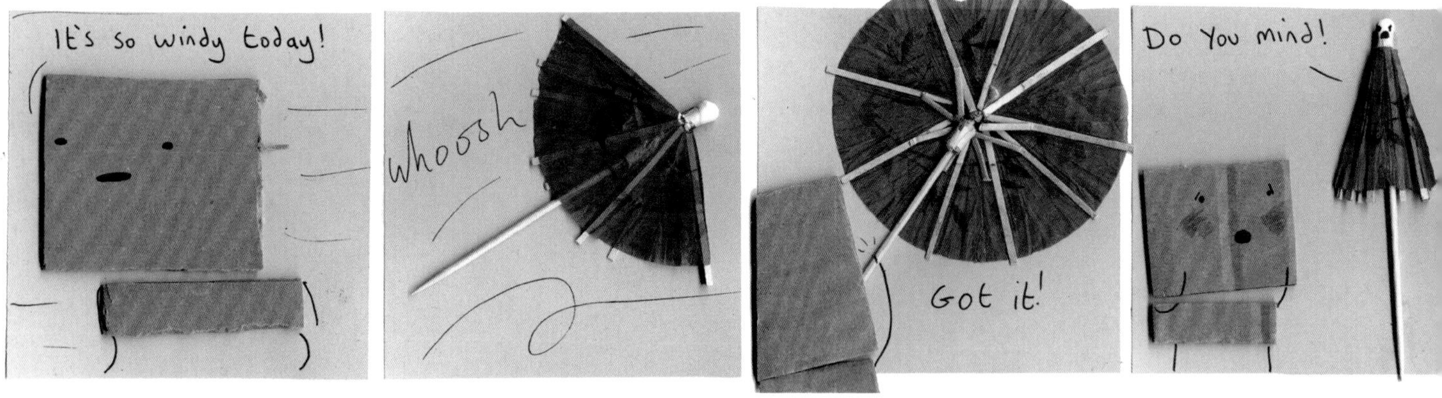
It's so windy today!
whoosh
Got it!
Do you mind!

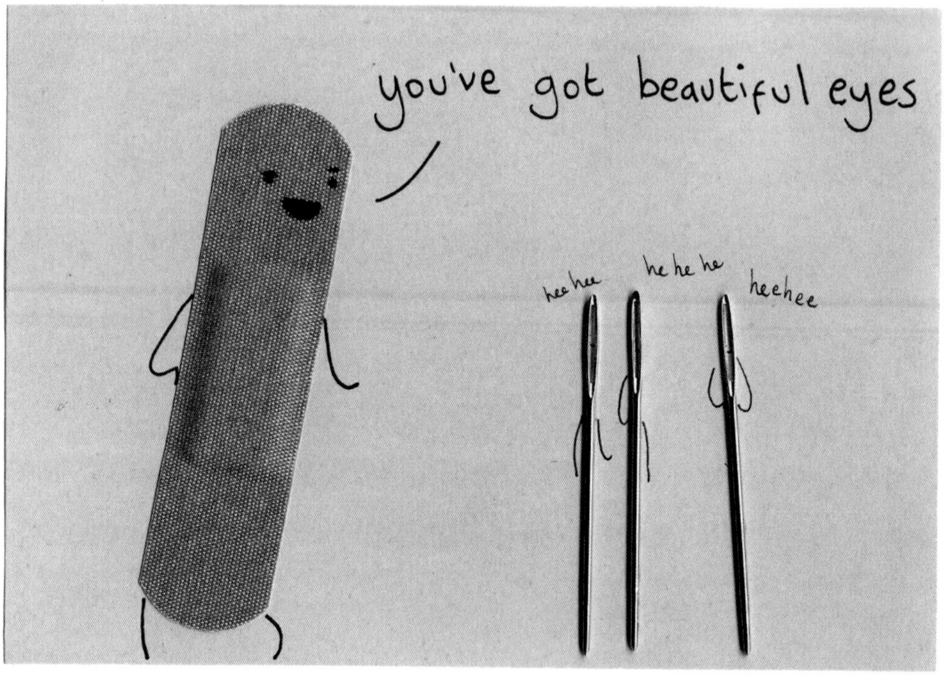
you've got beautiful eyes
heehee
he he he
heehee

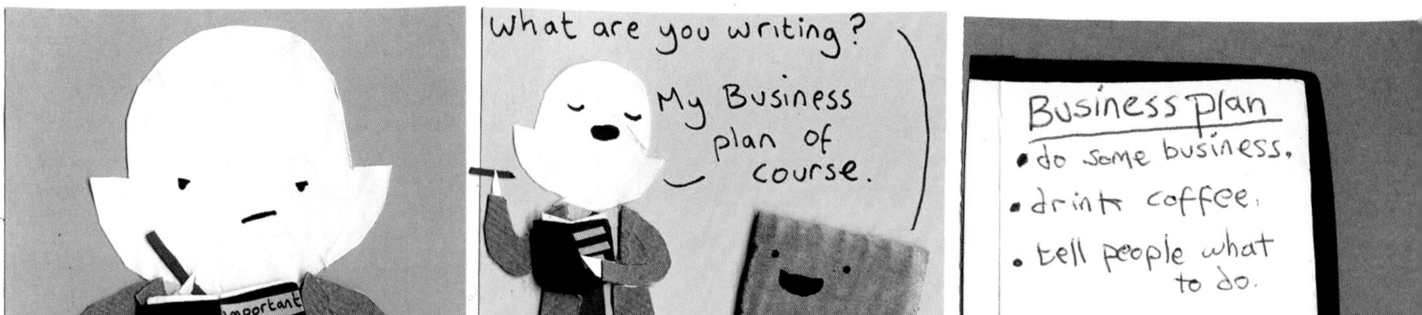
Important Business Stuff
What are you writing?
My Business plan of course.
Business plan
• do some business.
• drink coffee.
• tell people what to do.
• more coffee.
• write a business plan.
• coffee.

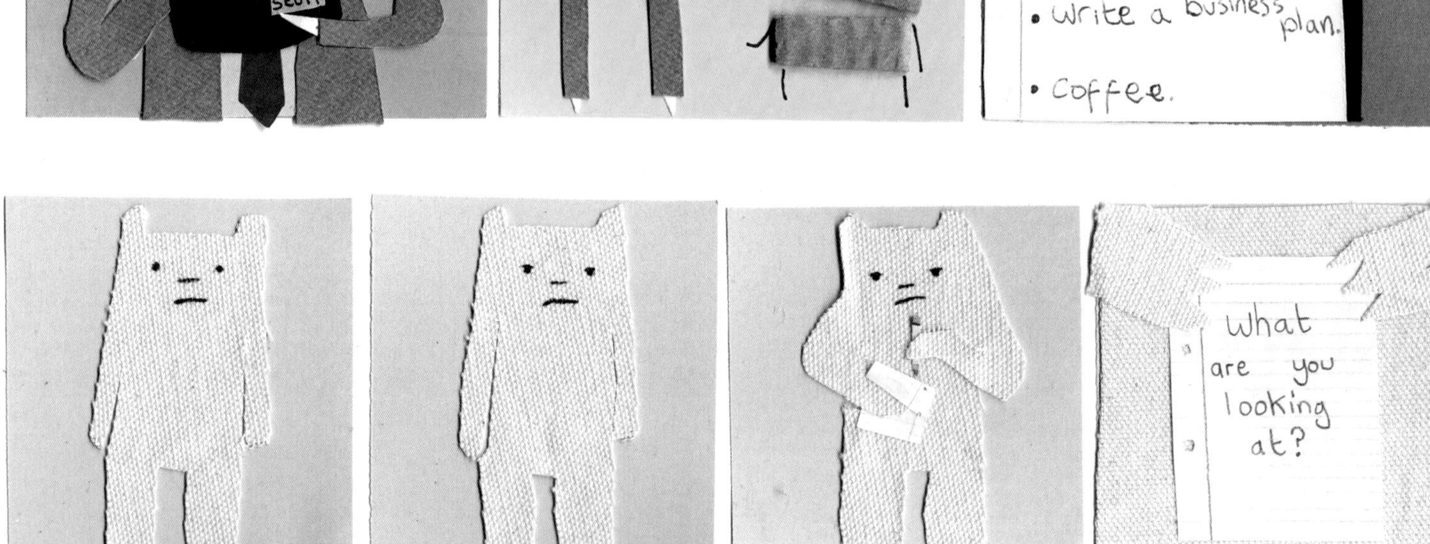
What are you looking at?

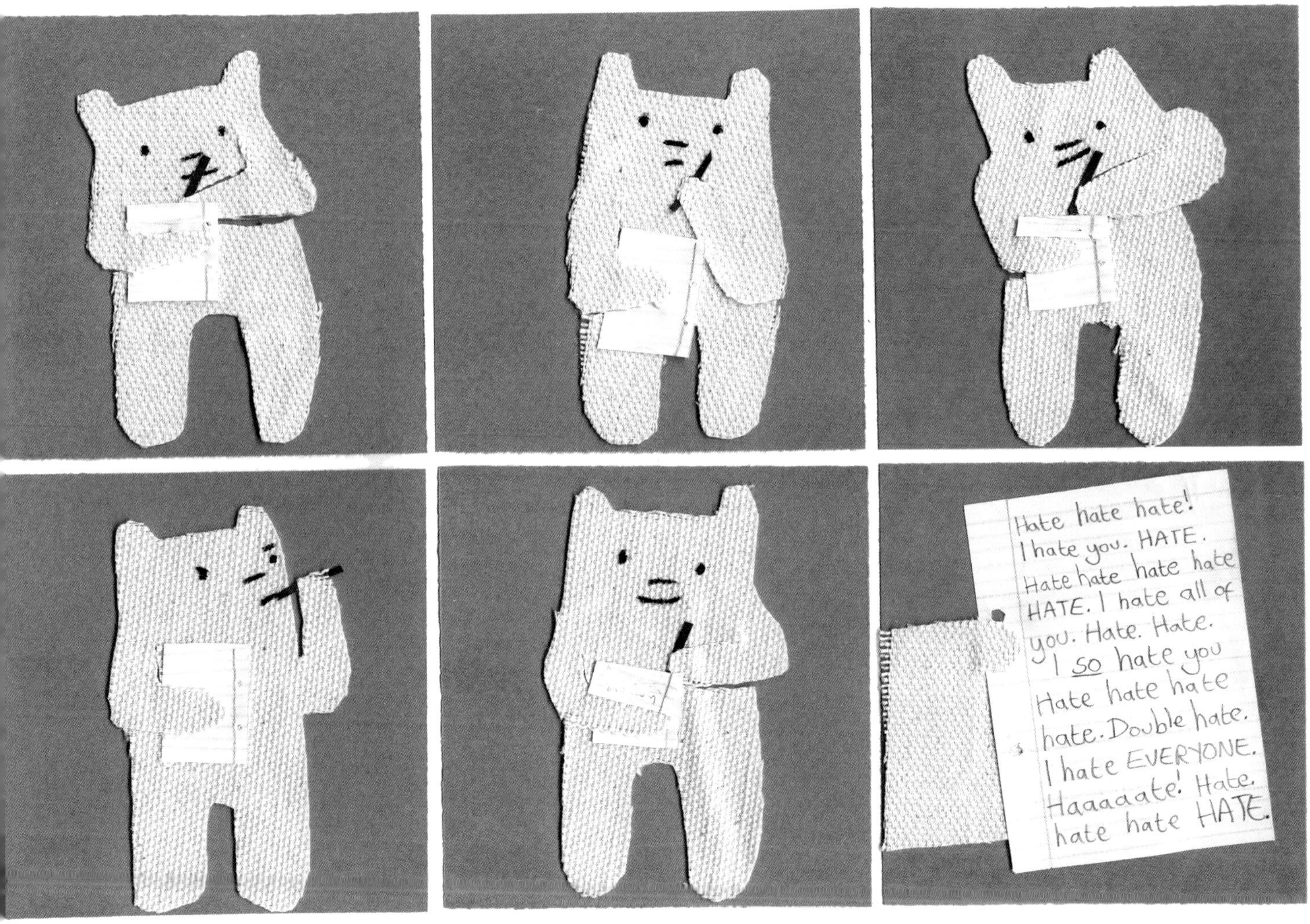
Hate hate hate!
I hate you. HATE.
Hate hate hate hate
HATE. I hate all of
you. Hate. Hate.
I so hate you
Hate hate hate
hate. Double hate.
I hate EVERYONE.
Haaaaate! Hate.
hate hate HATE.

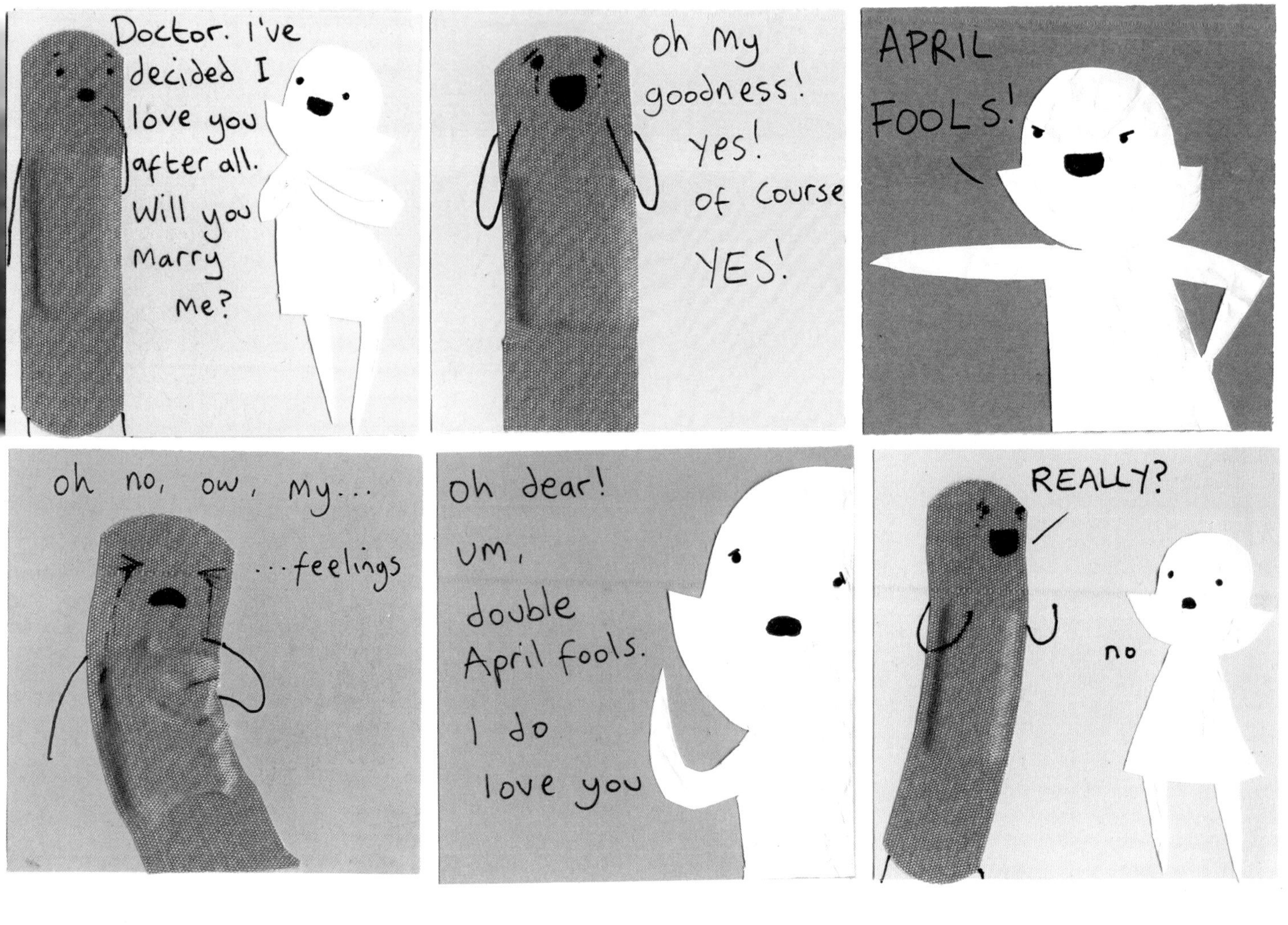
Doctor. I've decided I love you after all. Will you marry me?
oh my goodness! yes! of course YES!
APRIL FOOLS!
oh no, ow, my...
...feelings
oh dear! um, double April fools. I do love you
REALLY?
no

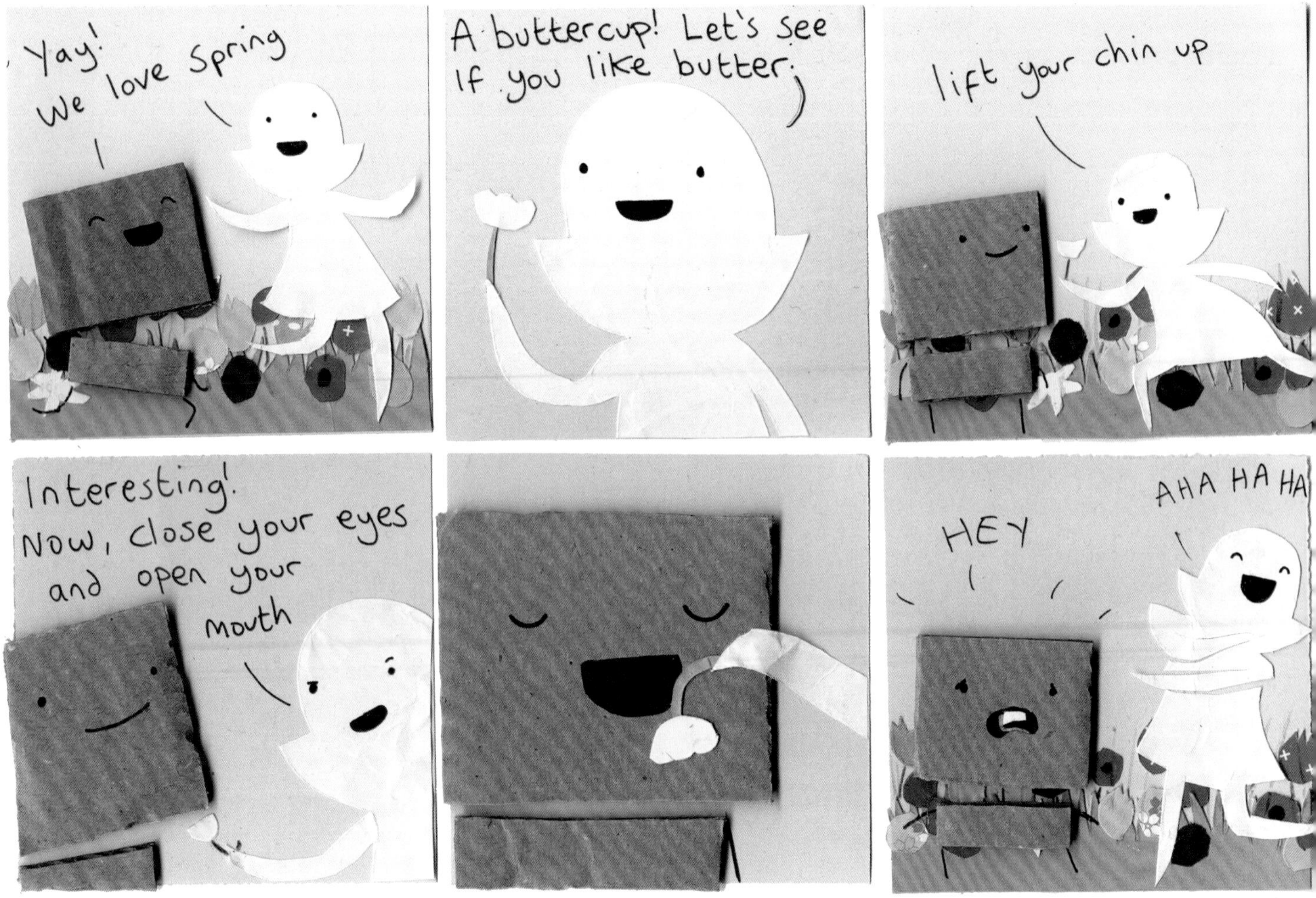
Yay!
We love Spring
A buttercup! Let's see If you like butter.
lift your chin up
Interesting!
Now, close your eyes and open your mouth
HEY
AHA HA HA

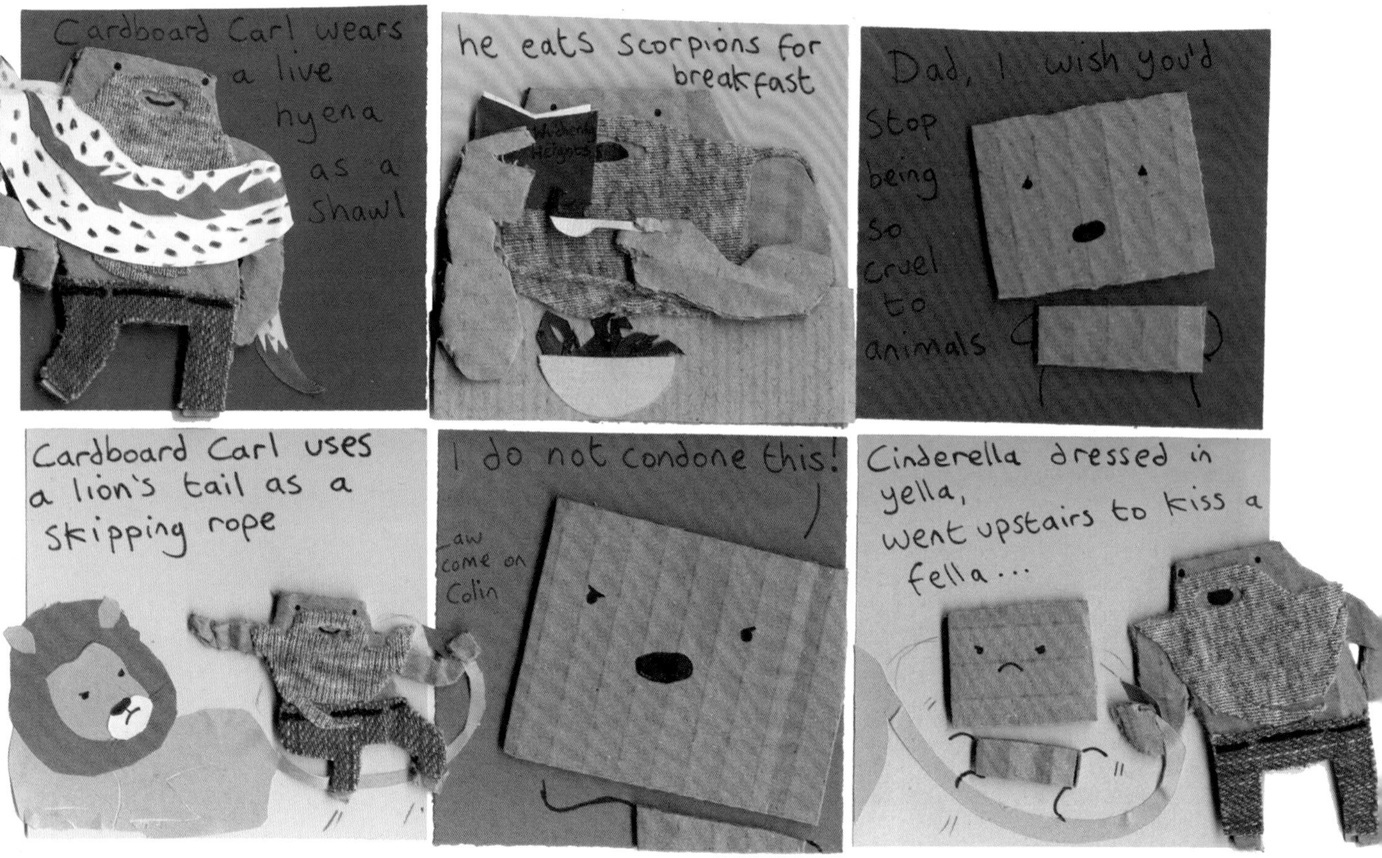
Cardboard Carl wears a live hyena as a shawl
he eats scorpions for breakfast
Dad, I wish you'd Stop being so cruel to animals
Cardboard Carl uses a lion's tail as a skipping rope
I do not condone this!
aw come on Colin
Cinderella dressed in yella, went upstairs to kiss a fella...

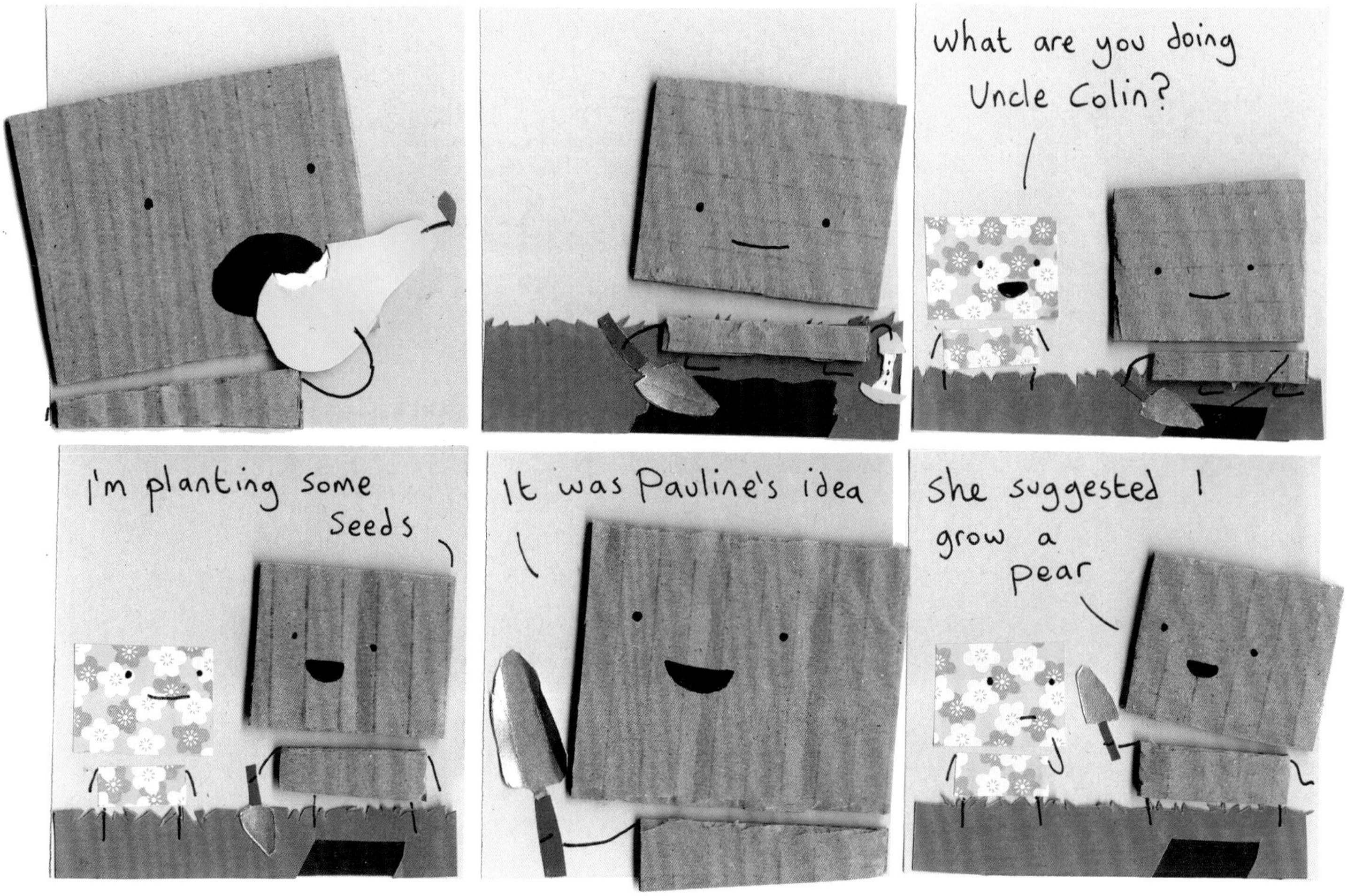
What are you doing Uncle Colin?
I'm planting some Seeds
It was Pauline's idea
She suggested I grow a pear

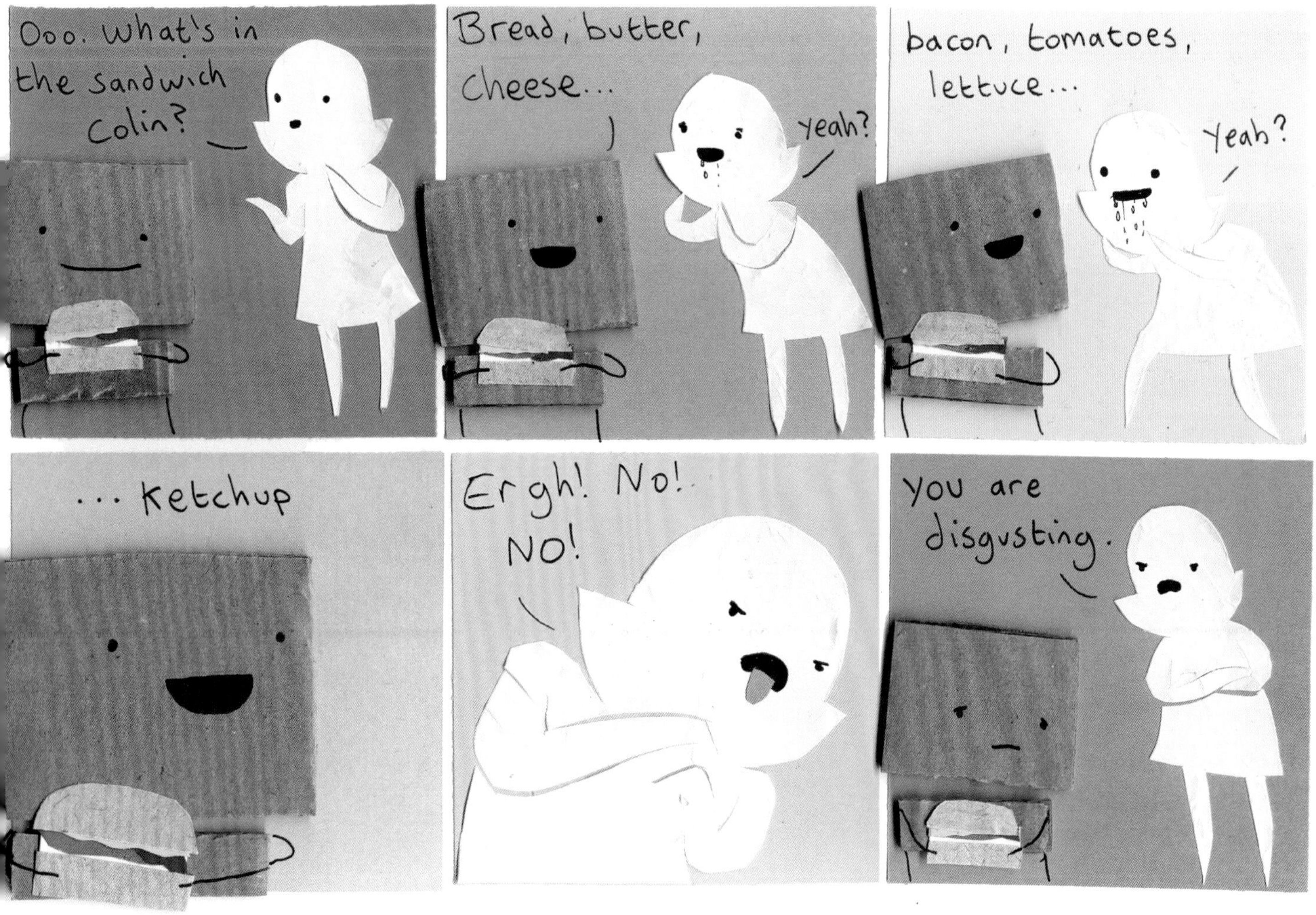
Ooo. What's in the sandwich Colin?
Bread, butter, Cheese...
Yeah?
bacon, tomatoes, lettuce...
Yeah?
... Ketchup
Ergh! No! NO!
You are disgusting.

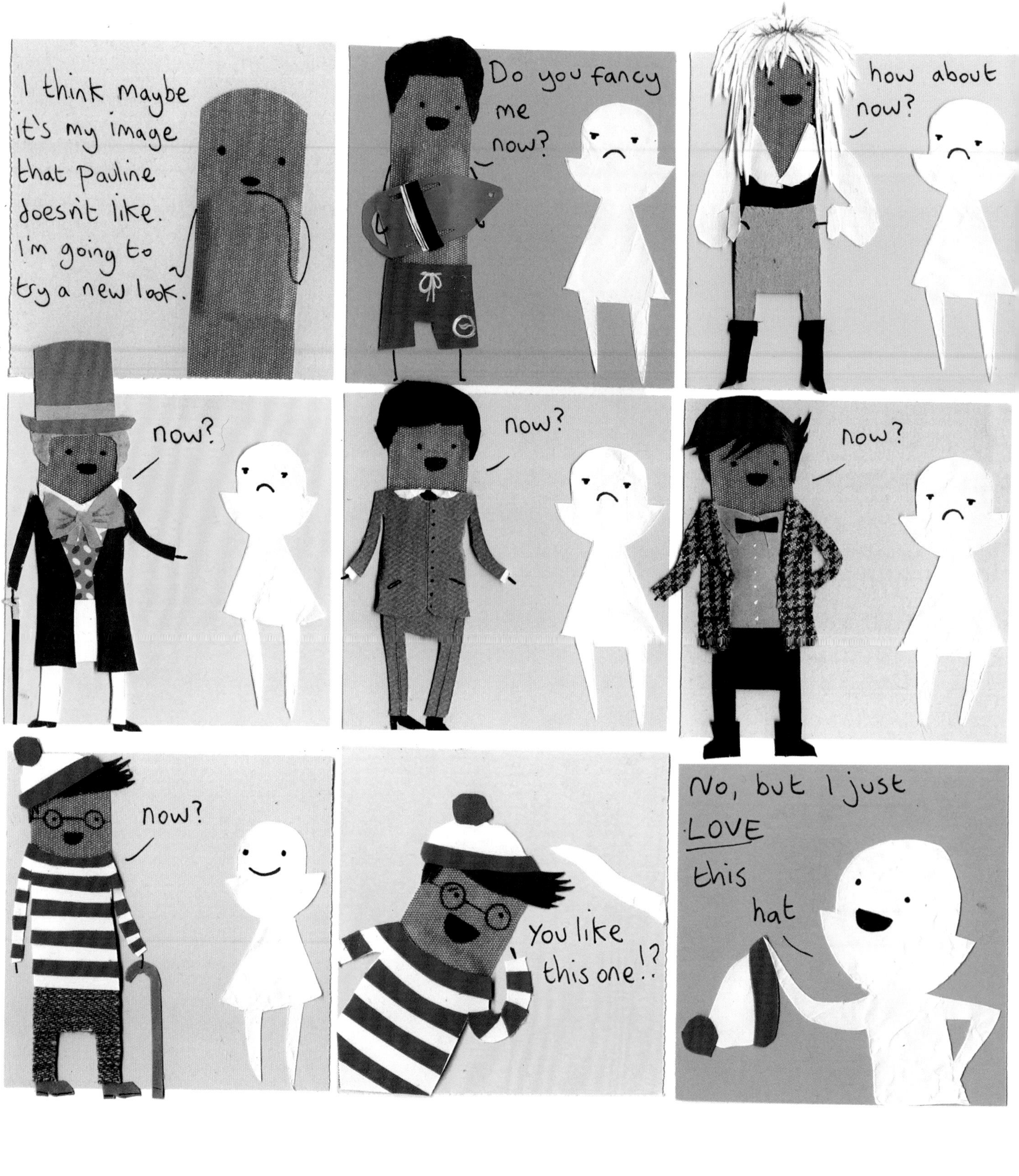

I think maybe it's my image that Pauline doesn't like. I'm going to try a new look.
Do you fancy me now?
how about now?
now?
now?
now?
now?
You like this one!?
No, but I just LOVE this hat

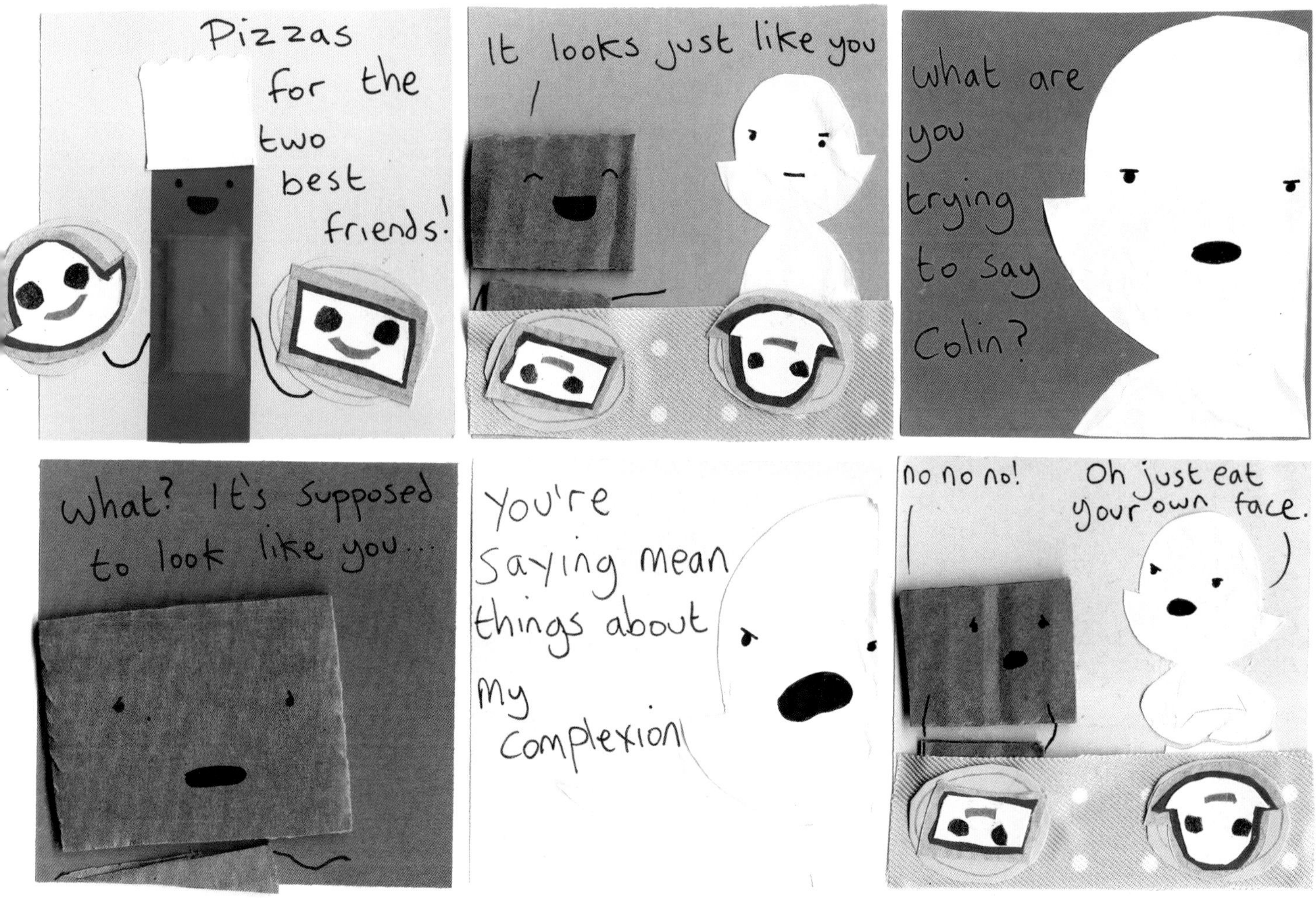

Pizzas for the two best friends!
It looks just like you
what are you trying to say Colin?
what? It's supposed to look like you...
You're saying mean things about my complexion
no no no!
Oh just eat your own face.

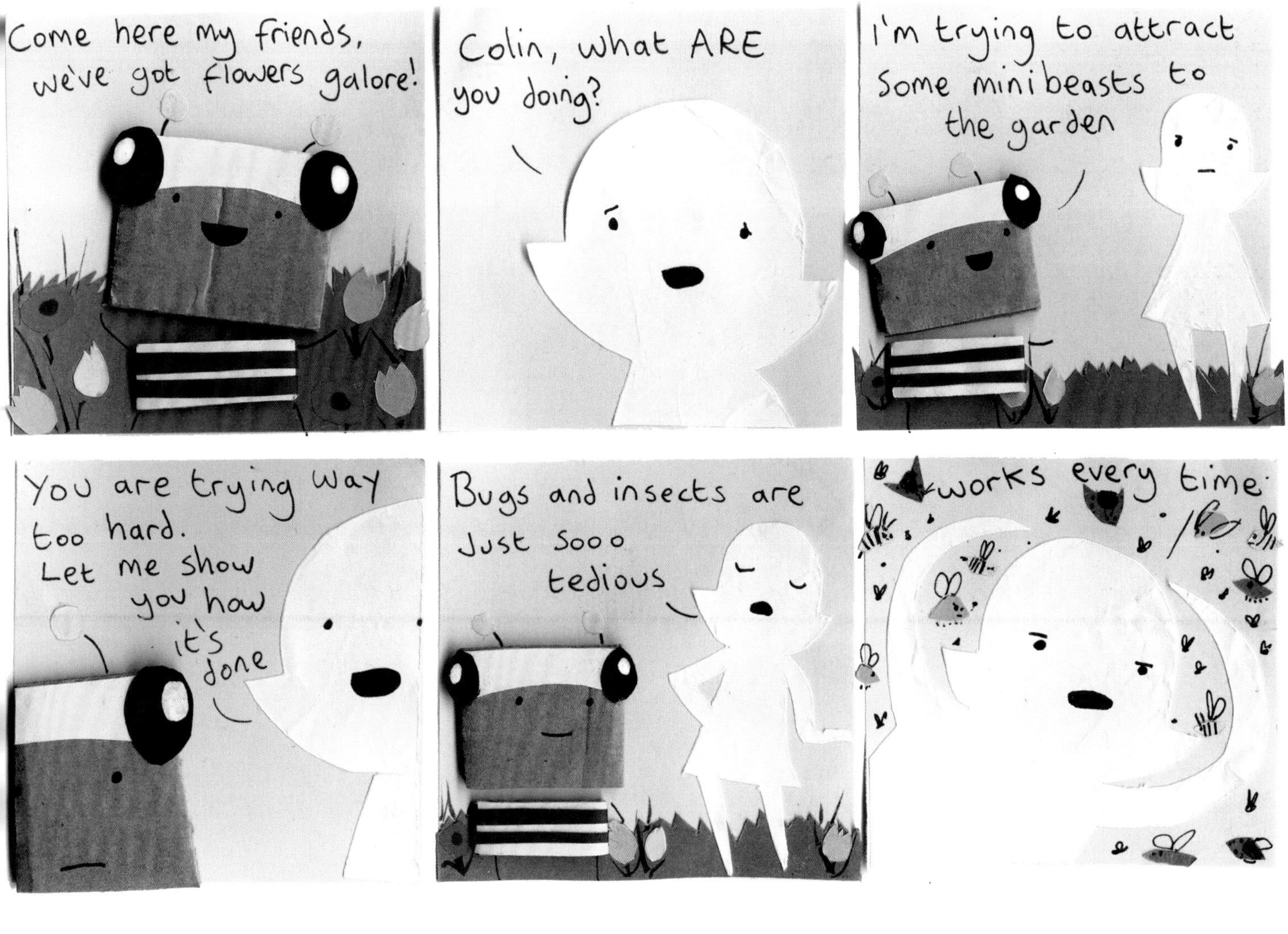

Come here my friends, we've got flowers galore!
Colin, what ARE you doing?
I'm trying to attract some minibeasts to the garden
You are trying way too hard. Let me show you how it's done
Bugs and insects are just sooo tedious
works every time.

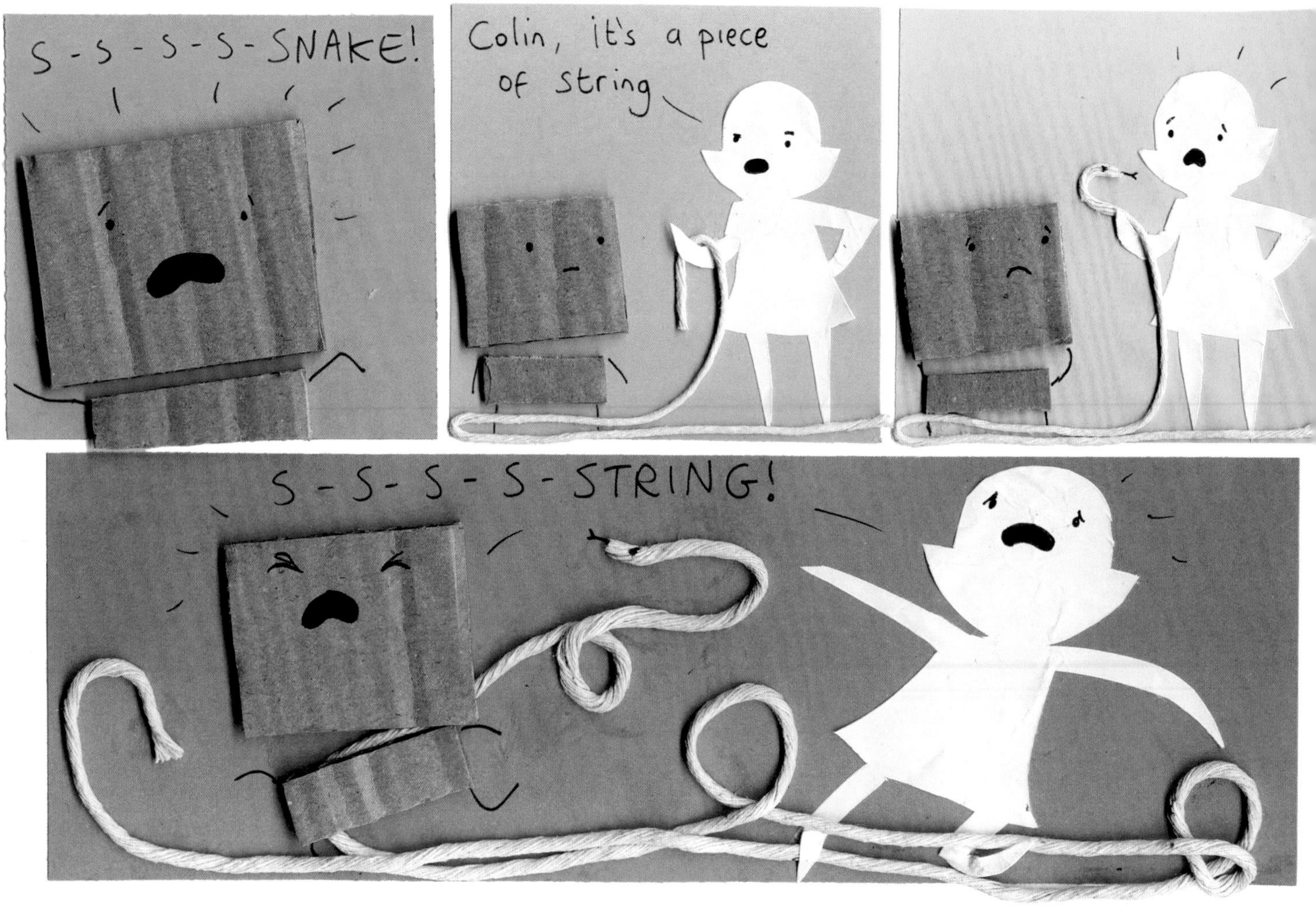
S-S-S-S-SNAKE!
Colin, it's a piece of string
S-S-S-S-STRING!

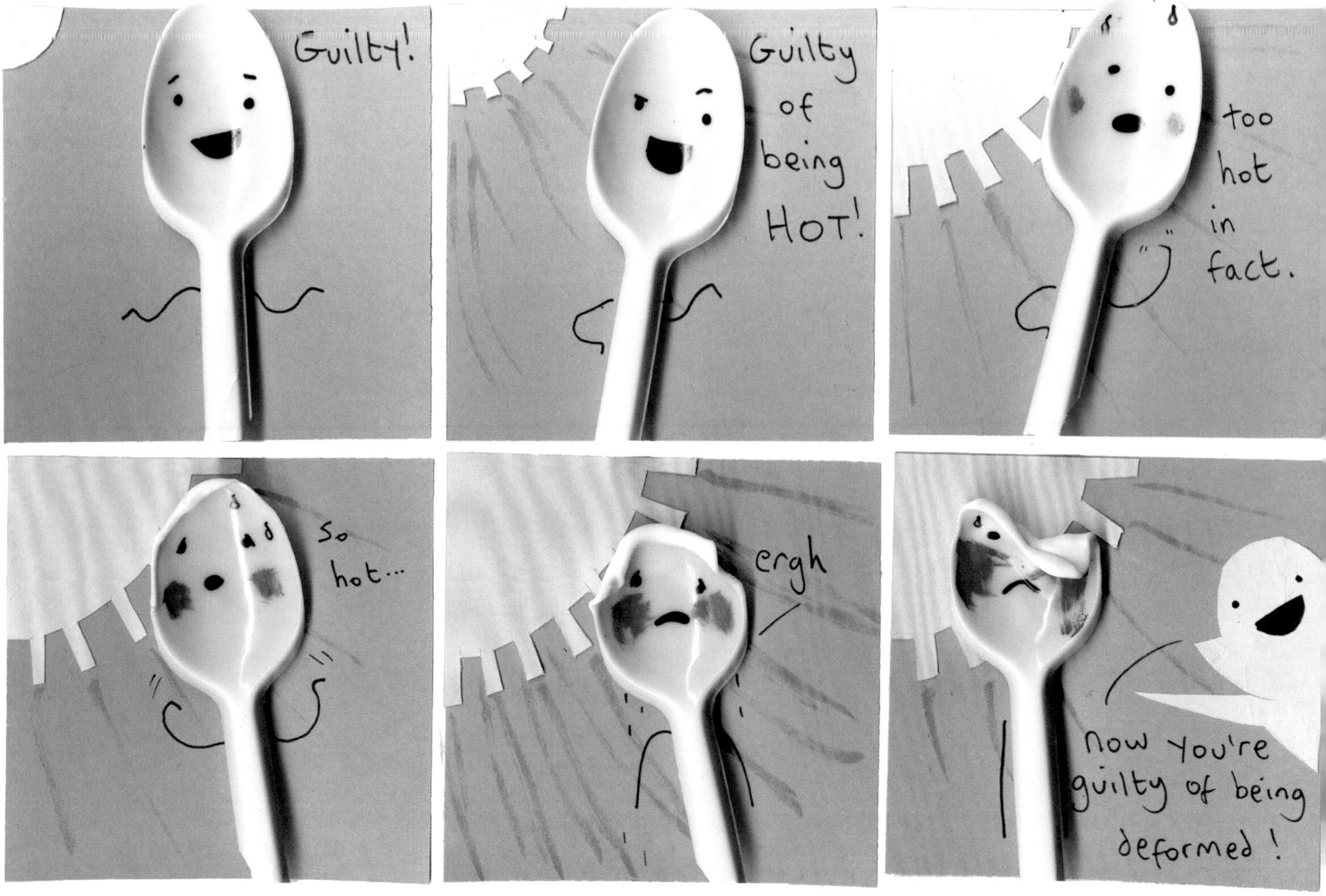
Guilty!
Guilty of being HOT!
too hot in fact.
So hot...
ergh
now you're guilty of being deformed!

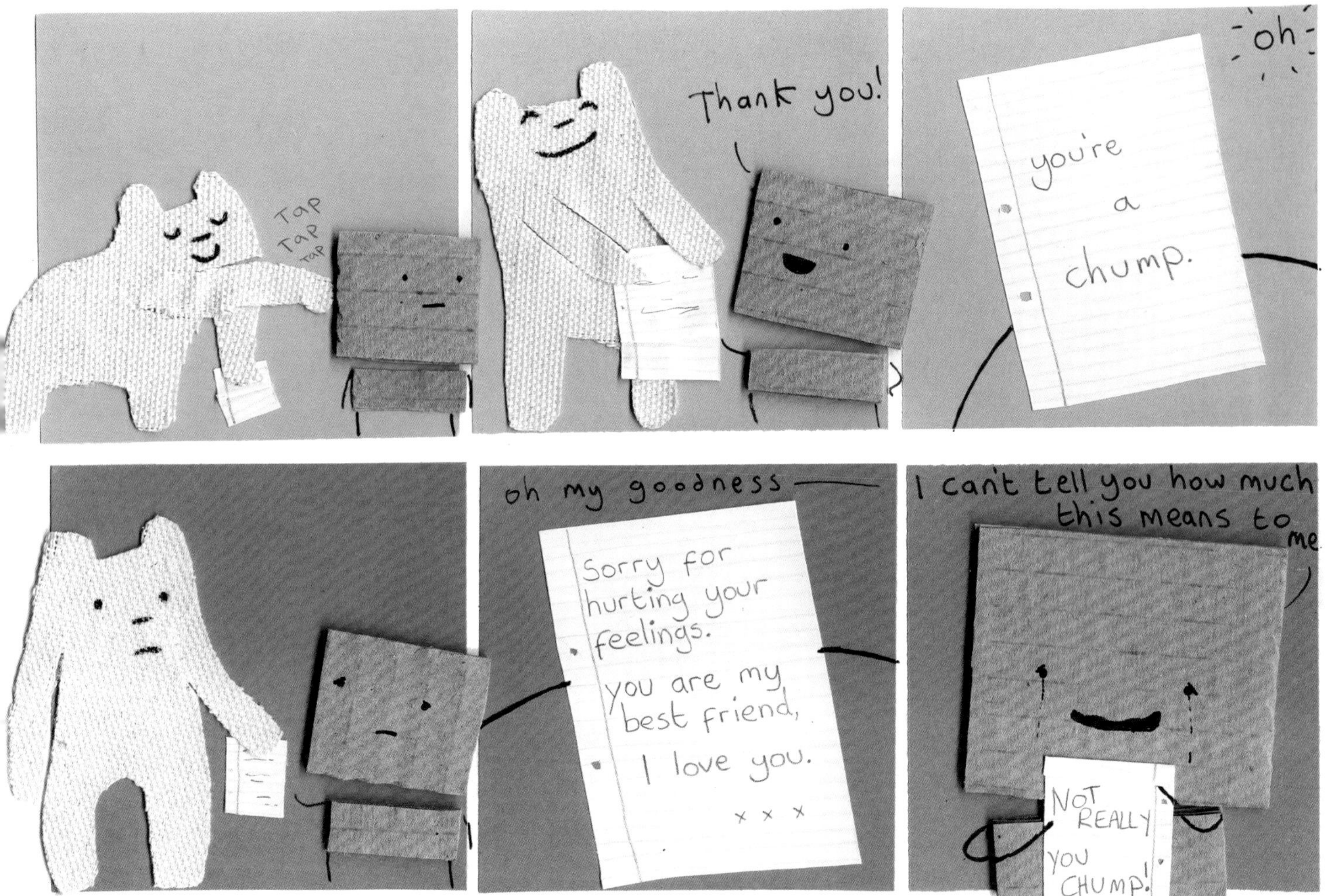
Tap Tap Tap
Thank you!
oh
you're a chump.
oh my goodness
Sorry for hurting your feelings.
you are my best friend,
I love you.
x x x
I can't tell you how much this means to me
NOT REALLY YOU CHUMP!

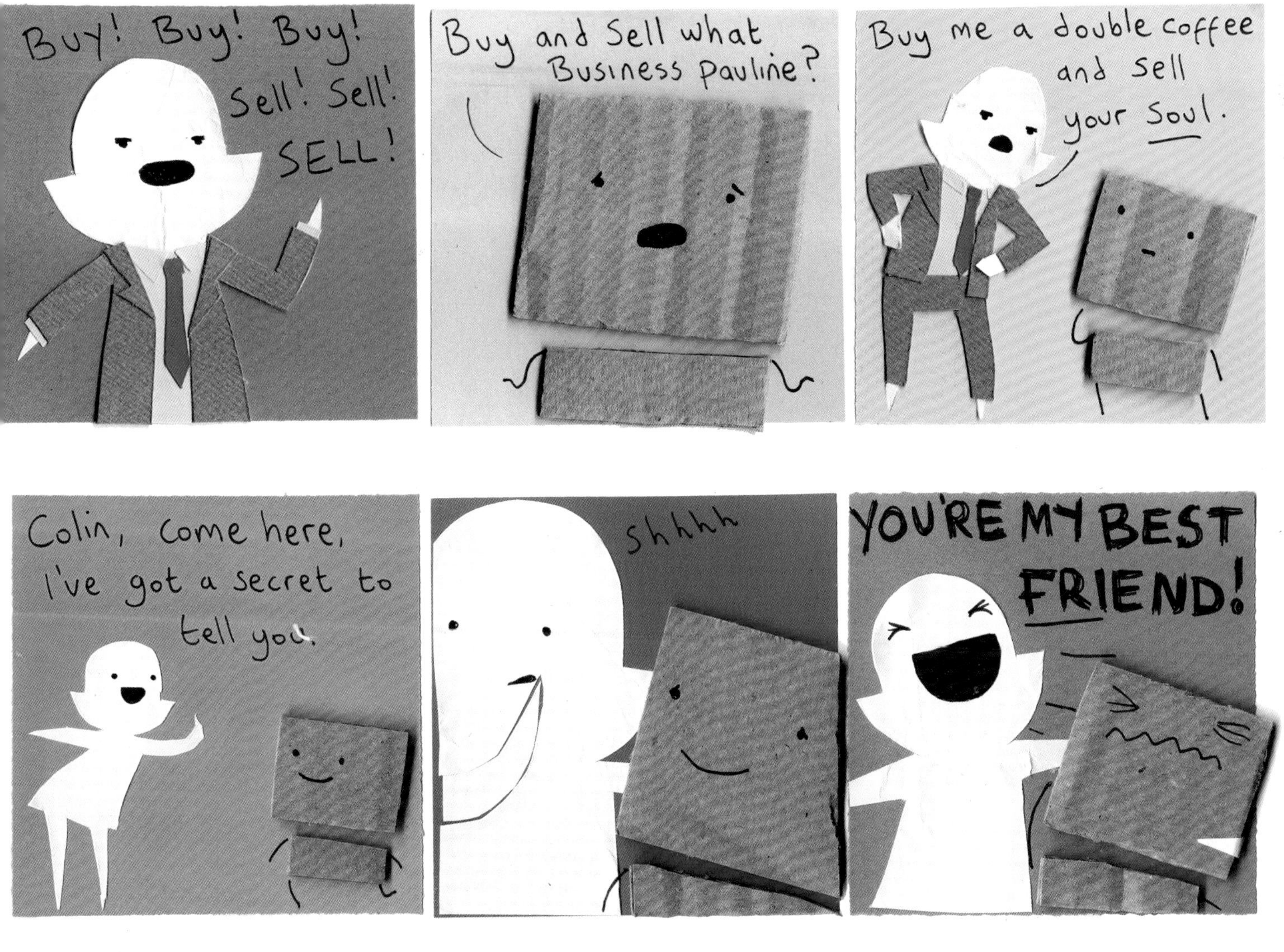
Buy! Buy! Buy!
Sell! Sell! SELL!
Buy and Sell what Business Pauline?
Buy me a double coffee and sell your Soul.
Colin, come here, I've got a secret to tell you.
shhhh
YOU'RE MY BEST FRIEND!

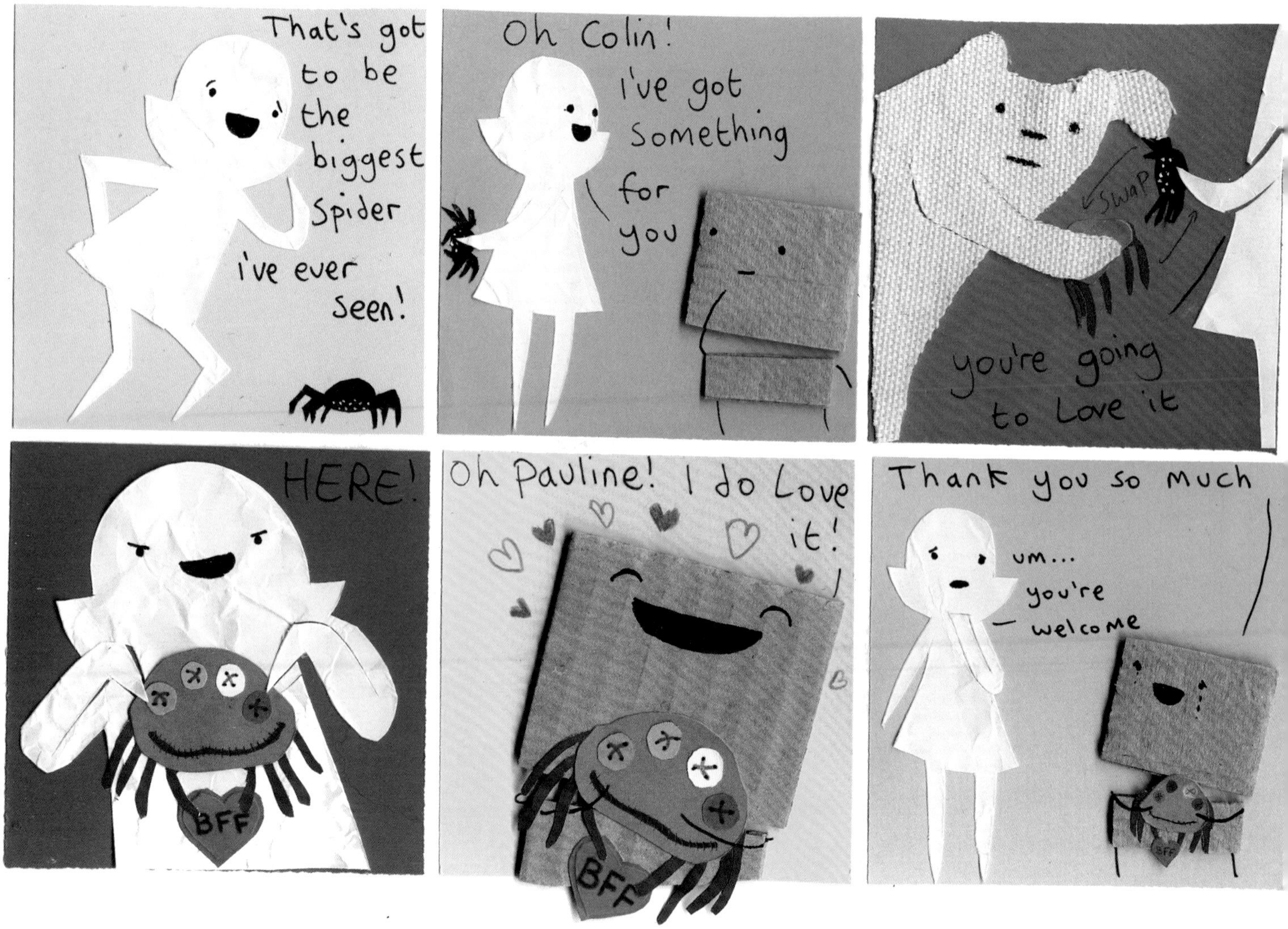
That's got to be the biggest Spider i've ever seen!
Oh Colin! i've got Something for you
you're going to Love it
SWAP
HERE!
Oh Pauline! I do Love it!
BFF
Thank you so much
um... you're welcome

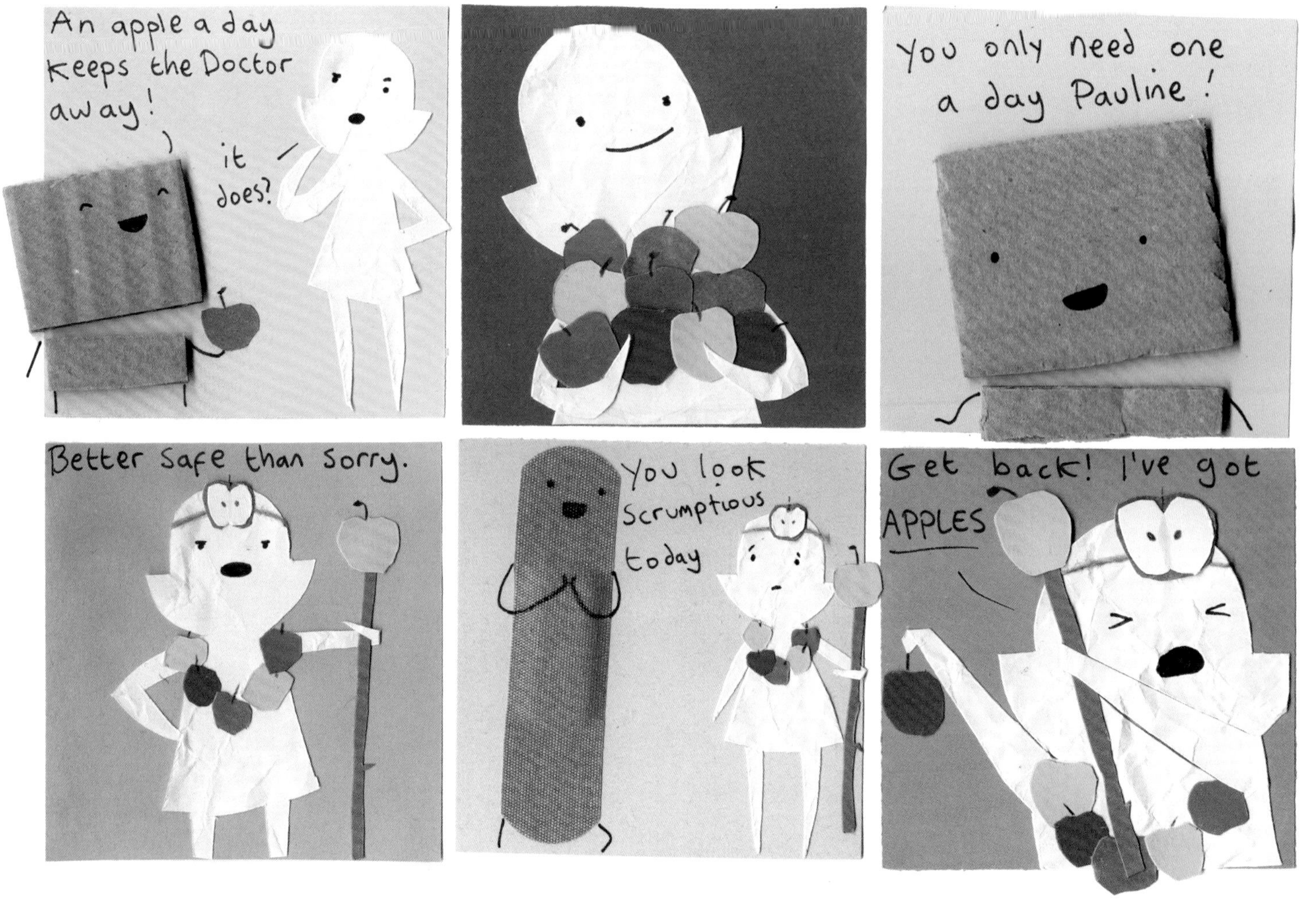
An apple a day keeps the Doctor away!
it does?
You only need one a day Pauline!
Better safe than sorry.
You look Scrumptious today
Get back! I've got APPLES

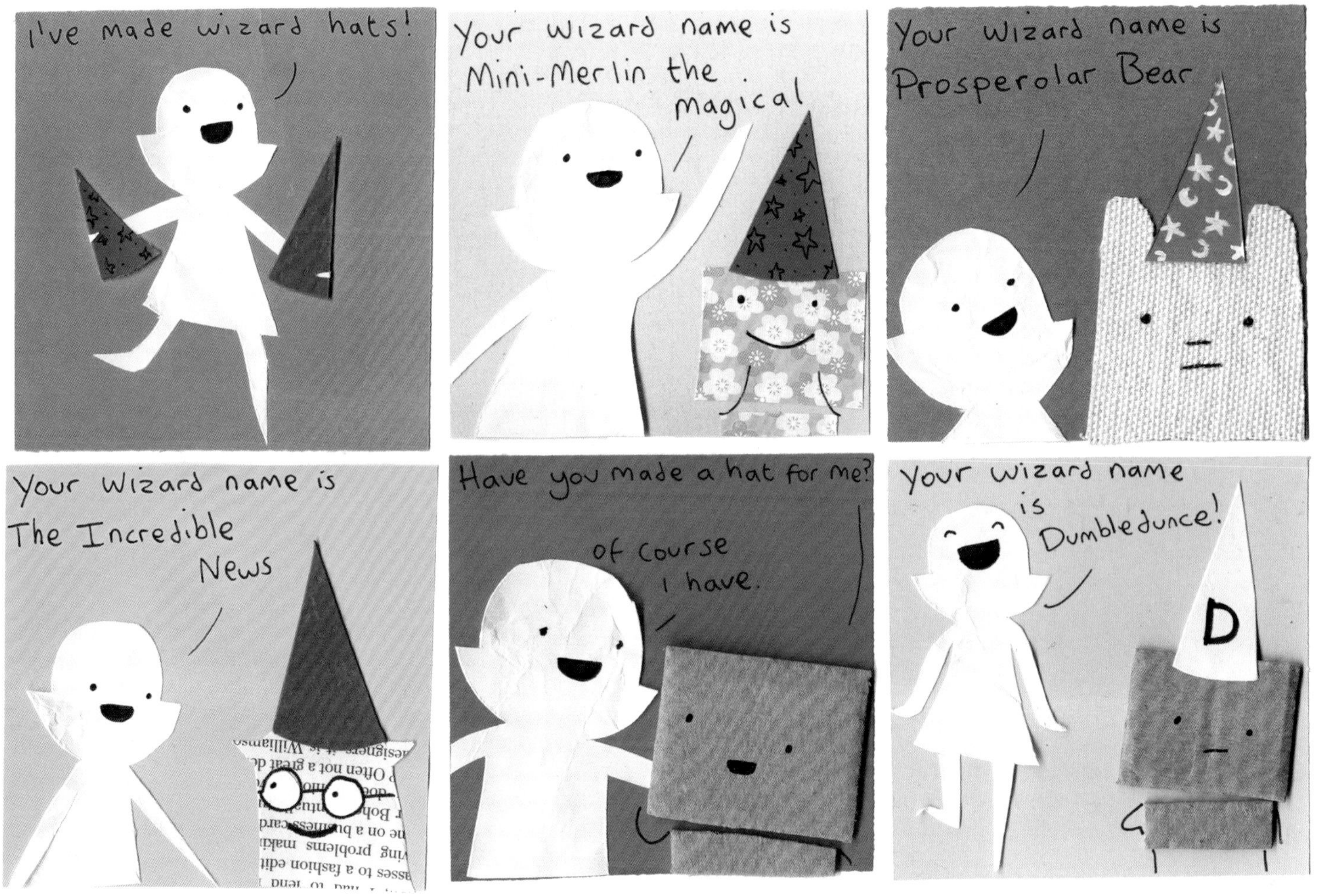
I've made wizard hats!
Your wizard name is Mini-Merlin the magical
Your wizard name is Prosperolar Bear
Your wizard name is The Incredible News
Have you made a hat for me?
of course I have.
Your wizard name is Dumbledunce!
D

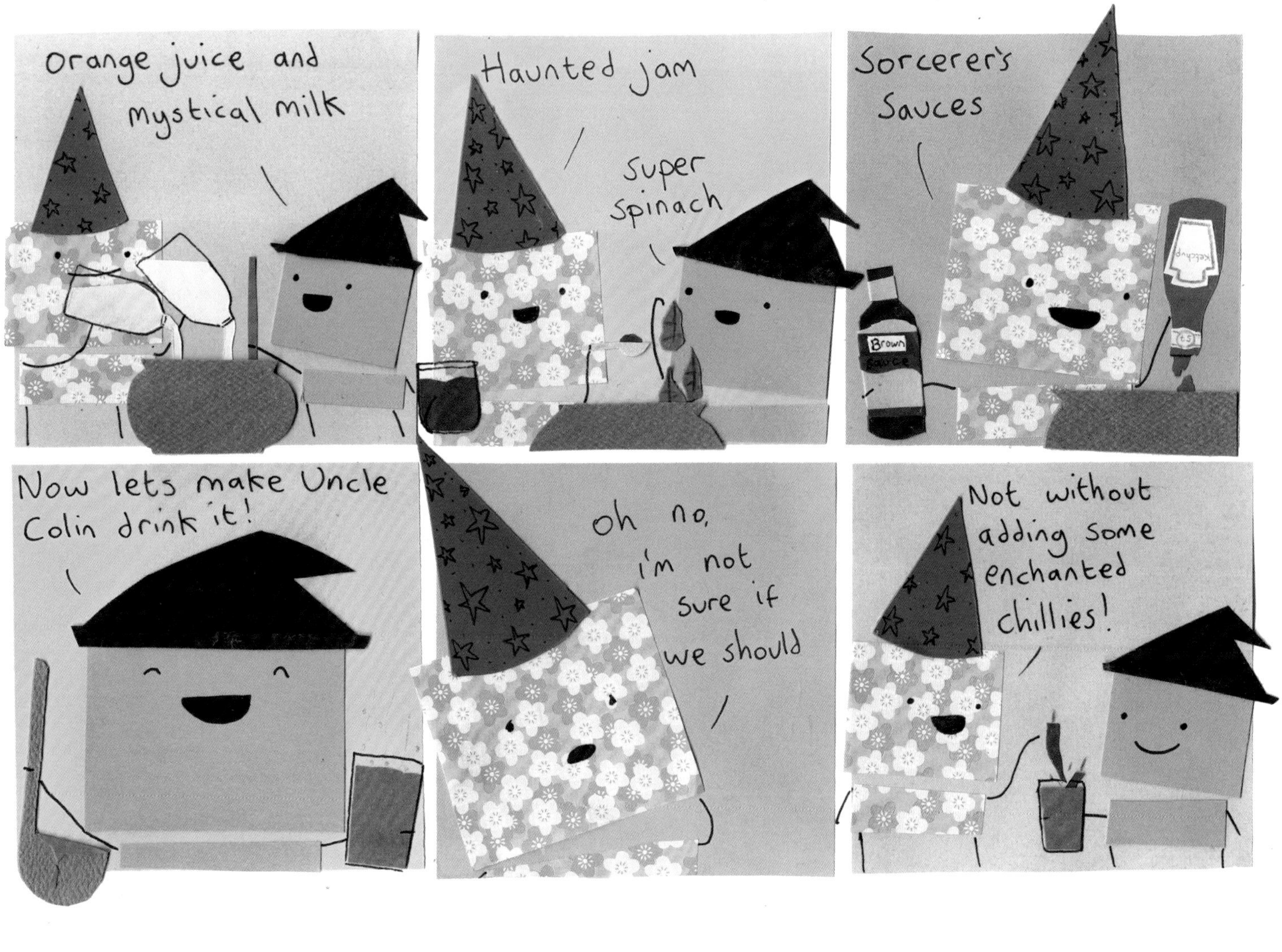
Orange juice and mystical milk
Haunted jam
Super spinach
Sorcerer's Sauces
Brown Sauce
Now lets make Uncle Colin drink it!
oh no, I'm not sure if we should
Not without adding some enchanted chillies!

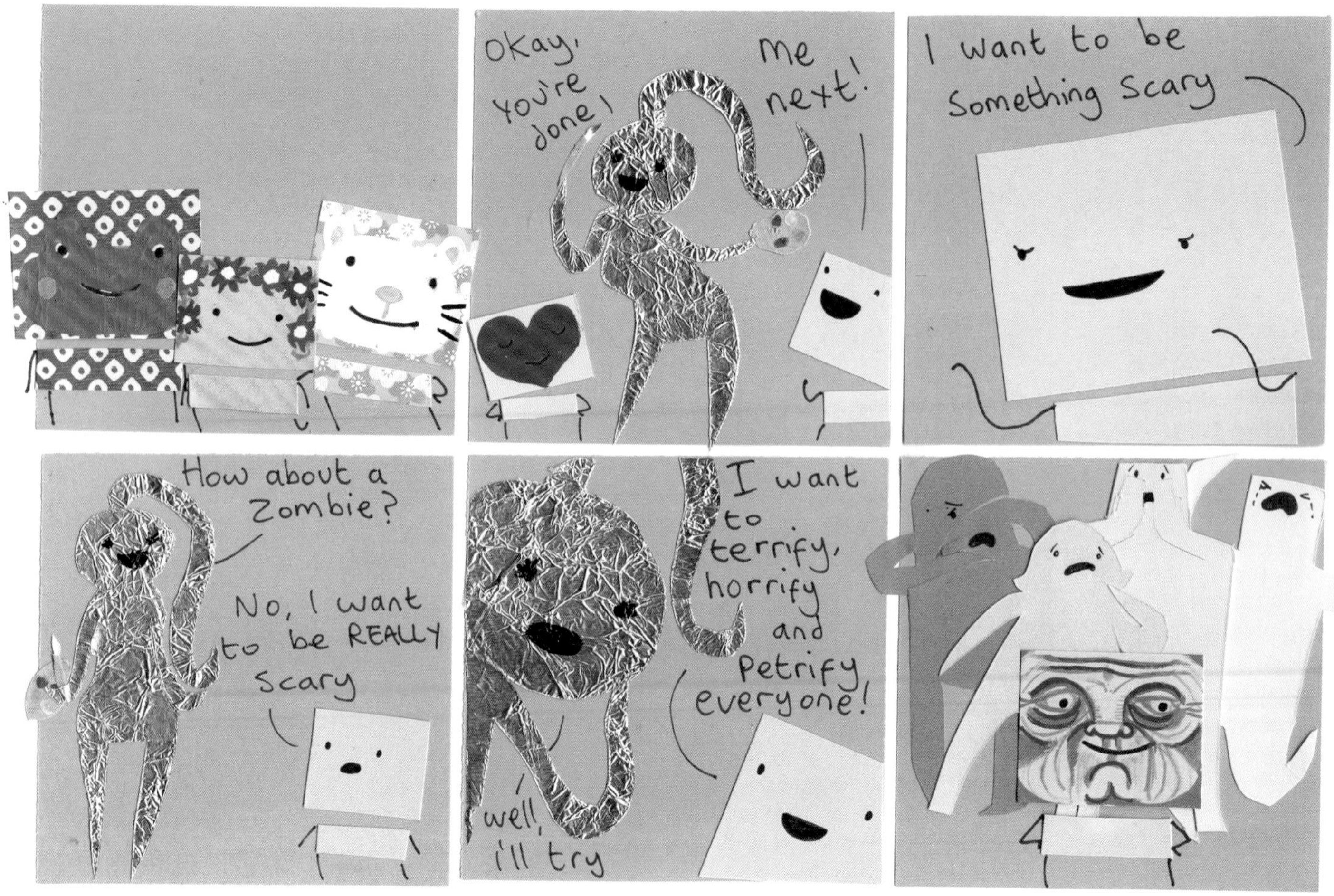

Okay, you're done!
Me next!
I want to be something scary
How about a zombie?
No, I want to be REALLY scary
I want to terrify, horrify and petrify everyone!
well, i'll try

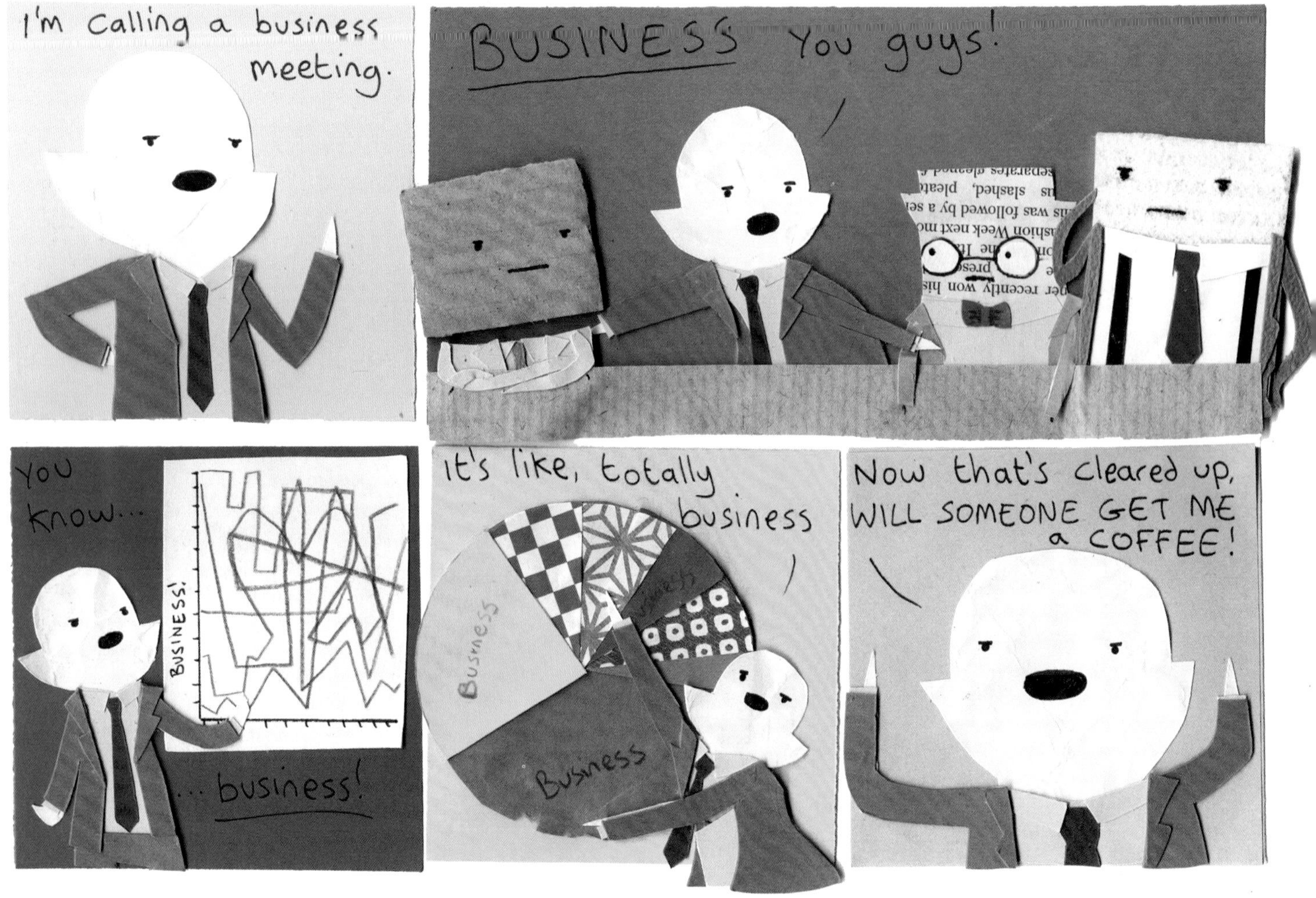

I'm calling a business meeting.
BUSINESS you guys!
You know...
BUSINESS!
...business!
It's like, totally business
Business
Business
Now that's cleared up, WILL SOMEONE GET ME a COFFEE!

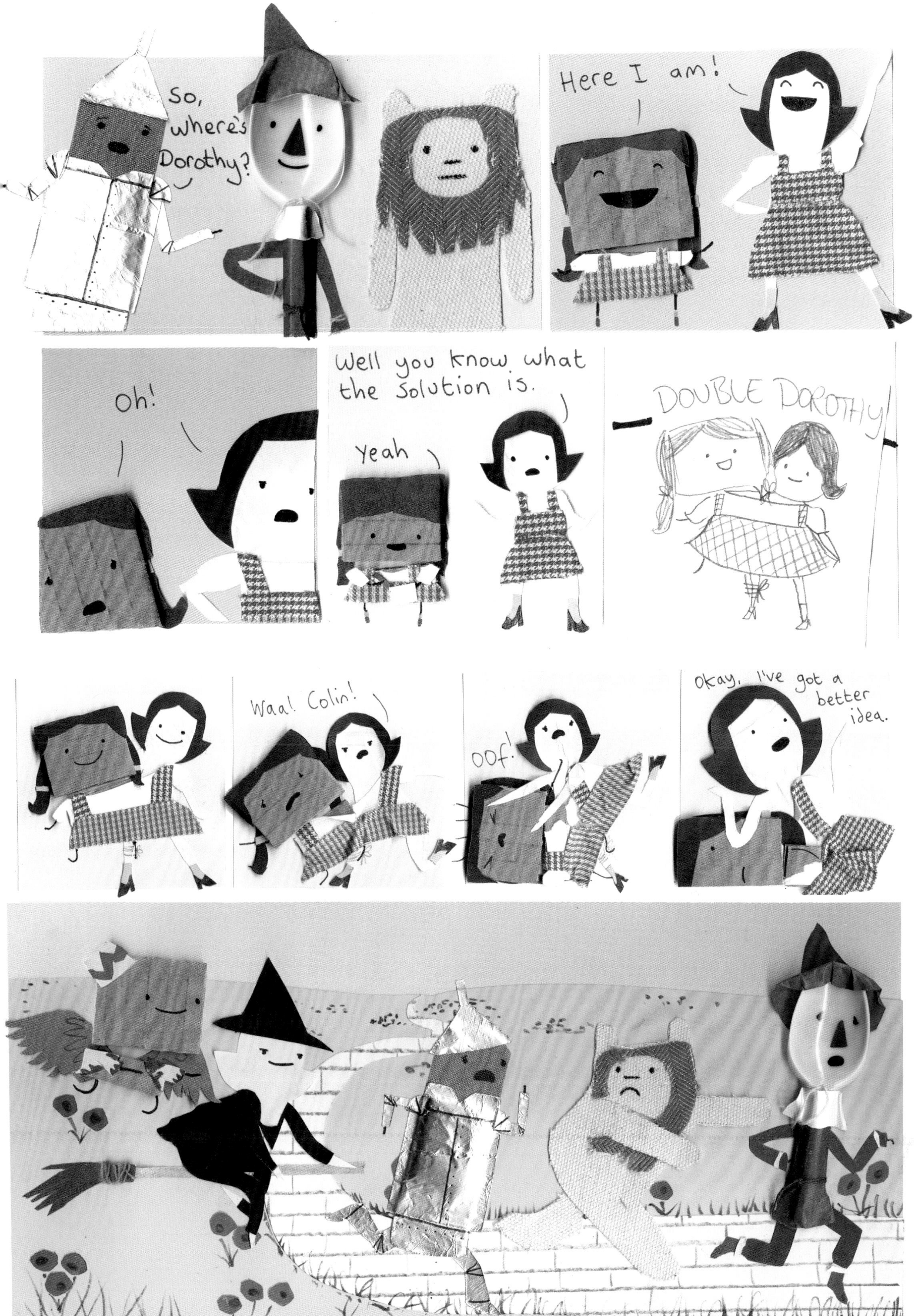

So, where's Dorothy?
Here I am!
Oh!
Well you know what the solution is.
Yeah
DOUBLE DOROTHY
Waa! Colin!
oof!
Okay, I've got a better idea.

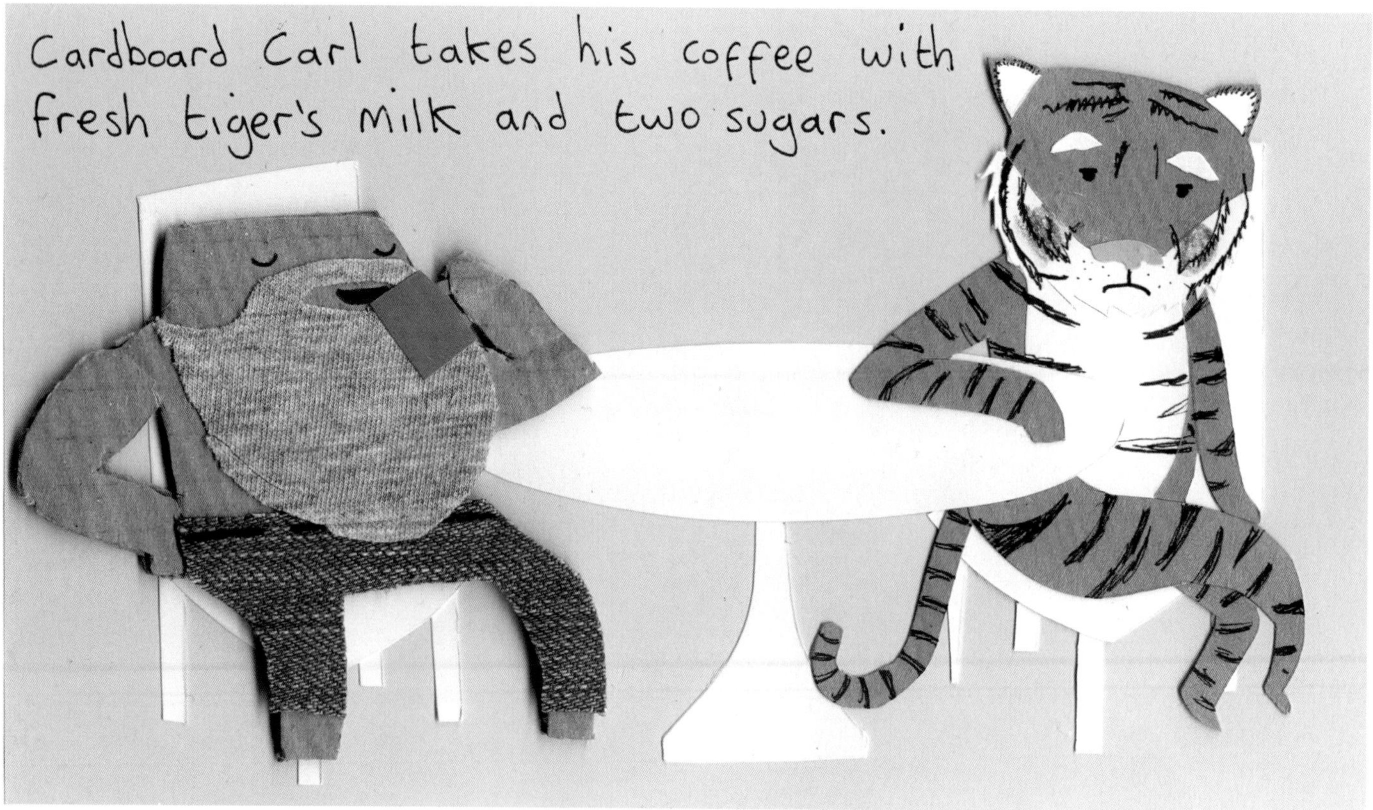
Cardboard Carl takes his coffee with fresh tiger's milk and two sugars.

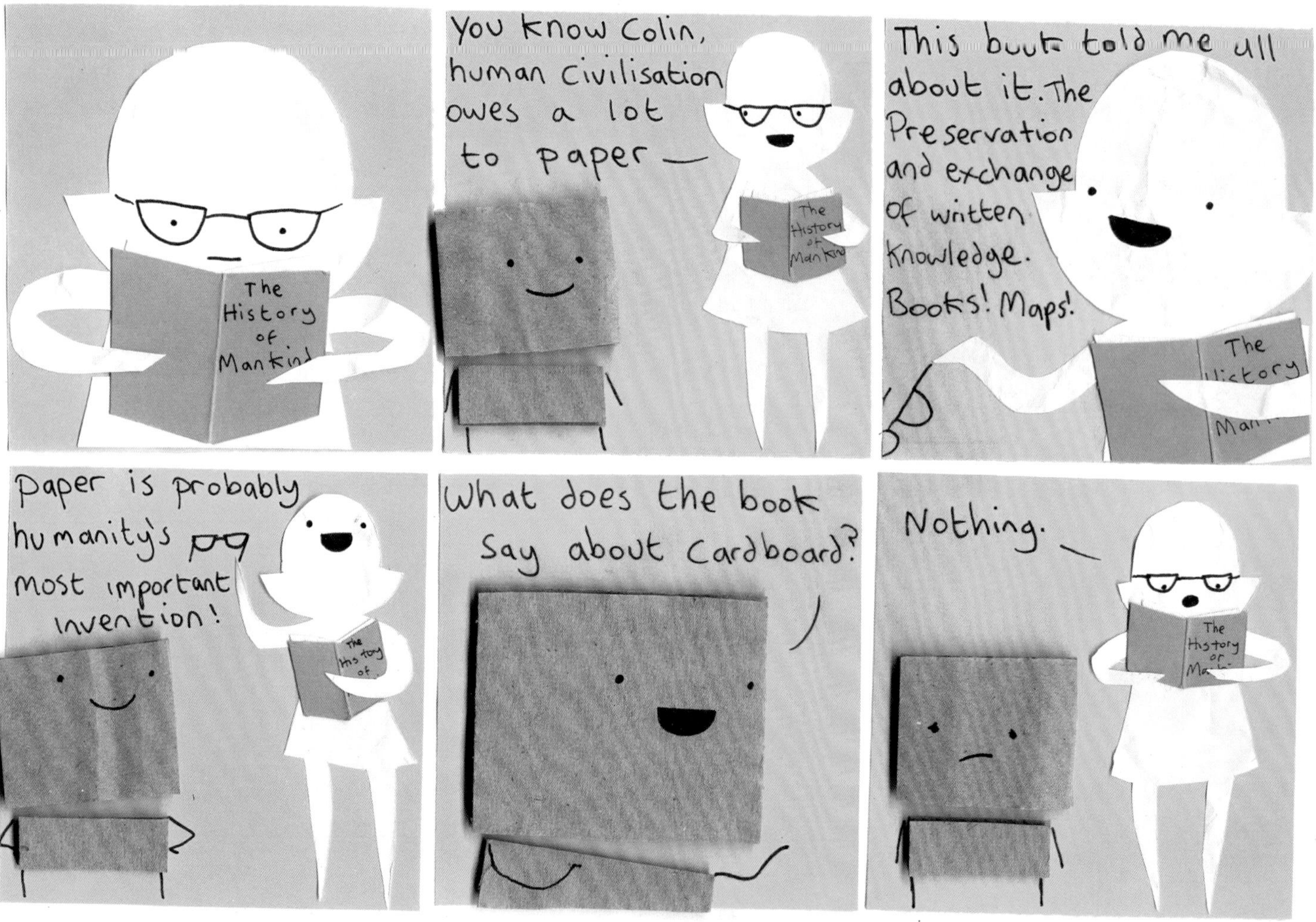
The History of Mankind
You know Colin, human Civilisation owes a lot to paper—
The History of Mankind
This book told me all about it. The Preservation and exchange of written knowledge. Books! Maps!
The History
Paper is probably humanity's most important invention!
The History of
What does the book say about Cardboard?
Nothing.
The History of

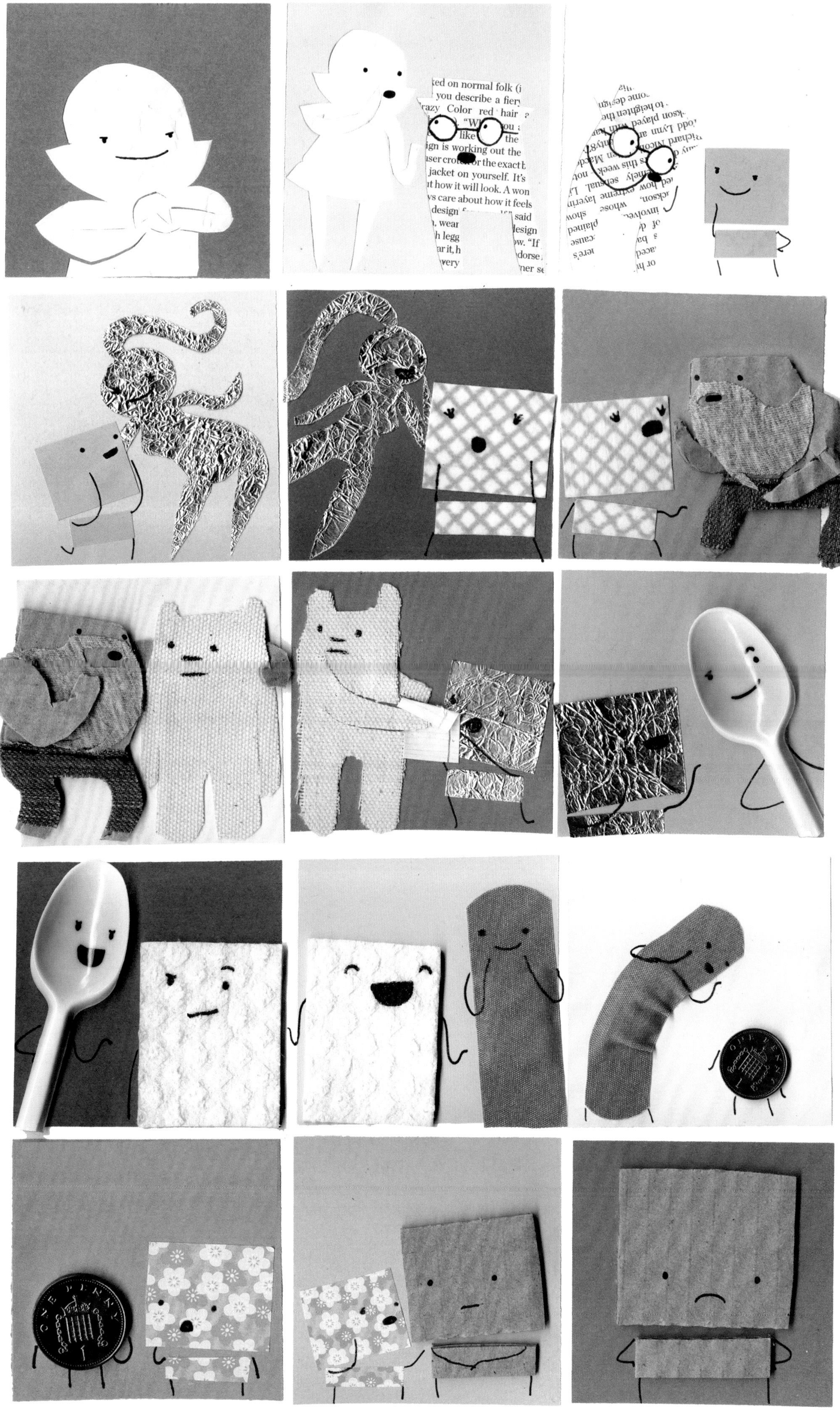

ked on normal folk (i
you describe a fiery
razy Color red hair
sign is working out the
jacket on yourself. It's
t how it will look. A won
ys care about how it feels
ONE PENNY

Cardboard Carl uses a Panther as a towel

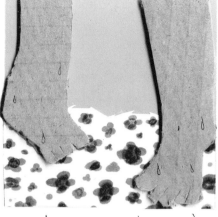

and a snow leopard as a bathmat.

His hair-towel is a Cheetah

Cardboard Carl's hand towel is a lynx

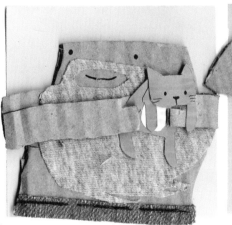

he uses a domestic cat as a flannel

and a kitten as a cotton ball.

let's play Grown Ups!

OU Oh im all grown up. I'm going out to buy some curtains

Ring-ring. Grown up here. No I don't need a new telephone thank you

You know, I actually AM a grown up.

Ha ha! That's just what a grown up would say!

Yeah but I really am

oh yes, me too me too. a real grown up!

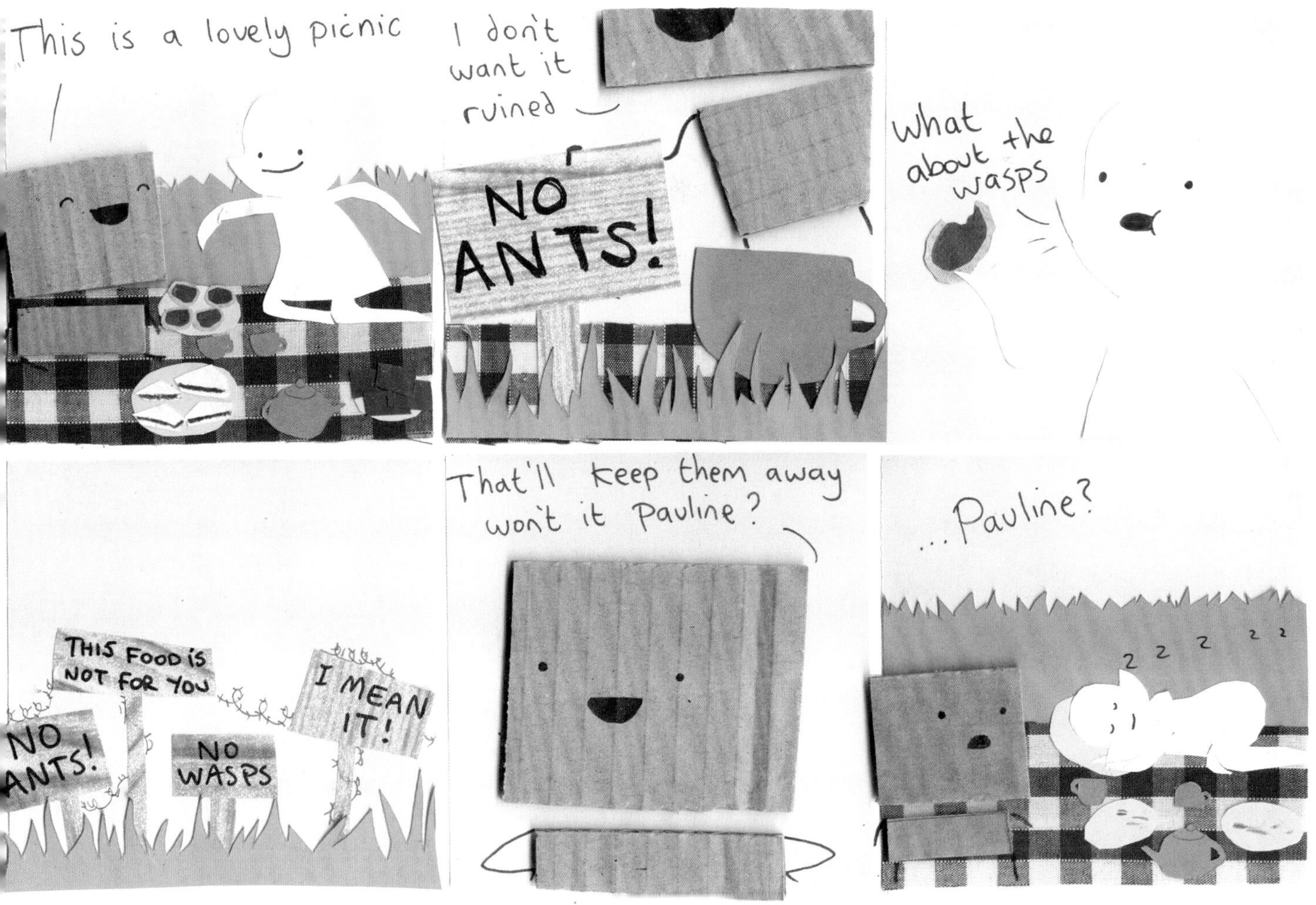
This is a lovely picnic
I don't want it ruined
NO ANTS!
What about the wasps
THIS FOOD IS NOT FOR YOU
NO ANTS!
NO WASPS
I MEAN IT!
That'll keep them away won't it Pauline?
...Pauline?
z z z z z z

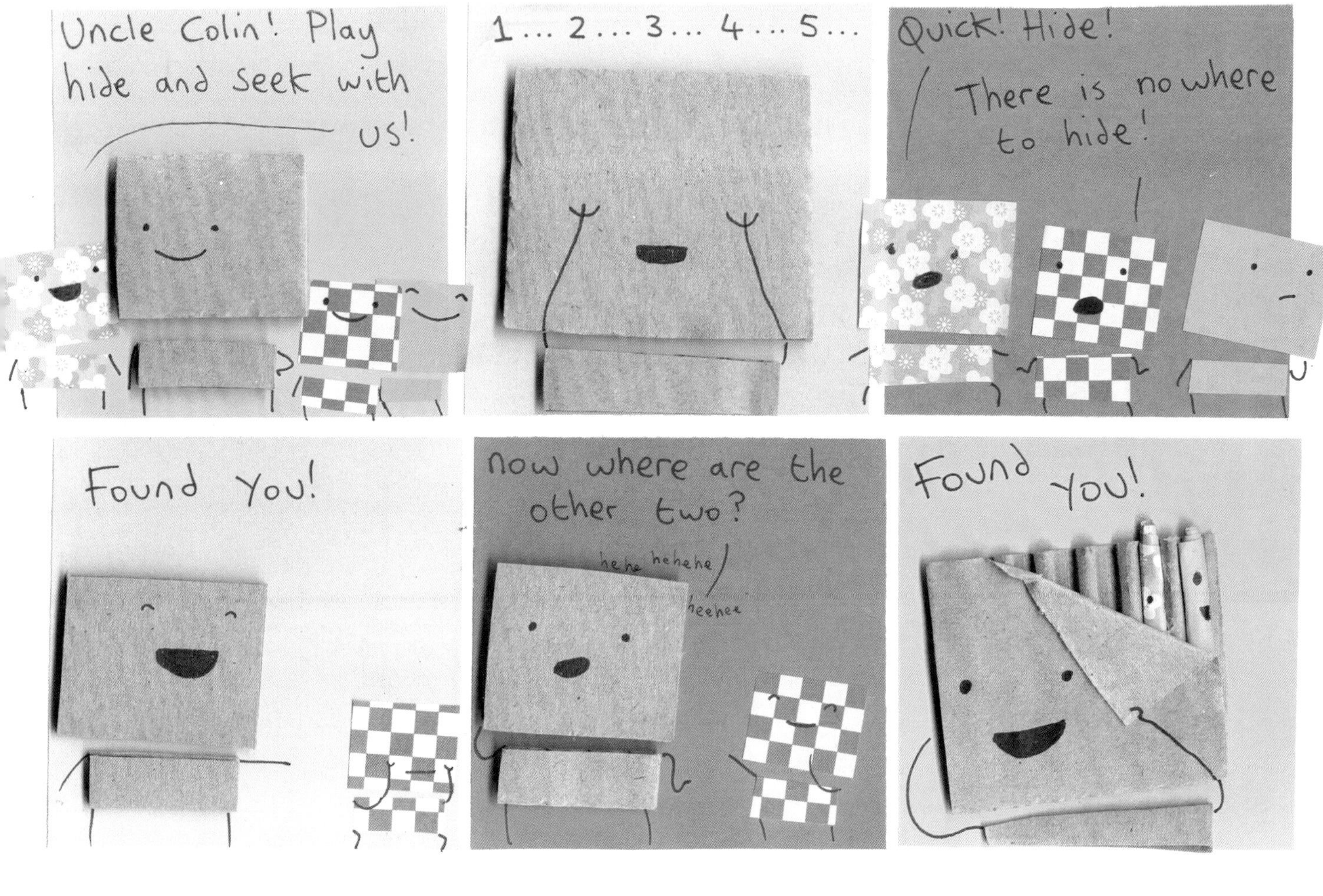
Uncle Colin! Play hide and seek with us!
1... 2... 3... 4... 5...
Quick! Hide!
There is nowhere to hide!
Found you!
now where are the other two?
hehe hehehe
heehee
Found you!

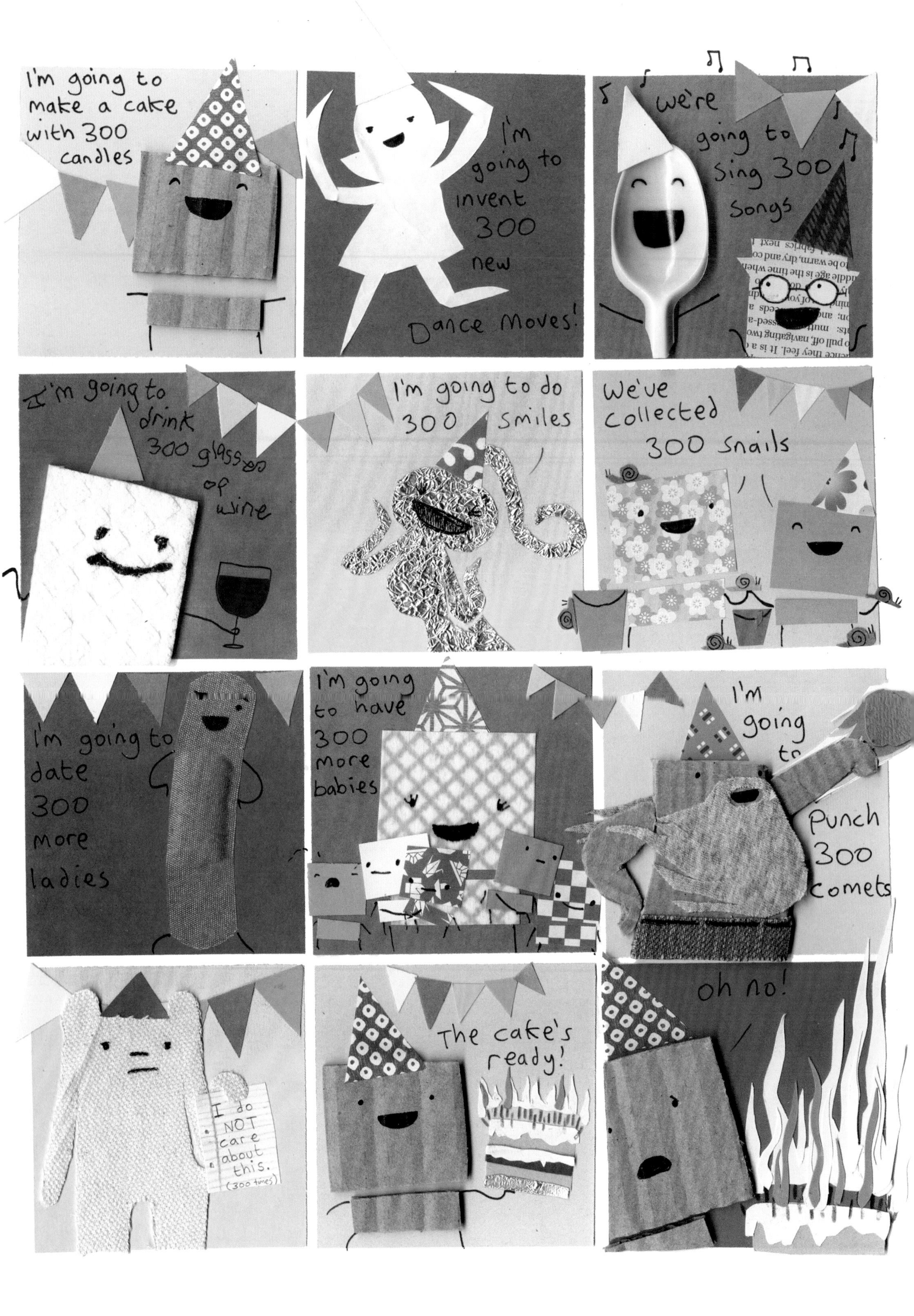
I'm going to make a cake with 300 candles
I'm going to invent 300 new Dance Moves!
We're going to sing 300 songs
I'm going to drink 300 glasses of wine
I'm going to do 300 smiles
We've collected 300 snails
I'm going to date 300 more ladies
I'm going to have 300 more babies
I'm going to Punch 300 comets
I do NOT care about this. (300 times)
The cake's ready!
oh no!

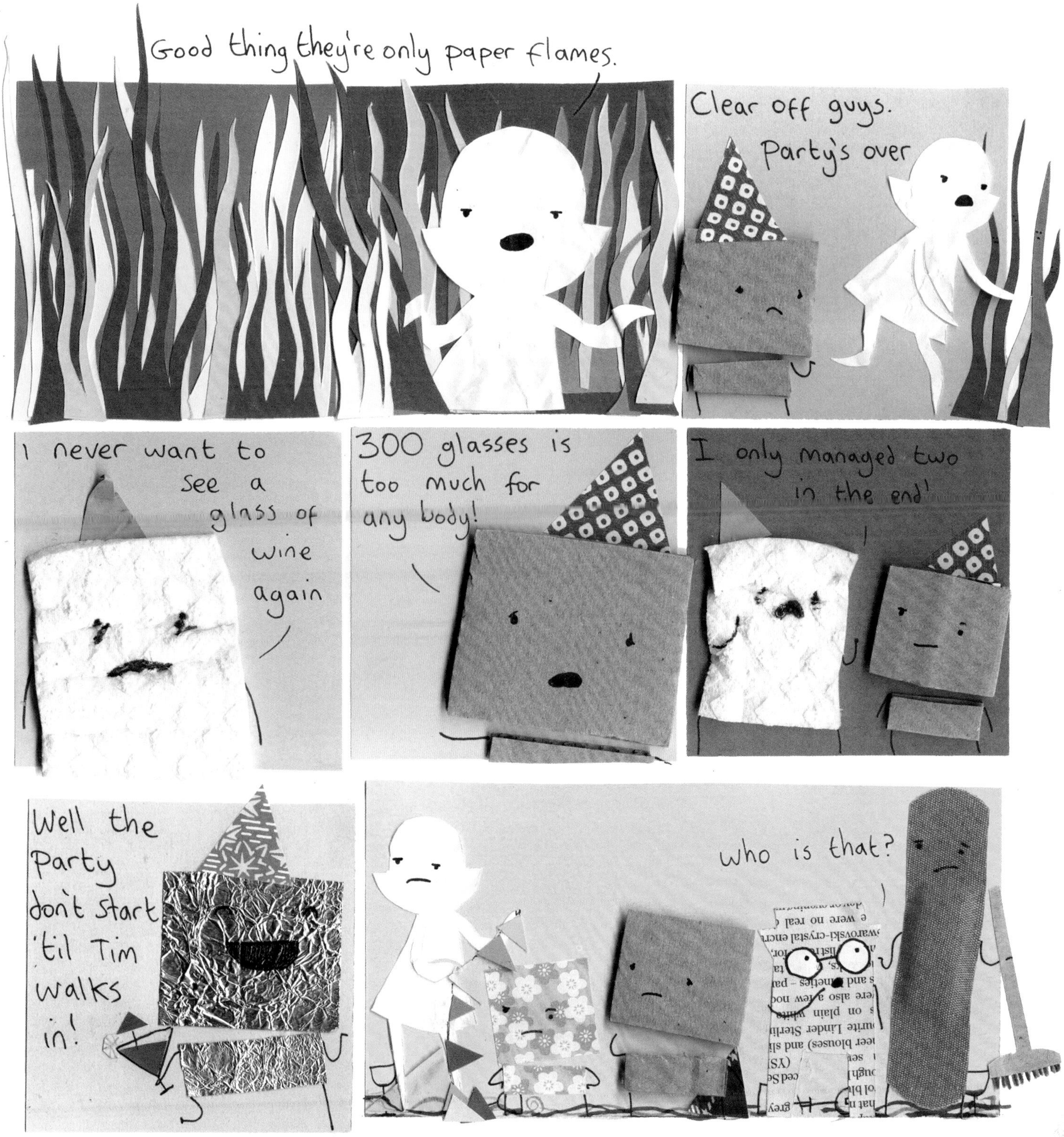
Good thing they're only paper flames.
Clear off guys. Party's over
I never want to see a glass of wine again
300 glasses is too much for any body!
I only managed two in the end!
Well the Party don't start 'til Tim walks in!
who is that?

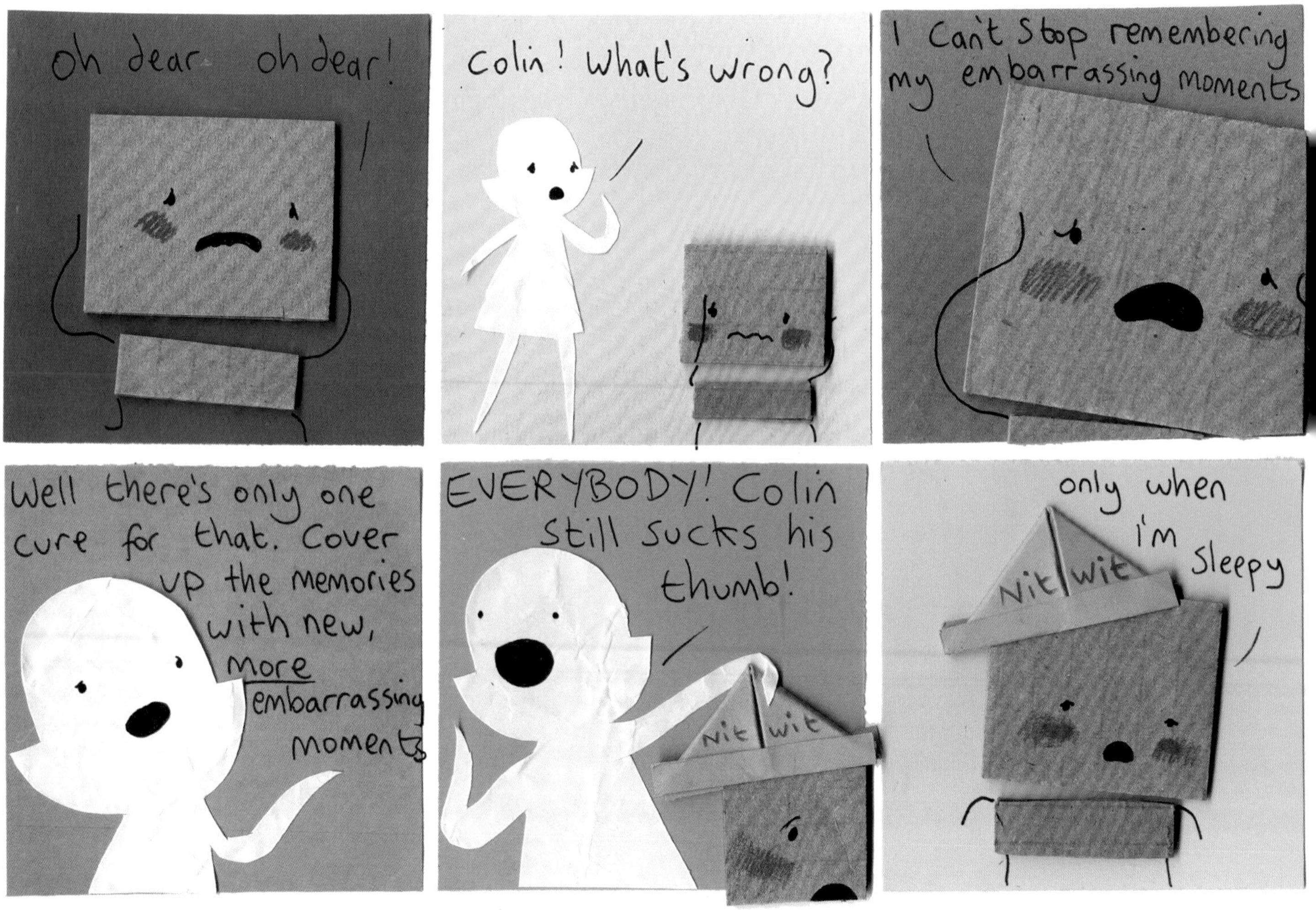
oh dear oh dear!
Colin! What's wrong?
I can't stop remembering my embarrassing moments
Well there's only one cure for that. Cover up the memories with new, more embarrassing moments
EVERYBODY! Colin still sucks his thumb!
Nit wit
only when I'm sleepy
Nit wit

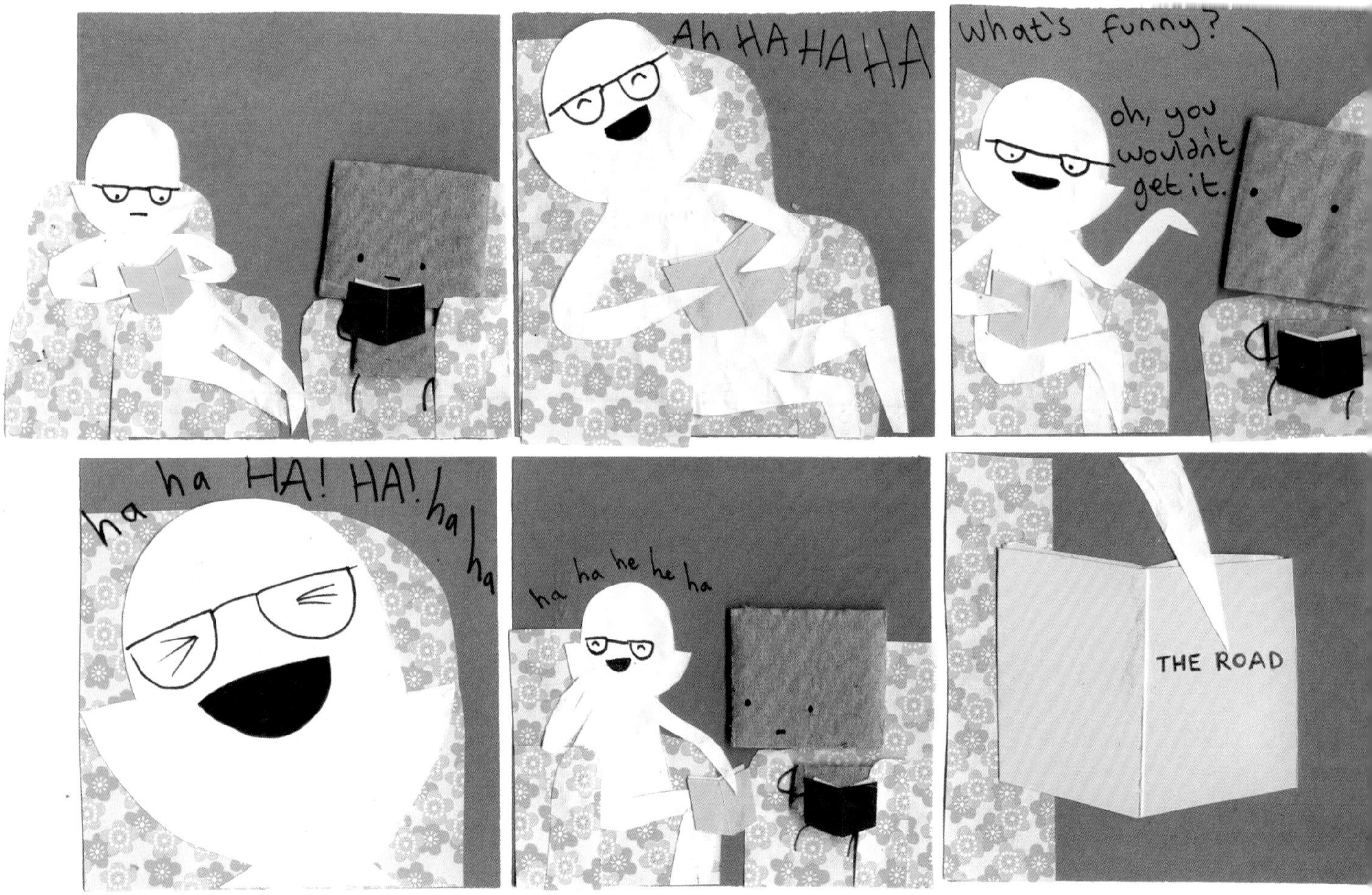
Ah HA HA HA
what's funny?
oh, you wouldn't get it.
ha ha HA! HA! ha ha ha
ha ha he he ha
THE ROAD

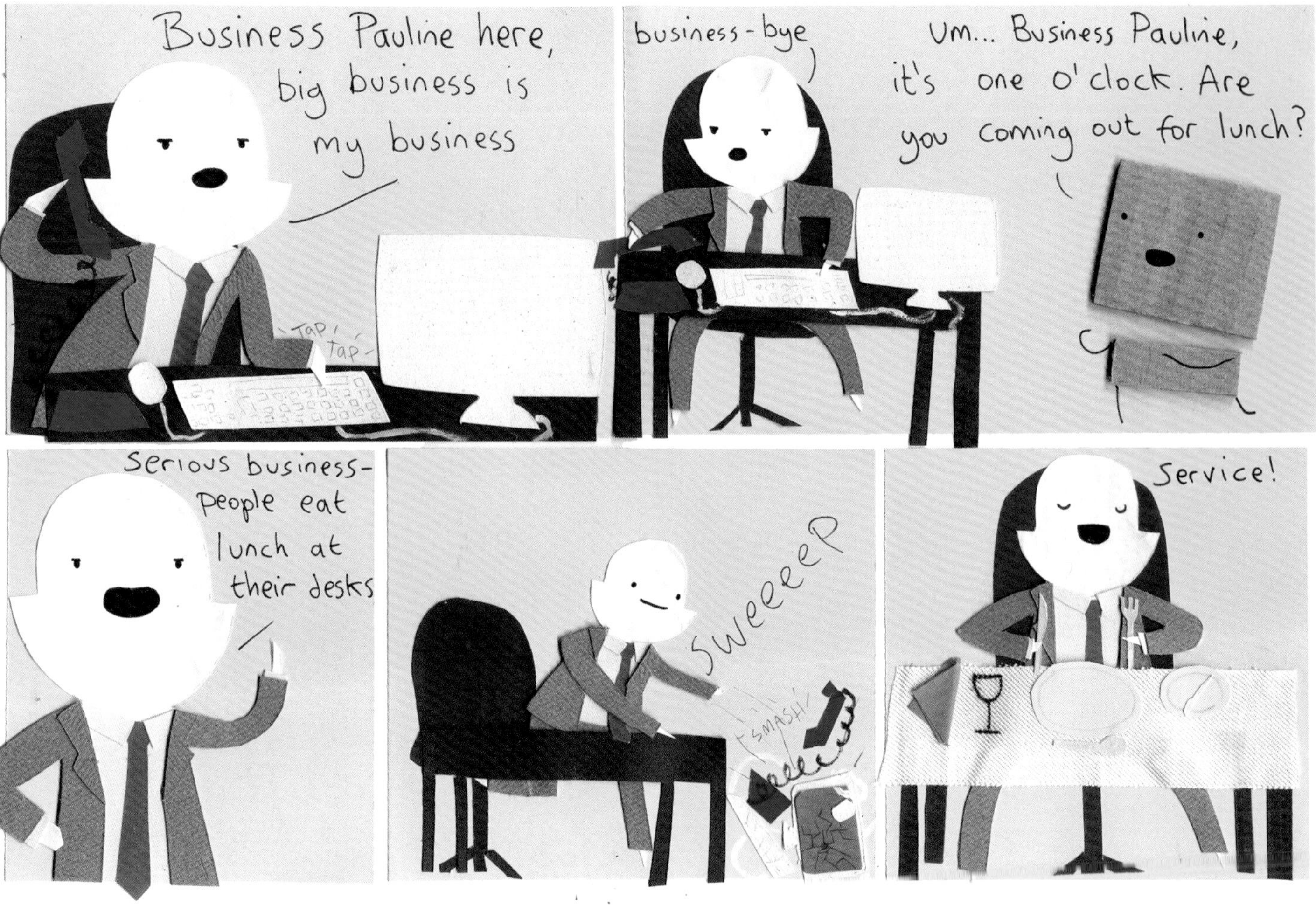
Business Pauline here, big business is my business
TAP! TAP!
business-bye
Um... Business Pauline, it's one o'clock. Are you coming out for lunch?
Serious business-people eat lunch at their desks
SWEEEEP
SMASH!
Service!

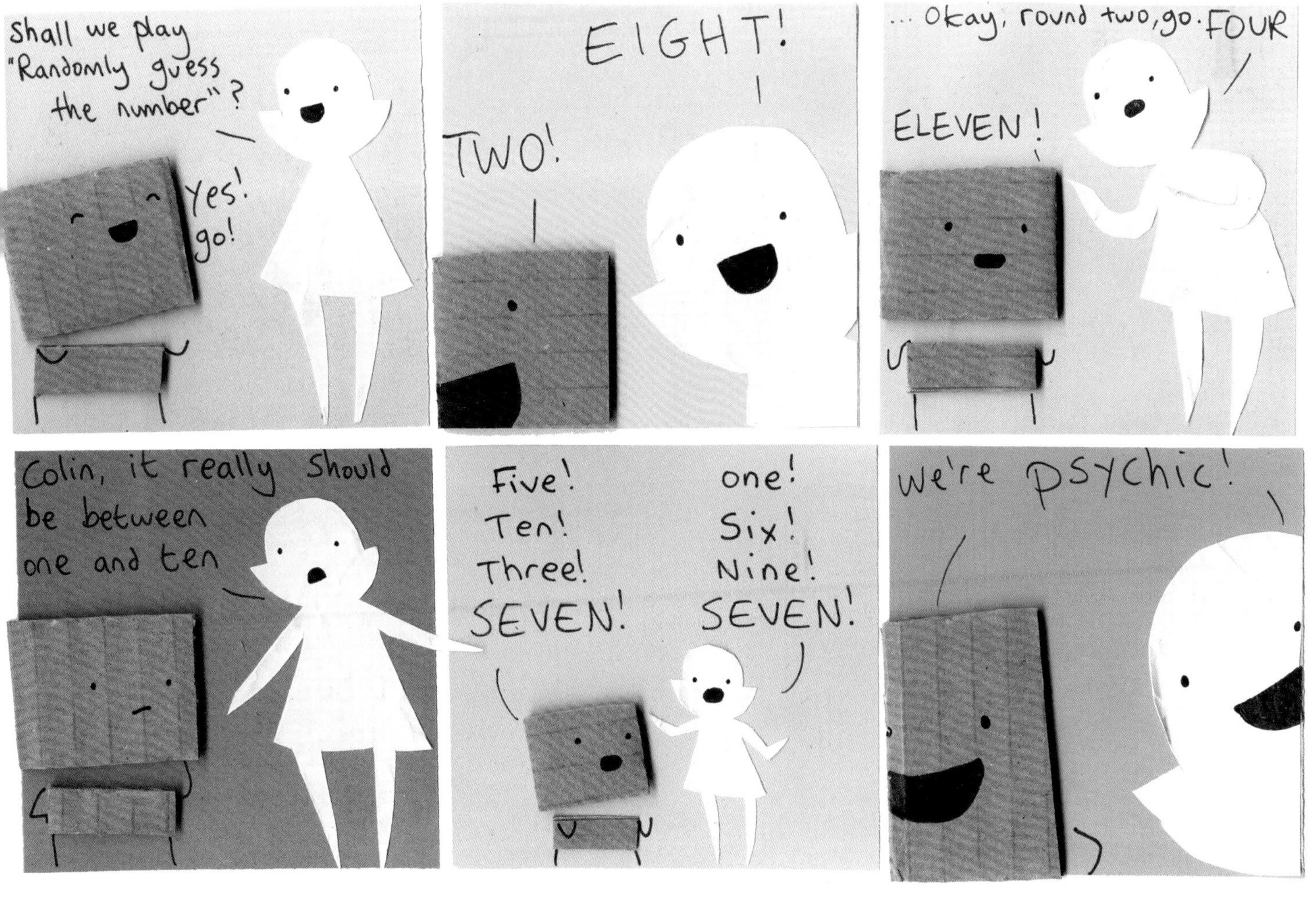
Shall we play "Randomly guess the number"?
Yes! go!
EIGHT!
TWO!
... Okay, round two, go.
FOUR
ELEVEN!
Colin, it really should be between one and ten
Five! Ten! Three! SEVEN!
one! Six! Nine! SEVEN!
we're psychic!

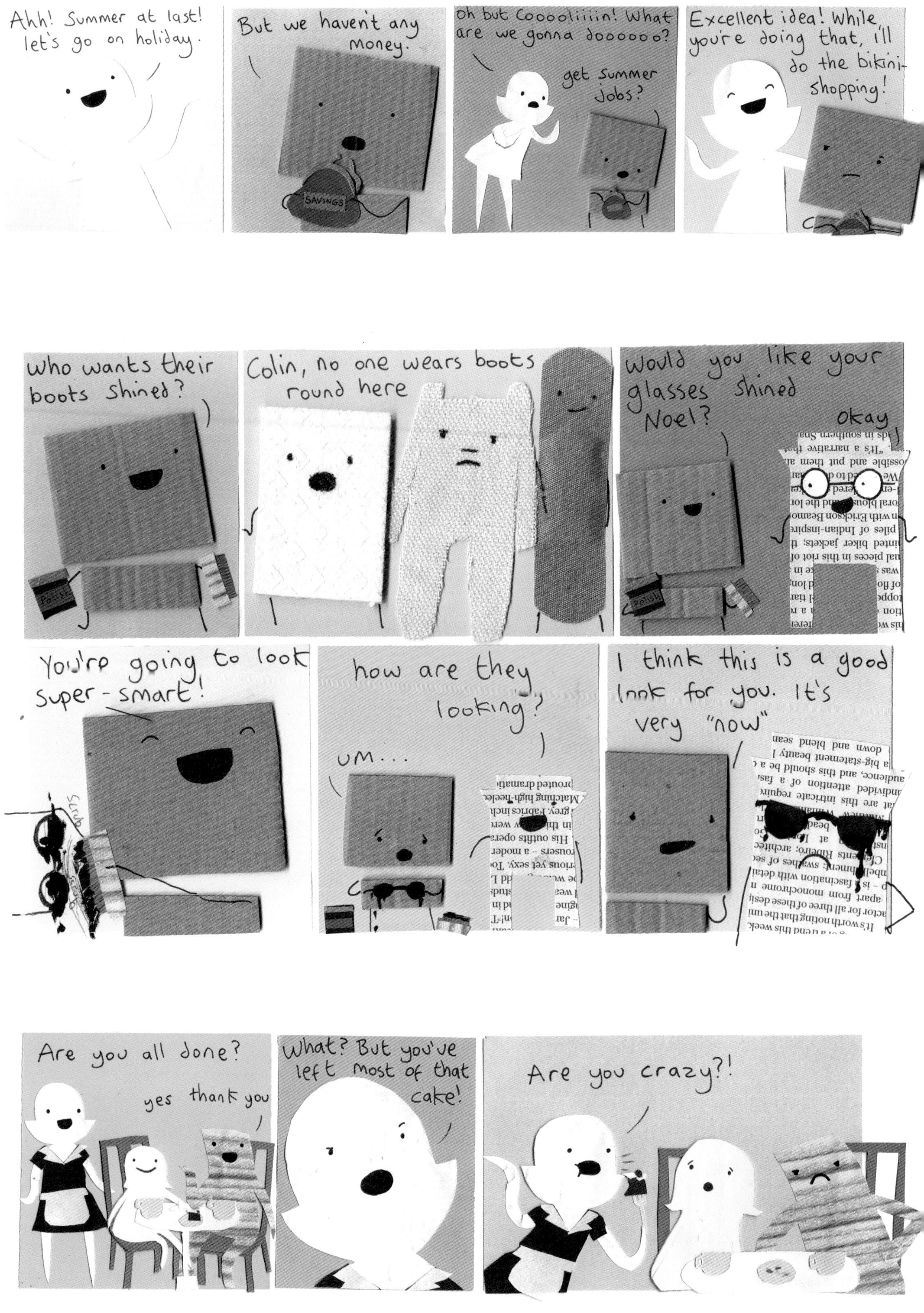
Ahh! Summer at last! let's go on holiday.
But we haven't any money.
SAVINGS
Oh but Coooooliiiiin! What are we gonna dooooooo?
get summer jobs?
Excellent idea! While you're doing that, I'll do the bikini-shopping!
who wants their boots shined?
Polish
Colin, no one wears boots round here
Would you like your glasses shined Noel?
Okay
Polish
You're going to look super-smart!
Scrub
how are they looking?
um...
I think this is a good look for you. It's very "now"
Are you all done?
yes thank you
What? But you've left most of that cake!
Are you crazy?!

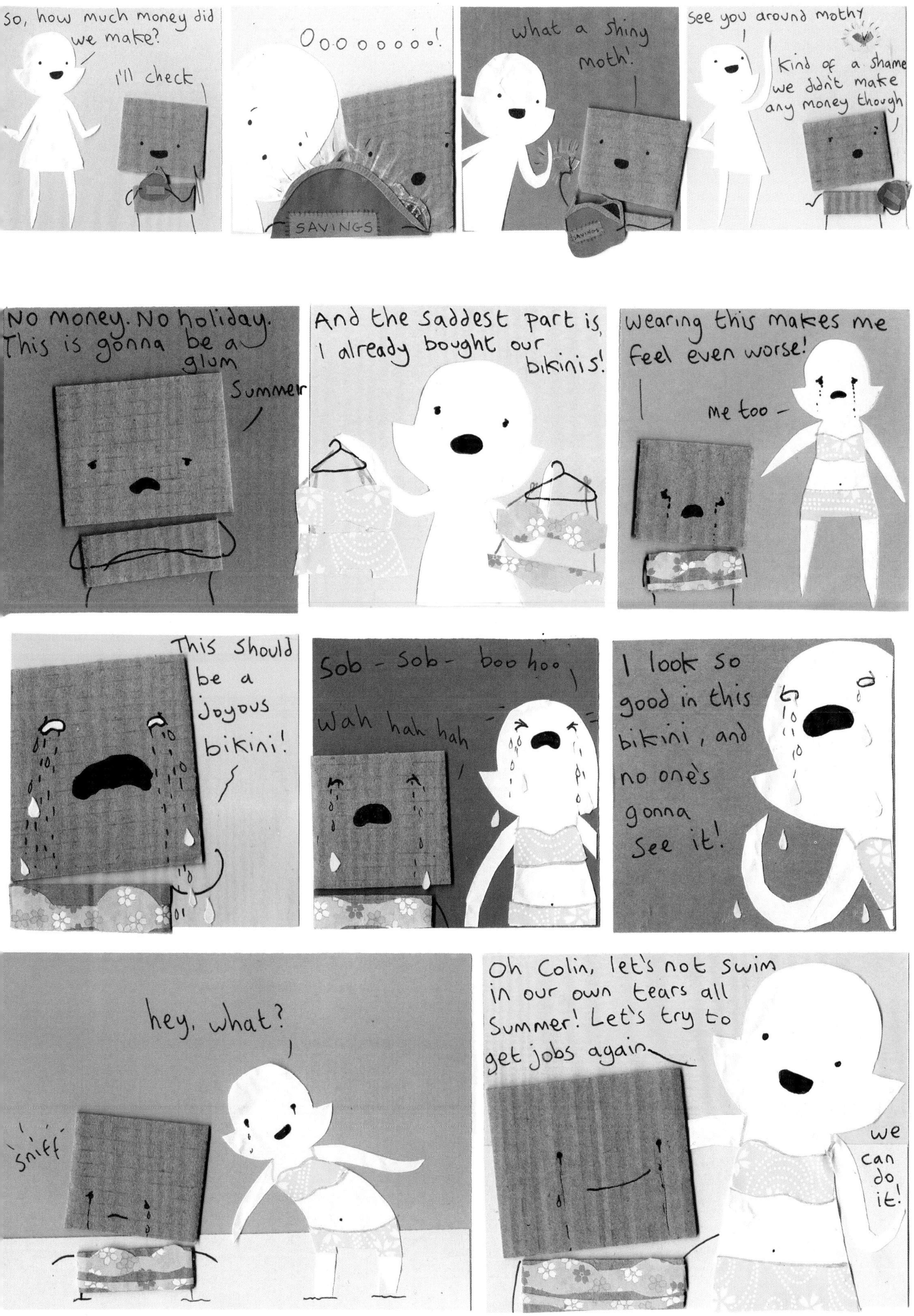
So, how much money did we make?
I'll check
Ooooooooo!
what a shiny moth!
See you around mothy
Kind of a shame we didn't make any money though
No money. No holiday. This is gonna be a glum Summer
And the saddest part is, I already bought our bikinis!
Wearing this makes me feel even worse!
me too
This should be a joyous bikini!
Sob - Sob - boo hoo
Wah hah hah
I look so good in this bikini, and no one's gonna see it!
hey, what?
sniff
Oh Colin, let's not swim in our own tears all Summer! Let's try to get jobs again
we can do it!

Dog Walking
- £5 per dog!
- exciting walking route!
- Pugs half price!

Baby-sitting
- £5 per baby!
- fine lullaby singing!
- well behaved kids half-price!

I'm going to help you today Doctor

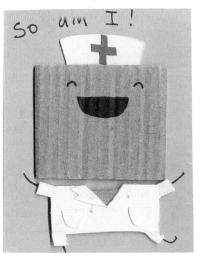

So um I!

Bob gings, it's my day off today!

maybe you've got some odd jobs we can do?

well,

Diagnosis creased!

diagnosis ugly!

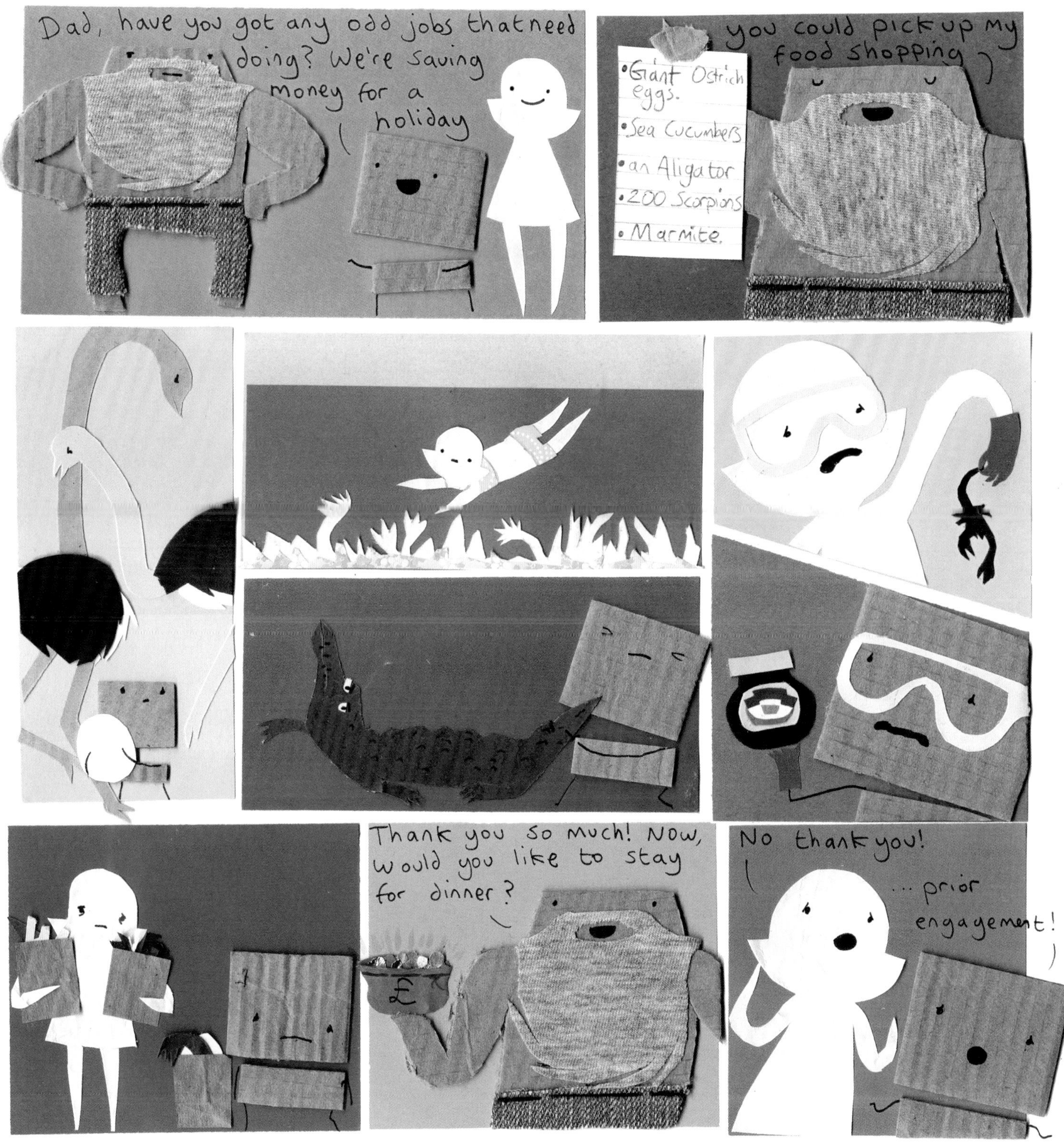

Dad, have you got any odd jobs that need doing? We're saving money for a holiday
You could pick up my food shopping
•Giant Ostrich eggs.
•Sea Cucumbers
•an Aligator
•200 Scorpions
•Marmite.
Thank you so much! Now, would you like to stay for dinner?
No thank you!
... prior engagement!

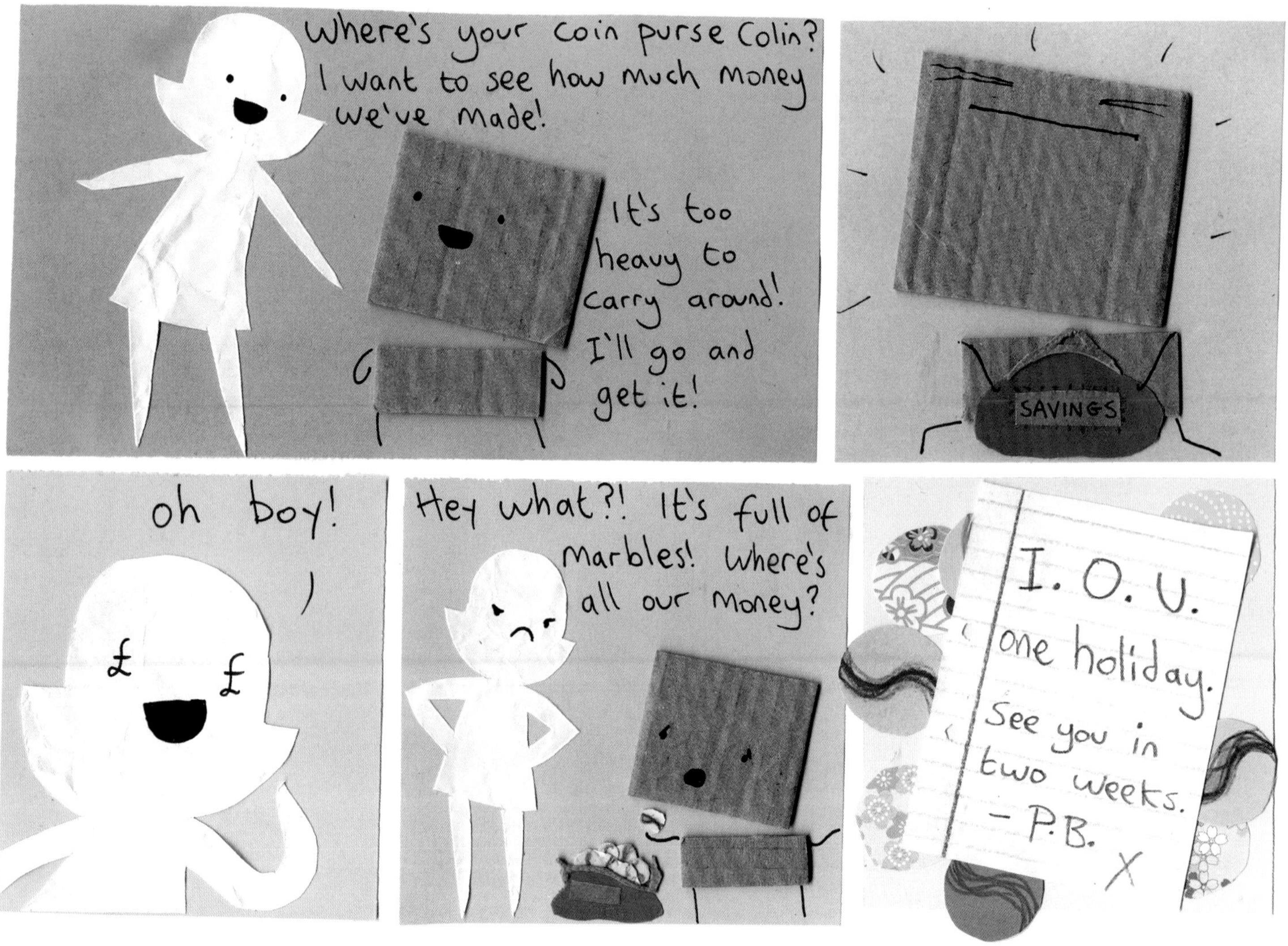
Where's your coin purse Colin? I want to see how much money we've made!
It's too heavy to carry around! I'll go and get it!
SAVINGS
oh boy!
Hey what?! It's full of marbles! Where's all our money?
I. O. U.
one holiday.
See you in two weeks.
- P.B.
X

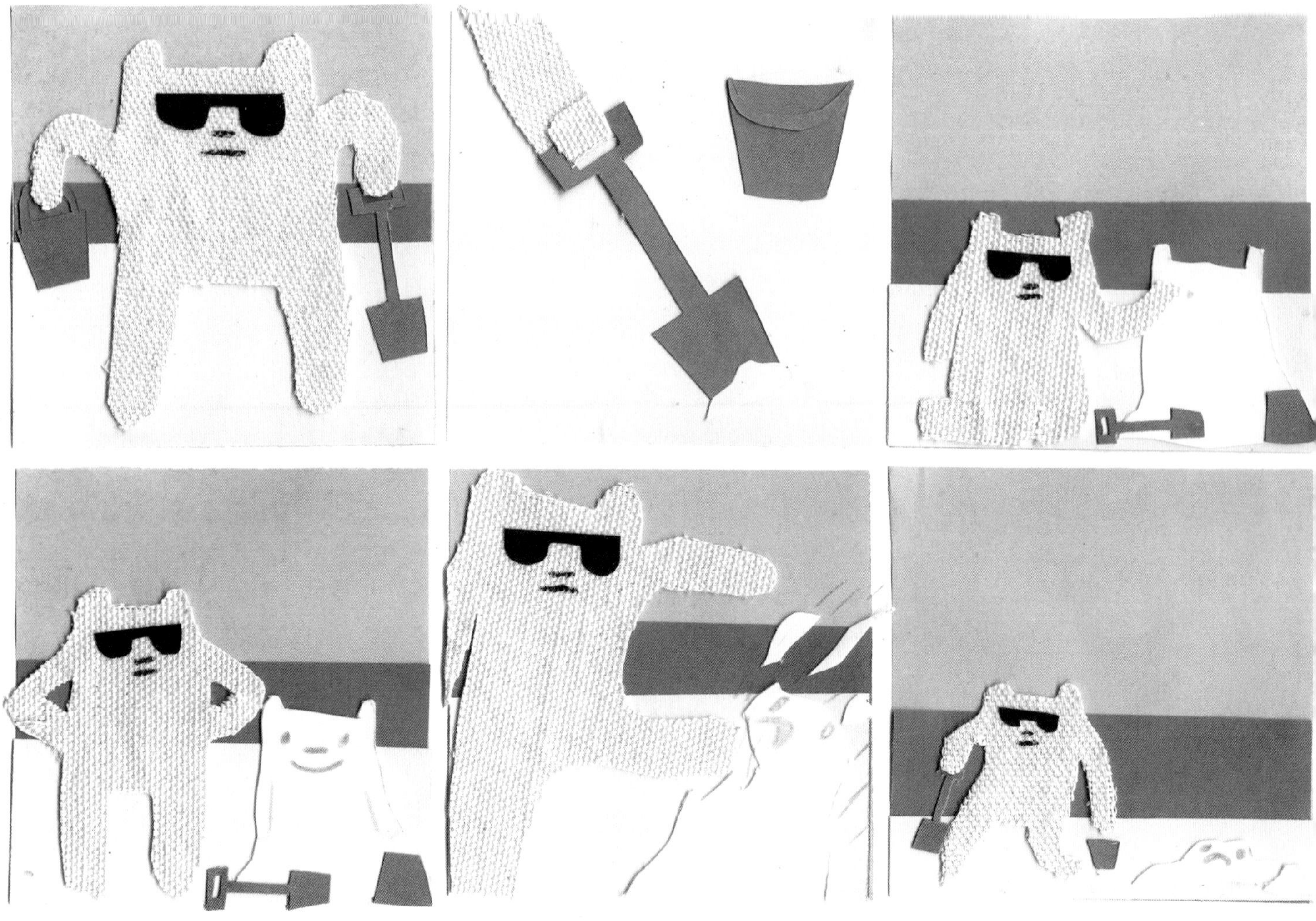

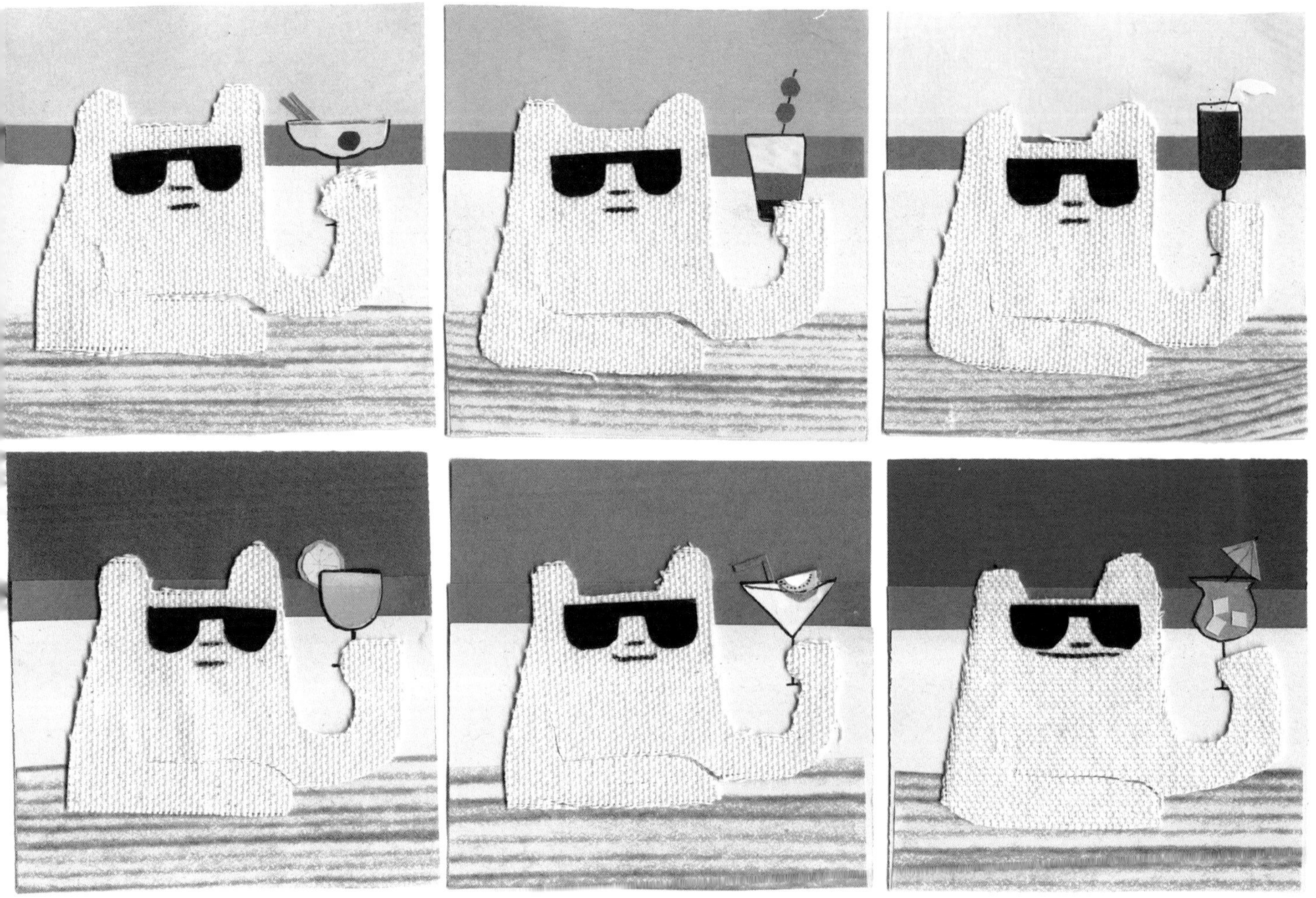

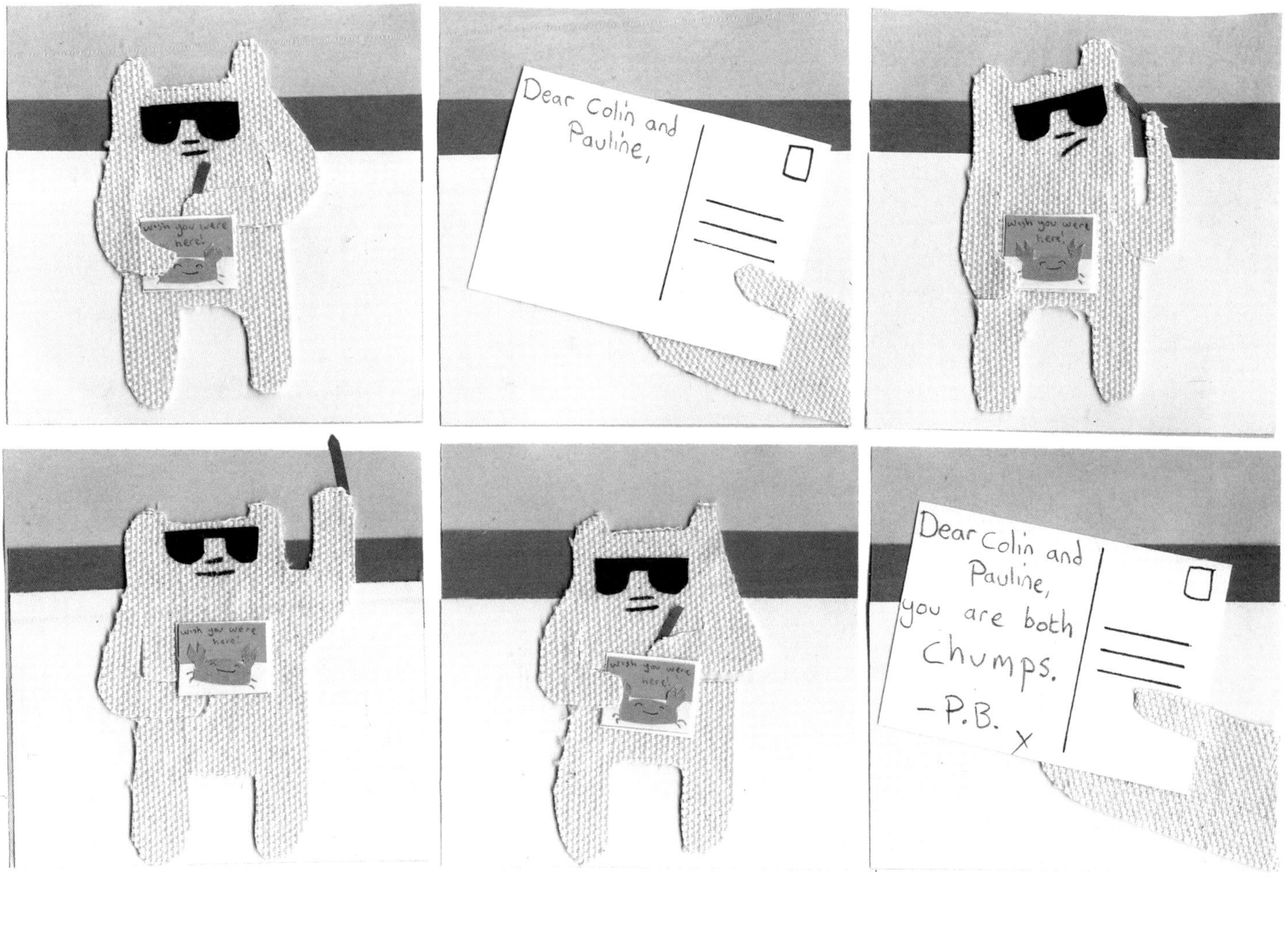
wish you were here!
Dear Colin and
Pauline,
wish you were here!
wish you were here!
wish you were here!
Dear Colin and
Pauline,
you are both
Chumps.
-P.B. x

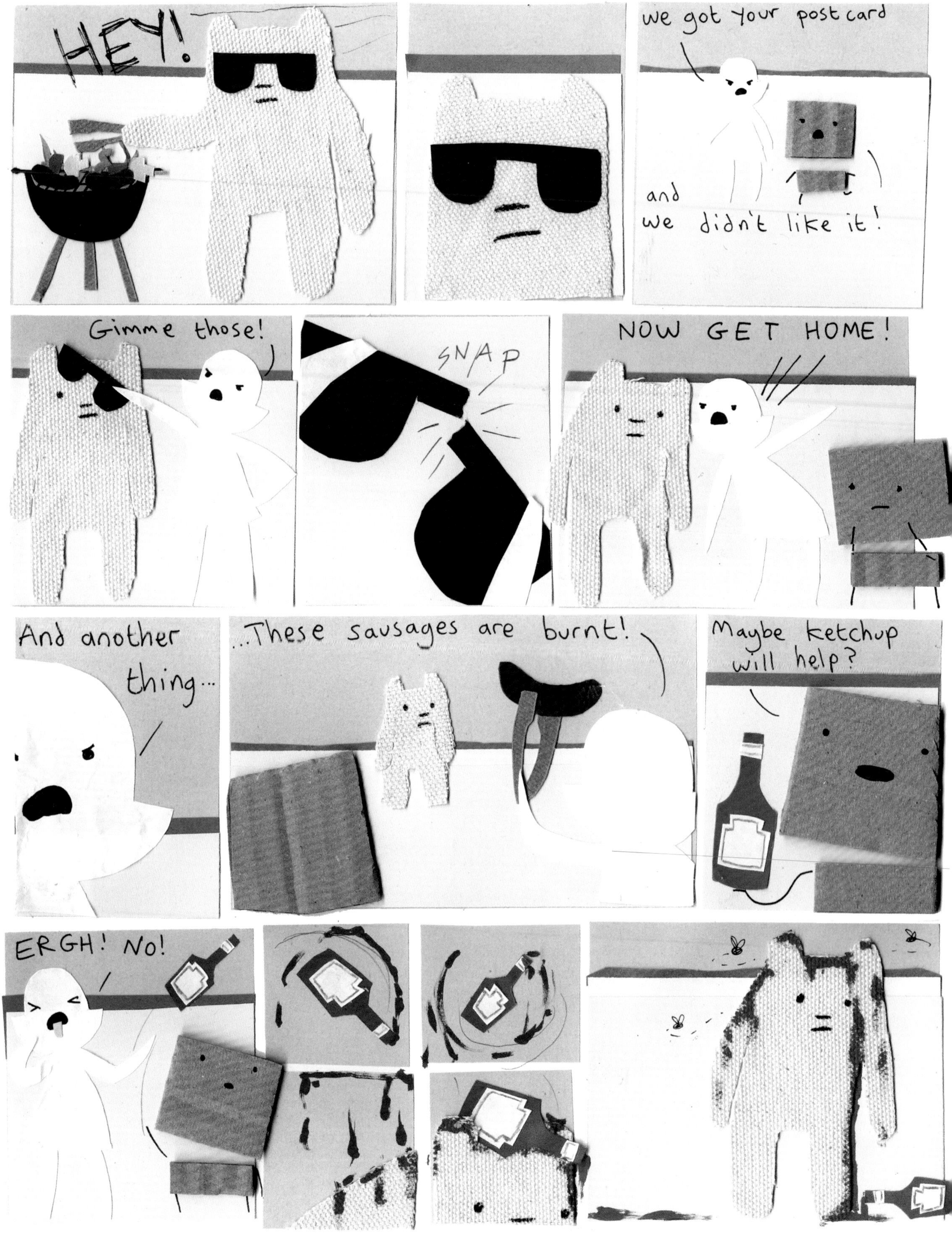
HEY!
we got your post card
and
we didn't like it!
Gimme those!
SNAP
NOW GET HOME!
And another thing...
...These sausages are burnt!
Maybe ketchup will help?
ERGH! NO!

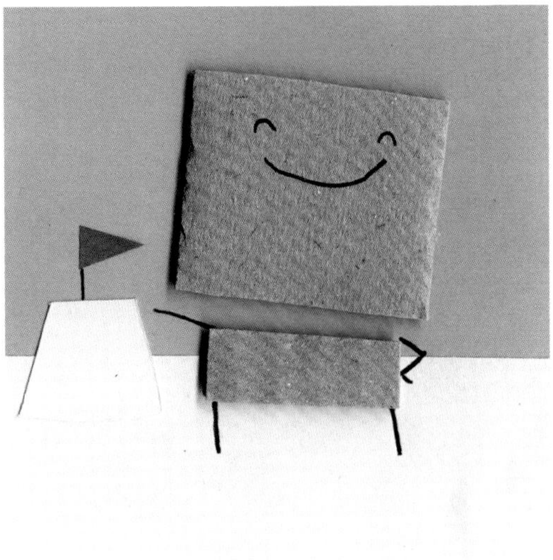
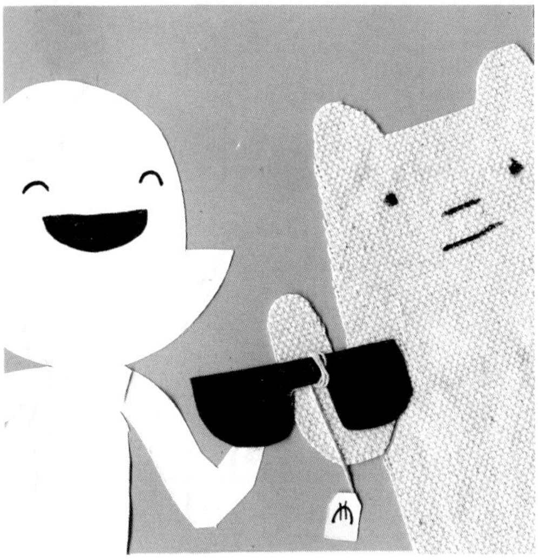
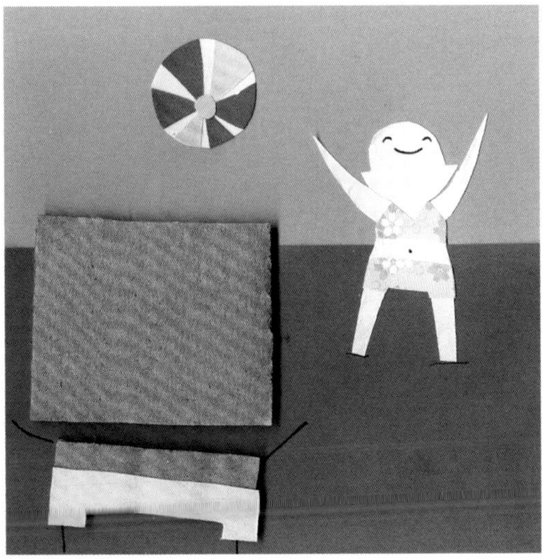
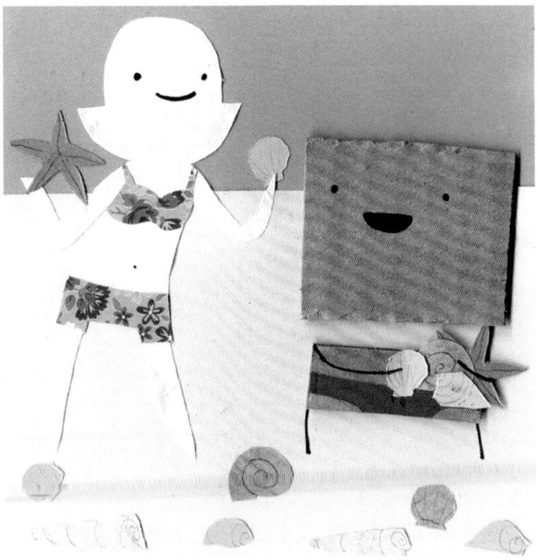
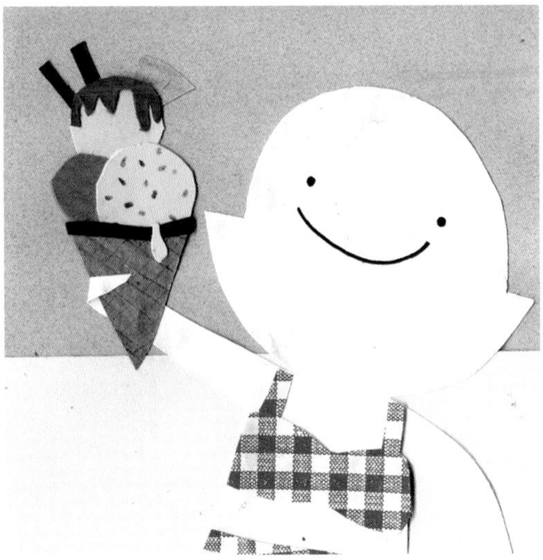
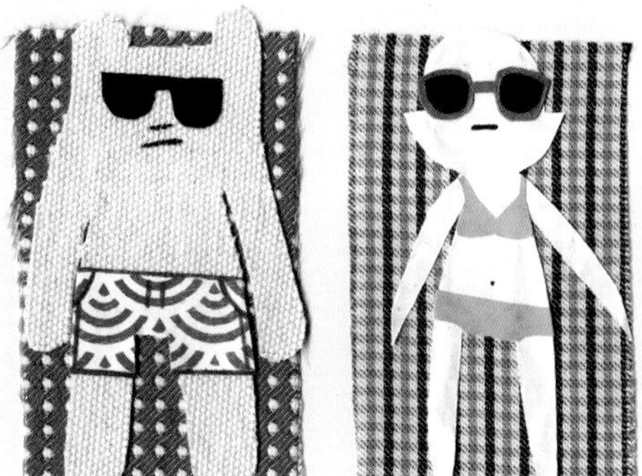
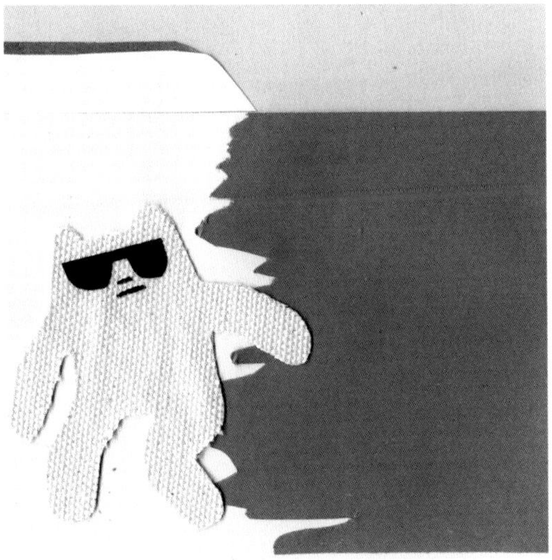
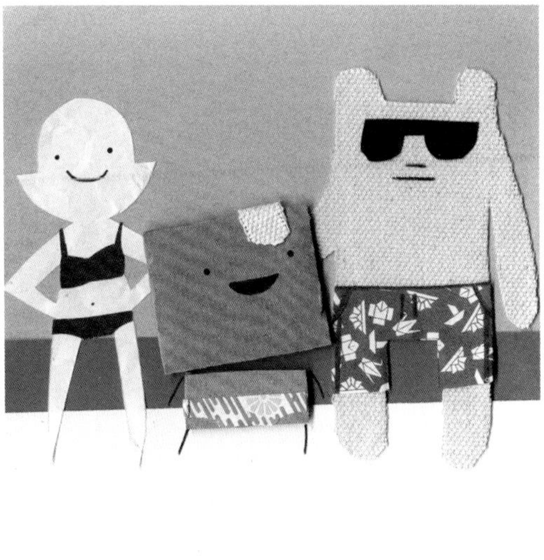

Bonus Material

CARDBOARD COLIN'S Family Tree

Granny Gingham
Grandpa Sponge

Nanna Crumples
Ted Wood

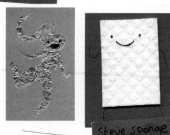

Silvia Foil
Steve Sponge

Trish Cloth

Cardboard Carl

Tim Foil

Janet

Cardboard Colin

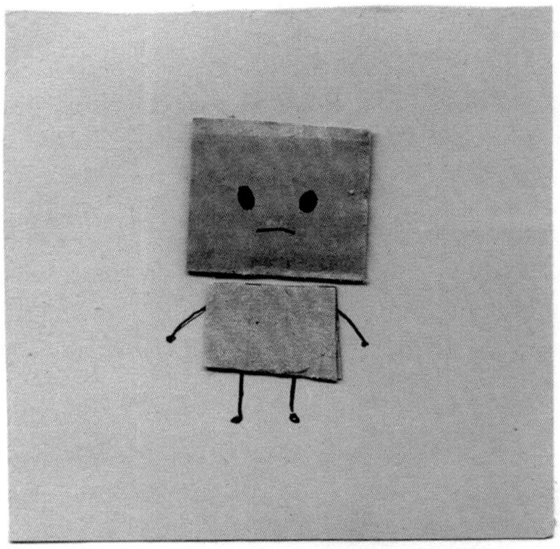

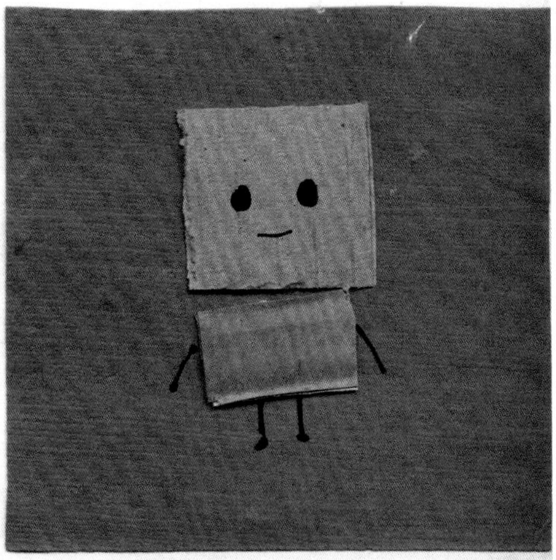

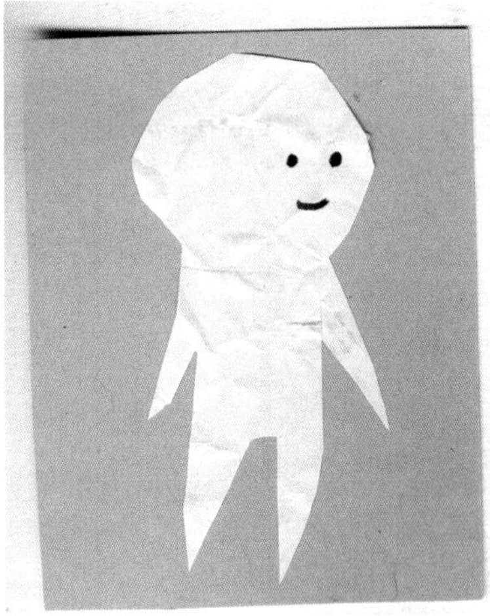

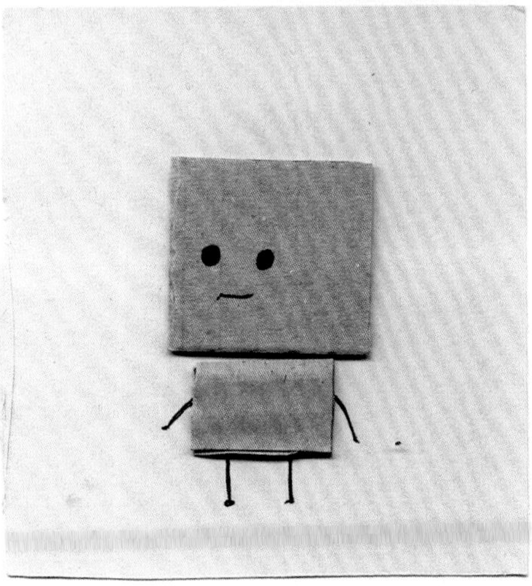

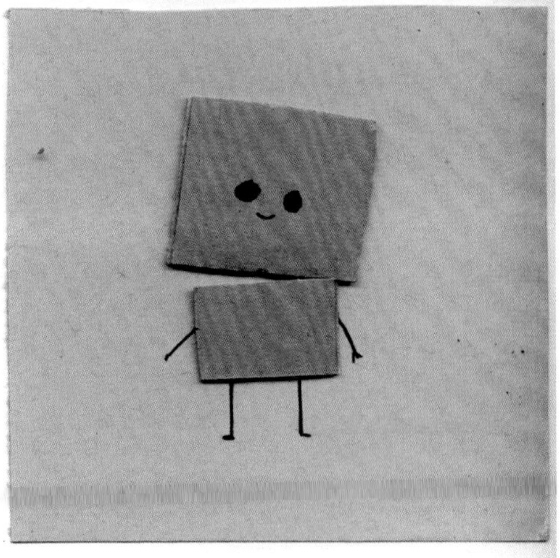

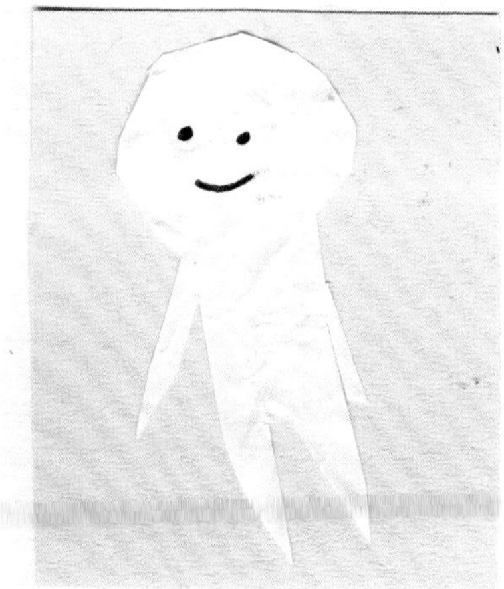

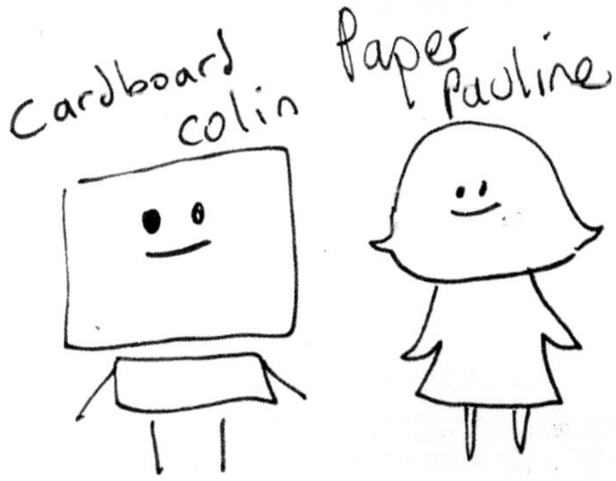
Cardboard colin
Paper Pauline

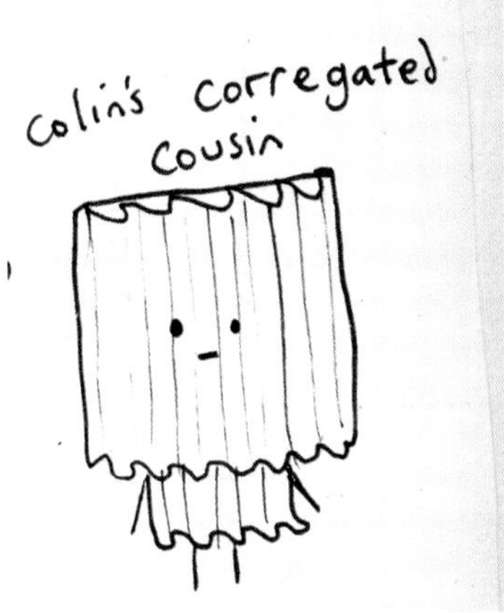
colin's corregated cousin

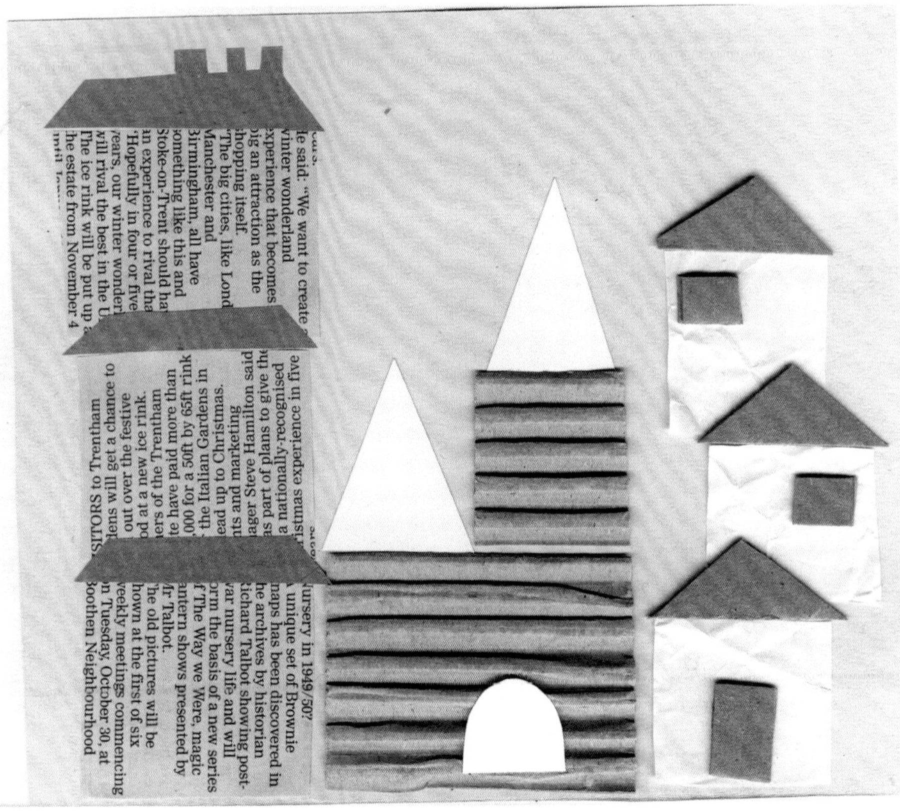

These were the initial designs for Cardboard Colin and Paper Pauline. Originally they were going to feature in a children's picture book about recycling.

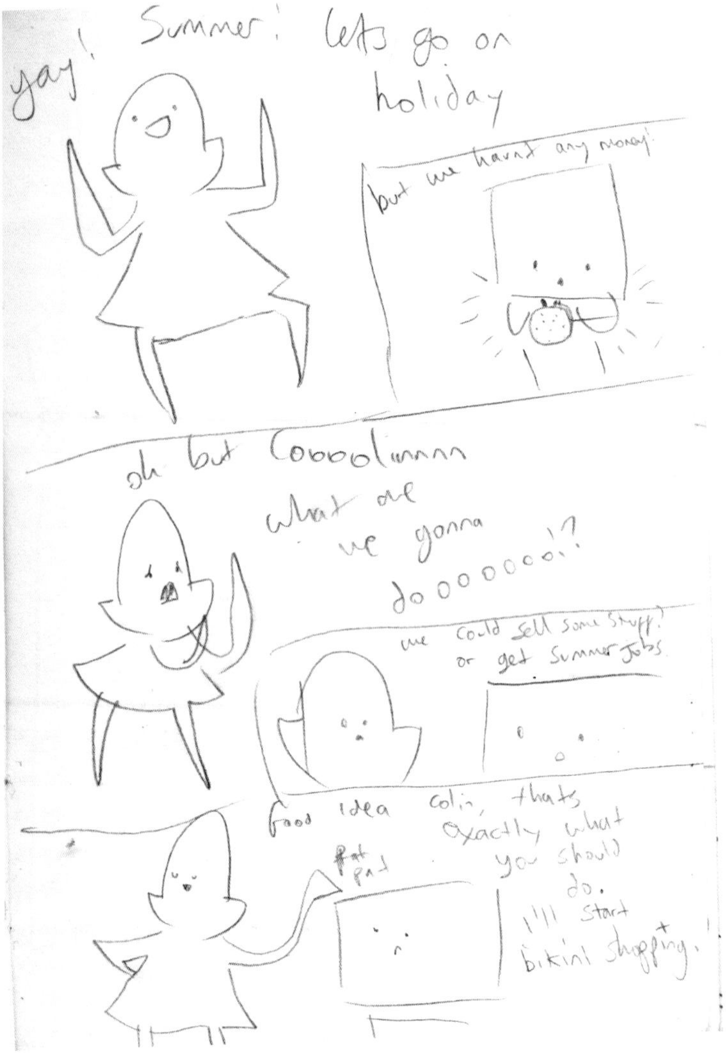
yay! Summer! lets go on holiday
but we havnt any money!
oh but Coooolinnnn what are we gonna dooooooo!?
we could sell some stuff? or get summer jobs
Good idea Colin, thats exactly what you should do. I'll start bikini shopping!
pat pat

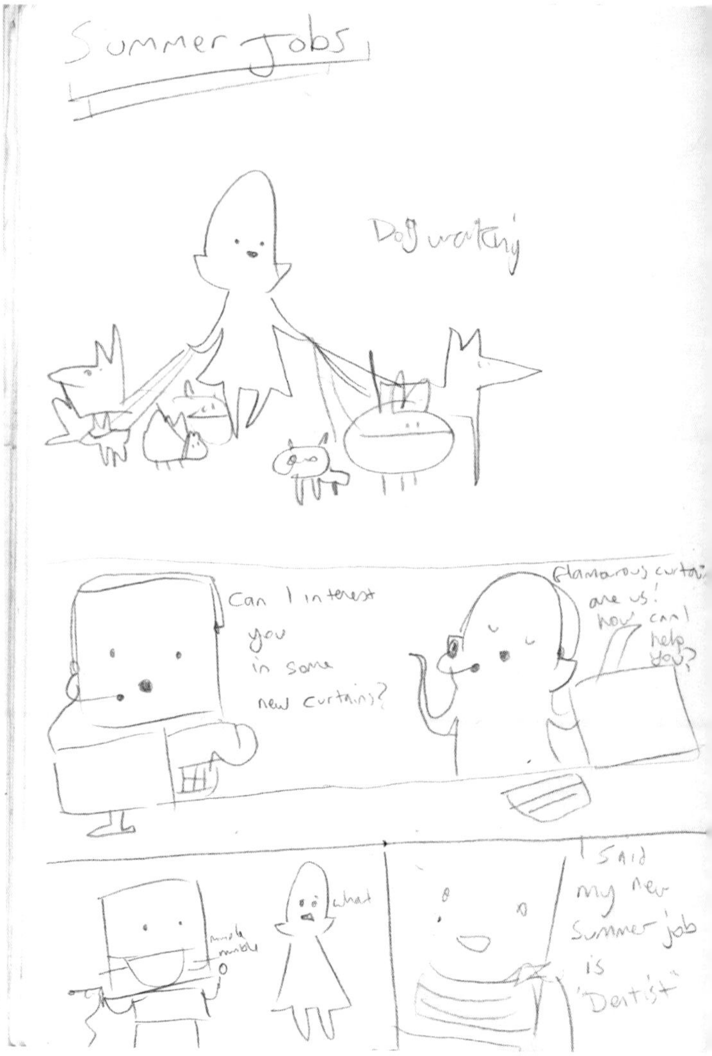
Summer Jobs
Dog walking
Can I interest you in some new curtains?
Glamorous curtains are us! how can I help you?
what
I said my new summer job is "Dentist"

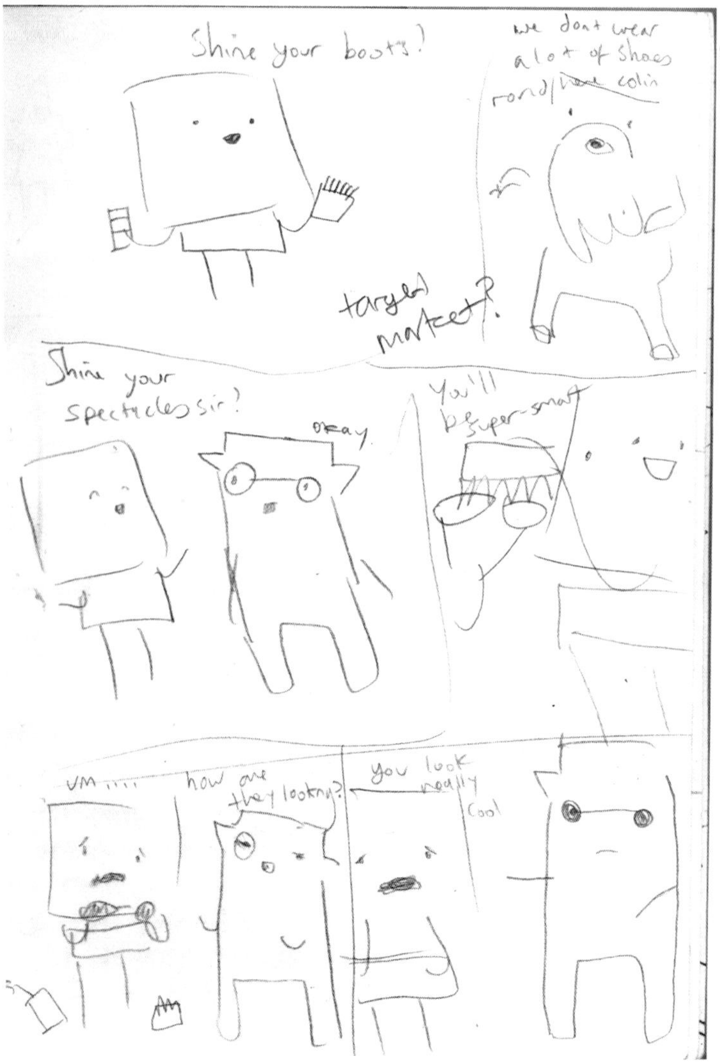
Shine your boots?
we dont wear a lot of shoes round here colin
target market?
Shine your spectacles sir?
okay
You'll be super-smart
UM....
how are they looking?
you look really cool

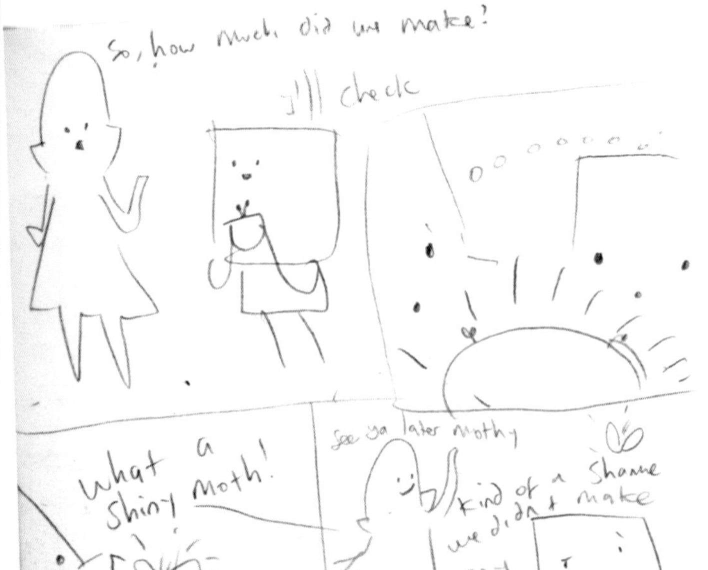
So, how much did we make?
I'll check
oooooooo
what a shiny moth!
see ya later mothy
kind of a shame we didnt make any money though

This summer holiday storyline ran between June and July in 2010. It was the first time I tried a longer story arc with Colin and Pauline. I think they benefited from it!

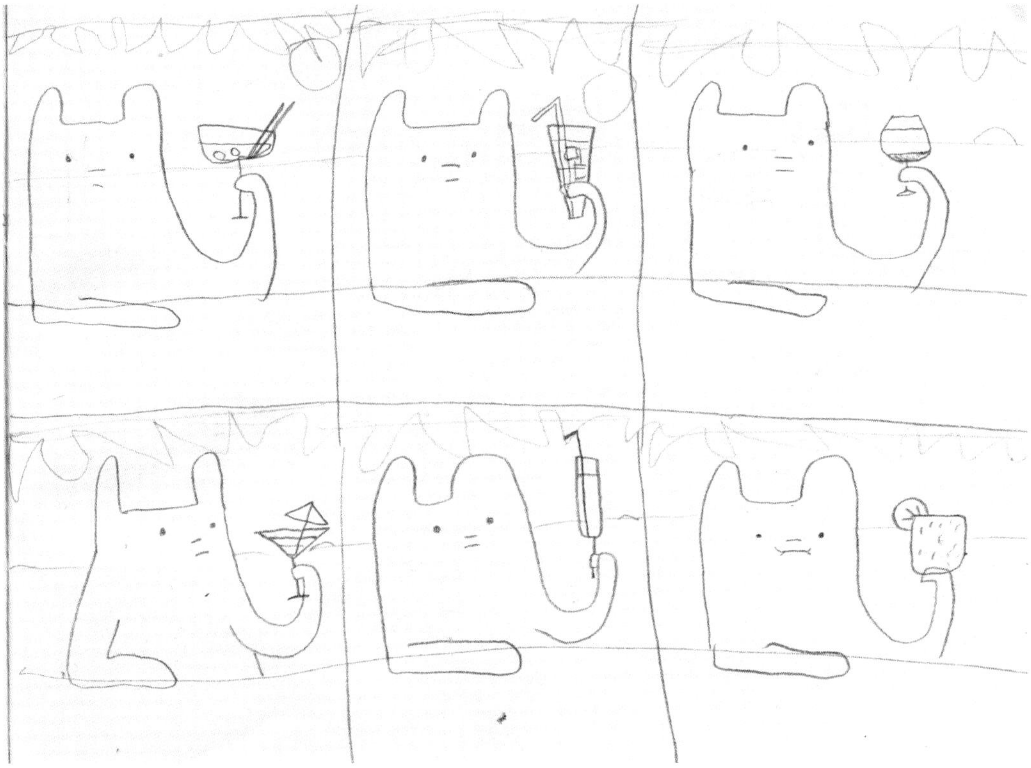

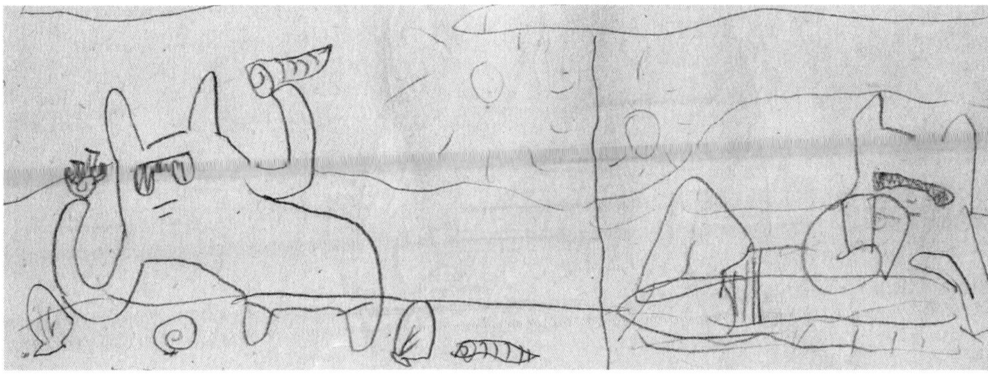

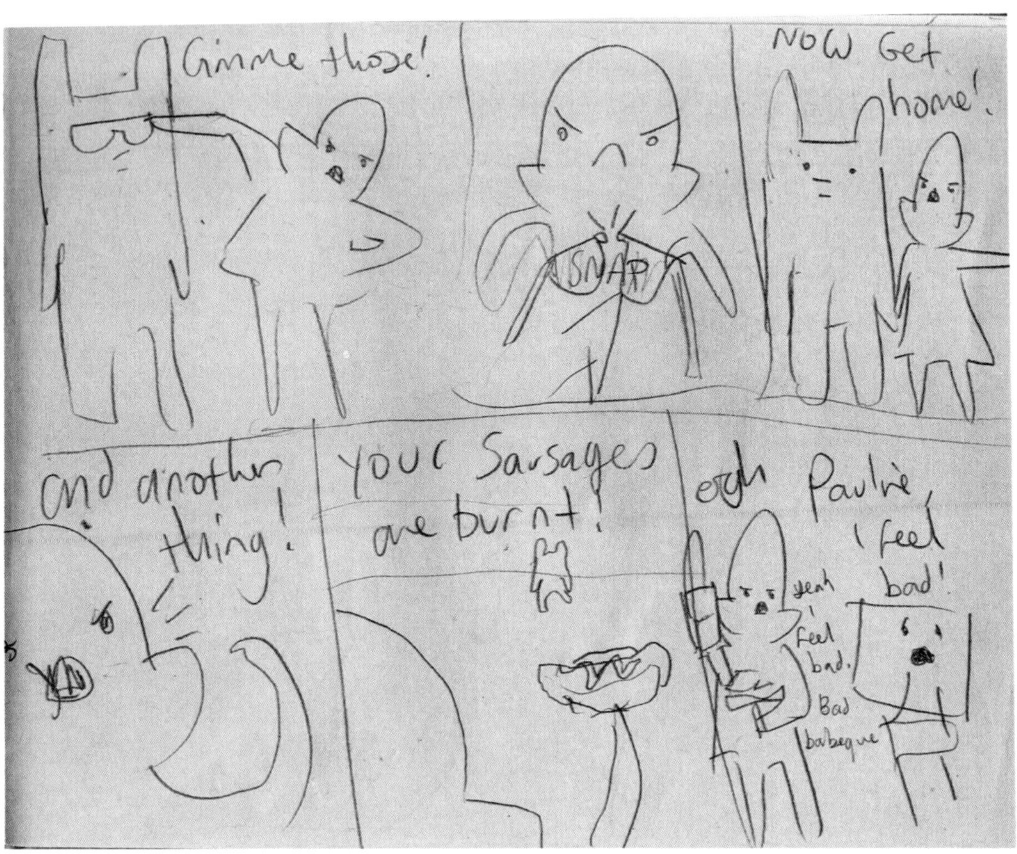
Gimme those!
SNAP
NOW Get home!
and another thing!
your Sausages are burnt!
erch Paulie, I feel bad!
yeah I feel bad.
Bad barbeque

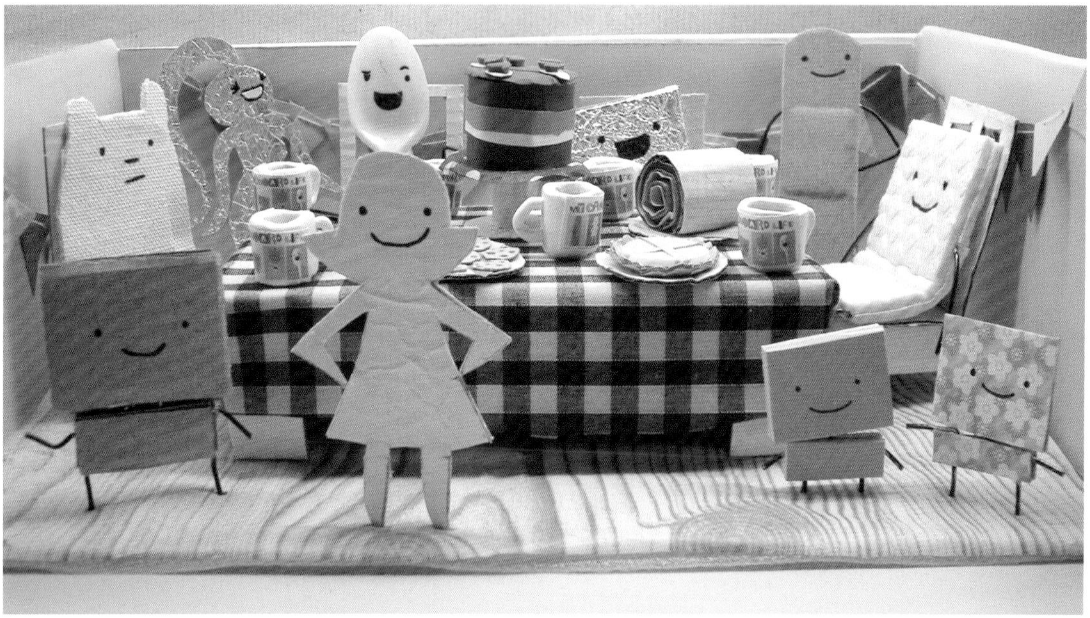

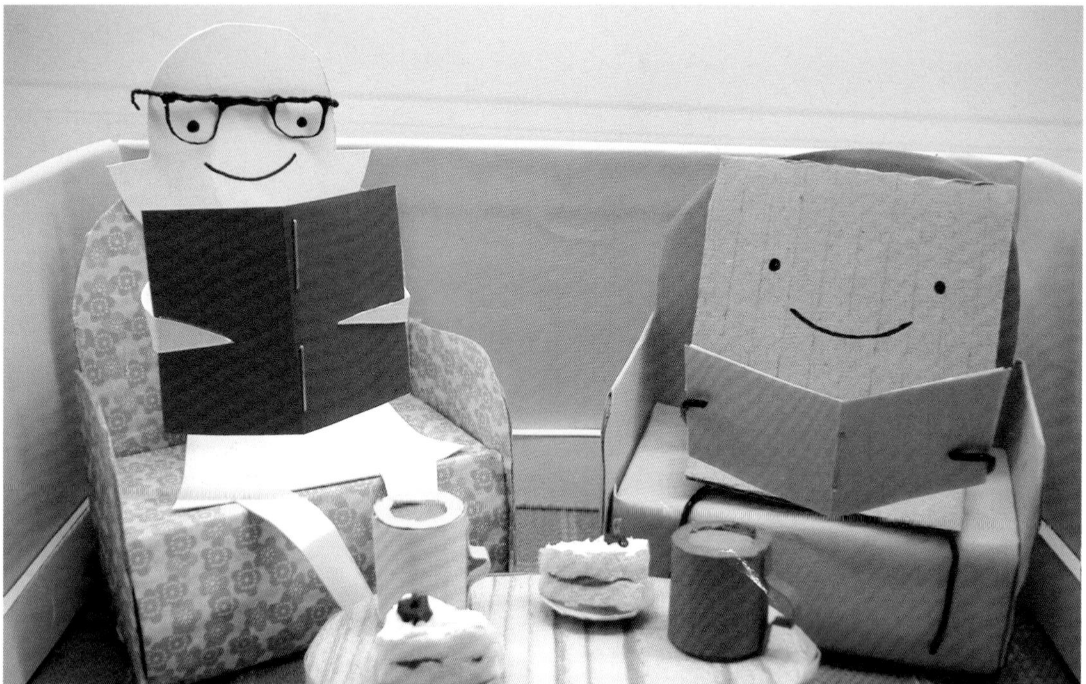

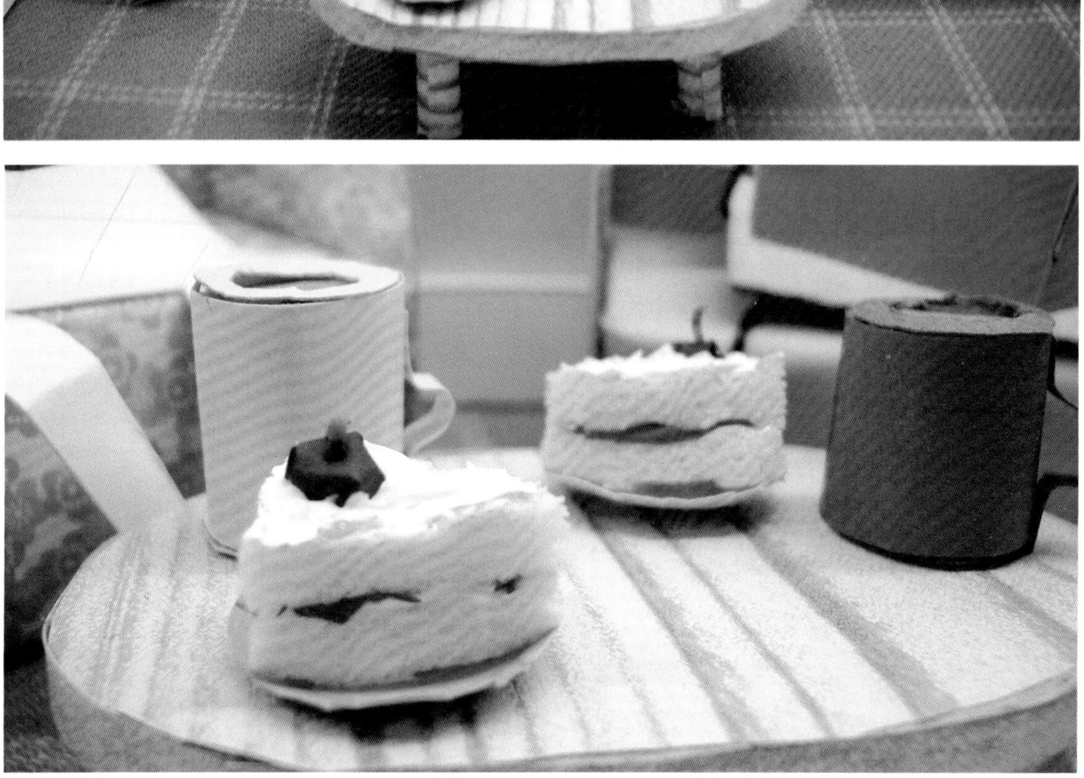

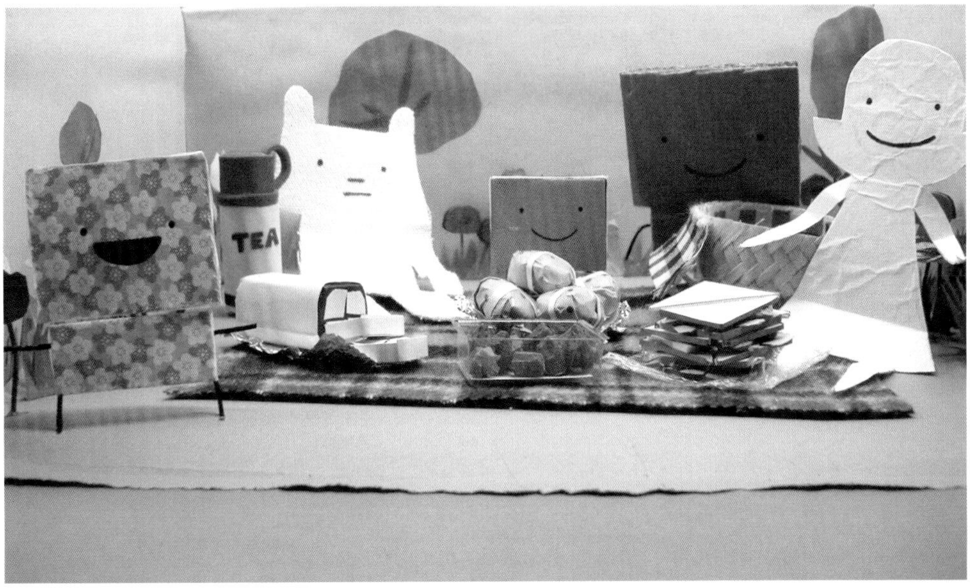
TEA

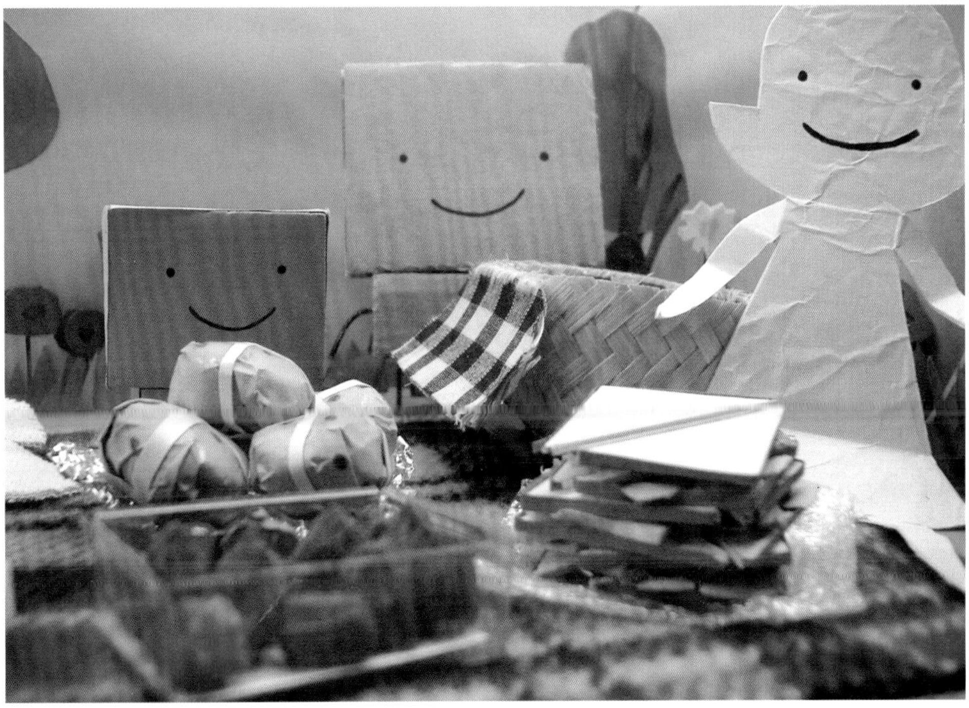

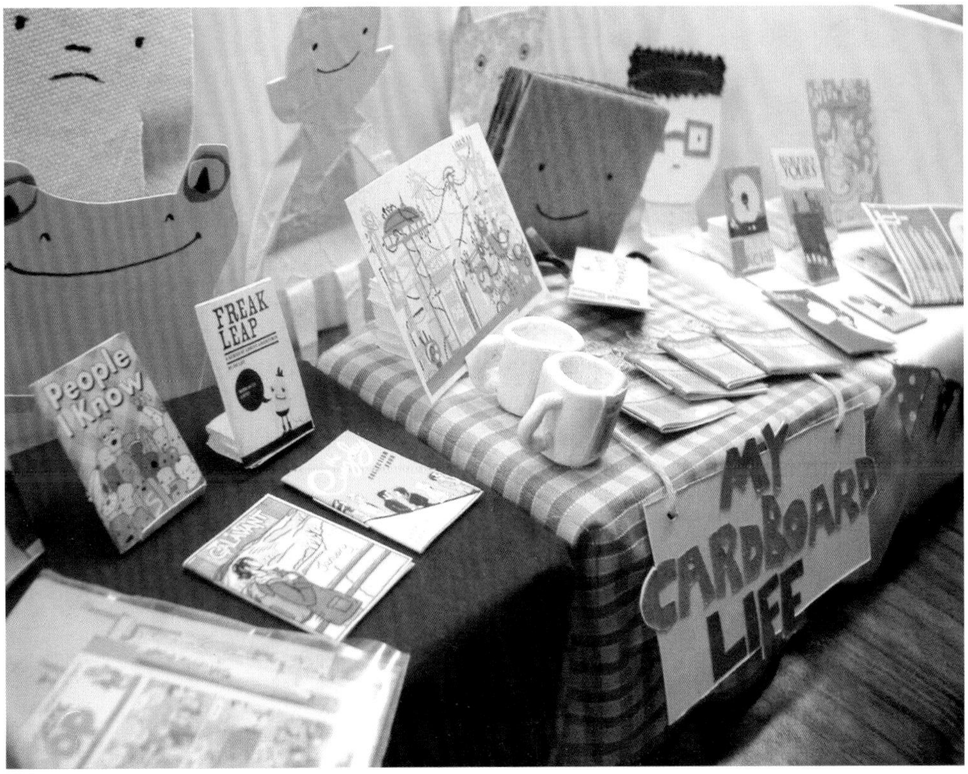
People I Know
FREAK LEAP
MY CARDBOARD LIFE

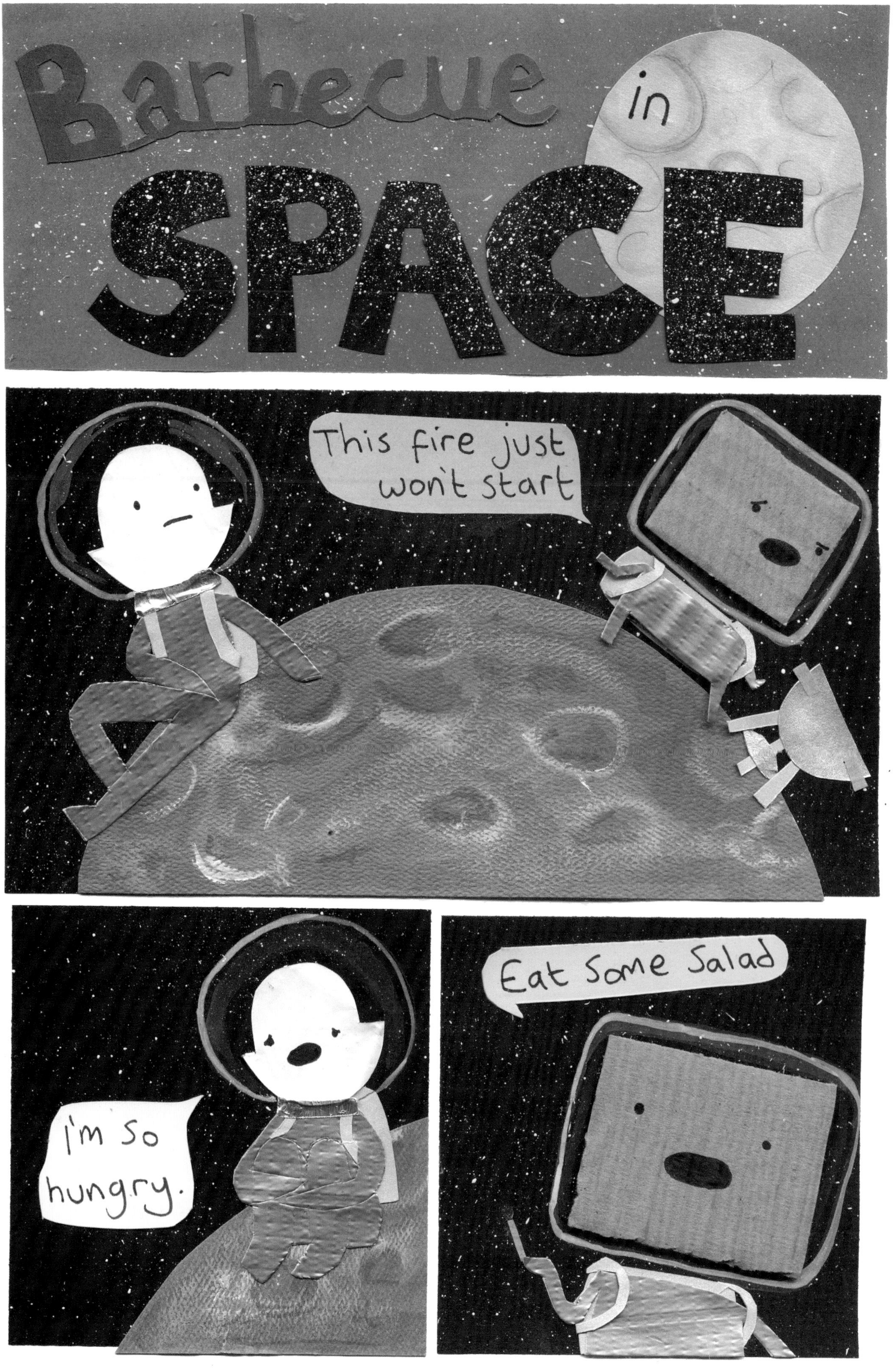
Barbecue in SPACE
This fire just won't start
I'm so hungry.
Eat Some Salad

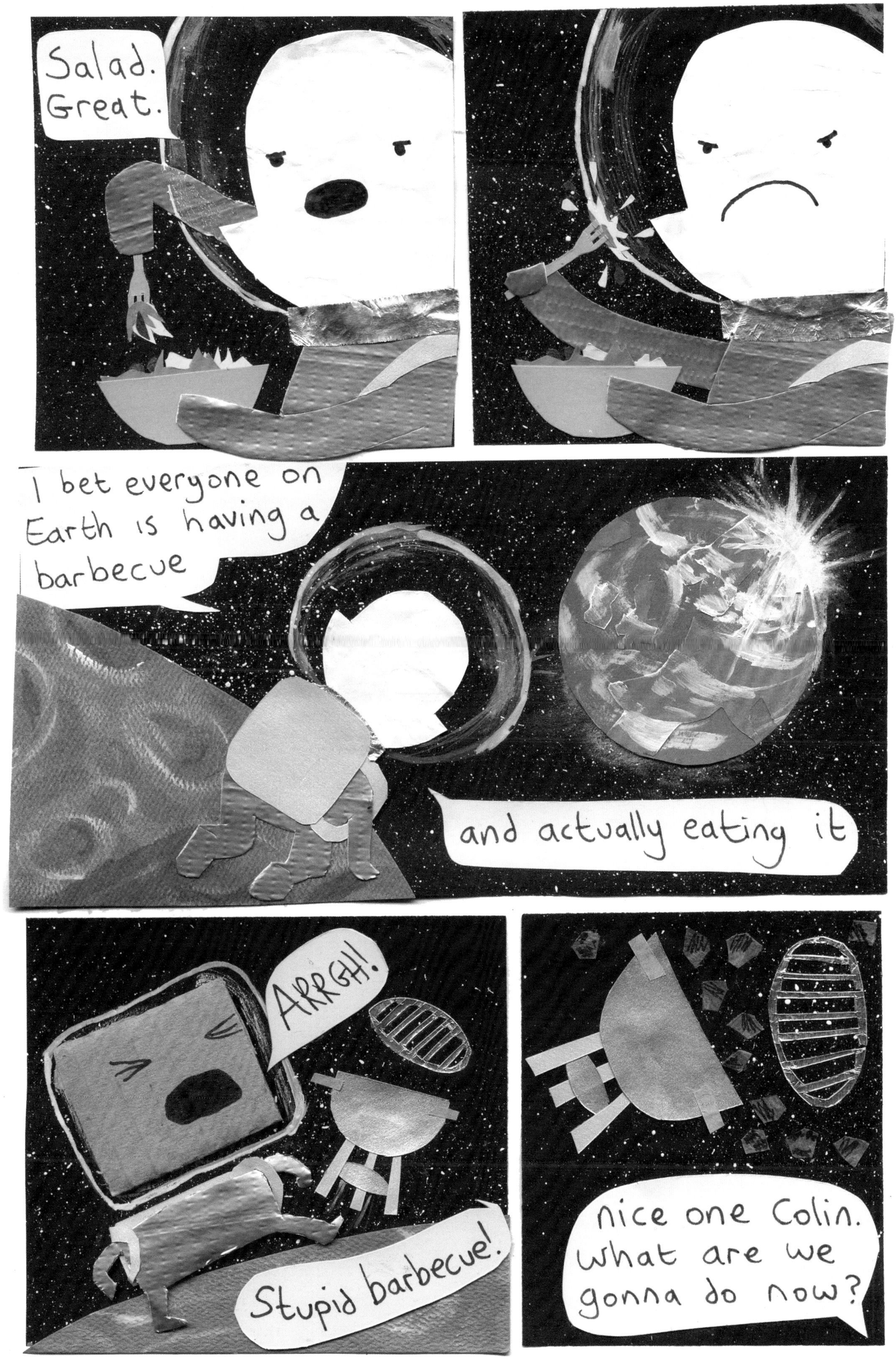
Salad. Great.
I bet everyone on Earth is having a barbecue
and actually eating it
ARRGH!
Stupid barbecue!
nice one Colin. What are we gonna do now?

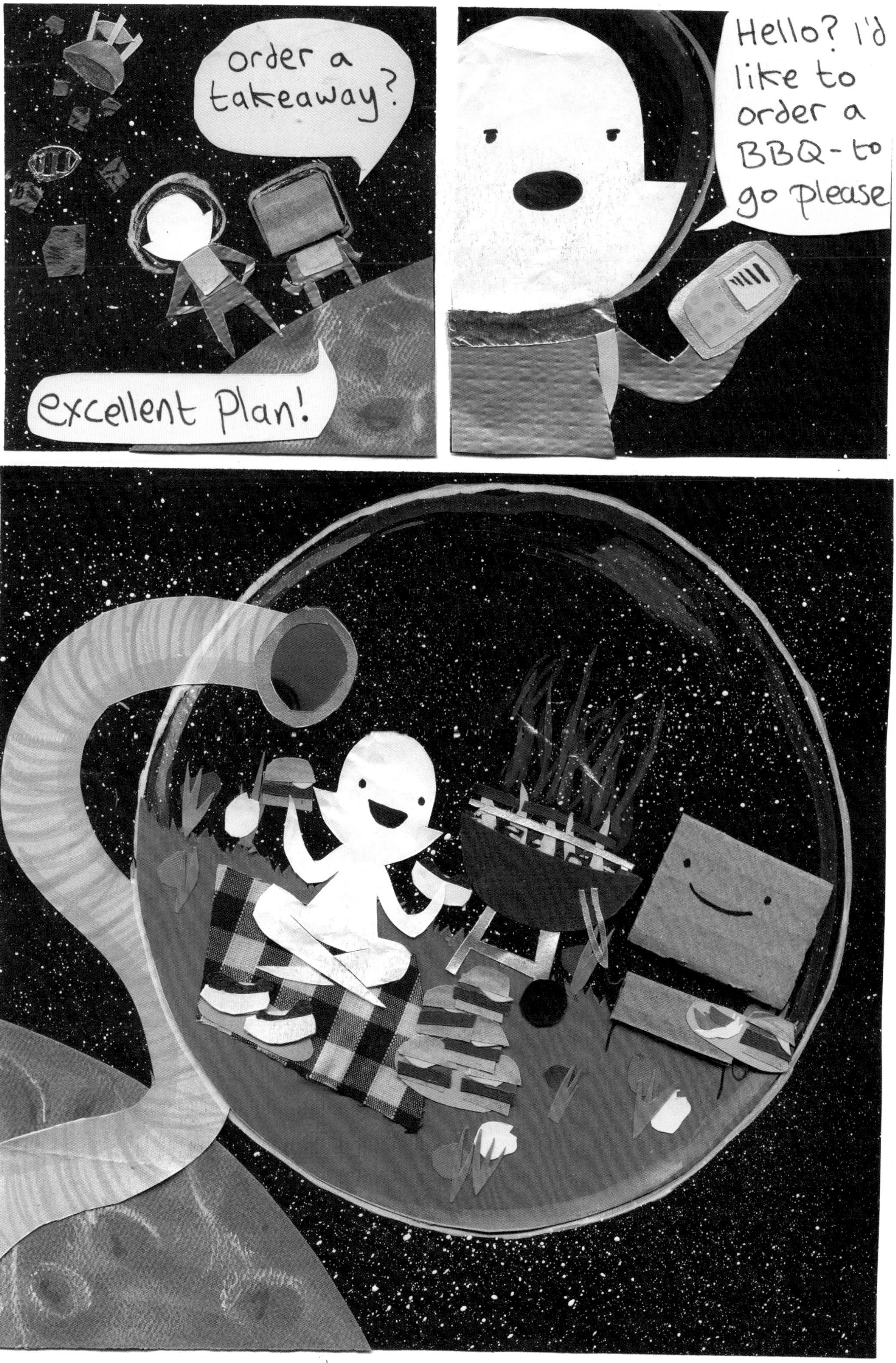
order a takeaway?
excellent Plan!
Hello? I'd like to order a BBQ-to go please